MYTHS OF
NATIVE AMERICA

Edited by
TIM McNEESE

Illustrated by
RICHARD HOOK

Four Walls Eight Windows
New York

Published in the United States by:
Four Walls Eight Windows
39 West 14th Street, Suite 503
New York, NY 10011

Visit our website at http://www.4w8w.com

Library of Congress Cataloging-in-Publication Data available on file.

ISBN: 1-56858-271-4

Cover design by Jerry Engelbach
Interior designed by Chris Bell
Maps by Richard Garratt

Printed by Printing Express Ltd., Hong Kong

10 9 8 7 6 5 4 3 2 1

Part 1
The NORTHEAST

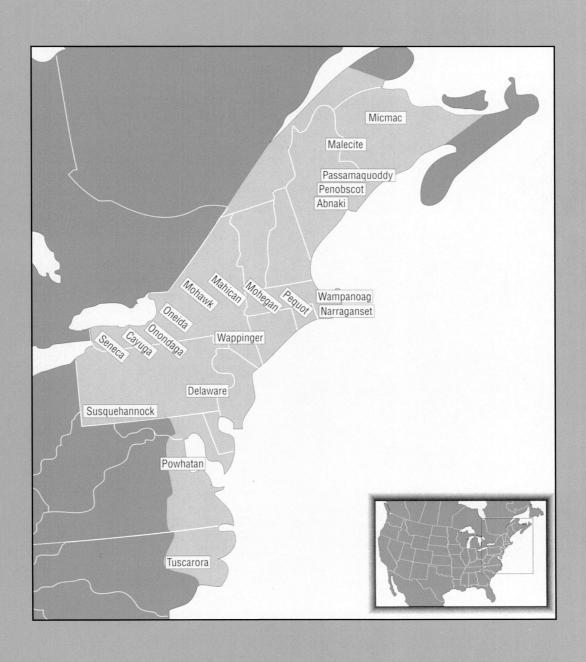

Micmac

Malecite

Passamaquoddy
Penobscot
Abnaki

Mohawk

Mahican

Mohegan

Pequot

Wampanoag
Narraganset

Oneida

Onondaga

Wappinger

Seneca

Cayuga

Delaware

Susquehannock

Powhatan

Tuscarora

TRIBES OF THE NORTHEAST

Although modern anthropologists continue to push back te earliest accepted date for Native American occupation of the great woodlands east of the Mississippi, a comfortable period lies somewhere between 5,000 and 7,000 years ago. In western New York a social order of natives arose called the Lamoka Culture. These ancient peoples utilized projectile points that have since been uncovered in other locales, including eastern Michigan,the Ohio valley and points east to the Atlantic coast. Their tools and weapons included bone and antler knives, fishing hooks, awls, hide scrapers and even whistles. Not only did they knap projectile points, they also busied themselves with polishing stones, including pestles and mortars.

To the east a neighbouring culture, the Laurentian Culture, developed at the same time and was longer lasting. Centred in eastern New York and extending east to New England and north to the St Lawrence River, this culture carved, beyond the usual kitchen tools, harpoons and slate spear points.

Such stone-based culture groups would over time give way to the Old Copper Culture, which peaked between 4,000 and 3,000 years ago and lasted for a couple of millennia. Centred on the Great Lakes, this hunting and fishing culture introduced an extensive use of metals. With copper ore in abundance in the region, the natives began to create from solid copper practical items for daily use, including knives, chisels, spear points and axes. Such metal items spread quickly throughout the eastern woodlands as they became prized trade goods. With these metal implements, the Native americans were able to make dug-out canoes. Other sorts of canoes, as well as a variety of different items, were made from birch bark. These people also began to develop forms of clay pottery.

Early Woodland Stage

Around 3,000 years ago,and lasting until about 500 years before Christ, another phase in the advancement of the prehistoric tribes of the Northeast developed: the Early Woodland Stage. At this time the Indians were noted for the building of earthen mounds. Among the most important mound-building cultures was the Adena (see page 84) which developed a highly centralized social structure and served as a culture of origin for Indian splinter groups that migrated over time to the east, as far as the Chesapeake region,and further north into modern-day New York state and New England. Such mound-building activities were possible only where tribes led a less nomadic, more sedentary life, and this was possible only when sustained farming could be practised.

This culture group became increasingly dependent on a permanent agricultural system. Certainly, hunting, fishing and the harvesting of coastal shellfish remained mainstays, even as agriculture made powerful inroads into their native diets. Vegetables common today, such as squash, were finding their way into the fare of these Northeastern tribes. They were also growing gourds, sunflowers and marsh elder. Over time these plants and vegetables provided between a third and nearly half of the daily food supply of many Northeastern tribes.

This new level of agricultural dependence speeded up to the growth of native populations simultaneously in the Northeastern region and in other parts of North America. with this sedentary lifestyle, tribes could develop more complex social, political and economic systems, bringing a new level of sophistication and a higher standard of living to the tribes of the region.

CONTENTS

INTRODUCTION

IN THE DAYS BEFORE the arrival and permanent settlement of Europeans in the early sixteenth century, the land that today comprises the continental United States was a vast wilderness, a place abundant with wildlife, where rivers carved their courses throughout its many ridges and mountains, verdant valleys and barren plains. This primeval region was the home of the earliest human inhabitants of North America.

When the European explorers arrived, the land was occupied by a patchwork quilt of varied tribal groups, each with its own unique arts, customs and social practices. These groups spoke many different languages, and communication between tribes was often difficult. This, together with a host of other factors, including the geography of where each tribe lived, caused these Native Americans to develop individual lifestyles.

This book presents a slice of the mythology and legends of eight regional groups of Native Americans: the Northeastern, the Southeastern, the Great Lakes and Ohio Valley, the Great Plains, the Southwest, the Western Range, the Pacific Northwest and the California culture groups.

The first two dominated the Eastern Woodland area of the modern-day United States before the coming of the Europeans. The tribes of the Northeast ranged throughout the region from Maine to the Great Lakes, stretching south to the Commonwealth of Virginia. Many of them hugged the Atlantic seaboard, extending their unique cultural influences from Massachusetts Bay to the tidewaters of the Chesapeake. The peoples of the Southeast included the mound-building tribes of the pre-Columbian Adena, Hopewell and Mississippian eras. They were scattered from the banks of the lower Mississippi River across the modern Gulf and Appalachian Mountain states of Tennessee, the Carolinas, Mississippi, Alabama and Georgia. These two regionally based, tribal–cultural groups shared common practices of daily life, from hunting to domestic agriculture. Yet each left its own mark on the land and on the history of the early occupation of North America.

Located along the banks of the Great Lakes and among the many rivers of the Ohio River valley, other tribes – many of them Algonquian in language stock – occupied the land, serving as rivals and enemies of the Iroquois of the Northeast. These tribes practised hunting, fishing and domesticated agriculture, and roamed about in birch-bark canoes. The region in which they lived included the modern-day states of Minnesota, Wisconsin, Michigan, Ohio, Indiana and Illinois.

Out on the boundless and nearly treeless prairies lived the cultural group known as the Great Plains tribes. These Native Americans spread their influence from the sage-brush lands of western Texas to the north as far as Canada. Tribes such as Sioux, Cheyenne, Blackfoot and Pawnee dominated the region and, by the

middle of the eighteenth century, had created a lifestyle that depended on the horse for transportation and the success of the buffalo hunt as the basis of its economy.

The remaining four groups of Native Americans historically and prehistorically occupied a vast region, including the western third of the continental United States, plus portions of the Canadian province of British Columbia, extreme northern elements of Mexico, including the Baja California peninsula, and sites as far north as the state of Alaska.

This region is a vast and varied one, allowing for much divergence of culture and societal structure among the Native Americans living there. Geographically, it is a land which boasts extraordinary extremes, from bitterly cold environs to hot, arid deserts. Topographically, these early inhabitants made their homes alongside majestic, snow-capped mountains, and along rich river systems which cut through vast valleys, often cutting their courses to the waters of the Pacific Ocean.

The tribes of the Southwestern culture group lived, as they still do, in an eerie land of painted deserts and red sandstone mesas, dotted by outcrops of tall saguaro cacti, which cast long shadows across the motionless scrubland of modern-day Arizona and New Mexico. These Native Americans are the people of the 'pueblo', the great apartment complexes of the ancient world, a name given by the Spanish exploring expeditions of the sixteenth and seventeenth centuries. They are a people with a history of early occupation in the region spanning thousands of years. Their predecessors – the human-dawn cultures of the Anasazi, Hohokam and Mogollon peoples – carved an existence in this hostile land which later generations, including the tribes of the Pueblo, Hopi, Zuni, Apache and Navajo, built upon, making for themselves dozens of oases in the barren lands of the region.

To the north lived the people of the Western Range, the region to the west of the great Rocky Mountains which split the continent along a seemingly endless divide, sending the waters of its eastern rivers to the Mississippi and those of its western streams to the Pacific Ocean and the Gulf of California. The Western Range encompasses two subregions and two Native American culture groups.

The first subregion is the Great Basin – an immense natural sink where rivers flow to nowhere and have no outlets, causing them to flow, evaporate and recondense into large, briny lakes such as Pyramid Lake, Walker Lake and, the largest of all, Great Salt Lake. In this arid and water-trapped region, tribes such as the Paiute, Shoshone and Ute made the best of their world, founding their culture and their place among the canyons and valleys of death.

The second subregion, the Plateau, boasted great, flowing riverine systems, heavy forests of oak and pine, and a Native American culture which thrived on the richness of the land, the abundant wildlife and the almost limitless supplies of riverine salmon. Here the tribes of the Nez Perce, Flathead, Sanpoil, Spokane, Yakima and Okanagan lived, creating a rich culture which traded extensively throughout the region and beyond, reaching, sharing and warring with their neighbours from the Great Plains to the east, the Pacific Northwest and the south, as well as the desperate tribes of the Great Basin.

Rounding out the culture groups of this vast land of mountains, lakes, rivers and brilliant sunsets were the peoples of the coastal region, those of the Pacific Northwest and California. It is here that Native Americans created for themselves a world unlike any other found in North America. These were the Northwestern tribes of conspicious wealth – Kwakiutl, Haida, Tlingit, Bella Bella and Nootka – those who practised the curious ritual of the potlatch, a wealthy man's game of revenge and consumption, where gifts become debts and repayment by the receiver sometimes led to his ultimate bankruptcy. It was a culture built on the abundance of salmon, where accumulation of all things material – houses, clothing, furniture, thousands of blankets in cedar chests – became the source of power and the benchmark of a man's prestige in his seaside community. While in southern California, the Native Americans lived lives of quietude, eking out an existence which included living in grass huts and eating insects.

For hundreds of years, these culture groups developed an elaborate oral tradition of legends, tales and myths concerning their ancestors, their gods, theirtribe- and the world of nature that surrounded them. These stories were passed from generation to generation, and many were not recorded in any permanent form until the eighteenth, nineteenth and even twentieth centuries. Much of this effort to preserve the oral heritage of Native Americans has been a co-operative one between Native American speakers and a host of ethnologists, linguists, dialecticians, army officers, explorers and anthropologists. Now this 'literature' of America's first people has been preserved for all time. In this volume there are sixty or so such stories, meant not only to entertain the reader but also to enlighten – to present the Native American and his world – for much of that world did not sur-vive the arrival of the Europeans to the New World. Here a remnant of that world remains, one that will, I trust, never be destroyed.

NOTE TO THE READER

THE STORIES INCLUDED in this book reveal both the differences and the similarities between the tribes of North America. While it is impossible to categorize all these legends into convenient pigeonholes of theme and subject, many reveal several key motifs.

In some of these tales, the protagonist, nearly always a male member of a tribe or a male animal, is involved in an adventure or experience that the narrator wishes his or her audience to apply to their lives or from which they can extract a message or certain information. Common motifs include visitations to supernatural lands, especially to the sky or stars; transformation experiences, wherein the protagonist becomes something new, such as a tree, a star or an animal; a contest, race or duel with an object at stake which is highly prized by the participants, such as immortality, beauty, great power or the maiden daughter of a great chief; dreams or visions with the protagonist experiencing a visitation or portent of some future event to come; 'numbskull' tales with half-witted characters who must laugh at their own stupidity or naïvety; taboo legends, featuring a character who decides to throw caution to the wind and do something which is forbidden or warned against; and tales of endless supplies of food, inspired by Native Americans whose diets were not always balanced and who experienced, from time to time, true hunger and near starvation.

◆

References in some citations to *JAFL* refer to the *Journal of American Folklore, BAE* to the *Bureau of American Ethnology and BAEAR to Bureau of American Ethnology Annual Report.*

Hopewellian Culture

This Early Woodland Stage of progress eventually gave way to another phase, which is known by anthropologists as the Middle Woodland Stage. Beginning about 100 BC and lasting until about AD 500-700, this phase witnessed the coming of the Hopewellian era. Still a mound-oriented culture, these tribes began planting and harvesting new crops that had made their way up from Central America and Mexico. Hopewellian mound sites have yielded for the modern anthropologist and archaeologist a great collection of artefacts that help to explain the lifestyles of such Native Americans. Copper tools were common among the Hopewell peoples. Other artefacts include wooden and stone tools and weapons, obsidian objects, carved stone pipes and statues. In a grave of one Hopewell mound, archaeologists unearthed a cache of 60,000 pearls.

These Hopewellian people were extraordinarily domesticated. Corn, beans and tobacco were soon added to their farming efforts Northeastern tribes in this era began building huts called wigwams – oval structures with curved, dome-like roofs. Tree saplings provided the framework for such houses, which were covered with large sections of bark or with animal skins. Trade flourished among the tribes. Tools were made out of copper, bone, antler and stone. Women created elaborate clay pottery. Northeastern Indian art included decorations on pottery and various forms of carving, including tobacco pipes whose bowls represented forest animals and human heads. The musical instruments produced included woodwinds, such as panpipes, and many varieties of drum and rattle.

It is not known why the Hopewellian Culture died out. Mound-building faded from the scene in the Northeastern region, although it continued to be prominent in the American Southeast, from the Mississippi River valley across to the coastal areas of modern-day South Carolina, Georgia and Florida.

In the Northeast, throughout the period from 1000 until the arrival of the Europeans in the sixteenth and seventeenth centuries, the culture became less monolithic, as various tribal identities developed, many of which were intact by te time of the European contact. Agriculture continued to dominate in the region, populations rose in number, the number and size of Northeastern settlements increased and their cultures became more inventive and creative. all across the north, form the great Lakes to modern-day New York and New England, through to the maritime provinces of modern-day Canada, tribal distinctions and familial clans developed. Languages such as the Algonquian, Iroquoian and Siouan took on their distinctive elements.

Indeed, the heyday of early, pre-Columbian tribal groups occurred in the years following 1250. During these centuries, the Eastern tribes continued to progress, advancing their political, economic and social structures, as well as their individual technologies, which gradually produced better weapons, tools, housing and means of transportation. By 1500, the intricate tribal structures founded across North America and particularly in the regions east of the Mississippi, as well as the American Southwest, were being deeply influenced or even destroyed with the coming of the Europeans.

Native Cultures of the Northeast

When English religious refugees landed in 1621 at Cape Cod in modern-day Massachusetts, they discovered a group of Native Americans unique to a place and time. The eastern Woodland tribes had already spread throughout the region stretching from the Atlantic seaboard to the Mississippi River in the west. One contemporary account, typical in its descriptiveness of a small party of local natives, Wampanoags, who were led by the famous Massasoit, a noted sachem (chief) to the tribe, reads as follows:

On this day came again the savage, and brought with him five other proper men. They had every man a deer's skin on him and the principal of them had a wild-cat's skin, or such like, on the one arm. They had most of them long hose up to their groins, close made, and above their groins to their waist another leather. They were altogether like the Irish trousers . . . On their heads long hair to the shoulders, only cut before, some trussed up before with a feather, broad wise, like a fan, another a fox tail hanging out. They were in their faces in part or in whole painted, some black, some red, some yellow, and some white, some with crosses, and other fanciful works. Some had skins on them and some naked, all strong, tall men in appearance.

Such encounters were a continuation of the process of early colonial contact between native populations and the Europeans, first brought on by visiting explorers such as Hudson, Verrazano and LaSalle, and by later arrivals such as the Pilgrim Fathers, who planted themselves along the Massachusetts coast and remained.

The native cultures that these early whites encountered were nothing like anything they had seen in the Old World. Though there were always tribal variations from one regional group to another, many of these native tribes had much in common with each other. In the North-east, the Woodland tribes, as described by the eyewitness account just quoted, wore a variety of distinct costumes. The men wore breechclouts in the summer, donning leggings and shirts of deer skin during the winter. Women wore deer-skin dresses and leggings, and everyone wore moccasins. Footwear designs varied from tribe to tribe, with most winter models being lined with rabbit fur. Some Atlantic coastal tribes wore grass and hemp skirts and robes adorned with wild turkey feathers sewn into the material.

For the most part, the tribes that comprise the Eastern Woodland ethnic groups may be divided into two language stocks: the Algonquian and Iroquoian. While some Algonquian tribes ranged to the west, as far as the region of the Great Lakes, several located themselves in the New England area. North of Maine were the Micmac peoples with their traditional lands encompassing the Canadian maritime provinces of Nova Scotia, Cape Breton Island and New Brunswick. Other Algonquian tribes included the Passamaquoddy and Penobscot tribes, which shared territory in Maine. These two, along with the Malecites and a few other, smaller tribes, are sometimes referred to as the Abenakis.

Early European contact with the Penobscot tribe resulted in a belief that this tribe was the centre of a great American kingdom. Later sixteenth- and early seventeenth-century New World maps began including a lavish city situated along the Norumbega River (the Penobscot River). According to the stories, the Penobscots were ruled by a great king named Bashaba, whose lands stretched to the south as far as Virginia. Subsequent explorations revealed that the Penobscots' village was a small one and their chief was in fact no king at all.

A smaller tribe in the New England area was the Wampanoags, whose history is inter-twined with the Plymouth Pilgrims and the founding of the Massachusetts Bay Colony. The tribe known as the 'People of the Small Bay', the Narrangansett, lived in Rhode Island. Neighbouring Connecticut (derived from the Indian word Quonoktacut, which translates as 'River Whose Water is Driven by Tides') was the homeland of the Mohegans, the Pequots and Wappinger tribes.

Modern-day New York, with its many rivers, lakes and ranging mountains, was the home of a variety of significant Indian groups, some Algonquin, others Iroquois. The Mahicans, who are sometimes confused with the Connecticut Mohegans, lived along the upper Hudson River country. Further to the south were the Delawares, who were known among themselves as the Lenni Lenape (which translates as 'Original People'). The use of such references made by certain tribes concerning themselves and their beginnings are common in Native American stories. Many tribes told creation myths and, in the process, explained how human life began not only on earth but also among their specific tribe or people.

The Iroquois

When Algonquian tribes spoke of their neighbours the Haudenosaunee, they referred to them as the Iruoquois, a word that means 'terrible people' or 'frightening people'. In time, the Haudenosaunee adopted the name for themselves. The Iroquoian language stock was shared by numerous tribes. In more modern times, when the term Iroquois is used, it applies to the five tribes who lived along the Mohawk River in central New York. These tribes came to unify themselves into a democratic confederacy known as the Five Nations. The original tribes of the Five Nations were the Senecas, Cayuga, Onondaga, Oneida and Mohawks. (Neighbouring Narragansetts gave the Mohawks their name, which means 'man-eaters', since the Mohawks had a reputation for occasional cannibalism.) In the early years of the eighteenth century, a sixth nation was added when the Tuscarora tribe was adopted into the confederacy after it had been driven from its North Carolina homelands by intruding Europeans and Anglo-Americans. The Tuscarora migrated north, joining up with the Oneida. They were officially accepted into the confederacy in 1715. Other Iroquoian tribes located in the Northeast included the Susquehanna, who ranged in southeastern Pennsylvania and the northern Maryland region, in the vicinity of the river that bears their name and flows into Chesapeake Bay.

The advent of the Five Nations confederacy came soon after the arrival of the first Europeans along the Atlantic in the later sixteenth century. Legend relates the coming of an Indian prophet named Dekanawida, who brought to the Iroquois a vision of a 'Great Peace'. This prophecy foresaw the confederacy, in which the tribes of the Iroquois would live together, united against common foes. A Mohawk chief named Hiawatha founded the Five Nations confederacy around 1570. He visit many Iroquois villages, preaching unity and condemning the practice of cannibalism. Hiawatha's message was not without its critics, most notably an Onondaga chief named Todadaho. According to legend, Hiawatha had to agree to an intertribal council which featured more Onondaga representatives than the other tribes were allowed. In addition, the Onondaga village was the first meeting site of the Five Nations. (Some Iroquois legends concerning Hiawatha portray Todadaho as a Medusa-like monster with snakes pouring out of his head which Hiawatha combs out.) Under the political arrangements inherent in the Five Nations agreement, member tribes retained their independence in self-governance, with the league having jurisdiction only in cases of inter-tribal concern.

Confederacies among Eastern Woodland tribes were not confined solely to the Iroquois confederacy of the Five Nations. Historically, various confederacies were formed periodically for purposes of defence. Some Algonquian tribes formed confederacies, the most notable among them being the Delaware Confederacy. Others included the Wabanaki Confederacy, which saw the unification of the Malecites, Micmacs, Penobscots, Passamaquoddys and others, and the Wappinger Confederacy, which brought together several smaller tribes in Connecticut and across the East River to Manhattan Island, where one member tribe, the Manhattans, sold the island to Dutch settlers for the oft-quoted bargain-basement price of twenty-four dollars. Yet the confederacy of the Five Nations was the most complicated union of related tribes, encompassing complex political and military concerns.

Iroquoian Intertribal Structures

Iroquois tribes established their social and familial structures around clans, each of which had an animal as its representative. Several interrelated families formed the basis of a clan. Members of the clan could claim common ancestors. Clan membership was always traced through the women of each family, thus making for a matrilineal society. In practical terms, this meant that a child born into his mother's Turtle clan, for example, would, after marrying, have children who were members of his wife's clan. The two original Iroquois clans were the Deer and the Wolf. Offshoots of the Deer would later include the Hawk, Heron and Snipe clans, while the Wolf clan produced the clans of the Derr, the Turtle and the Beaver. Intermarriage between members of the original Deer and Wolf clans was forbidden, which helped the tribes keep blood relatives from taking each other as husband and wife.

The Iroquois Long House

The Iroquois lived in fortified villages, surrounded by palisades and consisting of several 'long houses'. These bark-covered dwellings, known to the Iroquois as *ganonh'sees*, were built by the men of the tribe and owned by the women. They provided accommodation for anywhere from five to twenty families. On average, they were about sixty feet (eighteen metres) long with a width of eighteen to twenty feet (five to seven metres). The roof was often sloped or took on the shape of a barrel arch, with a line of ridge poles running the length of the house. The building's ridge peak was high, rising twenty feet (seven metres) from the earthen floor. The walls of the long house were a latticed framework covered with wide strips of birch bark measuring approximately four by six feet (one by two metres). In regions were birch was scarce, the Iroquois relied on elm, ash, cedar, basswood or hemlock. The walls of the long house were windowless, with doors at both ends. Such an arrangement proved cool and airy in the summer and snug in the winter. Inside, each family hung skins up for curtains, providing at least rudimentary privacy.

The Algonquian Wigwam

In contrast to the Iroquois multi-family dwellings, the Algonquins more often relied on the construction of wigwams, which tended to house fewer people and thus fewer families. Much smaller than the long houses of their neighbours, they were designed as bark-covered domes with the centre rising to a height slightly taller than an adult male standing erect. The outer dimensions of many Algonquian wigwams measured fourteen by twenty feet (four by seven metres)> A fire burned constantly inside, at the wigwam's centre, with an opening for smoke at the top of the wigwam. Along the outer wall, away from the central fire, the Algonquins slept on woven mats. Dried food and baskets hung from the support poles. While Iroquois men built their long houses, Algonquian women built their wigwams, just as many Plains women were responsible for the construction of their tepees (see page 125).

Food Sources of the Woodland Tribes

The diet of the peoples of the Eastern Woodland area was a varied one, supplied through agricultural endeavours, gathering, fishing and hunting. A strict delineation of sexual roles was practised: gathering and the raising of crops

were considered women's work, while catching fish, harvesting shellfish and hunting fell into the male domain.

The forested lands of the Northeastern region were teeming with wild game, creating a hunter's paradise prior to the arrival of the Euro-peans. The Algonquins hunted deer, caribou, moose, elk and bear, supplementing their diet with gathering and fishing. They also hunted smaller game, such as racoons, muskrats, porcupines, woodchucks and beaver, as well as a bevy of gamebirds including ducks, geese and grouse. Farming was difficult in the northern reaches because of the short growing season.

The Iroquois, located generally south of the Algonquins, relied on hunting and agriculture, raising a variety of crops including beans, squash and maize (the crops referred to as the 'Three Sisters'). As limited as this selection of crops sounds, the Indians in fact raised many kinds of corn (including a popping variety, which, when mixed with maple syrup, created a sweet delicacy that more modern Americans refer to as 'Cracker Jacks'), plus at least sixty types of bean and eight different varieties of squash. Add to their culinary repertoire such foods as potatoes, pumpkins and a plethora of berries, including strawberries, cranberries and blackberries, and throw in such exotic items as sunflowers, mushrooms and a variety of nuts, and you have the makings of a true tribal feast. Blander foods were often made more flavoursome by using natural seasonings, including wild onions and wild ginger. Salt was seldom used if at all; for the Onondaga to season their foods with sale was considered taboo.

In addition to a wide variety of foods, the Northeastern tribes had many different drinks on tap. The Iroquois, for example, had at least a dozen, including 'corn coffee' and teas made by boiling roots such as sassafras. Berries were squeezed and boiled into juicy libations. Some tribes cooked up a brew that tasted much like lemonade by harvesting the berries found on the staghorn sumac plant.

Hunting was more than a source of food; the hides of each hunter's catch were generally worked into clothing and furry sleeping covers. Typically, the men of the Northeastern Woodland tribes fished in the spring and summer, leaving the autumn season for their extensive hunting expeditions. (Winter was a sedentary season for nearly all the Northeastern tribes.) The chief weapon used by the Northeastern tribes in their hunting was the bow and arrow.

While hunting and fishing provided meat for the stewpots of both the Iroquois and the Algonquins, the women of many tribes practised a crude agriculture. The chief crop was corn. Nearly every tribe that grew corn had a story concerning this chief crop's origins. The Chippewa told a story of a stranger named Mon-daw-min who wrestled with a Chippewa hunter. When the hunter defeated his opponent, on the spot where Mon-daw-min died, there the first corn grew. (The legend is ironic, considering that the Chippewa did not traditionally grow corn!) Corn-growing became such an important source of food for the Iroquois that the word they used to describe it translates as 'our life'. Women and those children of the tribe old enough to work in the fields raised the maize. In preparation for their agricultural pursuits, the Northeastern tribes would notch a ring around the base of each tree that needed clearing, a practice known to the Europeans who later followed this method, which they referred to as 'girdling'. With a lack of fertilizers, these tribal agronomists planted crops in their fields for approximately twenty growing seasons and then, as the soil was sapped of its nutrients, cleared more land and began growing their crops once more on virgin land.

Nearly every activity of the Eastern Wood-land Indians was connected to some manifestation of the spirit world, including and especially corn production. Native tribes marked the planting, growing, cultivation and harvesting stages of corn with a festival. In fact, festivals marked the harvests of all crops.

Once harvest, these crops were often dried to preserve them. The Iroquois built wooden cribs where they stored their corn. Women also ground corn into meal, which would generally have a longer shelf life. Squash and pumpkins had their outers shells removed, and the dible portions were cut into long spirals and hung on pegs and sinew lines to dry. The Iroquois dug storage pits, lined them withe bark pieces and filled them with beans or meat or dried fruits, covering each pit with a slab of thick bark.

Eastern Woodlands Religion and Mythology

For all native cultures found in North America, religion played a dominant role in the day-to-day activities of each tribe and of its individual members. The Eastern Woodland tribes were no exception. Their religion was generally an extremely personal one, practical in nature, and having to do with an individual's daily needs. However, native religion is crowded with a pantheon of deities, both good and evil, and stratified hierarchies of various gods and goddesses. Superstition marked the perimeters of their religion and defined the rituals, festivals, dances and belief systems.

Like the ancient Greeks, Native Americans faced the daily potential of offending the supernatural forces who controlled their naturalistic lives. Appeasement to such dieties in the form of gifts and offerings was common. Failure to appeal to the appropriate supernatural being might bring drought, sickness, war or something as basic as a harsh northern wind.

Both the Iroquois and the Algonquins recognized an all-pervasive deity, a spirit that permeated the entire scope of the natural world around them. Though similar in nature, each greater tribal group gave their all-knowing deity a different name. The Iroquois called their great spirit Orenda; the Algonquins referred to their as Manitou. Their destinies depended on the responses of their greatest deity. However, unlike the Christian God, which many white missionaries likened to the natives' Orenda or Manitou, these supernatural beings were actually the embodiment of many spirits that lived and occupied all the objects common to each Indian's existence. Such a theology gave definition to Northeastern Indians' views of their own afterlife. Natives believed that their life after death would exist as a mirror image of their earthly lives, in much the same way as ancient Egyptians imagined theirs. Once one died, it was believed, life would continue in a spirit world where human needs such as eating and sleeping would continue. No Northeastern tribes believed in any sort of punishment in connection with their concept of the afterlife. The Iroquois, for example, had a belief in an underworld, but it was not the Hades of the Greeks; rather, it was a lovely ground where disease was non-existent and war was no longer waged. This underworld, it was believed, was where their ancestors resided, a place ruled by a being known as the Mother of Animals.

The Iroquois also wove intricate and elborate stories and myths into their religious framework, involving gods who took the form of various animals, which, on occasion, took human form. This idea led to the concept of animal-based clans such as the Deer, Wolf, Turtle and so on. Supreme among Iroquois gods was the thunder god, named Hinu. He was an even-handed god, kind to those who were deserving and a punisher of evil. The Iroquois courted Hinu's favour by burning tobacco in ceremonial rituals. (Incidentally, Hinu also provided the Iroquois people with an explanation of how the dinosaurs, whose gigantic bones native Americans occasionally discovered, disappeared from the earth. He had destroyed them long ago, since they would have proved a constand menace and danger to man.) Hinu makes an appearance in a variety of Iroquois myths, including some that have him residing behind Niagara Falls (Ne-ah-ga-rah to the Iroquois) and rescuing a young Indian girl from going over the Falls in her canoe (she later became the Maiden of the Mist).

Helping fill the ranks of the Iroquois dieties were Ka-tash-huaht, the North Wind, who brought cole and death to the tribes; Goweh, the war god, to whom only Iroquois could pray; Tarhuhyiawahku, the Holder of the Heavens, who created the Six Nationals of the Iroquois; and a host of others, including the good and evil twins Tsentsa and Taweskare, sons of the West Wind (Hinu's brother), who created the earth, and the Three Sisters, the trio of spirits who watched over the harvests of corn, beans and squash.

In addition, the Iroquois envisioned stories and myths that were sometimes crowded with lesser supernatural creatures, including wizards, pygmies, witches, giants made of stone and weird creates called Great Heads, which were little more than gigantic heads with a pair of legs in lieu of a neck to give them a threatening mobility. Despite modern expectations, pygmies

were not creates to be taken lightly. They had special powers to create massive rock formations, could turn stones into any shape of their choosing and were able to kill monsters infinitely larger than they, even giants. Such elfish creatures, as revealed in the myths, were always giving their assistance to hapless natives through their life's course.

The Algonquian concept of spirit power was, as we have already noted, embodied in the being they called Manitou, who, like the Iroquois Orenda, was understood to be multiple spirits, literally thousands in number, who in combination created a supernatural essence that permeated all things in nature. Thus their concept of Manitou was of many 'Manitous', each wielding its own level of power and potency. The highest power of Manitou was, for some tribes, called Kitshi Manitou, meaning chief in the Algonquian language. Other tribes, such as the Abenaki, believed in the existence of Kechi Niwaski, a god of good and giver of life. Tribal myths describe Kechi Niwaski as having created the first Abenaki from stone. Unhappy with their appearance, Kechi Niwaski carved another pair, male and female, from wood, then gave them life as flesh-and-blood humans.

Most noted among all Algonquian Manitous was a spirit known as Manabozho, wash translates variously as 'God of Light', 'Ruler of the Sun' and 'Great White Hare'. Commonly, Menabozho gave the sun power to make its daily course through the heavens. This god was capable of changing his shape, sometimes taking the form of a human and walking on earth. Some Algonquian tribes heralded the first arrivals of Europeans to their waters as the arrival of Manabozho as a man.

As in Iroquois mythology, Algonquian deities include good and evil twins, Malsum and Glooscap, who are similar to Tsentsa and Taweskare. In cause of their rivalries, Glooscap kills Malsum (or Malsumis), the maker of evil. In an underground world of magic, Malsum then takes on life as an evil wolf. There are many stories about Glooscap's adventures, and they often culminate in his leaving earth in a birch-bark canoe, paddling towards the heavens. Some tales end with the Algonquin anticipating the future second coming of Glooscap.

Additional supernatural and magical creatures may be found in Algonquian mythology in which ghosts eat humans, witches cast spells and sorcerers practise their arts with great powers at hand. As with many Native American tribes, the Algonquins believed in out-of-body experiences, which would allow a human being's body and spirit to separate, allowing spiritual adventures in other physical forms, as in the taking on of an animals's body. A designated caste of priests called shamans claimed to have the power to send their spirits, upon falling into a trance, on visitations to animals, or to the spirit world, where they might commune with an ancient ancestor or a recently departed soul. One caution an Algonquian magic man's visiting spirit had to remember was not to take food or drink from another spirit, as this action would forever separate the spirit from its physical body, which, once spiritless, would die.

Prophets, Magicians and Shamans

While shamans wielded great spiritual power as tribal holy men, other men filled additional roles as prophets, magicians and great healers known as herbalists. Algonquian magicians or sorcerers claimed power over some aspects of the physical world, including the ability to halt the coming of natural disasters. Such men performed incantations and rituals which called forth supernatural entities from the underworld. Sometimes their ceremonies involved wild, gyrating dances. They claimed the ability to remove evil spirits from a possessed member of their tribe.

Algonquins sought the services of not only magicians but tribal doctors as well. Herbalists sometimes practised their tribal medicine as individuals, while others became members of a medical society. These practitioners of the heal-ing arts had a great working knowledge of the natural medicinal properties of a wide variety of locally grown plants and used them in potions and as curative powders and other medicines.

False Face Societies

Similar healers could be found among the Iroquois as well. Some of their medicine men formed a special group called the False Face Society, whose purpose was not only to heal the diseased but to keep them from getting sick in the first place. To do this, they carved wooden masks which bore hideous and contorted facial features designed to protect the tribe by scaring off the evil spirits that carried disease. While each mask was handmade and no two were every exactly alike, there were about a dozen basic false-face designs. Some featured twisted mouth formations, others had protruding tongues and still others had thick lips and mocking looks. To gain membership of the False Face Society, it was necessary only to dream that you were a member. After such a dream, the candidate hosted a banquet and was accepted into the society. All members of the False Face Society were male, with only one exception. A women served as the Keeper of the False Faces. Her role was particularly significant since she was the only one of the tribe who knew the identities of each member of the False Face Society.

In action, members of the False Face Society would enter the lodge of a sick person and carry out a series of incantations, dancing around the victim, shaking turtle-shell rattles and sprinkling ashes all about the place. To ward off disease in general from their villages, False Face Society members performed additional incantations, generally each spring and autumn, designed to scare away the evil spirits intent on doing physical harm to unwary villagers.

Other tribes also wore masks, but not necessarily from the same reasons as the Iroquois False Face Society. The Delaware tribe, for example, used masks in their corn rituals and ceremonies. (Such masks were also worn by the Iroquois members of the Huskface Society, who made their face covering out of cornhusks rather than wood.) Algonquin corn masks were always prevalent at the annual Corn Harvest Dance, as a tribute to the Mother Corn deity.

MYTHS AND LEGENDS
OF THE NORTHEAST

THE FIRST PEOPLE AND THE FIRST CORN

Penobscot and Passamaquoddy

A LONG TIME AGO, Klos-kur-beh, the Great Teacher, lived all alone. He was visited one day by a mean who claimed to be his nephew. He stood before Klos-kur-beh saying, 'The foam of the waters bore me as a child. The winds blew about and caused the waves of the sea to foam. The sun warmed the sea foam and the warmth produced life. I am that life. I am a healthy and young being, and I have come to live with you and give you aid in all the things that you do.'

At noon on another day, Klos-kur-beh was visited by a young maiden. She stood before the Great Teacher and the youthful man and called them both 'her offspring'. She spoke on: 'I have come to live with you, my children. I bring love with me which I will give to you. I am also strong, and I have the power to grant this gift. If you give me love and give me my heart's desire, all the world will love me, including the animals. You may find comfort in me for I am young and strong. I was born out of a beautiful plant. The dew fell on a leaf, warmed by the sun. Its warmth produced life and I am that life.'

Klos-kur-beh prayed a song of praise to the Great Spirit for the arrival of the young man and the maiden. Soon afterwards, the two became husband and wife and she produced the first children in the world. She was the first mother. Klos-kur-beh taught the two many things about life and performed mighty works in their presence. When he determined that his work with them was completed, he left them and travelled in the Northland, waiting for the day when he felt it was time to return to them.

The numbers of people continued to multiply and increase. A famine fell upon the people and the First Mother became increasingly sorrowful. She began to distance herself from her husband and stayed away from him from morning until the evening cast long shadows. Since he loved her very much, her husband was saddened to watch First Mother grieve.

One day he followed after his wife when she left him that morning. He trailed her to the ford of a river and waited along its bank for her to return. When she returned later in the day, she began to sing for joy as she crossed the river. It seemed that she was happy as long as her feet remained in the water. When she emerged on the opposite bank, her husband noticed a long green blade behind her right foot. She stopped down and pulled the blade out, throwing it aside. Then she began to sadden once again.

When the husband followed her to their home, he encouraged her to come outside and look at the beauty of the setting sun. As they watched the sun, their

Source

Natalie Curtis
Burlin, *The
Indians' Book*,
New York:
Harper and
Brothers, 1907,
pp. 3–6

seven children joined them, crying to their mother, 'We are hungry, mother, and it will soon by nightfall. Will you bring us some food?' The First Mother began to cry and reassured them that they would have plenty to eat in seven moons. Her husband did not understand what she meant nor what he could possibly do to make his beautiful wife happy again. 'There is nothing you can do to make me happy,' she said to him.

Desperate for answers, the husband left home and travelled to the Northland, where he took counsel with the Great Teacher, his old mentor. After receiving counsel for seven suns, the husband returned to his wife, prepared to do for her whatever she asked of him. This pleased the First Mother and she gave him the following instructions: 'First, you must kill me, then allow two men to drag my body all over a field, all the time dragging me by my hair. In the middle of the field, they must bury my bones. After the passing of seven moons, they must return to the field and collect all they find there rising from the soil. They must eat what they find, for it is my flesh. Do not eat my bones, but burn them instead. The smoke which rises up will give you and my children great peace. Do not eat all of my flesh, but save a portion of it to plant in the ground the next year.'

The next morning, the husband did as First Mother had instructed and he killed her. According to her instructions, two men dragged her body over a fallow field until her flesh was all worn off, leaving them with her bones, which they buried.

After the passing of seven moons, her husband returned to the field where her body had been dragged and found it covered with beautiful green plants reaching to the sky. After removing the fruit of the plant and eating it, he discovered it to be sweet. He named the fruit Skar-mu-mal – "corn". In the middle of the field, where his wife's bones had been buried, he found another plant, this one shorter and with broad, brown leaves. Tasting it, he found it bitter. He named the plant Utar-mur-wa-yeh – 'tobacco".

All the people of the village came out to the field and harvested the corn and the tobacco. Once the crops were gathered in, the people of the tribe called for help from Klos-kur-beh, who helped them divide their harvest evenly among them. When Klos-kur-beh arrived and found the great harvest in the field where First Mother had been dragged, he said: "With this, the words of First Mother have been fulfilled. She claimed to have been born on the leaf of a beautiful plant. She said that she had the power to be loved by all people in the world and now so shall she be. Care well for the fruit of the green plants for they are the flesh of First Mother. Burn the other plant and the smoke will awaken your mind. These plants are filled with the goodness of the heart of First Mother. Remember her when you eat and when the smoke rises before you. Learn to share with one another, for them shall you know the love of the First Mother.'

THE MAGIC MOCCASINS

Passamaquoddy

THREE BROTHERS LIVED near the banks of a beautiful lake. Each of the three thought he was superior in all ways to his other two brothers. Sometimes the brothers were visited by an elderly women who was nearly blind and could barely walk. She was always hungry. When the Old Woman had eaten, however, she could perform amazing things and could grant magical powers to anyone she fancied. The youngest of the three brothers, Joseph, treated the Old Woman well and he became one of her favourites. After he gave her a meal one day, she told him to take his axe and make a pair of wooden moccasins. 'Wear these,' she said to him, 'and you will run faster than any bird.' Joseph made himself such a pair of moccasins and, sure enough, when he put them on, he could run amazingly fast. He could out-run the fastest animals in the forest. He kept the Old Woman supplied with meat since he could easily outrun game animals and capture them with his hands.

When the other two brothers saw the gift of speed the Old Woman had given him, they were jealous. They did not know that his speed came from the wooden moccasins until they secretly watched him put them on in the forest when he thought he was alone.

Joseph kept his wooden moccasins in a birch-bark box. When his brothers found wooden chips where Joseph had carved his magic shoes, they gathered up the chips and made magical moccasins of their own. These moccasins allowed them to run faster than even Joseph! When Joseph saw his brothers in their wooden shoes, he knew they had spied on him and had come to know his secret.

When Joseph fed the Old Woman next, she thanked him by giving him instructions to carve a dug-out canoe. She promised that such a craft would allow him to glide through the water with great swiftness. Just a she told him, Joseph made the dug-out canoe. He was able to fly about the water in the canoe, catching many large fish and water-birds. Again his brothers were jealous of Joseph. They began to keep a close watch on him just as before and finally found some of the wooden chips made when Joseph carved his dug-out. The two brothers began to fashion their own canoe. It, too, was magical and even faster than Joseph's. With it they were able to catch even whales out in the mighty sea.

Joseph was angered by what his brothers had done and he met with the Old Woman, feeding her once again. She encouraged him to build another canoe. 'In this canoe,' she said, 'you will be able to fly through the sky as a bird.' Joseph build the new dug-out and, when he had completed his work, carefully gathered up the wooden chips and burned them all. Once he had completed his work, he sat in his new canoe and was soon flying off into the distant sky. Joseph flew over many new and wonderful lands, flying over strange places and watching strange people below. He travelled great distances, over tall mountains and great oceans. When he had completed his journeys, he returned to his village and there he lived at peace for the remainder of his days.

When the two brothers saw the gift of speed the Old Woman had given Joseph, they were jealous.

Source
John Prince, 'Notes on Passamaquoddy Literature', *Annals of the New York Academy of Science*, 23 (1901), 381–5; 11 (1898), pp. 369–75

THE STORY OF THE GREAT CHENOO

Micmac and Passamaquoddy

O F THE OLD TIME. An Indian, with his wife and their little boy, went one autumn far away to hunt in the northwest. And having found a fit place to pass the winter, they built a wigwam. The man brought home the game, the woman dressed and dried the meat, and the small boy played at shooting birds with bow and arrow; in Indian-wise all went well.

One afternoon, when the man was away and the wife gathering wood, she heard a rustling in the bushes, as though some beast were brushing through them, and, looking up, she saw with horror something worse than the worst she had feared. It was an awful face glaring at her – a something made of devil, man and beast in their most dreadful forms. It was like a haggard old man with wolfish eyes; he was stark naked; his shoulders and lips were gnawed away, as if, when made with hunger, he had eaten his own flesh. He carried a bundle on his back. The woman had heard of the terrible Chenoo, the being who comes from the far, icy north, a creature who is a man grown to be both devil and cannibal, and saw at once that this was one of them.

Truly she was in trouble; but dire need gives quick wit, as it wa with this woman, who, instead of showing fear, ran up and addressed him with fair words, as 'My dear father', pretending surprise and joy, and, telling him how glad her heart was, asked where he had been so long. The Chenoo was amazed beyond measure at such a greeting where he expected yells and prayers, and in mute wonder let himself be led into the wigwam.

She was a wise and good woman. She took him in; she said she was sorry to see him so woebegone; she pitied his sad state; she brought a suit of her husband's clothes; she told him to dress himself and be cleaned. He did as she bade. He sat by the side of the wigwam, and looked surly and sad, but kept quite. It was all a new thing to him.

She arose and went out. She kept gathering sticks. The Chenoo rose and followed her. She was in great fear. 'Now,' she thought, 'my death is near; now he will kill and devour me.'

The Chenoo came to her. He said, 'Give me the axe!' She gave it, and he began to cut down the trees. Man never saw such hopping The great pines fell right and left, like summer saplings; the boughs were hewed and split as if by a tempest. She cried out, '*Noo, tabeagul boohsoogul!* – My father, there is enough!' He laid down the aze; he walked into the wigwam and sat down, always in grim silence. The woman gathered her wood, and remained as silent on the opposite side.

She heard her husband coming. She ran out and told him all. She asked him to do as she was doing. He thought it well. He went in and spoke kindly. He said, '*N'chilch* – My father-in-law', and asked where he had been so long. The Chenoo stared in amazement, but when he heard the man talk of all that had happened for years his fierce face grew gentler..

They had their meal; they offered him food, but he hardly touched it. He lay down to sleep. The man and his wife kept awake in terror. When the fire burned up and it became warm, the Chenoo asked that a screen should be placed before him. He was from the ice; he could not endure heat.

Source
Charles G. Leland, *The Algonquin Legends of New England*, Boston: Houghton, Mifflin, and Company, 1884, pp. 233–44

For three days he stayed in the wigwam; for three days he was sullen and grim; he hardly ate. Then he seemed to change. He spoke to the woman; he asked her if she had any tallow. She told him they had much. He filled a large kettle; there was a gallon in it. He put it on the fire. When it was scalding hot, he drank it all off at a draught.

He became sick; hew grew pale. He cast up all the horrors and abominations of earth, things appalling to every sense. When all was over he seemed changed. He lay down and slept. When he awoke he asked for food and ate much. From that time he was kind and good. They feared him no more.

They lived on meat such as Indians prepare. The Chenoo was tired of it. One day he said, '*N'toos* (my daughter), have you no *pela weoos*? (fresh meat)'. She said, 'No.' When her husband returned the Chenoo saw that there was black mud on his snow-shoes. He asked him if there was a spring of water near. The friend said there was one half a day's journey distant. 'We must go there tomorrow,' said the Chenoo.

And they went together, very early. The Indian was fleet in such running. But the old man, who seemed so wasted and worn, went on his snow-shoes like the wind. They came to the spring. It was large and beautiful; the snow was all melted away around it; the border was flat and green.

Then the Chenoo stripped himself and danced around the spring his magic dance; and soon the water began to foam, and anon to rise and fall, as if some monster below were heaving in accord with the steps and the song. The Chenoo danced faster and wilder; then the head of an immense *taktalok* (lizard) rose above the surface. The old man killed it with a blow of his hatchet. Dragging it out he began again to dance. He brought out another, the female, not so large, but still heavy as an elk. They were small spring lizards, but the Chenoo had conjured them; by magic they were made into monsters.

He dressed the game; he cut it up. He took the heads and feet and tails and all that he did not want, and cast them back into the spring. 'They will grow again into many lizards,' he said. When the meat was trimmed it looked like that of the bear. He bound it together with withies; he took it on his shoulders; he ran like the wind; his load was nothing.

The Indian was a great runner; in all the land was not his like; but now he lagged far behind. 'Can you go no faster than that?' asked the Chenoo. 'The sun is setting; the red will be black soon. At this rate it will be dark before we get home. Get on my shoulders.'

The Indian mounted on the load. The Chenoo bade him hold his head low, so that he would not be knocked off by the branches. 'Brace your feet,' he said, 'so as to be steady.' Then the old man flew like the wind – *nebe sokano'v'jal samastuk-teskugul chel wegwasumug wegul*; the bushes whistled as they flew past them. They got home before sunset.

Then the spring was at hand. One day the Chenoo told them that something terrible would soon come to pass. An enemy, a Chenoo, a woman, was coming like wind, yes – on the wind – from the north to kill him. There could be no escape from the battle. She would be far more furious, made and cruel than any male, even one of his own cruel race, could be. He knew not how the battle would end; but the man and his wife must be put in a place of safety. To keep them from hearing the terrible war-whoops of the Chenoo, which is death to mortals, their ears must be closed. They must hide themselves in a cave.

Then he sent the woman for the bundle which he had brought with him, and which, had hung untouched on a branch of a tree since he had been with them. And he said if she fought aught in it offensive to her to throw it away, but certainly to bring him a smaller bundle that was within the other. So she went and opened it, and that which she found therein was a pair of human legs and feet, the remains of some earlier horrid meal. She threw them far away. The small bundle she brought to him.

The Chenoo opened it and took from it a pair of horns – horns of the *chepitch-calm* (dragon). One of them has two branches; the other is straight and smooth. They were golden-bright. He gave the straight horn to the Indian; he kept the other. He said that these were magical weapons, and the only ones of any use in the coming fight. So they waited for the foe.

And the third day came. The Chenoo was fierce and bold; he listened; he had no fear. He heard the long and awful scream – like nothing of earth – of the enemy, as she sped through the air far away in the icy north, long ere the others could here it. And the manner of it was this: that if they without harm should live after hearing the first deadly yell of the enemy they could take no harm, and if they did but hear the answering shout of their friend all would be well with them. But he said, 'Should you hear me call for help, then hasten with the horn, and you may save my life.'

They did as he bade: they stopped their ears; they hid in a deep hold dug in the ground. All at once the cry of the foe burst on them like screaming thunder; their ears rang with pain: they were well-nigh killed, for all the care they had taken. But then the heard the answering cry of their friend, and were no longer in danger from more noise.

The battle begun, the fight was fearful. The monsters, by their magic with their range, rose to the size of mountains. The tall pines were torn up, the ground trembled as in an earthquake, rocks crashed upon rocks, the conflict deepened and darkened; no tempest was every so terrible. Then the male Chenoo was heard crying, '*N'loosook! choogooye! abog unumooe!* – My son-in-law, come and help me!'

He ran to the fight. What he saw was terrible! The Chenoos, who upright would have risen far above the clouds as giants of hideous form, were struggling on the ground. The female seemed to be the conqueror. She was holding her foe down, she knelt on him, she was doing all she could to thrust her dragon's horn into his ear. And he, to avoid death, was moving his head rapidly from side to side, while she, mocking his cries, said 'You have no son-in-law to help you. – *Neen nabujje*ole – I'll take your cursed life, and eat your liver.'

The Indian was so small by these giants that the stranger did not notice him. 'Now,' said his friend, 'thrust the horn into her ear!' He did this with a well-directed blow; he struck hard; the point entered her head. At the touch it sprouted quick as a flash of lightning, it darted through the head, it came out of the other ear, it had became like a long pole. It touched the ground, it struck downward, it took deep and firm root.

'Now,' said the Chenoo, 'thrust the horn into her ear!'

The male Chenoo bade him raise the other end of the horn and place it against a large tree. He did so. It coiled itself round the tree like a snake, it grew rapidly; the enemy was held hard and fast. Then the two began to dispatch her. It was long and weary work. Such a being, to be killed at all, must be hewed into small pieces; flesh and bones must all be utterly consumed by fire. Should the least fragment

remain unburnt, from it would spring a grown Chenoo, with all the force and fire of the first.

The fury of battle past, the Chenoos had become of their usual size. The victor hewed the enemy into small pieces, to be revenged for the insult and threat of eating his liver. He, having roasted that part of his captive, at it before her; while she was yet alive he did this. He told her she was served as she would have served him.

But the hardest task of all was to come. It was to burn or melt the heart. It was of ice, and more than ice: as much colder as ice is colder than fire, as much harder as ice is harder than water. When placed in the fire it put out the flame, yet by long burning it melted slowly, until they at least broke it to fragments with a hatchet, and then melted these. So they returned to the camp.

Spring came. The snows of winter, as water, ran down the rivers to the sea; the ice and snow which had encamped on the inland hills sought the shore. So did the Indian and his wife; the Chenoo, with softened soul, went with them. Now he was becoming a man like other men. Before going they built a canoe for the old man: they did not cover it with birch bark; they made it of moose skin. In it they placed a part of their venison and skins. The Chenoo took his place it; they took the lead, and he followed.

And after winding on with the river, down rapids and under forest boughs, they came out into the sunshine, on a broad, beautiful lake. But suddenly, when midway in the water, the Chenoo lay flat in the canoe, as if to hide himself. And to explain this he said that he had just then been discovered by another Chenoo, who was standing on the top of a mountain, whose dim blue outline could just be seen stretching far away to the north.

'He has seen me,' he said, 'but he cannot see you. Nor can he behind me now, but should he discover me again, his wrath will be roused. Then he will attack me; I know not who might conquer. I prefer peace.'

So he lay hidden, and they took his canoe in tow. But when they had crossed the lake and come to the river again, the Chenoo said that he could not travel further by water. He would walk the woods, but sail on streams no more. So they told him where they meant to camp that night. He started over mountains and through woods and up rocks, a far, roundabout journey. And the man and his wife went down the river in a spring freshet, headlong with the rapids. But when they had paddled round the point where they meant to pass the night, they saw smoke rising among the trees, and on landing they found the Chenoo sleeping soundly by the fire which had been built for them.

This he repeated for several days. But as they went south a great change came over him. He was a being of the north. Ice and snow had no effect on him, but he could not endure the soft airs of summer. He grew weaker and weaker; when they had reached their village he had to be carried like a little child. He had grown gentle. His fierce and formidable face was now like that of a man. His wounds had healed; his teeth no longer grinned wildly all the time. The people gathered round him in wonder.

He was dying. This was after the white men had come. They sent for a priest. He found the Chenoo as ignorant of all religion as a wild beast. At first he would repel the father in anger. Then he listened and learned the truth. So the old heathen's heart changed; he was deeply moved. He asked to be baptized, and as the first tear which he had ever shed in all his life came to his eyes he died.

HOW A MEDICINE MAN TURNED A MAN INTO A TREE

Passamaquoddy

THIS IS AN ANCIENT LEGEND concerning a Passamaquoddy woman who was always travelling through the forests. She ate many different varieties of tree and bush as she travelled until she became pregnant from eating one. As she grew larger with child, she stopped her forest travels and built herself a wigwam along the banks of a clear, swiftly running stream. Finally, one night, she gave birth to her child. Although her first thoughts were to kill the infant, she decided instead to make a small bark canoe and place her baby inside it. Then she set the canoe into the stream and watched as the canoe carried her child away. As the canoe floated out of sight, the child was safe inside. When the canoe floated alongside a village, one of the maidens discovered the canoe and found the baby inside. She took the baby home with her. Then something strange began to take place. Every morning in the village, a child died. No one could explain why this was happening.

Soon a curious woman watched as the rescued child toddled off each night to the river and returned soon afterwards. She watched the child closely and discovered that when he returned to his own wigwam, he was carrying a small tongue in his hand, which he roasted over a fire and ate. Only then did the child lie down to sleep for the night.

When, on the following morning, the word circulated throughout the village that another Indian child had died, the watchful woman spoke to the parents of the dead child, advising them to examine their child's mouth. Sure enough, the dead baby's tongue had been cut out, which had caused the baby to bleed to death.

Immediately, a tribal council was held to determine the fate of the young killer. Some wanted him cut to pieces and his body parts cast into the river, while others wishes to burn the child until its body was nothing but ashes. While the council members deliberated, another child was killed by the rescued child, its tongue removed and roasted. Then the child promised everyone that he would murder no more children.

Then the child began mysteriously to grow so that he was suddenly a lrage boy. He told the people of the village that he intended to remove one of his own bones from his side. When he attempted this, all of his bones came tumbling out of his body at the same time. With his bones out of his body, the young boy began to grow very large.

In time, the young boy became a great medicine man of the Passamaquoddies. He had great gifts and powers which he used at the request of the villagers. When his tribe moved to another encampment site, he remained in the old one. Before moving, his people built him a new wigwam, where they continued to visit him even after they moved away from him. Usually, when he was visited by someone with a request for help, he would say to them, 'You must turn me over and examine me, for there you will find the medicine you need.'

One day, a young brave visited the Medicine Man, requesting a love elixir from him to attract a women to him. The Medicine Man instructed the youth to turn him over. Underneath the Medicine Man lay an herb which the youth was told he must keep for ever.

Source
J. Walter Fewkes, 'How the Medicine Man was Born, and How He Turned a Man into a Tree', *JAFL*, 3 (1884), pp. 273–5

Immediately the young maidens of the camp began to follow the brave around. He found it impossible ever to be alone, due to the young women constantly giving him their attention. When the problem became too much for him, he returned to the Medicine Man and gave him back his herb.

A second young brave visited the MEdicine Man asking him for eternal life.

'Make me live as long as the earth exists,' he said to the conjuror.

The Medicine Man replied, 'What you have asked for is not easy, yet I shall endeavour to fulfil your request. Turn me over.'

The visitor found another herb beneath the MEdicine Man. He ordered the brave to go at once to a site away from the encampment, a bar and barren place where no vegetation grew. The young warrior did as the conjuror instructed him finding a destitute spot where no plants grew. As the young stood on the spot, a change began to occur. He soon watched with horror as branches began to appear all over his body. Shortly, he was transformed into a cedar tree and doomed to stand on that spot, for ever, continuing to live without end, serving no good purpose for anyone.

HOW A YOUNG MAN DIED FROM LOVE

Passamaquoddy

O F THE OLDEN TIME. Two brothers went hunting in the autumn, and that as far as the head waters of the Penobscot, where they remained all winter. But in March their snow-shoes gave out, as did their moccasins, and they wished that a woman were there to mend them.

When the younger brother returned first to the lodge, the next day – which he generally did, to get it ready for the elder – he was astonished to find that someone had been there before him, and that, too, in the housekeeping. For garments had been mended, the place cleaned and swept, a fire built and the pot was boiling. He said nothing of this to his brother; but returning the next day at the same time, found that all had been attended to, as at first. And again he said nothing; but in the morning, when he went forth to hunt, he did but go a little way and, returning, watched, from a hidden place, the door. And there came a beautiful and graceful girl, well attired, who entered the wigwam. And he, stepping softly, looking through a hole in the hut, saw her very busy with her housekeeping.

Then he entered, and she seemed to be greatly alarmed and confused; but he calmed her, and they soon became good friends, sporting together very happily all day long like children, for indeed, they were both young.

When the sun's height was little and his shadows long, the girl said, 'I must go now. I hear your brother coming, and I fear him. But I will return tomorrow. Addio!'

So she went, and the elder brother knew nothing of what had happened. The next day she came again, and once more they played in sunshine and shadow until evening; but ere she went he sought to persuade her to remain always. And she, as if in doubt, answered, 'Tell they brother all, and it may be that I will stay an serve ye both. For I can make the snow-shoes and moccasins which ye so much need,

Source

Charles G. Leland, *The Algonquin Legends of New England*, Boston: Houghton, Mifflin, and Company, 1884, pp. 295–9

and also canoes.' Then she departed with the day, and the elder, returning, heard from his brother all that had happened, and said, 'Truly I should be glad to have someone here to take care of the wigwam and make snow-shoes.'

So she came in the morning, and hearing from the younger that his brother had consented to her coming was very glad, and went away, as in haste. But she returned about noon, drawing a toboggin (sled) piled up with garments and arms, for she was a huntress. Indeed, she could do all things as few women could, whether it were cooking, needlework or making all that men need. And the winter passed very pleasantly, until the snow grew soft, and it was time for them to return. Till she came they had little luck in hunting, but since her coming all had gone well with them, and they now had a wonderful quantity of furs.

Then they returned in a canoe, going down the river to their village. But as they came near it the girl grew sad, for she had thrown out her soul to their home, though they knew it not, by means of a vision. And suddenly she said, as they came to a point of land, 'Here I must leave. I can go no further. Say nothing of me to your parents, for your father would have but little love for me.' And the young men sought to persuade her, but she only answered sorrowfully, 'It cannot be.' So they came home with their furs, and the elder was so proud of their luck and their strange adventure that he could not hold his peace, but told all.

Then his father was very angry, and said, 'All my life have I feared this. Know that this woman was a devil of the woods, a witch of the Mitche-hant, a sister of the Oonahgamess (goblins and ghosts).' And he spoke so earnestly and so long of this thing that they were afraid, and the elder, being persuaded by the sire, went forth to slay her, and the younger followed him afar. So they sought her by the stream, and found her bathing, and, seeing them, she ran up a little hill. And, as she ran, the elder shot an arrow at her. Then there was a strange flurry about her, a fluttering of scattered feathers, and they saw her fly away as a partridge. Returning, they told all this to their father, who said, 'You did well. I know all about these female devils who seek to destroy men. Verily this was a she-Mikumwess (prankster).'

But the younger could not forget her, and longed to see her gain; so one day he went into the woods, and there he indeed found her, and she was as kind as before. Then he said, 'Truly it was not by my goodwill that my brother shot at you.' And she answered, 'Well do I know that, and that it was all by your father; yet I blame him not, for this is an affair of N'karnayoo, the days of old; and even yet it is not at an end, and the greatest is to come. But let the day be only a day unto itself; the things of tomorrow are for tomorrow, and those of yesterday are departed.' So they forgot their troubles, and played together merrily all day long in the woods and in the open places, and told stories of old times till sunset. And as the Kah-kah-goos, or Crow, went to his tree, the boy said, 'I must return'; and she replied, 'Whenever you would see me, come to the woods. And remember what I say. Do not marry anyone else. For your father wishes you to do so, and he will speak of it to you, and that soon. Yet is is for your sake only that I say this.' Then she told him word by word all that his father had said; but he was not astonished, for now he knew that she was not as other women; but he cared not. And he grew brave and bold, and then he was above all things. And when she told him that if he should marry another he would surely die, it was as nothing to him.

Then returning, the first thing his father said was, 'My son, I have provided a wife for you, and the wedding must be at once.' And he said, 'It is well. Let it be so.' Then the bride came. For four days they held the wedding dance; four days they feasted. But on the last day he said, 'This is the end of it all,' and he laid him down on a white bearskin, and a great sickness came upon him, and when they brought the bride to him he was dead.

Truly the father knew what ailed him, and more withal, of which he said nothing. But he liked the place no longer, and he and his went away therfrom, and scattered far and wide.

THE WOMAN AND THE SERPENT

Passamaquoddy

OF OLD TIMES. There was a very beautiful woman. She turned the heads of all the men. She married, and her husband died very soon after, but she immediately took another. Within a single year she had five husbands, and these were the cleverest and handsomest and bravest in the tribe. And then she married again.

This, the sixth, was such a silent man that he passed for a fool. But he was wiser than people thought. He came to believe, by thinking it over, that this woman had some strange secret. He resolved to find it out. So he watched her all the time. He kept his eye on her by night and by day.

It was summer, and she proposed to go into the woods to pick berries, and to camp there. By and by, when there were in the forest, she suggested that he should go on to the spot where they intended to remain and build a wigwam. He said that he would do so. But he went a little way into the woods and watched her

As soon as she believed that he was gone, she rose and walked rapidly onwards. He followed her, unseen. She went on, till, in a deep, wild place among the rocks, she came to a pond. She sat down and sang a song. A great foam, or froth, rose to the surface of the water. Then in the foam appeared the tail of a serpent. The creature was of immense size. The woman, who had laid aside all her garments, embraced the serpent, which twined around her, enveloping all her limbs and body in his folds. The husband watched it all. He now understood that, the venom of the serpent having entered the woman, she had saved her life by transferring it to others, who died.

He went on to the camping ground and built a wigwam. He made up two beds; he built a fire. His wife came. She was earnest that there should be only a single bed. He sternly bade her lie by herself. She was afraid of him. She laid down and went to sleep. He arose three times during the night to replenish the fire. Every time he called here and there was no answer. In the morning he shook her. She was dead. She had died by the poison of the serpent. They sunk her in the pond where the snake lived.

Source
Charles G. Leland, *The Algonquin Legends of New England*, Boston: Houghton, Mifflin, and Company, 1884, pp. 273–5

THE ORIGIN OF INDIAN SUMMER

Penobscot

IN DAYS LONG PAST, as the Penobscot Indians say, an elderly man named Zuni paid a call to the Chief of the Sky Spirits requesting his aid. He had been ill in the spring of the year when all the others in his tribe were busying themselves with the plaint of seeds. His illness had lingered and kept him from planting. By summer's end, the people of his village had harvested their corn and other vegetables. They had dried them for their winter's food. However, due to his illness, Zuni was not supplied with food for the cold, wintry season. He had nothing for his food.

In desperation, he visited the Chief of the Sky Spirits and spoke to him: 'I was ill when the spring planting was done and remained ill all summer. Now the harvest has come and gone and winter is approaching. I am not prepared. I have no food. I have come to you for help. Wheat am I to do now?'

The Chief of the Sky Spirits took pity on the old man and gave him an immediate response. 'Although the season of planting and harvesting has passed, go, now, and plant your seeds. I will make certain that you will have food for the winter.'

With this advice and a promise from the Chief of the Sky spirits, Zuni returned home and went immediately into his field and planted his seeds. Despite the fact that it was autumn, the season remained warm. No sooner had he finished his planting than the vegetables in his new garden were fully grown and ready for Zuni to begin harvesting. Within seven days, Zuni had gathered up all his new vegetables and his abundance was equal to any other man of his village. Only when he had completed his gathering did winter come.

Now the Penobscot people have a name for the warm days of autumn. They call them Indian summer.

Source

Frank G. Speck, 'Penobscot Tales', *JAFL*, 48 (1935), pp. 95_6

GREAT HEAD AND THE TEN BROTHERS

Iroquois

FAR AWAY IN A REMOTE SPOT an orphaned family of ten boys lived with their uncle. The older brothers went out every day to hunt, but the younger ones, not yet fitted for so rigorous a life, remained at home with their uncle, or at least did not venture much beyond the immediate vicinity of their lodge. One day the hunters did not return at their usual hour. As the evening passed without bringing any sign of the missing youths, the little band at home became alarmed. At length the eldest of the boys left in the ledge volunteered to go in search of his brothers. His uncle consented, and he set off, but he did not return.

In the morning another brother said, 'I will go to seek my brothers.' Having obtained permission, he went, but he also did not come back. Another and another took upon himself the task of finding the lost hunters, but of the searchers as well as of those sought for there was no news forthcoming. At length only the youngest of the lads remained at home, and to his entreaties to be allowed to seek

Source

Lewis Spence, *The Myths of the North American Indians*, London: George G. Harrap & Co., 1914 pp. 232–5

for his brothers the uncle turned a deaf ear, for he feared to lose the last of his young nephews.

One day when uncle and nephew were out in the forest the latter fancied he heard a deep groan, which seemed to proceed from the early exactly under his feet. They stopped to listen. The sound was repeated – unmistakably a human groan. Hastily they began digging in the earth, and in a moment or two came upon a man covered with mould and apparently unconscious.

The pair carried the unfortunate one to their lodge, where they rubbed him with bear's oil till he recovered consciousness. When he was able to speak he could give no explanation of how he came to be buried alive. He had been out hunting, he said, when suddenly his mind became a blank, and he remembered nothing more till he found himself in the lodge with the old man and the boy. His hosts begged the stranger to stay with them, and they soon discovered that he was no ordinary mortal, but a powerful magician. At times he behaved very strangely. One night, while a great storm raged without, he tossed restlessly on his couch instead of going to sleep. At last he sought the old uncle.

'Do you hear that noise?' he said. 'That is my brother, Great Head, who is rid-ind on the wind. Do you not hear him howling?'

The old man considered this astounding speech for a moment, then he asked, 'Would he come here if you sent for him?'

'No,' said the other, thoughtfully, 'but we might bring him here by magic. Should he come you must have food ready for him, in the shape of huge blocks of maple wood, for that is what he lives on.'

The stranger departed in search of his brother Great Head, taking with him his bow, and on the way he came across a hickory tree, whose roots provided him with arrows. About midday he drew near to the dwelling of his brother, Great Head. In order to see without being seen, he changed himself into a mole, and crept through the grass till he saw Great Head perched on a rock, frowning fiercely. 'I see thee!' he growled, with his wild eyes fixed on an owl. The man-mole drew his bow and shot an arrow at Great Head. The arrow became larger and larger as it flew towards the monster, but it returned to him who had fired it, and as it did so it regained its natural size. The man seized it and rushed back the way he had come. Very soon he heard Great Head in pursuit, puffing and snorting along on the wings of a hur-ricane. When the creature had almost overtaken him he turned and discharged another arrow. Again and again he repulsed his pursuer in this fashion, till he lured him to the lodge where his benefactors lived. When Great Head burst into the house the uncle and nephew began to hammer him vigorously with mallets. To their surprise the monster broke into laughter, for he had recognized his brother and was very pleased to see him. He ate the maple blocks they brought him with a hearty appetite, whereupon they told him the story of the missing hunters.

'I know what has become of them,' said Great Head. 'They have fallen into the hands of a witch. If this young man –' indicating the nephew – 'will accompany me, I will show him her swelling, and the bones of his brothers.'

The youth, who loved adventure, and was besides very anxious to lean the fate of his brothers, at once consented to seek the home of the witch. So he and Great Head started off, and lost no time in getting to the place. They found the space in front of the lodge strewn with dry bones, and the witch sitting in the doorway singing. When she saw them she muttered the maic word, which turned living

The youth, who loved adventure, and was besides very anxious to learn the fate of his brothers, at once consented to seek the home of the witch.

people into dry bones, but on Great Head and his companion it had no effect whatever. Acting on a prearranged signal, Great Head and the youth attacked the witch and killed her. No sooner had she expired than he flesh turned into birds and beasts and fishes. What was left of her they burned to ashes.

Their next act was to select the bones of the nine brothers from among the heap, and this they found no easy task. But at last it was accomplished, and Great Head said to his companion, 'I am going home to my rock. When I pass overhead in a great storm I will bid these bones arise, and they will get up and return with you.'

The youth stood alone for a little while till he heard the sound of a fierce tempest. Out of the hurricane Great Head called to the brothers to arise. In a moment they were all on their feet, receiving the congratulations of their younger brother and each other, and filled with joy at their reunion.

THE WOMAN WHO MARRIED THE THUNDER

Passamaquoddy

ONCE A WOMAN WENT to the edge of a lake and lay down to sleep. As she awoke, she saw a great serpent, with glittering eyes, crawl from the water and stealthily approach her. She had no power to resist his embrace. After her return to her people her condition betrayed itself and she was much persecuted; they pursued he with sticks and stones, howling abuse.

She fled from the village, she went afar into wild places, and, sitting down on the grass, wept, wishing that she were dead. As she sat and wailed, a very beautiful girl, dressed in silver and gold, appeared and, after listening to her sad story, said, 'Follow me!'

Then they went up high into a mountain, through three rocks, until they cae into a pleasant wigwam with a very smooth floor. An old man, so old that he was all white, came to meet them. Then he, taking a short stick, bade her dance. He began to sing, and as he sang she gave birth, one by one, to twelve serpents. These the old man killed in succession with his stick as they were born. Then she became thin again and was in her natural form.

The old man had a son, Badawk, the Thunder, and a daughter, Psawk-tankapic, the Lightning, and when Thunder returned he offered to take her back to her own people, but she refused to go. Then the old man said to his son, 'Take her for your wife and be good to her.' So they were married.

In time she bore a son. When the boy could stand, the old man, who never leaves the mountain, called him to stand before him, while he fastened wings to the child. He was soon able, with these wings, to make a noise, which greatly pleased the grandfather. When a storm is approaching, the distant rumbling is the muttering thunder made by the child, but it is badawk, his father, who comes in the dark cloud and makes the roaring crash, while Psawk-tankapic flashes her lightnings.

In after-days, when the woman visited her people, she told them that they never need fear the thunder or lightning.

They came into a pleasant wigwam with a very smooth floor. An old man, so old that he was all white, came to meet them.

Source
George G. Leland, *The Algonquin Legends of New England*, Boston: Houghton, Mifflin, and Company, 1884, pp. 266–7

THE BOY MAGICIAN

Iroquois

IN THE HEART OF THE WILDERNESS there lived an old woman and her little grandson. The two found no lack of occupation from day to day, the woman busying herself with cooking and cleaning and the boy with shooting and hunting. The grandmother frequently spoke of the time when the child would grow up and go out into the world.

'Always go to the east,' she would say. 'Never go to the west, for there lies danger.'

But what the danger was she would not tell him, in spite of his importunate questioning. Other boys went west, he thought to himself, and why should not he? Nevertheless his grandmother made him promise that he would not go west.

Years passed by and the child grew to be a man, though he still retained the curiosity and high spirits of his boyhood. His persistent inquiries drew from the old grandmother a reluctant explanation of her warning.

'In the west,' said she, 'there dwells a bring who is anxious to do us harm. If he sees you it will mean death for both of us.'

This statement, instead of frightening the young Indian, only strengthened in him a secret resolution he had formed to go west at the first opportunity. Not that he wishes to bring any misfortune on his poor old grandmother, any more than on himself, but he trusted to his strong arm and clear head to deliver them from their enemy. So with a laugh on his lips he set off to the west.

Towards evening he came to a lake, where he rested. He had not been there long when he heard a voice saying, 'Aha, my fine fellow, I see you!'

The youth looked all round him, and up into the sky above, but he saw no one.

'I am going to send a hurricane,' the mysterious voice continued, 'to break your grandmother's hut to pieces. How will you like that?'

'Oh, very well,' answered the young man gaily. 'We are always in need of firewood and now we shall have plenty.'

'Go home and see,' the voice said mockingly. 'I dare say you will not like it so well.'

Nothing daunted, the young adventurer retraced his steps. As he neared home a great wind sprang up, seeming to tear the very trees out by the roots.

'Make haste!' cried the grandmother from the doorway. 'We shall both be killed!'

When she had drawn him inside and shut the door she scolded him heartily for his disobedience, and bewailed te fate before them. The young man soothed her fears, saying, 'Don't cry, grandmother. We shall turn the lodge into a rock, and so we shall be saved.'

Having some skill in magic, he did as he had said, and the hurricane passed harmlessly over their heads. when it had ceased, they emerged from their retreat, and found an bundance of firewood all round them.

Next day the youth was on the point of setting off towards the west once more, but the urgent entreaties of his grandmother moved him to proceed eastward – for a time. Directly he was out of sight of the lodge he turned his face once more to the west. Arrived at the lake, he heard the voice once more, though its owner was still invisible.

Source

Lewis Spence, *The Myths of the North American Indians,* London: George G. Harrap & Co., 1914, pp. 238–42

'I am going to send a great hailstorm on your grandmother's hut,' it said. 'What do you think of what?'

'Oh,' was the response, 'I think I should like it. I have always wanted a bundle of spears.'

'Go home and see,' said the voice.

Away the youth went through the woods. The sky became darker and darker as he neared his home, and just as he was within a bowshot of the little hut a fierce hailstorm broke and he thought he would be killed before he was able to reach shelter.

'Alas!' cried the old woman when he was safely indoors. 'We shall be destroyed this time. How can we save ourselves?'

Again the young man exercised his magic powers, and transformed the frail hut into a hollow rock, upon which the shafts of the hailstorm spent themselves in vain. At last the sky cleared, the lodge resumed its former shape, and the young man saw a multitude of sharp, beautiful spear-heads on the ground.

'I will get poles,' said he, 'to fit to them for fishing.'

When he returned in a few minutes with the poles he found that the spears had vanished.

'Where are my beautiful spears?' he asked his grandmother.

'They were only ice-spears,' she replied. 'They have all melted away.'

The young Indian was greatly disappointed, and wondered how he could avenge himself on the being who had played on him this malicious trick. 'Be warmed in time,' said the aged grandmother, shaking her head at him. 'Take my advice and leave him alone.'

But the youth's adventurous spirit impelled him to see the end of the matter, so he took a stone and tied it round his neck for a charm, and sought the lake once again. Carefully observing the direction from which the voice proceeded, he saw in the middle of the lake a huge head with a face on every side of it.

'Aha, uncle!' he exclaimed, 'I see you! How would you like it if the lake dried up?'

'Nonsense!' said the voice angrily. 'That will never happen.'

'Go home and see,' shouted the youth, mimicking the mocking tone the other had adopted on the previous occasions. As he spoke he swung his charmed stone round his head and threw it into the air. As it descended it grew larger and larger, and the moment it entered the lake the water began to boil.

The lad returned home and told his grandmother what he had done.

'It is of no use,' said she. 'Many have tried to slay him, but all have perished in the attempt.'

Next morning our hero went westward again, and found the lake quite dry and the animals in it dead, with the exception of a large green frog, who was in reality the malicious being who had tormented the Indian and his grandmother. A quick blow with a stick put an end to the creature, and the triumphant youth bore the good news back to his old grandmother, who from that time was left in peace and quietness.

THE FRIENDLY SKELETON

Iroquois

A LITTLE BOY LIVING in the woods with his old uncle was warned by him not to go eastward, but to play close to the lodge or walk towards the west. The child felt a natural curiosity to know what lay in the forbidden direction, and one day took advantage of his uncle's absence on a hunting expedition to wander away to the east. At length he came to a large lake, on the shores of which he stopped to rest. Here he was accosted by a man, who asked him his name and where he lived.

'Come,' said the strange, when he had finished questioning the boy, 'let us see who can shoot an arrow the highest.'

This they did, and the boy's arrow went much higher than that of his companion. The stranger then suggested a swimming match.

'Let us see,' he said, 'who can swim farthest under water without taking a breath.'

Again the boy beat his rival, who next proposed that they should sail out to an island in the middle of the lake, to see the beautiful birds that were to be found there. The child consented readily, and they embarked in a curious canoe, which was propelled by three swans harnessed to either side of it. Directly they had taken their seats the man began to sing, and the canoe moved off. In a very short time, they had reached the island. Here the little Indian realized that his confidence in his new-found friend was misplaced. The stranger took all his clothes from him, put them in the canoe and jumped in himself, saying, 'Come, swans, let us go home.'

The obedient swans set off at a good pace, and soon left the island far behind. The boy was very angry at having been so badly used, but when it grew dark his resentment changed to fear, and he sat down and credit with cold and misery. Suddenly he heard a husky voice close at hand, and, looking round, he saw a skeleton on the ground.

'I am very sorry for you,' said the skeleton in hoarse tones. 'I will do what I can to help you. But first you must do something for me. Go and dig by that tree, and you shall find a tobacco pouch with some tobacco in it, a pipe and a flint.'

The boy did as he was asked, and when he had filled the pipe he lit it and placed it in the mouth of the skeleton. He saw that the latter's body was full of mice, and that the smoke frightened them away.

'There is a man coming tonight with three dogs,' said the skeleton. 'He is coming to look for you. You must make tracks all over the island, so that they may not find you, and then hide in a hollow tree.'

Again the boy obeyed his gaunt instructor, and when he was safely hidden he saw a man come ashore with three dogs. All night they hunted him, but he had made so many tracks that the dogs were confused, and at last the man departed in anger. Next day the trembling boy emerged and went to the skeleton.

'Tonight,' said the latter, 'the man who brought you here is coming to drink your blood. You must dig a hole in the sand and hide. When he comes out of the canoe you must enter it. say, "Come, swans, let us go home," and if the man calls you do not look back.'

Source

Lewis Spence, *The Myths of the North American Indians*, London: George G. Harrap & Co., 1914, pp. 227–32

Everything fell out as the skeleton had foretold. The boy hid in the sand, and directly he saw his tormentor step ashore he jumped into the canoe, saying hastily, 'Come, swans, let us go home.' Then he began to sing as he had heard the man do when they first embarked. In vain the man called him back; he refused to look round. The swans carried the canoe to a cave in a high rock, where the boy found his clothes, as well as a fire and food. When he had donned his garments and satisfied his hunger he lay down and slept. In the morning he returned to the island, where he found the tyrant quite dead. The skeleton now commanded him to sail eastward to seek for his sister, whom a fierce man had carried away. He set out eagerly on his new quest,and a three days' journey brought him to the place where his sister was. He lost no time in finding her.

'Come, my sister,' said he, 'let us flee away together.'

'Alas! I cannot,' answered te young woman. 'A wicked man keeps me here. It is time for him to return home, and he would be sure to catch us. But let me hide you now, and in the morning we shall go away.'

So she dug a pit and hid her brother, though not a moment too soon, for the footsteps of her husband were heard approaching the hut. The woman had cooked a child, and this she placed before the man.

'You have had visitors,' he said, seeing his dogs snuffling around uneasily.

'No,' was the reply, 'I have seen no one but you.'

'I shall wait til tomorrow,' said the man to himself. 'Then I shall kill and eat him.' He had already guessed that his wife had not spoken the truth. However, he said nothing more, but waited till morning, when, instead of going to a distant swamp to seek for food, as he pretended to do, he concealed himself at a short distance from the hut, and at length saw the brother and sister making for a canoe. They were hardly seated when they saw him running towards them. In his hand he bore a large hook, with which he caught the frail vessel; but the lad broke the hook with a stone, and the canoe darted out on to the lake. The man was at a loss for a moment, and could only shout incoherent threats after he pair. Then an idea occurred to him, and, lying down on the shore, he began to drink the water. This caused the canoe to rush back again, but once more the boy was equal to the occasion. Seizing the large stone with which he had broken the hook, he threw it at the man and slew him, the water at the same time rushing back into the lake. Thus the brother and sister escaped, and in three days they had arrived at the island, where they heartily thanked their benefactor, the skeleton. He, however, had still another task for the young Indian to perform.

'Take your sister home to your uncle's lodge,' said he, 'then return here yourself, and say to the many bones which you will find on the island, "Arise,' and they shall come to life again.'

When the brother and sister reached their home they found that their old uncle had been grievously lamenting the loss of his nephew, and he was quite overjoyed at seeing them. On his recommendation they built a large lodge to accommodate the people they were to bring back with them. When it was completed, the youth revisited the island, bade the bones arise, and was delighted to see them obey his bidding and become men and women. He led them to the lodge he had built, where they all dwelt happily for a long time.

THE YOUNG MAN WHO WAS SAVED BY A RABBIT AND A FOX

Passamaquoddy

THERE DWELT A COUPLE in the woods, far away from other people – a man and his wife. They had one boy, who grew up strong and clever. One day he said, 'Father and mother, let me go and see other men and women,' They grieved but let him go.

He went afar. All night he lay on the ground. In the morning he heard something coming. He rose and saw it was a Rabbit, who said, 'Ha, friend, where go you?'

The boy answered, 'To find people.'

'That is what I want,' replied the Rabbit. 'Let us go together.'

So they went on for a long time, till they heard voices far off, and walking quietly came to a village.

'Now,' said the Rabbit, 'steal up unseen and listen to them!' The boy did so, and heard the people saying that a *kewahqu'* 'a cannibal monster', was to come the next day to devour the daughter of their sagamore. And having returned and reported this to the Rabbit, the latter said to the boy, 'Have no fear; go to the people and tell them that you can save her.' He did so, but it was long before they would listen to him. Yet at last it came to the ears of the old chief tha a strange young man insisted that he could save the girl; so the chief sent for him, and said, 'They tell me that you think you can deliver my daughter from death. Do so and she shall be yours.'

Then he returned to the Rabbit, who said, 'They did not send the girl far away because they know that the demon can follow any track. But I hope to make a track which he cannot follow. Now do you, as soon as it shall be dark, bring her to this place.'

The young man did so, and the Rabbit was there with a sled, and in his hand he had two squirrels. These he smoothed down, and as he did so they grew to be as large as the largest sled-dogs. Then all three went headlong, like the wind, till they came to another village.

The Rabbit looked about till he found a certain wigwam and then peered through a crevice into it. 'This is the place,' he said. 'Enter.' They did so; then the rabbit ran away. They found in the cabin an old woman, who was very kind, but who, on seeing them, burst into tears. 'Ah, my dear grandchildren,' she credit, 'your death is following you rapidly, for the *kewahqu'* is on your track and will soon be here. But run down to the river, where you will find your grandfather camping.'

They went and were joined by the Rabbit, who had spent the time in making many divergent tracks in the ground. The *kewahqu'* came. The tracks delayed him a long time, but at last he found the right one. Meanwhile, the young couple went on, and found an old man by the river. He said, 'Truly you are in great danger, for the *kewahqu'* is coming. But I will help you.' Saying this, he threw himself into the water, where he floated with outstretched limbs, and said, 'Now, my children, get on me.' The girl feared lest she should fall off, but being reassured mounted, when he turned into a canoe, which carried them safely across. But when they turned to look at him, lo! he was no longer a canoe, but an old Duck. 'Now my dear children,' he said, 'hasten to the top of yonder grey mountain.' The *kewahqu'* came

Source

George G. Leland, *The Algonquin Legends of New England*, Boston: Houghton, Mifflin, and Company, 1884, pp. 227–32

raging and roaring in a fury, but however he pursued, they were at the foot of the precipice before him.

There stood the Rabbit. He was holding up a very long pole; no pine was ever longer. 'Climb this,' he said. And, as they climbed, it lengthened, till they left it for the hill, and then scrambled up the rocks. Then the *kewahqu'* came yelling and howling horribly. seeing thefugitives far above, he swarmed up the pole. With him, too, it grew, and grew rapidly, till it seemed to be half a mile high. Now the *kewahqu'* was no such sorcerer that he could fly; neither had he wings' he must remain on the pole; and when he came to the top the young man pushed it afar. It fell, and the monster was killed by the fall thereof.

They went with the squirrel-sledge; they flew through the woods on the snow by the moonlight; they were very glad. And at last they came to the girl's village, when the Rabbit said, 'Now, friend, goodbye. Yet there is more trouble coming,and when it is with you I and mine will aid you. So farewell.' And when they were home again it all appeared like a dream. Then the wedding feast was held,and all seemed well.

But the young men of the village hated the youth, and desired to kill him that they might take his wife. They persuaded him to go with them fishing on the sea. Then they raised a cry, and said, 'A whale is chasing us! He is under the canoe!' and suddenly they knocked him overboard, and paddled away like an arrow in flight.

The young man called for help. A Crow came, and said, 'Swim or float as long as you can. I will bring you aid.' He floated a long time. The Crow returned with a strong cord; the Crow made himself very large; he threw one end of the cord to the youth; by the other he towed him to a small island. 'I can do no more,' he said, 'but there is another friend.' So as the youth sat there, starving and freezing, there came to him a Fox.

'Ha, friend,' he said, 'are you here?'

'Yes,' replied the youth, 'and dying of hunger.'

The Fox reflected an instant, and said, 'Truly, I have no meat; and yet there is a way.' So he picked from the ground a blade of dry grass, and bade the youth eat it. He did so, and found himself a moose (or a horse). Then he fed richly on the young grass till he had enough, when the Fox gave him a second straw, and he became a man again.

'Friend,' said the Fox, 'there is an Indian village on the mainland, where there is to be a great fest,a grand dance. Would you like to be there?'

'Indeed I would,' replied the youth.

'Then wait till dark, and I will take you there,' said the Fox. And when night came he bade the youth close his eyes and enter the river, and take hold of the end of his tail while he should draw. So in the tossing sea they went on for hours.

Thought the fox, 'We shall never get there.'

Said the Fox, 'Yes, we will, but keep your eyes shut.'

So it went on for another hour, when the youth thought again, 'We shall never reach land.'

Said the Fox, 'Yes, we shall.' However, after a time he opened his eyes, when they were only ten feet from the shore, and this cost them more time and trouble than all the previous swim ere they had the beach underfoot.

It was his own village. The festival was for the marriage of his own wife to one of the young men who had pushed him overboard. Great was his magic power,

They went with the squirrel sledge, flying through the woods on the snow by the moonlight.

great was his anger; he became strong as death. Then he went to his own wigwam, and his wife, seeing him, cried aloud for you, and kissed him and wept all at once. He said, 'Be glad, but the hour of punishment for the men who made these tears is come.' So he went to the sagamore and told him all.

The old chief called for the young men. 'Slay them all as you choose,' he said to his son-in-law; 'scalp them.' But the youth refused. He called to the Fox and got the straws which gave the power to transform men to beasts. He changed his enemies into bad animals – one into a porcupine, one into a hog – and they were driven into the woods. Thus it was that the first hog and the first porcupine came into the world.

GLOOSCAP THE DIVINITY

Wabanaki

NOW THE GREAT LORD GLOOSCAP, who was worshipped in after-days by all the Wabanaki, or the children of light, was a twin with a brother. As he was good, this brother, whose name was Malsumsis, or Wolf the younger, was bad. Before they were born, the babes consulted to consider how they had best enter the world. And Glooscap said, 'I will be born as others are.' But the evil Malsumsis thought himself too great to be brought forth in such a manner, and declared that he would burst through his mother's side. As they planned it so it came to pass. Glooscape as first came quietly to light, while Malsumsis kept his word, killing his mother.

The two grew up together, and one day the younger, who knew that both had charmed lives, asked the elder what would kill him, Glooscap. Now each had his own secret as to this, and Glooscap, remembering how wantonly Malsumsis had slain their mother, thought it would be misplaced confidence to trust his life to one so fond of death, while it might prove to be well to know the bane of the other. So they agreed to exchange secrets, and Glooscap, to test his brother, told him that the only way in which he himself could be slain was by the stroke of an owl's feather, though this was not true. And Malsumsis said, 'I can die only by a blow from a fern-root.'

It came to pass in after-days that Kwah-beet-a-sis, the son of the Great Beaver, or, as others say, Miko the Squirrel, or else the evil which was in himself, tempted Malsumsis to kill Glooscap; for in those days all men were wicked. So taking his bow he shot Ko-ko-khas the Owl, and with one of his feathers he struck Glooscap while sleeping. Then he awoke in anger, yet craftily said that it was not by an owl's feather, but by a blow from a pine-root, that his life would end.

Then the false man led his brother another day far into the forest to hunt, and, while he again slept, smote him on the head with a pine-root. But Glooscap arose unharmed, drove Malsumsis away into the woods, sat down by the brook-side and, thinking over all that had happened, said, 'Nothing but a flowering rush can kill me.' But the Beaver, who was hidden among the reeds, heard this, and hastening to Malsumsis told him the secret of his brother's life. For this Malsumsis promised to bestow on Beaver whatever he should ask; but when the latter wished for wings

Source
George G. Leland, *The Algonquin Legends of New England*, Boston: Houghton, Mifflin, and Company, 1884, pp. 15–17

like a pigeon, the warrior laughed and scornfully said, 'Get thee hence; though with a tal like a file, what need hast thou of wings?'

Then the Beaver was angry, and went forth to the camp of Glooscap, to whom he told what he had done. Therefore Glooscap arose in sorrow and in anger, took a fern-root, sought Malsumsis in the deep, dark forest and smote him so that he fell down dead. And Glooscap sang a song over him and lamented.

How Glooscap Caught the Summer

Algonquin

A LONG TIME AGO glooscap wandered very far north to the Ice-country, and, feeling tired and cold, sought shelter at a wigwam where dwelt a great giant – the giant Winter. Winter received the god hospitably, filled a pipe of tobacco for him and entertained him with charming stories of the old time as he smoked. All the time Winter was casting his spell over Glooscap, for as he talked drowsily and monotonously, he gave forth a freezing atmosphere, so that Glooscap first dozed and then fell into a deep sleep – the heavy slumber of the winter season. For six whole months he slept; then the spell of the frost arose from his brain and he awoke. He took his way homeward and southward, and the farther south he fared the warmer it felt, and the flowers began to spring up around his steps.

At length he came to a vast, trackless forest, where, under primeval trees, many little people were dancing. The queen of these folk was Summer, a most exquisitely beautiful, if very tiny, creature. glooscap caught the queen up in his great hand and, cutting a long lasso from the hide of a moose, secured it round her tiny frame. Then he ran away, letting the cord trail loosely behind him.

The tiny people, who were the Elves of Light, came clamouring shrilly after him, pulling frantically at the lasso. But as Glooscap ran the cord ran out, and pull as they might they were left far behind.

Northward he journeyed once more, and came to the wigwam of Winter. the giant again received him hospitably, and began to tell the old stories whose vague charm had exercised such a fascination upon the god. But Glooscap in his turn began to speak. Summer was lying in his bosom, and her strength and heat sent forth such powerful magic that at length Winter began to show signs of distress. The sweat poured profusely down his face,and gradually he commenced to melt, as did his dwelling. Then slowly nature awoke, the song of birds was heard, first faintly, then more clearly and joyously. The thin green shoots of the young grass appeared, and the dead leaves of last autumn were carried down to the river by the melting snow. Lastly the fairies came out, and Glooscap, leaving Summer with them, once more bent his steps southward.

Source

Lewis Spence, *Bthe Myths of the North American Indians,* London: George G. Harrap & Co., 1914 pp. 147–9

PART 2
THE SOUTHEAST

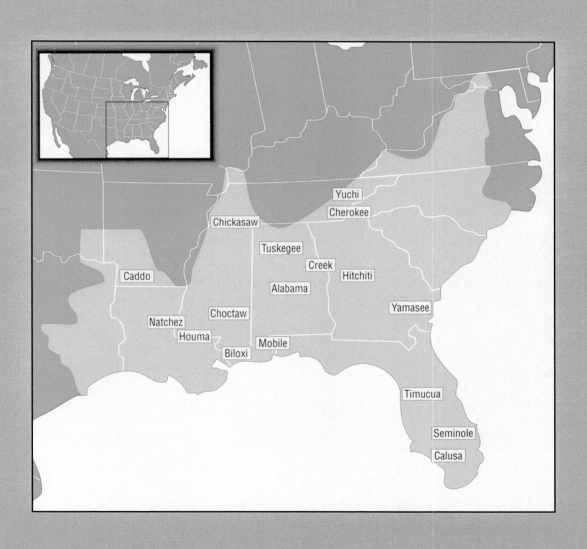

TRIBES OF THE SOUTHEAST

The southeastern region of the United States was the homeland of a wide variety of Indian tribes prior to the coming of Europeans to the New World. This vast setting, which stretched east and west from the Atlantic coast to the Mississippi River and north and south from the Ohio River to the Gulf of Mexico, witnessed the comings and goings of several variant language families. The primary language stock of these Southeastern tribes was the Muskogean branch. Tribes who spoke a dialect rooted in this language source included the Creeks, Hitchitis and Yamasees of modern Georgia; the Seminoles in Florida; the Chickasaws, Choctaws and Houmas of Mississippi; and the Alabamas and Mobiles of the state named after the former. Other less well-known tribes of the Muskogean family included the timucuas of northern, coastal Florida and the Calusas of the southern Florida peninsula.

Yet despite the predominance of Indians of a Muskogean-based tongue in the southeast, other native groups, speaking other language stocks, were located in the region. Perhaps the largest and most readily known group were the Cherokees, who ranged through North Carolina and Tennessee. They spoke a language based on Iroquois stock. In Mississippi, the Biloxi tribal language was Siouan in origin, as was also that of the Yuchis, whose traditional lands were located in northern Georgia.

Most of these tribes were located on their traditional lands before the arrival of the first Europeans and their cultures were firmly fixed historically. Pottery had been produced by most of these tribes for over 3,000 years. around ad 700, an extremely dominant culture arose in the Southeast, which archaeologists refer to as the Mississippian Culture or the Middle Mississippian. It developed along the banks of several key Southeastern river systems, including the Illinois,

Tennessee, the lower Ohio and the middle Mississippi. How exactly this culture developed is unclear, but many anthropologists consider the Mississippians to embody the third era of what has come to be known by archaeologists as the mound-builders.

Mount-building was a practice of various native cultures in the southeast dating back thousands of years. The original mound-builders, who practised this earthen architecture from around 2,500 years ago, are referred to as the Adenas, a name that derives from the region in Ohio where early Indian mounds were discovered. The Adenas constructed cone-shaped mounds of earth, burying their dead in an above-ground earthen mound. Some of their early mounds were constructed in the shapes of animals, such as bears, frogs and birds.

The second phase of mound-building is known as the Hopewell era, which began about 2,000 years ago. The name is derived from the mounds uncovered in the nineteenth century on an Ohio farm located in Ross County and owned by M.C. Hopewell. At his request, archaeologists were allowed to dig into nearly three dozen such mounds on his property, in which they unearthed a variety of relics, including utensils and bones of local origin. However, the mounds also revealed the extensive trade contacts of these ancient Indians as they contained Atlantic coastal shells, bracelets, earrings and breastplates made from copper mined in the Lake Superior region and obsidian fragments from west of the Mississippi River.

The Hopewell Culture practised the architecture of constructing mounds on a greater scale than their predecessors did. Their mounds were larger, and the contents discovered by archaeologists reveal more wealthy societies than those common to the Adenas. In addition, their mounds were more elaborate, consisting of earth-works that involve intricate patterns of circles, squares, rectangles and octagons. Some mound systems stretched for three or four miles (five or six kilometres) in length. Construction of such mounds would have required the recruitment of a vast workforce, pressed into labour by a power-ful centralized government.

By AD 700, or perhaps a century or so earlier, the third phase of mound-building began to develop. The Mississippian Culture serves histori-cally as the immediate predecessor of the more modern tribes, such as the choctaws, Chickasaws, Natchez and others. This culture was centred in the Southeastern states of Mississippi, Alabama and Tennessee.

Perhaps the most recognizable change in the Mississippi mound-building from that of the Hopewell and the Adenas was the construction of earthen pyramids. While earlier mounds were seemingly constructed as burial sites, the Missis-sippian pyramids served as temples and, occasionally, as the base for a chieftain's dwelling.

During the Mississippian phase, corn was introduced from Mexico, and the Indians began developing a serious agriculture. As a result of this sedentary culture, native cities began to develop, such as the impressive city of Cahokia, located in the region where the Mississippi and Missouri rivers join one another. Cahokia was situated on the eastern bank of the Mississippi River, opposite modern-day St Louis, It covered six square miles (more than fifteen square kilo-metres) and boasted an ancient population of approximately 25,000 people. archaeologists have unearthed at least eighty-five mounds at the Mississippian site. Considering that this culture did not have a practical use of the wheel or animals to carry heavy loads, this building accomplishment is stupendous. The mounds were created by the labours of thousands of workers, who carried baskets of earth up the incline, depositing their load at the mound's ever-increasing summit. Over time, the city declined and was eventually abandoned. The reasons for its collapse as an ancient population centre are not clear.

The Mississippian stage of mound-building had reached its peak during the 1500s. As these large, sedentary centres, such as Cahokia, fell

apart, the people scattered and dispersed into smaller tribal units, remaining largely agricultural and, to an extent, still village-oriented.

The Survival of the Natchez Culture

One mound culture that did survive until the arrival of the Europeans was that of the Natchez. By the time of the Spanish explorer DeSoto arrived on the lower Mississippi in the 1540s, the Natchez numbered about 4,000 natives living in at least nine town settlements scattered along the river. such villages were ruled, even by the final decades of the 1600s, by a powerful chief known as the Great Sun. The village where the Great Sun lived was known as the Great Village, near modern-day Natchez, Mississippi. The tribal belief was that the chief was a descendant of the sun and he was treated with a deference often associ-ated with that given to Aztec or Inca rulers.

Below this nobility in the Natchez Culture were the common people, referred to by contem-porary French explorers and missionaries of the day as 'Stinkards'. While these two castes were tightly drawn, they did have significant contact with one another. Records indicate that by tribal law all noblewomen who married had to marry a Stinkard. Their children were considered aristo-cracy. However, a nobleman who married a Stinkard woman produced Stinkard children. This fact indicates that the blood lines were traced through the female, creating a matrilineal structure. The Natchez Culture did not survive white contact – the last remnants of the mound-building culture in the American Southeast.

Daily Life Among the Natchez

The Natchez were a settled, agricultural society. Their chief crop was corn, yet their diet was as varied as that of many of the Northeastern tribes. In addition, they harvested wild river rice and gathered a wide variety of edible seeds. Hunting provided meat for their diets. Contact with the Spanish and French introduced new foods to the Natchez. In fact, over time, especially after con-tact with Europeans, the Natchez named their lunar months of the year after important crops, foods and animals. In order, the list of months was as follows: Deer, Strawberries, Little Corn, Watermelons, Peaches, Mulberries, Great Corn, Turkeys, Bison, Bears, Cold Meal, Chestnuts and Nuts. (Items such as watermelons and peaches had European origins.)

Natchez Villages

The houses of the Natchez were grander than those of neighbouring tribes. Built as great rectangles, they used bent tree saplings to provide a curving roof, reminiscent of the Conestogas and prairie schooners used by Americans in later centuries. The roofs were covered with grasses, creating a thatched look. The walls consisted of pliable reeds and sticks, which were woven horizontally through wooden poles set in the ground. When this great basket of a house was completed, the people covered the framework with mud, that was then whitewashed over, creating homes that were cool in summer and snug in the mild winters of the Southeast. Such dwellings were dark because no windows were included. A fire burned constantly inside and was used for cooking and heat. Since the Natchez generally died not include a smoke hole in the roof of their houses, an ashen cloud generally hovered about the house, escaping through the door. Often the Natchez surrounded their villages with fortifications, which included wooden perimeter fencing. Such villages frequently also had a great community house and a temple that dominated the scene.

The Chief of the Natchez

While nearly all North American Indian tribes boasted a ruling structure that was dominated by chiefs, the Natchez system was an extraordinary one in this regard. As already noted, the people of the tribe referred to their leader as the 'Great Sun'. He symbolized a divine leader on earth who received complete deference from those he ruled as the head of the Natchez Sun clan. To them, he was a god. Eight men of the tribe carried the Great Sun in a sedan chair of sorts. At his approach, all bowed. No one was to ever turn his or her back to the Great Sun. He was installed at the tope of one of the Natchez mounds, from

where he served as a tribe's religious and political leader. His lodge was built on top of a mound. His dwelling place was off limits to commoners, the so-called Stinkards, and could be entered only by a handful of tribal elders and the chief's wives, known as the 'Honoured People', which made up the tribal aristocracy. Yet so important was the chief himself that, when a Great Sun died, his wife and closest associates were executed, allowing them to continue serving their great ruler in the afterlife.

A visiting French explorer, a Jesuit priest named Pierre Charlevoix who had contact with the Natchez in the 1720s, presents an eyewitness account of the Great Sun at work:

> Every morning as soon as the Sun appears, the great chief comes to the door of his cabin, turns himself to the east, and howls three times, bowing down to the earth. Then they bring hum a calumet [smoking pipe], which served only for this purpose. He smokes, and blows the smoke of his tobacco towards the Sun; then he does the same thing towards the other three parts of the world. He acknowledges no superior but the Sun, from which he pretends to derive his origin. He exercises an unlimited power over his subjects, can dispose of their goods and lives, and for whatever labours he requires of them they cannot demand any recompense.

This tight class structure was rounded out by the Great Sun's kin, known as Little Suns. Dominant among them was the chief's next youngest brother. Military leaders for the Natchez came from this clan. The women of the Sun clan also carried a relative weight, for they had the power and responsibility to appoint new chiefs when Great Suns died.

The Great Sun exerted a theocratic control over his people, so much so that even in death, the Natchez continued to sacrifice on behalf of their ruler-god. When a Great Sun died, an elaborate ceremony followed, resulting in the deaths of those closest to him. During elaborate funerary rites, the Great Sun's wives, servants and lodging guards were killed so they could accompany him to the afterworld. Others could volunteer to die as well if they wished to follow their leader in his

next life. During a prescribed ritual, generally taking place four days after the Great Sun's death, those marked for death ate a tobacco-based mixture, which caused them to pass out. Once unconscious, family members strangled them to death. All the fires of the Natchez village were extinguished. Another was set, as the villagers burned the Great Sun's lodge to the ground. Then their chief's body was buried. However, months later, village priests dug up his bones and placed them in a sacred basket, which was then housed in the tribal temple. During this ceremony, the men guarding the temple were also executed, so they could protect their royal leader in his new, spiritual domain.

The mount-building culture of the Natchez did not survive the arrival of Europeans in North America. By the 1720s, relations with French traders had deteriorated into war and acts of retaliation. Through an alliance of the French and the Choctaws, neighbours of the Natchez, the mound-builders were defeated. Most were killed and a few hundred were shipped down the Mississippi, where they were eventually sold into slavery in the French West Indies. A lucky few fled and were later absorbed into the tribes of the Creek, Cherokee and Chickasaw Indians.

With the elimination of the Natchez people, other tribes of the Southeast rose in significance. The Natchez were the last of the mound-building societies of ancient America. While other tribes – including the Chickasaws, Choctaws and Cherokees – were still building mounds in the 1700s, these cultures were in a state of change and flux, which eventually resulted in their abandonment of mound-building.

The Five Nations

In time, the arrival of Europeans to the Southeast spelled disaster for all the tribes of Naive Americans. The Natchez were not even the first victims of European contact, as Floridan tribes including the Apalachees Calusas and Timucuas had been destroyed by the Spanish in earlier years. Several tribes did retain dominant power in the Southeast, however, until the nineteenth century. Among them and foremost were those tribal groups which banded together to form the confederacy known as the Five Civilized Tribes. This

union included the Cherokees, chickasaws, Choctaws, creeks and the group known as the Isty-Semole, a mixed group of refugee Creeks and escaped slaves, who, by the middle of the 1700s, had found one another in the swamps of Florida, creating a tribe known for their hunting abilities and a lack of agriculture. The Isty-Semole, a name given them by the Northern Creeks meaning 'wild men', became known as the Seminoles, which translates as 'runaways'.

As these tribes took on the culture and ways of whites, their life patterns altered dramatically. By the 1820s and 1830s, the Five civilized Tribes were not only practising the white man's agriculture, with modern tools and equipment, but were also building Anglo-American houses, using skills and crafts including blacksmithing, a Cherokee leader, named Sequoyah, even invented a Cherokee alphabet, which led to the publishing of a tribal newspaper, the writing of a Cherokee constitution of government (which mirrored the US Constitution) and well-delineated legal codes to be followed by all members of the tribe.

However, despite the assimilation of white culture and practices by these tribes, this did not save the tribes from tragedy at the hands of whites. Throughout the 1820s and 1830s, the United States government forced the removal of each of the five tribes from their homelands in alabama, Georgia, Mississippi, Tennessee and Florida to reservation lands west of the Mississippi River. These forced marches, at the direct hands of US Army soldiers, are a dark chapter in United States – Native American relations. The results were the irretrievable disruption of new ways of life for the tribes and also fragmentation of their ancient heritage.

Warfare Among the Southeastern Tribes

As with nearly all the tribes of North America, the Indians of the Southeast were constantly in conflict with one another. Warring was considered necessary as a gauge of one's prowess as a male member of the tribe. Southeastern peoples developed a standing arsenal of both offensive and defensive weapons and tactics. Among those weapons that were common among Southeastern tribes were the ubiquitous bow and arrow, as well as a wide variety of war clubs, darts, scalping knives, tomahawks and shields. After extensive contact and trade with Europeans, these tribes had also gained access to the gun. The erection of wooden fences or palisades ringing the perimeter of an encampment helped to protect a village from raids by a fractious enemy. At the gate or entrance of such a palisade, a tribe often placed a pair of guards. Anyone not doing his duty as a watchman might receive a beating from other warriors wielding heavy clubs.

In preparation for battle, many Southeastern tribal warriors went through an elaborate process of rituals. In some tribes, once was had been decided on, a war leader danced three times around his lodge to the beat of a war drum. all members of the tribe who wanted to join the fight then expressed their interest. (Rarely did all the warriors of a given tribe participate in the same warring party; frequently more than one raiding party at a time might be following the 'warrior's path'. Once the party was formed, warriors prepared their weapons and gathered food for their expedition. A ritual fast was observed and warriors went through a litany of ceremonies to prepare themselves and to receive blessings from above. Warriors commonly slathered bear grease on their hair, while the women of the tribe decorated the men's bodies and faces with paint, feathers, beadwork and copper ornaments. Generally, swan's feathers were given to a tribe's ordinary warriors, while war leaders were adorned with eagle's feathers. A war dance was held, which might stretch on for two or three days, followed by a great feast for the warriors, while their relatives fasted. Most veteran war leaders began their march at daybreak, the warriors sending musket volleys into the air, followed closely by great war whoops.

Once on their way, the warrior band remained silent at all times while following the forest paths. Certain taboos and superstitions marked their time. For example, warriors were not to lean against trees and, if they sat, were to squat on rocks. Any warrior who experienced a bad dream might be sent back to the tribe's village, as such visions were considered omens.

Even the sounds of certain birds in the woods might be enough to indicate doom for the war party and the entire effort might be completely abandoned.

A warrior wore little into combat. Among the Creek and Chickasaw tribes, for example, a warrior wore a breechclout, a belt and moccasins. After having his face painted red and black, he and his group set out for combat. Such warriors typically carried with them a blanket, leather strips and cords for repairing clothing and moccasins, and some dried corn in a leather bag for a quick meal, literally, on the run. Weapons might include a bow and arrows, a knife, a tomahawk, a war club and a spear. By the early 1700s, such warriors might carry a musket or rifle acquired through trade with European merchants, or even a flintlock pistol or two.

Warriors sometimes went to great lengths to engage an enemy. A British observer, noting Southeastern war practices in the early eighteenth century, describes a common form of Indian raid:

> A body of Indians will travel four or five hundred miles to surprise a town of their enemies, travelling by night only, for some days before they approach the town. Their usual time of attack is at break of day, when, if they are not discovered, they fall on [the town] with dreadful slaughter, and scalping, which is to cut off the skins of the crown of the temples, and taking the whole head of hair along with it as if it was a night cap: sometimes they take the top of the scull with it; all which they preserve, and carefully keep by them for a trophy of their conquest. Their caution and temerity is such, that at the least noise, or suspicion of being discovered, though at the point of execution, they will give over the attack, and retreat back again with precipitation.

Southeastern warriors made no hesitation about scalping not only male members of an enemy's tribe but the women and children as well. Less honour was attached to the latter, however. Once an enemy was defeated, a ritual followed. After killing an enemy, warriors marked signs on nearby trees as a testimonial of the murderous event. Once scalped, the body was frequently carved up, with some of the pats being carried by victorious braves back to their village.

The activity of scalping increased a warrior's status with his people. Any captives taken during an engagement were often returned to the victor's camp, where the women of the tribe paid in tobacco for the privilege of whipping the prisoners. Typically, prisoners were forced to perform for the tribe, singing and dancing for days on end until they were presented to the relatives of warriors who had been killed by their enemy. Female captives had their hair cut off and were often kept as slaves for life. Males were subjected to a horrific trial which included many blows from war clubs and a scalping. Then they were fastened to a square of thick branches, a fire was set under them and they were burned to death, sacrificed on behalf of the victorious tribe.

Southeastern Indian Mythology

The mythology of the Southeastern tribes is a rich heritage of stories, tales and legends. As the Natchez tribe was an early casualty of European contact, their myths reach the modern reader in a form that was probably corrupted and distorted by many subsequent transformations. The same may be said of the legends of other Southeastern tribes, including the Creeks. Although the Creeks' culture survived white contact, the result was often a combining of ancient Creek stories with European stories, as well as with African-American tales introduced by black slaves. For example, the Creeks' stories of the trickster rabbit bear an uncanny resemblance to the tales that the Southern writer Joel Chandler Harris wrote in his famous *Uncle Remus* stories, which included such whimsical characters as Brer Rabbit, Brer Fox and Brer Wolf.

Many of the tales of the Southeast bring human beings into direct contact with nature and the animal world. This is, of course, a tendency in much of the Native American literature. For example, for a warrior male to practise his skill at the hunt he needed to have at his disposal both personal courage and technical skill. These powers came from the spirit world and, more directly, from the animals themselves. Animal powers granted to hunters, generally through dreams or

vision quests, provided supernatural assistance. All this of great importance to the would-be warrior. His status in the tribe depended on his skill at the hunt. As his hunting skills improved, and this would occur only when he received an infusion of animal prowess and skill, so did his position in his tribe.

Animal spirits could not only improve gaming technique and prowess but also grant other skills to humans. Visions and dreams could give specific skills, such as curative powers. Tribal doctors and medicine men received from the animal spirits their knowledge of how to cure disease or grant immunity from an otherwise deadly contagion. These healers, therefore, were seen as spiritual leaders, since they gained their art from animals. Others might become prophets and seers of the future among the tribe. Again, the mythology reflects such a belief. Among the South0-eastern tribes, simple events in nature took on great significance. Indian prophets might see significance in the howling of a dog or a wolf, or the hoot of a night owl in a distant tree.

Cosmic events, such as shooting stars, might announce troubles for the tribe, including a war or an epidemic. Among the Cherokees, when a person sneezed, it was interpreted as a sign of good luck. In several Southeastern tribes, prophets were divided into different classes, each having specific special skills One group, called the 'Knowers', was considered capable of predicting the future. Often twin brothers were likely candidates for becoming such prophets. The famous nineteenth-century Shawnee chief Tecumseh had a twin brother, Tenskatawa, who was known throughout the Southeast as the Prophet.

Cogmogonic Tales

Woven into the tapestry of Indian legends are tales considered to be cosmogonic in nature. These are designed to explain where something originated from or how it came into being. They seek to answer common, almost mundale questions, such as where strawberries, fish or pine trees come from, as well as more cosmic concerns, including the origins of the Milky Way galaxy, the heavenly bodies, the earth, disease and the existence of evil and sin.

Such stories often interweave simple and complex plot lines. Naturally, to the modern, scientifically minded reader, many seem naïve. For example, a Cherokee story seeks to explain how man received the use of fire. The Thunders had original control of fire and kept it in a hollow sycamore tree. After many failed attempts to recover it were made by various animals of the forests, it was finally stolen by a lowly water spider, who carried a live coal on its back in a web-woven bowl. In such stories, often a small creature is presented as a heroic figure. Other tales explain how disease was created by the animal kingdom as a way of combating man.

Sometimes the legends explained the cosmic in the simplest terms. Meteors hurtling across the night sky might be interpreted as snakes or lions on their way to new worlds. Eclipses might be explained as the work of giant toads eating away at the sun or the moon. Rainbows were, to the Southeastern story-teller, great serpents whose arched bands cut off rainfall from the earth.

Southeastern Indian Deities and Animal Spirits

As with all native cultures, the Southeastern Indians recognized a pantheon of gods and goddesses. Serving as the supreme deity for the Creeks was a being known as Hisagita-imisi, which translates as 'The Preserver of Breath'. Such a god was directly associated with the son. On earth, he was represented by a fire spirit. Other spirits existed on earth, including the four winds, thunder and lightning. Spirits were found in animals and plants and their powers were, as has been previously mentioned, transferable to human beings. Various varieties of snake were greatly honoured by Southeastern tribes, and other animals were accorded similar prestige. Eagles and hawks were highly regarded. Owls, and one variety of red-headed woodpecker, were known for their powers to see the future.

Southeastern Religion

Although there were many variations between the Southeastern tribes, their religion shared many of the same roots. Both the Chickasaws and the Creeks recognized a supreme being who lived above the earth in the Sky World and effected connection between the two spheres. The spirits of deceased human beings could expe-rience an afterlife. Their souls were throughout to be wanderers and travellers, always moving west, where the sun died each day. Souls considered worthy found their way to the Sky World, where they could reside with the supreme beings. Evil individuals were doomed to wander in the west for ever, where witches and ghosts dwelled.

According to Creek and Chickasaw beliefs, all humans had two souls. It was the inner soul, called the *shilup* or 'inside shadow', that spirited its way to the afterlife. Some received comfort, while others, such as those who committed murder, were relegated to a hellish place. To provide for the journey to the afterlife, Southeastern tribes buried their dead with food, clothing and the weapons and tools necessary to complete the trip. The alternate soul, known as the *shilombish* or 'outside shadow', remained on earth, taking the form of a ghost. Such a spirit could take on animal form, disguising itself as an owl, fox or other creature of the forest.

MYTHS AND LEGENDS
OF THE SOUTHEAST

THE CEDAR TREE
Yuchi

AN UNKNOWN MYSTERIOUS BEING once came down upon the earth and met people there who were the ancestors of the Yuchi Indians. To them this being taught many of the arts of life, and in matters of religion admonished them to call the sun their mother as a matter of worship. Every morning the sun, after rising above the horizon, makes short stops, and then goes faster until it reaches the noon point. So the Unknown inquired of them what was the matter with the sun. They denied having any knowledge about it, and said, 'Somebody has to go there to see and examine it.' 'Who would go there, and what could he do after he gets there?' The people said, 'We are afraid to go up there.' But the Unknown selected two men to make the ascent, gave to each a club, and instructed them that as soon as the wizard who was playing these tricks on the sun was leaving his cavern in the earth and appeared on the surface, they should kill him on the spot. 'It is a wizard who causes the sun to go so fast in the morning, for at sunrise he makes dashes at it, and the sun, being afraid of him, tries to flee from his presence.'

The two brave men went to the rising place of the sun to watch the orifice from which the sun emerges. The wizard appeared at the mouth of the cave, and at the same time the sun was to rise from another orifice beyond it. The Wizard watched for the fiery disc and put himself in position to rush and jump at it at the moment of its appearance. When the wizard held up his head, the two men knocked it off from his body with their clubs, took it to their tribe and proclaimed that they had killed the sorcerer who had for so long a time urged the sun to a quicker motion. But the wizard's head was not dead yet. It was stirring and moving about, and to stop this the man of mysterious origin advised the people to tie the head on the uppermost limbs of a tree. They did so, and on the next morning the head fell to the ground, for it was not dead yet. He then ordered them to tie the head to another tree. It still lived and fell to the ground the next day. To ensure success, the Unknown then made them tie it to a red cedar tree. There it remained, and its life became extinct. The blood of the head ran through the cedar. Henceforth the grain of the wood assumed a reddish colour, and the cedar tree became a medicine tree.

Source
Albert S. Gatschet. 'Some Mythic Stories of the Yuchi Indians', *American Anthropologist* (OS), 6 (1893), pp. 279–82

ADOPTION OF THE HUMAN RACE

Natchez

IN THE VERY BEGINNING, Moon, Sun, Wind, Rainbow, Thunder, Fire and Water together met a very old man whom they later discovered was the Chief of the Sky Spirits. Thunder asked him, 'Can you make the human beings of the world children of mine?' 'No, never,' said the Wise Old One. 'The human beings may not be your children, but they may become your grandchildren.' 'Can you make the human beings of the world children of mine?' asked the Sun. 'No, they may not be children of yours,' replied the Old One. 'They may, however, become your friends and your grandchildren. They may receive much light from you.' Moon asked of the Old Man, 'Can you make the human beings of the world children of mine?' 'No, I may not do such a thing,' said the Old One. 'They may be your nephews and friends.' Fire then took his turn and asked, 'Can you make the human beings of the world children of mine?' The Wise Old One gave his reply: 'No, I may not make them your children, but they may be your grandchildren, also. It will be your purpose to give them warmth and heat to cook their food.' Wind asked the same question: 'Can you make the human beings of the world children of mine?' And again the Wise Old One answered, 'No, they may not be made your children, but as I have told the others, they may become your grand-children. You will keep them healthy by blowing away the foul air and with it the diseases which make the human beings sick.' The rainbow asked as well and the Old One told him, 'They may not be your children, but you will be there for them to clean themselves when they are soiled and dirty. By doing so, you will give them long life.'

After telling them each these things, the Wise Old One reminded each of them, 'I have given you instructions concerned how each of you may give help and comfort to the human beings of the world. And ever must you remember that the children of earth – the human race – are my children.'

'And ever must you remember that the children of earth – the human race – are my children' said the Wise Old One.

Source
John R. Swanton, 'Adoption of the Human Race', *BAE Bulletin*, 42 (1945–5), p. 240

HOW RABBIT FOOLED ALLIGATOR

Creek

LONG AGO, when the animals could talk as human beings do today, an alligator of extraordinary good looks lay in the warm sun on a log in the everglades. Mr Rabbit soon came hopping along and addressed the alligator: 'Have you ever seen the devil, Mr Handsome Alligator?' 'No,' said Mr Alligator. 'I have not seen the devil, but if I did, I would not fear him.' 'Well, I have seen the devil,' said Mr Rabbit. 'And he spoke of you.' The Alligator then asked, 'Well, what did the devil have to say?' 'The devil was certain that you feared him so much you would not even look at him.'

The Alligator assured the Rabbit that he was not afraid of the devil and he asked Mr Rabbit to give that message to him next time he saw him. The Rabbit replied, 'The day after tomorrow, you could crawl up the hill and tell him your-self, Mr Alligator. But I don't think you will be willing to make the trip.' 'But I

Source
John R. Swanton, 'How Rabbit Fooled Alligator', *BAE Bulletin*, 88 (1929), pp. 115-16

will,' said the Alligator. 'In fact, let's go tomorrow rather than wait.' 'Fine,' said Mr Rabbit. 'Now you should know that when you climb the hill tomorrow, if you see smoke, don't worry. That just means that the devil is on his way to meet you.' 'I will be prepared to meet him,' said Mr Alligator. 'And if you witness deer galloping past you and birds flying swiftly past, don't worry.' The Alligator continued to assure Mr Rabbit that he would not worry and was not afraid of meeting the devil. The Rabbit continued, 'If you hear the crackle of fire nearby and if the grass around you smokes and burns, do not be afraid, for it will only be the devil walking nearby. In fact, when the heat is intense around you, that is the best time to see the devil.' Finally, Mr Rabbit left Mr Alligator, who continued sunning himself on his log.

The next day, Mr Rabbit returned and began encouraging Mr Alligator to begin his crawl up the hill, assuring him that he would be close behind him. Once they reached the top, Rabbit instructed Alligator to wait in the tall grass on the hill. Soon, Alligator was alone as Rabbit scampered away. As Rabbit hopped down the hill, he laughed and laughed. He knew Alligator was now a great distance from his home in the swamp.

On his way down the hill, Rabbit came upon a low burning tree stump. Rabbit picked up some coals and carried them back up the hill, setting the tall grass on fire with Mr Alligator nearby. Soon a fire was burning through the tall grass, coming closer and closer to Mr Alligator. Rabbit moved out of the tall grass to a sandy spot where he could watch the fire and talk to the Alligator.

Soon the smoke from the fire was thick across the hill top. Birds flew away and the forest animals began to stampede away and down the hill. Rabbit could hear Alligator call his name: 'Mr Rabbit, are you there?' Rabbit reassured him: 'Do not be afraid, Mr Alligator, it is only the devil drawing near.' As the fire grew and became quite hot, Alligator again called out to Rabbit, 'What is that noise I hear, Mr Rabbit?' 'It is the devil's breath,' said Rabbit. 'Just remain where you are, and do not be afraid. The devil is very near you.'

Then the fire began to burn the grass near Alligator. As Rabbit watched, he was rolling around in laughter. Soon, the fire was burning Alligator and he writhed in pain at the heat and flames. Rabbit continued to encourage Alligator to remain calm and not to move. 'The devil is very close now, Mr Alligator. You must not be afraid or you will miss your opportunity to see him face to face.'

But Alligator could not wait any longer. He began crawling out of the burning grass and down the hill towards the swamp. He was covered with burns and was choking on the smoke of the fire. Meanwhile, Rabbit continued laughing at the trick he had played on Alligator. He called out to him, 'Wait, Mr Alligator, wait. If you leave now, you will miss seeing the devil. You must be afraid of him, after all.' When he reached the bottom of the hill, Alligator slipped into the swampy water, his skin charred and roasted. No longer was he a handsome alligator. He had been tricked by Rabbit and he was always careful after that never to trust Mr Rabbit again or even any member of the Rabbit's family.

INCEST OF THE SUN AND MOON

Cherokee

THE SUN WAS A YOUNG WOMAN and lived in the east, while her brother, the Moon, lived in the west. The girl had a lover who used to come every month in the dark of the Moon to court her. He would come at night, and leave before daylight, and although she talked with him she could not see his face in the dark, and he would not tell her his name, until she was wondering all the time ho it could be. At last she hit upon a plan to find out, so the next time he came, as they were sitting together in the dark of the *asi* (wigwam), she slyly dipped her hand into the cinders and ashes of the fireplace and rubbed it over his face, say-ing, 'Your face is cold; you must have suffered from the wind,' and pretending to be very sorry for him, but he did not know that she had ashes on her hand. After a while he left her and went away again.

The next night when the Moon came up in the sky his face was covered with spots, and then his sister knew he was the one who had been coming to see her. He was so much ashamed to have her know it that he kept as far away as he could at the other end of the sky all the night. Ever since he tries to keep a long way behind the Sun, and when he does sometimes have to near her in the west he makes himself as thin as a ribbon so that he can hardly be seen.

Source
James Mooney,
'Myths of the
Cherokees',
BAEAR, 19:2
(1900),
pp. 256–7

THE THEFT OF FIRE

Cherokee

IN THE BEGINNING there was no fire and the world was cold, until the Thunders (Ani'-Hyun'tikwala'ski), who lived up in Galun'lati, sent their lightning and put fire into the bottom of a hollow sycamore tree which grew on an island. The animals knew it was there, because they could see the smoke coming out at the top, but they could not get to it on account of the water, so they held a coun-cil to decide what to do. This was a long time ago.

Every animal that could fly or swim was anxious to go after the fire. The Raven offered, and because he was so large and strong they thought he could surely do the work, so he was sent first. He flew high and far across the water and alighted on the sycamore tree, but while he was wondering what to do next, the heat had scorched all his feathers black, and he was frightened and came back without the fire. The little Screech Owl (Wa'huhu') volunteered to go, and reached the place safely, but while he was looking down into the hollow tree a blast of hot air came up and nearly burned out his eyes. He managed to fly home as best he could, but it was a long time before he could see well, and his eyes are red to this day. Then the Hooting Owl (U'guku) and the Horned Owl (Tskili') went, but by the time they got to the hollow tree the fire was burning so fiercely that the smoke nearly blind-ed them, and the ashes carried up the wind made white rings about their eyes. They had to come home again without the fire, but with all their rubbing they were never able to get rid of the white rings.

Now no more of the birds would venture, and so the little Uksu'hi snake, the

Source
James Mooney,
'Myths of the
Cherokees',
BAEAR, 19:2
(1900),
pp. 240–1

black racer, said he would go through the water and bring back some fire. He swam across to the island and crawled through the grass to the tree, and went in by a small hole at the bottom. The heat and smoke were too much for him, too, and after dodging about blindly over the hot ashes until he was almost on fire himself, he managed by good luck to get out again at the same hole, but his body had been scorched black, and he has ever since had the habit of darting and doubling on his track as if trying to escape from close quarters. He came back, and the great blacksnake, Gule'gi (the Climber), offered to go for fire. He swam over to the island and climbed up the tree on the outside, as the blacksnake always does, but when he put his head down into the hold the smoke chocked him so that he fell into the burning stump, and before he could climb out again he was as black as the Uksu'hi.

Now they held another council, for still there was no fire and the world was cold, but birds, snakes and four-footed animals, all had some excuse for not going, because they were all afraid to venture near the burning sycamore, until at last Kanane'ski Amai'yehi (the Water Spider) said she would go. This is not the water spider that looks like a mosquito, but the other one, with black downy hair and red stripes on her body. She can run on top of the water or dive to the bottom, so there would be no trouble to get over to the island, but the question was, How could she bring back the fire?

'I'll manage that,' said the Water Spider. So she spun a thread from her body and wove it into a little bowl, which she fastened on her back. Then she crossed over to the island and through the grass to where the fire was still burning. She put one little coal of fire into her bowl and came back with it, and ever since we have had fire, and the Water Spider still keeps her *tusti* bowl.

The Origin of Animals (Clans)

Tuskegee and Creek

The origin of animals (clans).

THE OLD-TIME BEINGS were gathered together. They began acting in different ways and showing different qualities. Master of Breath observed them. Some began jumping upon trees and running about. Someone asked, 'What sort of beings are those?'

'They are like panthers,' someone answered.

'Henceforth they shall go about as panthers,' said Master of Breath. Then again, some began leaping and running.

'What are they like?' someone asked.

'Like deer,' it was said.

'Henceforth they shall go about as deer,' said Master of Breath. Then again, some went hopping high among the leaves of trees and alighted on the branches.

'What are they like?' asked somebody.

'Like birds,' someone answered.

'They shall be birds,' said Master of Breath. Then again, some were very fat and when they walked they made a great noise on the ground.

'What are they like?' asked someone.

'Like bears,' was the answer.

Source
Frank G. Speck, 'The Creek Indians of Taskigi Town', *American Anthropological Society Memoirs*, 2, 2 (1907), pp. 146ff

'They shall be bears, then,' said Master of Breath. Then again, one started off to run but could not go fast. When he came back he had black stripes near his eyes.

'What will that be?' it was asked.

'It is like a raccoon,' said one.

'That kind shall be racoons,' said Master of Breath. Then one was so fat and round-bodied that when he started off he could hardly walk.

'What is that kind?' it was asked.

'It is like a beaver,' someone answered.

'They shall be the beavers,' said Master of Breath. Then again, one kind was fat and could not run very fast. When this one had gone off to a distance and returned, someone asked, 'What is that like?'

'Like a milk.'

'They shall go about as minks,' said Master of Breath. Then again, one was very swift when he started to run. He darted back and forth very quickly.

'What is he like?' was the question.

'Like a fox,' came the answer.

'That kind shall be foxes,' said Master of Breath. Then again, one was very strong and could pull up saplings by the roots. He went off to a distance and returned. Then someone asked, 'What is he like?'

'Like the wind,' was the answer.

'That kind shall be wind,' said Master of Breath. Then again, one started off into the mud. When he had come back out of it, someone asked, 'What is he like?'

'Like a mud-potato,' it was answered.

'Such shall be mud-potatoes,' said Master of Breath. Then again, one of them had short legs and his back was covered with ridges. When he started out and returned, someone asked, 'What is he like?'

'Like an alligator,' was the answer.

'That kind shall be alligators,' said Master of Breath. Then again, one with stripes on his back went running off, and when he came back, someone asked, "What is he like?'

'Like a skunk,' was the answer.

'That kind shall be skunks,' said Master of Breath. Then again, one went away jumping, and when he came back to the starting place, someone asked, 'What is he like?'

'Like a rabbit,' was the answer.

'That kind shall be rabbits,' said Master of Breath. Then again, one went off squirming along on the ground. When he returned, someone asked, 'What is he like?'

'Like a snake,' was the answer.

'That kind shall be snakes,' said Master of Breath.

Master of Breath, after he had given them their forms on the earth, told them not to marry their own kind, but to marry people of other clans. All the red people know what clans they belong to and do not marry in their own clan. If they did they would not increase.

THE ORIGIN OF EARTH

Tuskegee

BEFORE THE BEGINNING, water was to be found everywhere. Only water was visible and there were no human beings, animals or even the earth to be seen. Only the birds were in existence and they flew above the water.

One day the birds held a council to decide whether they should remain where only the water existed or seek out land. Some of the birds wanted land so that food would be more plentiful. Others among the birds were content being surrounded by water, saying it was all they had ever known and they did not want to change. Since they could not agree among themselves, the birds appealed to the Eagle, who was to be their chief. He was to decide whether they would remain in a water world or go and seek out land.

After deciding in favour of land, the Eagle asked the birds who among them might go out and search for land. The dove volunteered first and was soon off in flight. Four days passed before his return. He told the other birds, 'I flew for four days and could find no land anywhere.'

At that moment, Crawfish swam near the bird council and they asked him if he was willing to help the birds find land.

Agreeing, Crawfish swam beneath the water, only to return after four days had passed. With his return, he held in his claws some soil, which he showed to the birds. He said he had discovered land far beneath the waters. He took the dirt and formed it into the shape of a ball. He gave it to Chief Eagle and the Chief flew off with the ball of dirt.

Four days later, Chief Eagle returned and announced to the bird council that he had created an island with the ball of soil. 'Follow me,' he told the birds. All the birds followed after Chief Eagle until they arrived near a small island. As they watched, the little island began to grow ever bigger. As the land grew, the waters began to recede, until the island grew even more. Other islands appeared, some connecting to one another. The larger islands slowly formed into one earth.

Once the earth had been formed, the Great Spirit placed the Tuskegee people on it first as the earth's first human beings. All this happened a long, long time ago.

Source
John R. Swanton, 'Creation', *BAE Bulletin*, 42 (1924–5), p. 487

EARTH-DIVER

Creek and Yuchi

THE TIME WAS, in the beginning, when the earth overflowed with water. There was no earth, no beast of the earth, no human being. They held a council to know which would be best, to have some land or to have all water. When the council had met, some said, 'Let us have land, so that we can get food,' because they would starve to death. But others said, 'Let us have all water,' because they wanted it that way.

So they appointed Eagle as chief. He was told to decide one way or another. Then he decided. He decided for land. So they looked around for someone whom they could send out to get land. The first one to propose himself was Dove, who thought that he could do it. Accordingly they sent him. He was given four days in

Source
Frank G. Speck, 'The Creek Indians of Taskigi Town', *American Anthropological Society Memoirs*, 2, 2 (1907), pp. 145–7

which to perform his task. Now when Dove came back on the fourth day, he said that he could find no land. They concluded to try another plan. Then they obtained the services of Crawfish (Sakdju). He went down through the water into the ground beneath and he too was gone four days. On the fourth morning he arose and appeared on the surface of the waters. In his claws they saw that he held some dirt. He had at last secured the land. Then they took the earth from his claws and made a ball of it. When this was completed they handed it over to the chief, Eagle, who took it and went out from their presence with it. When he came back to the council, he told them that there was land, an island. So all the beasts went in the direction point out and found that there was land there, as Eagle had said. But what they found was very small. They lived there until the water receded from this earth. Then the land joined into one.

The Hero with the Horned Snake

Cherokee

LONG AGO, MAGIC SNAKES lived on the earth. They were giant snakes with a skin which shone brightly in the sun. Each snake had two horns and carried great power. It was considered a bad sign when one even saw one of these snakes. When anyone ran from one of these snakes, the snake used its magic to lure its victim to it and would then eat it. Killing such a creature was nearly impossible. Only a shaman or hunter who possessed great skill and cunning could kill any of these dreadful two-horned snakes. Such hunters could kill the beast only by shooting an arrow into its skin, piercing the snake's seventh stripe.

One day the Cherokees captured a young Shawnee brave. To gain his freedom, the Shawnee lad agreed to hunt down and kill one of the two-horned snakes. The young warrior hunted across the land, searching in dark caves and over the rugged Tennessee Mountains, until he found one. Immediately, the youth prepared to make the kill. He built a fire circle by burning pine cones. Approaching the snake, the Shawnee brave fired an arrow into the monster, shouting, 'Freedom or death!' The arrow struck the seventh stripe. Then the youth jumped into the ring of fire where he would be safe from the snake. When venom flowed out of the snake, it streamed towards the young Shawnee, but the fire circle stopped its advance. Because he had committed this act of bravery, the Cherokees freed their Shawnee captive, as they had promised.

Several days later, some Cherokee warriors went to the site where the Shawnee lad had killed a two-horned snake. They collected the snake's remains, including the bones and skin, placing them inside a sacred bundle. These things they kept in the bundle as a source of good fortune for the future of the tribe, for their children and grandchildren.

When venom flowed out of the snake, it streamed towards the young Shawnee, but the fire circle stopped its advance.

Source
H. Kate, 'The Hero with the Horned Snake', *JAFL*, 2 (1889), p. 55

THE WALNUT-CRACKER

Creek

MANY, MANY YEARS AGO in western Georgia, there lived a Southeastern Creek-Hitchiti Indian names Walnut-cracker. Members of his tribe named him this because he spent many of his days at one place collecting, cracking and eating walnuts. He would crack the walnuts with a small stone. Every day, even into the evenings, Walnut-cracker sat and ate walnuts. For years, this activity was all Walnut-cracker did until his death. When he died, the men of his tribe buried his body near the spot where Walnut-cracker had cracked and eaten his walnuts all those years.

One day, some time after the death of Walnut-cracker, a Creek brave was passing through the forest, near the spot where Walnut-cracker had laboured and died. There he discovered a large mound of walnuts and, as he was hungry, he sat himself down and cracked open several walnuts, eating the tasty nut meat. Later that same day, the Creek hunter returned and cracked open even more walnuts, eating them as well. While he sat and worked at Walnut-cracker's old spot, another Creek warrior happened to walk by and heard the sound of someone cracking walnuts. He approached and, peering through the evening darkness, thought he saw Walnut-cracker once more at his work.

Bewildered and surprised, the warrior ran back to his village and told the people that he had seen Walnut-cracker cracking walnuts once again at his old haunt. The man asked his people, 'Could Walnut-cracker's ghost be at work?' The Creek warrior's family all decided to visit the place where Walnut-cracker had lived. Were they surprised when they, too, saw someone squatting among the rocks, cracking walnuts? They, also, thought the man they saw was Walnut-cracker.

One member of the Creek warrior's family had been a good friend of Walnut-cracker. He was a lame man and asked his clansmen to carry him to the spot where Walnut-cracker's 'ghost' had been spotted. 'Carry me on your back,' he asked. 'I must see if the one you have seen is my friend Walnut-cracker.'

So Lame Man was carried to the spot and he saw through the darkness a figure sitting cracking walnuts. 'Take me closer,' said Lame Man, and his bearer carried him closer. The hunter could not hear the men approaching since he was busy cracking walnuts. Still Lame Man told his carrier, 'Take me even closer, so I may see him.'

When Lame Man came very close to the mysterious figure, the hunter heard him approach and leapt up, taking his bow and arrows, running away. In surprise and fear, when the hunter leapt up and ran, do did those watching him. In fear, Lame Man's bearer dropped him and ran back to his village. Frightened, Lame Man jumped to his feet and ran to catch up with his people. It appeared that his fear had cured him of his lameness. In fact, he ran so fast that he outran everyone else, arriving back at their lodge before they arrived. After this frightful encounter, Lame Man was able to walk for the rest of his days

As for Walnut-cracker, his 'ghost' was never seen again.

'Could Walnut-cracker's Ghost still be at work?'

Source
John R. Swanton, 'The Walnut-cracker', *BAE Bulletin*, 88 (1929), pp. 115–16

JOURNEY TO THE UNDERWATER LODGE

Creek

A CHIEF SENT HIS SON with a message to another chief, and delivered to him a vessel as the emblem of his authority.

The son stopped to play with some boys who were throwing stones into the water. The chief's son threw his vessel upon the water and it sank. He was frightened. He was afraid to go to the neighbouring chief without the vessel, and he did not like to return home and tell his father of the loss. He jumped into the stream and, reaching the spot where the vessel had sunk, he dived into the water. His playmates waited a long time for him, but he did not reappear. They returned and reported his death.

When the chief's son was beneath the surface of the stream the Tie-snakes seized him and bore him to a cave and said to him, 'Ascent yonder platform.' He looked and saw seated on the platform the king of the Tie-snakes. The platform was a mass of living Tie-snakes. He approached the platform ad lifted his foot to ascend, but the platform ascended as he lifted his foot. Again he tried, with the same result. The third time he tried in vain. The Tie-snakes said, 'Ascend.'

He lifted his foot the fourth time and succeeded in ascending the platform and the king invited him to sit by his side. Then the king said to him, 'See yonder feather; it is yours,' pointing to a plume in the corner of the cave. He approached the plume and extended his hand to seize it, but it eluded his grasp. Three times he made the attempt and three times it escaped him. On the fourth attempt he obtained it.

'Yonder tomahawk is yours,' said the Tie-snakes' king.

He went to the place where the tomahawk was sticking and reached out his hand to take it, but in vain. It rose of itself every time he raised his hand. He tried four times and on the fourth trial it remained still and he succeeded in taking it.

The king said, 'You can return to your father after three days. When he asks where you have been, reply, "I know what I know," but on no account tell him what you do know. When he needs my aid walk towards the east and bow three times to the rising sun and I will be there to help him.'

After three days the Tie-snake carried him to the spot where he had dived into the stream, lifted him to the surface of the water and placed his lost vessel in his hand. He swam to the bank and returned to his father, who was mourning him as dead. His father rejoiced over his son's wonderful restoration.

He informed his father of the Tie-snake king and his message of proffered aid. Not long afterwards his father was attacked by his enemies. He said to his son, 'You understand what the king of the Tie-snakes said. Go and seek his aid.'

The son put the plume on his head, took the tomahawk, went towards the east and bowed three times to the rising sun.

The king of the Tie-snakes stood before him.

'What do you wish?' he said.

'My father needs your aid.'

'Go and tell him not to fear. They will attack him, but they shall not harm him or his people. In the morning all will be well.'

Source
John R. Swanton, 'Myths and Tales of the Southeastern Indians', *BAE Bulletin*, 88 (1929), pp. 34–5

The son returned to his father and delivered the message of the king of the Tie-snakes.

The enemy came and attacked his town, but no one was harmed. Night came. In the morning they beheld their enemies each held fast in the folds of a Tie-snake, and so all were captured and the chief made peace with his foes.

THE BIRDS AND THE ANIMALS PLAY BALL

Cherokee

A LONG TIME AGO, the animals challenged the birds to a game of ball. 'We will defeat you,' said the animals, but the birds responded, 'We are willing to play a ball game with you and we will win.' Both animals and birds began planning for the event and a day was chosen for the game to be played.

When the animals gathered for their game, they chose the bear, the deer and the terrapin or turtle to play the ball game. The bear was chosen for his weight and size, for he was heavier than even all the birds put together. The deer was a swift runner. The terrapin was chosen for his thick shell. The animals were certain they would win the ball game. The birds were equally certain. They selected the eagle, the hawk and the raven as their players. These birds were known for their swiftness in flight. They could see great distances. Each had a sharp beak, which was strong and capable of tearing.

Before the game began, the birds were sitting in the tree tops, smoothing down their feathers, as they watched the animals on the forest floor. As they watched, two tiny creatures began climbing towards them. They were no bigger than mice. 'May we play in the game today?' they asked the chief of the birds. When the chief saw they had four legs, he asked them, 'Since you have four feet, whey don't you play for the animals?' 'We wish to play on your side,' they said. 'Besides, the animals will not let us play on their side. They laughed at us when we asked them.' Feeling sorry for the tiny creatures, the bird chief asked the others if the two could play with them. The birds – including eagle and hawk – agreed.

'But how can they play on our side?' the birds asked. 'These two creatures have no wings.' Another bird answered, 'We will make wings from the skin of the drum.' The skin was that of a groundhog. The birds removed the skin and fashioned a pair of leather wings for one of the two creatures. In doing so, they created the first bat.

The chief of the birds then gave them instructions concerning the ball game. 'When I toss you the ball, you be certain to catch it and do not let it fall to the ground.' As the bat practised, he caught the ball and then flew around the trees, zigzagging as he flew. He flew very fast and in many directions. He was careful not to drop the ball. Even before the game began, the birds were glad they had made the creature his wings.

But the birds asked, 'What shall we do for the other creature? We have no more drum leather to make him a pair of wings, too.' After thinking long and hard, the birds came up with another idea. 'If we have no more skin to make him wings, let us just pull his skin until it can be made into wings.' With that, the eagle

Source

James Mooney, 'The Cherokee Play Ball', *BAEAR*, 24 (1907), pp. 575–86 and hawk, since they were large and strong, grabbed up the little creature and began pulling on his skin with their powerful beaks. Soon, his fur between his front and hind feet was stretched out, making wings for him to fly. In this way, the birds created the first flying squirrel.

When the ball game began, the flying squirrel caught it and flew it to another tree far above the animals below. He then flew it over to the eagle. After catching it, the eagle threw it to another bird. As the game went on, the birds kept the ball away from the animals, throwing it back and forth to one another.

Finally, however, one of the birds dropped the ball. As it dropped towards the ground, the bat flew down swiftly and grabbed it! The bat continued flying, zigzagging past the animals, so that even the fast deer could not catch him. When the bat threw the ball into the goal, he had won the game for his friends, the birds.

THE MILKY WAY

Seminole

LONG, LONG AGO, the Maker of Breath blew his wind across the sky, creating the Milky Way. This path serves as the route in the sky for fallen warriors to help them find the City in the West, the place were good souls may go after an honourable death. The Seminole believe that when a Seminole soul dies, the Milky Way shines brighter to give him a clear path to the spirit world.

To walk along the path of the Milky Way, a warrior must have led a good life. It is important that he was a person whom many people liked and respected. He must not have engaged in stealing or lying or spoken evil of another. He must have been a brave individual who knew honour in his days. Once a departed soul arrives in the City in the West, he will always remain there. The Seminoles do not believe that such souls haunt the earth and come back to visit people after their deaths. When a good soul travels the Milky Way, he rides in the boat of the Big Dipper. This boat carries the souls of good Seminoles to the City in the West.

However, anyone who died whose soul was evil could not rise up into the sky, but had to remain on earth, buried in the ground. Such spirits may not escape and remain near their graves. The Seminoles have a fear of such sites and will always avoid them if possible. Seminoles seem to know when they are in the presence of such evil souls, even when their graves are obscured by bushes and under-growth.

Along the path of the Milky Way live both Rain and Rainbow. The Seminole word for rainbow is stops-the-rain, since the rain disappears when the rainbow appears. The Seminoles believe that when the sun is in an eclipse, it is because toad-frog is moving across the sky, eating pieces of the sun until it disappears. The Seminole hunters kill toad-frogs with their arrows to help prevent such eclipses from occurring.

When a Seminole soul dies, the Milky Way shines brighter to give him a clear path to the spirit world.

Source
R.F. Greenlee, 'The Milky Way', *JAFL*, 58 (1945) pp. 138–40

THE ORIGIN OF POISON

Choctaw

LONG AGO A CERTAIN VINE grew along the edges of bayous, in shallow water. This vine was very poisonous, and often when the Choctaw would bathe or swim in the bayous they would come in contact with the vine and often become so badly poisoned that they would die as a result.

Now the vine was very kind and liked the Choctaw and consequently did not want to cause them so much trouble and pain. He would poison the people without being able to make known to them his presence there beneath the water. So he decided to rid himself of the poison. A few days later he called together the chiefs of the snakes, bees, wasps and other similar creatures and told him of his desire to give them his poison. For up to that time no snake, bee or wasp had the power it now possesses, namely that of stinging a person.

Source
David Bushnell,
'Myths of the
Louisiana
Choctaw',
*American
Anthropologist*,
12 (1910),
pp. 526–35

The snakes and bees and wasps, after much talk, agreed to share the poison. The rattlesnake was the first to speak and he said, 'I shall take the poison, but before I strike or poison a person I shall warn him by the noise of my tail (*intesha*); then if he does not heed me I shall strike.'

The water moccasin was the next to speak: 'I also am willing to take some of your poison; but I shall never poison a person unless he steps on me.'

The small ground rattler was the last of the snakes to speak: 'Yes, I will gladly take of your poison and I will also jump at a person whenever I have a chance.' And so it has continued to do ever since.

MEN VISIT THE SKY TO SEE GOD

Seminole

ALONG, LONG TIME AGO, five Seminole warriors began a journey to visit the sky in hopes of seeing the Great Spirit. They walked a long distance on their trip, travelling ever to the east. After a month of walking, they reached the end of land. At the earth's edge, they tossed their belongings over and then they, too, disappeared over the rim. After falling down for some time, they began to rise upwards towards the sky. They passed along the air for a long time, always towards the west. At long last, they landed near the lodge of a very old woman. She spoke to them in a feeble voice, asking, 'Tell me, for whom are you looking?' 'We are in search of the Great Spirit,' they replied. 'You may not see him now,' the Old Woman said. 'You may remain here for the time being.'

That evening the five Seminole warriors took a walk away from the Old Woman's lodge. While out walking, they came upon a group of winged, white-robed angels. These celestial men were playing a ball game similar to one the Seminoles played on earth. At this sight, two of the five Seminoles decided they would like to become angels and not return to earth. Their desire was granted when the Great Spirit appeared, saying to them, 'So be it!'

Source
R.F. Greenlee,
'Men Visit the
Sky to See God',
JAFL, 58
(1945): p. 143

To prepare the two Seminoles for their new home, the Great Spirit placed them in a large cooking pot with a fire burning beneath it. The two men were cooked until only their bones remained. Then the Great Spirit took the bones out of the pot and put them back into their proper shape. He then placed white robes on both of them and brought them back to life with the touch of his magic stick. They had received their wish to remain and become Men-Angels. At this, the Great Spirit turned to the other three Seminoles and asked them what they wanted to do. 'With your permission, we wish to return to our earthly Seminole encampment,' they said. 'Collect your belongings and go to sleep immediately,' ordered the Great Spirit. This they did, and when they awoke, they were once again in their home village. 'We have returned,' the three warriors told their people. 'We will never journey to the sky again for we are happy to be here on earth.' These words they spoke to the chief of the Seminoles.

NANIH WAIYA
Choctaw

IN ANCIENT DAYS the ancestors of the Choctaws and the Chickasaws lived in a far western country, under the rule of two brothers, named Chahta and Chikasa. In the process of time, their population becoming very numerous, they found it difficult to procure subsistence in that land. Their prophets thereupon announced that far to the east was a country of fertile soil and full of game, where they could live in ease and plenty. The entire population resolved to make a journey eastward in search of that happy land In order more easily to procure subsistence on their route, the people marched in several divisions of a day's journey apart. A great prophet marched at their head, bearing a pole which, on camping at the close of each day, he planted erect in earth, in front of the camp. Every morning the pole was always seen leaning in the direction they were to travel that day. After the lapse of many moons, they arrived one day at Nanih Waiya. The prophet planted his pole at the base of the mound. The next morning the pole was seen standing erect and stationary. This was interpreted as an omen from the Great Spirit that the long-sought-for land was at last found. It so happened, the very day that the party camped at Nanih Waiya, that a party under Chikasa crossed the creek and camped on its east side. That night a great rain fell, and it rained several days. In consequence of this all the low lands were inundated, and Nanih Waiya Creek and other tributaries of Pearl River were rendered impassable.

After the subsidence of the waters, messengers were sent across the creek to bid Chikasa's party to return, as the oracular pole had proclaimed that the long-sought-for land was found and the mound was the centre of the land. Chikasa's party, however, regardless of the weather, had proceeded on their journey and, the rain having washed traces of their march from off the grass, the messengers were unable to follow them up and so returned to camp. Meanwhile, the other divisions in the rear arrived at Nanih Waiya and learned that here was the centre of their new home and that their long pilgrimage was at last finished. Chikasa's party, after their separation from their brethren under Chahta, moved on to the Tombigbee, and eventually became a separate nationality. In this way the Choctaws and the Chickasaws became two separate though kindred nations.

Source
Henry S. Halbert, 'Nanih Waiya, the Sacred Mound of the Choctaws', *Publications of Mississippi Historical Society*, 2 (1899), pp. 230–33

THE MAN WHO BECAME A DEER

Choctaw

ONE NIGHT A HUNTER killed a doe and soon afterward fell asleep near the carcass. The next morning, just at sunrise, the hunter was surprised and startled to see the doe raise her head and to hear her speak, asking him to go with her to her home.

At first he was so surprised that he did not know what to reply, so the doe again asked him whether he would go. Then the hunter said that he would go with her, although he had no ideas where she would lead him. So they started and the doe led the hunter through forests and over high mountains, until at last they reached a large hole under a rock, which they entered. Here the hunter was led before the king of all the deer, an immense buck, with huge antlers and a large black spot on his back.

Soon the hunter became drowsy and finally he fell asleep. Now all around the cave were piles of deer's feet, antlers and skins. While the hunter was asleep the deer endeavoured to fit to his hands and feet deer's feet which they selected for the purpose. After several unsuccessful attempts, the fourth set proved to be just the right size and were fastened firmly on the hunter's hands and feet. Then a skin was found that covered him properly, and finally antlers were fitted to his head. And then the hunter became and deer and walked on four feet after the manner of deer.

> To the great astonishment of all, the deer spoke.

Many days passed, and the hunter's mother and all his friends thought he had been killed. One day when they were in the forest they found his bow and arrows hanging on a branch of the tree beneath which he had slept beside the body of the doe. All gathered around the spot and began singing, when suddenly they saw a herd of deer bounding towards them through the forest. The deer then circles about the singers. One large buck approached closer than the others and the singers, rushing forwards, caught it. To the great astonishment of all it spoke, whereupon they recognized the voice of the lost hunter

Source

David Bushnell, 'The Choctaw of Bayou Lacomb, St Tammany Parish, LA', *BAE Bulletin*, 48 (1909), p. 32

Greatly distressed, the hunter's mother begged her companions to remove from her son the deer skin and antlers and feet, but they told her he would certainly die if they should do so. She insisted, however, saying she would rather bury her son than have him remain a deer. So her friends began tearing away the skin, which already had grown to the hunter's body, and as they continued their efforts to remove it, the blood began to flow. Finally the hunter died. Then his body was taken back to the village where it was buried with the ceremony of a great dance.

FALSE BRIDEGROOM

Caddo

ONE TIME THERE LIVED an old man and woman who had two beautiful twin daughters. These girls heard of a chief who lived in another village, and rumours of his great wealth and his fame as a great chief had travelled far. The girls asked their parents if they might not go to the chief and offer themselves in marriage. Their parents consented, and so the girls started to the chief's village. They did not know just where the village was, but they started in the direction that they thought it was, and decided to ask the first person they met to direct them. They travelled along for a time and then met a man with a turkey in his hand coming down the road. They stopped him and began to talk to him. 'We want to marry this famous chief, for we hear that he is good and very wealthy, but we do not know him. We have never seen him, we have not even been to his village and perhaps we would not know him if we should see him.' The man grinned to himself and said, 'I am the chief, and I live just a little way from here; I have been away attending a council. Well, I must say that I am willing, but wait here while I run on home and tell my grandmother.'

The girls waited. They thought it strange that so great a chief should have to tell his grandmother, but they said nothing. The man, who was no other than Owl, ran on to his home and, calling his grandmother, said, 'Clean up the lodge and put it in order. I am going to bring home two girls whom I am playing a joke on. They think I am the rich chief and want to marry me.' After they had cleaned the lodge, for it was very disorderly, Owl said, 'I am going to put this turkey which I have brought home over my bed; when you get up in the morning ask me which turkey you shall cook and pretend to point to one, and I will say, 'No, take this.' Then the girls will think that we have many turkeys and many good things to eat.'

Owl went back for the girls and brought them to his grandmother's lodge. They were pleased, for everything looked neat and nice, and so they married Owl. Every day Owl came in with the turkey, and he always pretended to have been out hunting. Really he had been at the council, and the chief gave him the turkey for allowing him to sit on his back. At all councils the chief always sat on Owl's back, and so he gave Owl a turkey every time to repay him for his trouble and the pain of holding him so long.

Source

George A. Dorsey, 'Traditions of the Caddo', *Carnegie Institution*, 41 (1905), pp. 67–8

After many moons the twins grew weary of nothing but turkey and they began to suspect something, so one day they followed Owl when he went away. They followed and saw him go to a large grass lodge. They peeped through an opening, there they saw Owl sitting in the middle of the lodge with the chief sitting on his head. They gave a scream. Owl recognized their voices and jumped up, throwing the chief off his head, and ran home. He gave his grandmother a terrible scolding for leeting the girls follow him and find him out. The girls felt so ashamed when they discovered how they had been fooled that they slipped off to their home and told their father and mother their experience.

TAR-BABY

Biloxi

THE RABBIT AND THE FRENCHMAN were two friends. The Rabbit aided the Frenchman, agreeing to work a piece of land on shares. The first season they planted potatoes. The Rabbit, having been told to select his share of the crop, chose the potato vines and devoured them all. The next season they planted corn. This year Rabbit said, 'I will eat the roots.' So he pulled up all the corn by the roots, but he found nothing to satisfy his hunger. Then the Frenchman said, 'Let us dig a well.' But the Rabbit did not wish to work any longer with his friend. Said he to the Frenchman, 'If you wish to dig a well, I shall not help you.'

'Oho,' said the Frenchman, 'you shall not drink any of the water from the well.'

'That does not matter,' replied the Rabbit, 'I am accustomed to licking the dew from the ground.' The Frenchman, suspecting mischief, made a tar-baby, which he stood up close to the well. The Rabbit approached the well, carrying a long piece of cane and a tin bucket. On reaching the well he addressed the tar-baby, who remained silent.

'Friend, what is the matter? Are you angry?' said the Rabbit.

Still the tar-baby said nothing. So the Rabbit hit him with one forepaw, which stuck there.

'Let me go or I will hit you on the other side,' exclaimed the Rabbit. And when he found that the tar-baby paid no attention to him, he hit him with his other forepaw, which stuck to the tar-baby.

'I will kick you,' said the Rabbit. But when he kicked the tar-baby, the hind foot stuck.

'I will kick you with the other foot,' said the Rabbit. And when he did so, that foot, too, stuck to the tar-baby. Then the Rabbit resembled a ball, because his feet were sticking to the tar-baby and he could neither stand nor recline.

Just at this time the Frenchman approached. He tied th legs of the Rabbit together, laid him down and solded him. Then the Rabbit pretended to be in great fear of a briar patch.

'As you in such fear of a briar patch,' said the Frenchman, 'I will throw you into one.'

'Oh, no,' replied the Rabbit.

'I will throw you into the briar patch,' responded the Frenchman.

'I am much afraid of it,' said the Rabbit.

'As you are in such dread of it,' said the Frenchman, 'I will throw you into it.' So he seized the Rabbit and threw him into the briar patch. The Rabbit fell at some distance from the Frenchman. But instead of being injured, he sprang up and ran off, laughing at the trick which he had played on the Frenchman.

Source
J.O. Dorsey, 'Two Biloxi Tales', *JAFL*, 6 (1893), pp. 48–9

ALLIGATOR POWER
Choctaw

ONE WINTER THERE WERE many hunters living in a village, all of whom, with one exception, had killes a great many deer. But one had met with very poor luck and although he often succeeded in getting close to deer, just ready to draw his bow on them, they always contribed to escape unharmed. He had been away from his village three days and during that time had seen many deer, but he had not been able to kill a single one. On the third day, when the sun was overhead, the hunter saw a huge alligator resting on a dry, sandy spot.

This alligator had been without water for many days, and ws dry and shrivelled and so weak that he could scarcely speak. He was able, however, to ask the hunter where water could be had. The hunter replied, 'In that forest, only a short journey hence, is a clear, deep pool of cold water.' 'But I cannot travel alone; I am too weak to go so far. Come nearer that we may talk and plan. I cannot harm you; have no fear,' said the alligator.

At last the hunter went nearer and listened to the alligator, who said, 'I know you are a hunter, but all the deer escape from you. Now, carry me to the water and I will then make you a great hunter and tell you how to kill many, many deer.' The hunter hesitated, as he feared the alligator, and then he said, 'I will carry you, but not unless I may bind your legs so you cannot scratch and your mouth so you cannot bite me.' The alligator rolled over on his back and held up his legs, saying, 'I am helpless; bind me and do with me as you will.'

Then the hunter bound with a cord the alligator's legs and mouth. Then he lifted the animal to his shoulder and carried him to the water. When they reached the pool the hunter loosened the cords and the alligator plunged into the water. It went down, then returned to the surface three times, then went down again and remained a long time. At last he rose again to the surface and spoke to the hunter, saying, 'You brought me to the water; now listen, and if you do as I counsel you will become a great hunter. Take your bow and arrows and go into the woods. You will first meet a small doe, but do not kill it. Next you will meet a large doe, but you must not shoot this one, either. Then you will see a small buck, but this likewise must be spared. Lastly you will encounter a very large, old buck. Go very close to it and kill it, and ever afterward you will be able to kill many deer.'

The hunter did as the alligator told him and never again was without venison in his camp.

The hunter lifted the bound alligator to his shoulder and carried him to the water.

Source
David Bushnell, 'The Choctaw of Bayou Lacomb, St Tammany Parish. LA', *BAEB*, 48 (1909), pp. 32–3, and John Swanton, 'Myths and Tales of the Southeastern Indians', *BAEB*, 88 (1929), p. 34

THE CELESTIAL CANOE
Alabama

MANY AGES AGO, the Alabama peoples witnessed the arrival of a magical canoe near their encampment. The canoe held several young maidens, who stepped out of the craft, joyously singing. The women ran about, freely enjoying themselves, playing a ball game with one another. When they had finished their sport, they tiredly reboarded the canoe and sailed out of sight once again. Several more times the maidens returned in their magical canoe, each time

Source
John R. Swanton, 'The Celestial Canoe', *BAE Bulletin*, 42 (1924–5), p. 138

visiting the earth near the Alabama village. Each time they sang, danced and played ball until they tired of their performance and returned into the sky aboard their sky canoe.

During one of the canoe's visits, a young Alabama warrior watched secretly as the sky maidens played and sang. While playing ball, one of the girls came close to him, fetching the ball. As she came near him, she did not know he was there. Suddenly, he jumped out from behind the bushes and grabbed her by the hand. Panic ensued among the sky visitors, and they hurried to their canoe and disappeared into the heavens, leaving one of their group behind. The Alabama warrior made the sky maiden his wife. In time, she produced several children for him. As his family grew in number, the Alabama warrior made two canoes, a large one for his family and a smaller one for just himself.

One day, his children were hungry and they spoke to their father: 'We are hungry. Will you hunt a deer and give us some fresh meat?' In response, the father headed off into the woods to hunt, but after a short span of time, he returned to his lodge with no deer in hand. At their mother's request, the children asked their father, 'Go hunt a fat deer for us.' Again, the Alabama warrior left his family to go hunt, this time intending to further from his lodge in search of game. After he left his family and his lodge, the mother took her children and placed them in the large canoe her husband had built. She then sang her magic song and the canoe began magically to float into the sky. But the father heard the singing and returned to his lodge in time to catch the floating canoe and pull it back down to earth.

Another day, the mother repeated her attempt to escape from earth with her children. This time she placed her children in the large canoe and herself in the smaller canoe. As she sang, the canoes began to rise. Again, her husband returned from his hunting in time to take hold of the larger canoe and bring it down with his children inside. However, the mother continued her celestial song and soon floated high into the sky, until she and the canoe disappeared.

The husband soon missed his wife, as did his children. After several weeks had passed, he and his children climbed inside the large canoe and sange the song she had sung. The canoe began to float and they soon found themselves sailing through the sky and beyond the clouds. Soon, they arrived in a sky place and stepped out of their canoe. They came upon an old grandmother sitting outside her lodge. The Alabama husband asked her if she had seen his wife. 'My children wish to see their mother, for they miss her greatly.' The Old Woman spoke: 'She is over yonder, where she dances and sings continuously. If you would like to eat before you go to her, I will cook you a meal of squash.' The husband and his children decided to eat with her. Soon, she brought them a single cooked squash. As they began to eat, they knew it would not be enough for all of them. However, they were surprised when they saw that as they ate the squash, a great squash appeared in its place, as if by magic! Since they were very hungry, the man and his children ate and ate. When they finished eating, there was more food available for them. The Old Grandmother then fed the children corn.

Then the father left with his children and walked to another lodge, where he asked about his wife. 'She is here,' he was told. 'She spends all her time singing and dancing.' At that moment, the mother came dancing by her family, but she did not recognize them. Again, she danced by and this time her children tossed pieces of corn to make her notice them. Still she did not stop or notice them. The mother did smell the corn, however, which reminded her of her life on earth. 'I smell the scent of earth.' But she continued her dancing and did not see her children. When she danced by again, her children threw pieces of corn at her and this time she realized they were nearby.

When she saw them, she ran to them, hugging them all, for she had missed them, too. Her husband took her and his children and loaded them in the canoes and took them back to his earthly lodge.

However, his wife did not want to remain on earth. One day, when her husband was out hunting again, she took her children and placed them in her magic canoe. She sang her songs and the canoe rose into the sky. This time, the father did not return to pull the canoe down and he lost his children forever. His wife and his children becme permanent sky people.

After losing his wife and children, the Alabama warrior returned to his people and found another wife among the maidens of the village. He married her knowing that she would always remain on earth with him and would never sail off into the sky.

PART 3
THE GREAT LAKES REGION

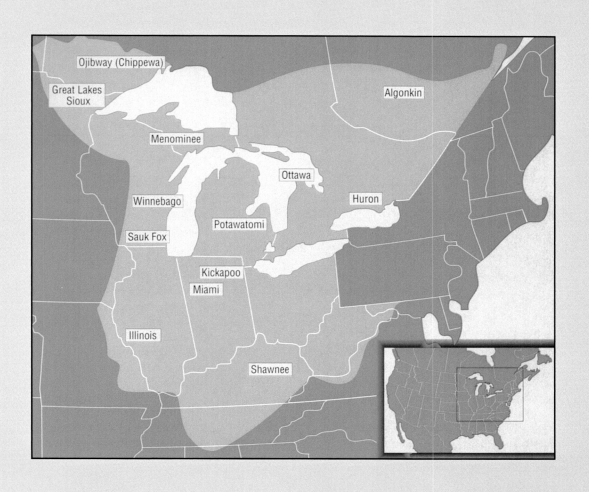

Anthropologists date the occupation of the Great Lakes region by human beings to approximately 10,000 BC. The ancient peoples who wandered into this region were Palaeo-Indians who hunted the great mastodons. Little evidence of these nomadic hunters exists today. What does remain are Stone Sage tools and weapons. These include Vlovis-style projectile points, common to many parts of North America in the Palaeolithic era. Mastodon-hunting remained the primary occupation of these hunters until about 7000 BC, when the great shaggy beasts began to die out. Changes in the climate not only brought the mastodons to the edge of extinction but changes the lifestyles of the ancient Indians.

The Great Lakes region witnessed the rise of a new anthropological age, known as the Neolithic. Between 7000 and 4500 BC the Aqua-Plano group of Native Americans dominated the region. With the disappearance of the mastodon, these Neolithic peoples continued to work with stone and hunted smaller game, including elk, caribou and deer. By 4500 BC two relatively distinct cultural groups had developed: the Boreal Archaic and the Old Copper.

The Boreal Archaic could be found from the Upper Great Lakes east to the Atlantic Ocean. This period marked the transition of Woodland Indians from an emphasis on the making of stone implements to an extended emphasis on woodworking. Thriving in the pine and hard-wood forests of the Great Lakes, these Native Americans developed woodworking tools, such as axes and stone adzes. Such Neolithic axes were used for a variety of purposes, including making dug-out canoes.

Perhaps as an offshoot of the Boreal Archaic cultural group, the Copper Culture developed after 4500 BC. Reaching a peak during the millennium between 4000 and 3000 BC, it was centred

in the region of the western Great Lakes, primarily in the modern-day state of Illinois and north to Lake Superior. Here Native Americans began working raw copper into many different items. These were alternately functional, including spears, axes, knives, awls and wedges for splitting tree trunks, and decorative, resulting in the creation of copper bracelets, pendants and beads. Copper Culture Indians not only fashioned copper into tools, weapons and trinkets through hammering raw ore, they annealed the metal – a process that includes heating the ore and working the softened copper. They were also woodworkers, who built their dug-out canoes from the same lakeland forests as their Boreal neighbours.

In time, the Old Copper Culture withered away, while the Boreal Archaic group continued to develop. By 1500 BC the Boreal Archaic had given way to the Late Archaic, which marked the early stages of the Woodland Cultures. Around 3,000 years ago, the Early Woodland stage saw the advent of the Adena cultural group, which was noted for its burial mounds.

The Adena Culture spread up and down the Ohio River valley. These cultures are marked by larger population groups, an advanced style of pottery making, highly stylized cloth weaving, a more sedentary lifestyle, the development of rectangular-shaped houses and a clear delineation of status and rank among members. The Adena cultural group, however, was overshadowed by the eventual development of the Hopewellian Culture, which rose up among Woodland Indians about AD 500–700. Although the cultural age lasted only a few hundred years, these Native Americans were involved in greater trade among themselves and with their neighbours. They built elaborate burial mounds, worked implements out of stone, copper and bone, and carved intricate items of utility and pleasure, including musical instruments, tobacco pipes, eating utensils and jewellery.

Between 1000 and 1600 the Great Lakes region and the Ohio River valley tribes developed into those that were in place by the time of the arrival of the European explorers. Those tribes located in southern Wisconsin developed from the Hopewellian Culture into the Effigy Mound Culture, noted for the burial sites shaped like animals and birds. (The Great Serpent Mound in southwest Ohio is an example.) In the lands of modern-day Minnesota and the Great Lakes region, tribal groups developed, speaking a variety of languages, including dialects of Siouan, Algonquian and Iroquoian. About 1000, the Winnebago migrated from the upper Mississippi valley into northeastern Wisconsin. All such tribes were by this time practising organized agriculture, as well as relying on the hunt and fishing the myriad lakes and streams of this vast northern region. Although not all tribes fit into one generalized description or cultural group, the peoples who occupied the Great Lakes region and the lands north of the Ohio River are generally known today as those belonging to the Algonquian group.

The Algonquins

The term 'Algonquin' may be used in several different, and even confusing, ways. Linguists use the label to identify those tribes who spoke a regional variation of a major language group. From the Algonquian language stock, words familiar to English speakers today have come down to us: hickory, moccasin, moose, papoose, powwow, sachem, squash, squaw, tomahawk, totem and wigwam, for example. Others use the name to identify a large culture group located in the American Northeast, from New England west to the Great Lakes. Anthropologists divide the cultural group known as the Algonquins into subcultures, including the New England Algonquins, the Hudson River group, the Middle Atlantic group, the Southern group, the Great Lakes group, the Prairie group, the Canadian Woodland group and the Canadian Subarctic group. This chapter is concerned with the Algonquins found in the Great Lakes and Prairie

culture groups. The individual cultural groups are represented by specific tribes, each of which ranged in a limited region. Those tribes that are included in the Great Lakes group were the Chippewa, Algonquin, Menominee, Ottawa and Potawatomi. As the group name indicates, they ranged through the Lakes country, especially in the lands of modern-day Michigan. The Prairie Algonquins were the tribes Fox, Kickapoo, Sauk, Illinois, Miami and Shawnee, whose homes were usually to be found in modern-day Wisconsin, Illinois and Indiana. These and other Algonquins were among the first Indians to make contact with the British and French explorers and settlers of the seventeenth and eighteenth centuries. Traditionally, the Algonquins became allies of the French in Canada, while their neighbours in the Northeast, the Iroquois, allied themselves with the British. Throughout the seventeenth and eighteenth centuries the slow but continuous movement of whites pushed the Algonquins further west. The Great Lakes Algonquins were among the last of the subcultural groups to feel this pressure, but they too, by the nineteenth century, found themselves being removed by the United States government to relocation sites, primarily reservations in Oklahoma.

Algonquian Society

In looking at the Algonquian lifestyle and social structure, it is possible to see a reliance on intertribal confederacies. These unions often provided the military structure for protecting the tribes, as well as the legal system for their members. Such confederacies were not as well organized as neighbouring Iroquois unions, serving rather as a loose connection between Algonquian villages and towns.

Most such confederacies were led by a grand sachem, a chief of great wisdom and varying authority. Grand sachems in some villages had power no greater than that of a mediator of disputes, while in others they might have the power of an almighty monarch. However, most Algonquian tribes in the Great Lakes region were led, instead, by a dual leadership of two chiefs, one a war chief and the other a peace chief. War chiefs were chosen by the tribe's membership, while the position of peace chief was often hereditary.

Some Great Lakes Algonquian tribes had a third chief who was a shaman, a holy medicine man who organized and led the tribe's religious ceremonies.

Tribal organization among the Algonquins often included bands comprising extended families who hunted and lived together throughout the year. A tribe's bands traditionally came together each summer for important celebrations and ceremonies. Even when the band structure was in place among a tribe's members, an essential element of tribal social organization was the moiety. Moieties resulted in the dividing of clans into two groups; each was responsible for various functions within a tribe. They also served as the opposing teams during a tribe's sporting games. Families who intermarried within a tribe were generally part of the same clan, another subdivision of a band. Such clans often identified themselves through symbols such as animals or elements. These symbols were known as totems. Totems were considered sacred by their clan and thought to have great power, as well as providing protection for band members.

Algonquian Wigwams

As has already been discussed earlier in this book (see page 14), typical housing among Algonquian tribes was the rounded, bark-covered wigwam. We shall take time now to elaborate on the subject here.

Generally, there were three different types of wigwam: domes, conical and an extended conical pattern. The domed wigwam was found among the Chippewas. The structure was circular or oval and measured about fifteen feet (five metres) in diameter. Approximately eighteen to twenty saplings were used to build the wigwam's framework, with the poles set approximately two feet (just under a metre) apart. The poles were bent into the circle's centre and those opposite each other were lashed together with strips of cedar bark, forming supporting arches.

Wigwams were covered with a natural sheathing. Often, cat's tails were sewn together to form the walls of the wigwam, while strips of bark were placed on top of the lashed poles to form a roof for the dwelling. Various woods were used, but birch was considered ideal. This wood

was light and hearty, and the birch pieces were easily removed, rolled up and transported when a band uprooted and moved to a new campsite. Such a dwelling was relatively cool in summer. When winter came, the Algonquins covered the wigwams with an additional layer of bark over the outer walls, piled mountains of autumn leaves all around their houses and stacked evergreen branches on top and around the entire structure.

At the top of these primitive yet snug houses, a smoke hole was left open so that the home's campfire might emit its smoke. Inside the wigwam, woven mats of cat's tails covered the floor. Additional mats provided bedding.

The second variety of wigwam, called the conical wigwam, was not used by the Algonquins of the Great Lakes region but by tribes located in New England. This wigwam resembled the tepees of the Great Plains tribes, but was covered with sections of birch bark rather than buffalo hides.

The third type, called by the Chippewa *wigwassawigamig*, was found commonly among the Algonquins. Anthropologists refer to this as an 'extended conical' because of its shape. Rather than the framework consisting of poles stacked together in the shape of a cone, a *wigwassawigamig* featured a ridge pole about six to eight feet (two to three metres) in length, with poles leaning into it, providing the frame for the wigwam. This house, like the other two types of wigwams, was also covered in sheets of birch bark.

The Algonquins built other lodges, some smaller and some quite large. Each had a specific purpose. Smaller wigwams might serve as sweat lodges or places where shamans prophesied. Larger lodges provided the meeting houses for the bands. Often these larger structures stood twenty to thirty feet (seven to nine metres) in width and were 200 feet (sixty metres) in length. Such buildings served to house all the members of a large band of Algonquins.

When the Algonquins built their villages, they provided protection for their homes and families by erecting a palisade or stockade around their encampment. Such 'forts' were either circular or square and often featured drainage ditches around them to keep rainwater from flooding a village site.

Food Sources

The Algonquian tribes practised a combination of hunting, formal agriculture, gathering and fishing to feed themselves. They did not raise any domesticated animals for eating, although they used dogs on hunting expeditions. Hunters and fishermen provided fresh meat, especially in non-winter months. Large and small animals alike filled the cooking pots and fire pots of the Algonquins. Deer was a mainstay, as well as bear, moose and elk. Tribes to the north hunted caribou too. Smaller animals, such as rabbit, squirrel and even beaver, were hunted, and gamebirds – duck, goose, turkey and partridge – were hunted and trapped.

Traps included snares and deadfalls, these latter used in killing larger animals. A typical deadfall involved the erection of a pair of logs standing on end with a third post – sometimes called a samson post by Europeans – resting on the ends of the support posts. The end of a large log was placed gingerly across the support pole. The entire contraption was designed to collapse at the slightest touch. Bait was placed beneath the large log. Many an unwary bear or deer set off such traps. Snares were used typically to catch small animals and gamebirds. A limber tree sapling was bent over and attached to a trigger device, then a piece of cord or rope was set in a loop on the ground below the trigger. Bait was set on the opposite end of the trigger and when a gamebird, for example, wandered by and took the bait, the trigger was sprung, the sapling jerked up and, it was hoped, snagged the bird.

While hunters on land chased down or captured their quarry, Algonquian fisherman traversed the lakes, rivers and streams of the region to catch fish. The Great Lakes teemed with fish; the sturgeon was the largest, weighing hundreds of pounds. These fishermen used a variety of methods in their work, including nets, traps, spears and harpoons. They ran lines with hooks on their ends, fashioned from bone or antler. Bird wishbones were used to make crude fish hooks. The Algonquins also caught larger fish using bone gorges – straight pieces of bone with their ends sharpened and the fishing line tied in the bone's centre. When the fish took in the gorge, it turned sideways after being swallowed,

leaving them caught on the line. The Algonquins trapped eels for food as well. This activity usually took place in the spring, when the eels migrated. To catch them, the Indians built weirs, or wooden fences, across shallow streams, so that their prey was funnelled into narrow chutes flanked by waiting fishermen in dug-out canoes. The shallow, narrow waters were difficult for the eels to manoeuvre in and they were caught in large numbers. Once the eels were speared, the women on shore skinned them and smoked them over low fires.

Among the domesticated crops raised by the Algonquins were corn, beans and squash, the most common crops of the Native Americans, as well as pumpkins. A band's summer encampment was generally located on a site where at lest limited farming could be carried out. Corn, beans and squash were often planted side by side, with bean vines clinging to corn stalks, snaking their way ever upwards.

Because corn was grown among the Algonquian groups, hominy was a natural food they produced. Hominy is made by cooking whole ears of corn with wood ash or lye. Once cooked, the corn hulls were picked off and washed to remove the lye, before the removed hulls were boiled again.

They also collected wild berries, such as cranberries and blueberries, roots and other edible plants. Where freshwater lakes and ponds were located, the Algonquins harvested wild rice. This 'wild' plant was eaten extensively by the tribes of the Great Lakes region. They gathered the stalks of rice, beating them with wooden sticks, This caused the grain to fall to the bottom of their canoes, which were lined with reed mats for collecting the rice. Since the Algonquins competed with the water gamebirds for rice, they harvested it just before it was fully ripe. It was then dried and threshed by being stamped on. The women of the tribes stored the grin in birch-bark storage containers, which were buried underground, where the grain might be kept many months before being eaten.

Algonquins sweetened their meals by tapping maple trees for their sap, from which they produced both maple syrup and sugar. The work was done by the women and children of each band. A maple tree was gashed along one side and flat spiles were driven into the cut. These spiles, or spouts, became the conduits for the tree's sap, which oozed into birch-bark containers. The women then boiled the sap until it produced syrup or continued the heating process until it crystallized, creating maple sugar. Many Algonquins used water to dilute maple syrup, producing a sweet drink. Sometimes the liquid was fermented, making an alcohol, but this custom was not common.

Cooking these various food stuffs and meats was generally kept simple. Freshly slain meat was skewered on green sticks and grilled over an open fire. Meat was occasionally fried, but this technique was not popular among most bands and may have been learned from their European neighbours. Algonquin women hung cooking skins over their fires, boiling the meat inside. Wooden cooking vessels were also suspended over a cooking fire on a stick, the opposite end of which was anchored by a heavy stone.

Transportation

Before the arrival of the Europeans in the New World, Native Americans did not use horses for transportation. The tribes of the Great Lakes region did have a natural advantage in developing a viable transport system thanks to the many lakes and rivers that cut through their homelands. They were able to make use of these by building canoes, which were small, lightweight, sleek and reasonably manoeuverable.

Just as the Great Plains tribes were noted for their tepees, eagle-feather bonnets and horse-bound buffalo hunts, the Northeastern tribes, including the Algonquins, were noted for their birch-bark canoes. By paddling their canoes, the Lakes country Native Americans could travel great distances, going far from home.

Canoes did not come in a standard size or design. Some were built with low bows and sterns, and these were ideal for travel on calmer rivers since they were sleek and fast, their design exerting little wind resistance. Others were built for plying the waters of the Great Lakes and other large bodies of water, where the waves might be sharper and higher. There, the canoes were built with high bows and sterns. The length of a canoe also varied widely. A common model

was built to accommodate two people at best, while longer designs resulted in a canoe that could hold as many as ten, sitting in rows of two abreast. Northeastern and Great Lakes canoes varied, then, from ten or twelve feet (three or four metres) in length to fifty or sixty feet (fifteen to eighteen metres).

Native American canoes were built from several different types of wood – spruce, elm and especially birch. Bark was peeled directly from standing trees in lengthy strips and sections. A typical canoe's framework was made from pieces of white cedar, since this wood splits easily. The frame was then covered with birch-bark pieces. Birch bark did not change its shape through stretching or shrinking. The pieces were laced together with strips of split roots of black spruce. Black-spruce gum was then heated until it had the consistency of a thickish syrup before being spread over the canoe's seams and cracks, to make them watertight. The insides of these canoes were lined with strips of white cedar. Bow-shaped sticks of cedar or maple were placed across the canoe's middle length to give the canoe a wider shape across its gunwales. Paddles were often carved out of maple as well.

Building even such a simple craft was not a one-day task. Canoe-building generally required the efforts of at least two men and perhaps four women, working for two to three weeks. The women harvested and prepared the spruce for the boat and were responsible for sewing and sealing the birch-bark pieces. Once completed, these crafts were light enough for a man to carry one measuring as long as eighteen feet. Inside a typical canoe, Indians kept a birch-bark 'bucket' for bailing out water, spare pieces of birch bark and spruce root and pine gum for emergency repairs, and a heavy stone tied to a piece of cordage for use as an anchor. When paddling a canoe, Algonquins sat in the bottom of the boat, often on a deer skin. Rarely did these crafts have any seats.

Algonquian Clothing

As with all other Native American tribes, the Algonquins wore as many clothes as they needed to suit the weather. In the warm and humid summer months, most Indians wore less than in the colder seasons. Children generally wore no clothing until they reached the age of ten. By then they were considered adults.

The women of the Ohio country and Great Lakes tribes generally wore dresses of deer skin, hemmed below the knee. Such dresses were wrapped around a woman and held in place by a belt. Women wore leather leggings in the winter and typically wore moccasins all year round. Also, in cool weather the women wore pairs of cape sleeves, which were joined at the back of the neck. Often such clothing – dresses, skirts, capes – was fringed.

Most Algonquian men wore less than the women, regardless of the weather. A typical summertime costume was a breechclout and moccasins, although footwear was optional. Such breechclouts were mere strips of leather, approximately three feet (one metre) in width, which were run through a leather belt and between the warrior's thighs. However, if a day's activities were to be spent in the forests, a brave often wore leggings for protection. Leggings were not necessarily the same as trousers, however. Some leggings came up to only just below the knees; others covered the thighs as well.

In winter Algonquian men wore fur skins for warmth. Robes of fur were draped over the shoulders and might be supplemented on extremely cold days with rabbit-skin blankets. To help them walk through snowy landscapes, Algonquian men wore moose-hide boots, sometimes over their moccasins. Such boots were cut and sewn from the hind leg of a moose, just where the animal's hock bends. This provided the boots with a natural heel. Moccasins might also be stuffed with padding to help keep a brave's feet warm, with deer or moose hair or cat's-tail fluff being used most often.

Moccasins were worn all year round and were typically of two different designs. One was constructed from a single piece of leather, cut and sewn down the middle to make footwear that was slightly boot-shaped. The other model, which mirrored the more modern concept of the moccasin, was sewn from three pieces of deer-skin. It included stitching that formed the puckered moccasin top, plus a thin band of hide sewn in a tube along the moccasin's heel. A leather drawstring was run through the tube which could be

tightened and tied to make the footwear fit more snugly.

In addition to wearing moccasins, Algonquins wore snow-shoes in winter. These lightweight 'shoes' were attached to the moccasins or fur boots and were sometimes up to three feet (one metre) in length. Snow-shoes were cut from a green piece of wood, generally ash, which formed the frame. This wooden strip was heated and bent in the shape of either a large teardrop or an oval. An intricate pattern of thwarts and meshing filled in the space of the shoe. Commonly, men's snow-shoes featured two thwarts, one that crossed in front of the wearer's toes and the other behind the heel of his moccasin. Sinew was then woven beneath the moccasin to provide support. Additional webbing was included both behind and in front of the moccasin, with the closest netting in front to keep the snow off the wearer's foot as much as possible. A leather thong curved above the middle of the snow-shoe to hold the moccasin in place while walking.

Women and children wore a different model of snow-shoe called a 'bear-paw'. These shoes were smaller and designed for short walks within the camp. They were barely eighteen inches (fifty centimetres) long, about one foot (thirty centimetres) in width and were oval-shaped with the shoe's front slightly wider than the back. These shoes were less elaborate and did not have nearly as much webbing as did the warrior's snow shoe.

Men and women alike decorated their clothing with paints, feathers, freshwater shells and porcupine quills. Often, they dyed their feathers in vegetable and wood-root shades to give them a more colourful appearance. They sometimes created elaborate patterns with paints and quills. Contact with whites later allowed them to replace quills and shells with glass beads.

Algonquian Headgear and Hairstyles

Algonquian men and women did not tend towards elaborate head-dresses or feathered bonnets, as was the custom of other Native American tribes, although how they displayed their hair was of great importance to them. Hair for the

Algonquins was a symbol of independence and individual power.

Hairstyles varied between men and women. The women generally wore their hair in braids, topped with a smallish cap or headband of decorated shells. The men wore a variety of styles, depending o the custom of their individual tribes, bands and clans. Some men wore their hair long, tied off in two braids or pulled up into two great hanks of hair, minus the braids. Others affected the roach cut, which required braves to pluck out their hair except for a wide strip left running down the middle of the scalp from the forehead to the nape of the neck

Often Algonquin men maintained a scalp lock, a longer piece of hair left in the middle of the roach. This extra length of hair was maintained for the convenience of, and perhaps as a taunt for, any enemy who might have opportunity to scalp a brave in battle. Scalp locks were treated in various fashions, from simple letting them fall loose, dangling down from the roach, to tying them up so that they stood above the general hair line of the roach.

In winter, both men and women wore a variety of fur caps. Occasionally they wore an entire fur skin, complete with the head of the animal, such as a fox or otter. These caps were tied around the sides of the head, leaving the top of the head exposed. This type of headgear may have been the progenitor of the racoon cap that was worn by American pioneers and frontiersmen of the eighteenth and early nineteenth centuries.

As for feathers as hair decorations, the Algonquins did not wear them often or in any considerable numbers. Warriors recognized for their valour in combat might wear a single feather on their heads. Such a feather might be cut in such a way so as to indicate a specific deed in battle. Unlike the Indians of the Great Plains, the Algonquins did not accumulate feathers as symbolic trophies or make elaborate eagle-feather bonnets.

Algonquins at War

When the Algonquins went to war, they approached the art in much the same way as their neighbours. Generalized war between the tribe and a neighbour, whether another tribe or a white settlement, was organized by tribal leaders or by the leaders of established raiding parties. Such fighting did not usually include large warrig parties or what might be called large-scale battles. Raiding was a common activity, and one that consumed much of a brave's time and effort. Generally, raids against a neighbouring tribe were organized by one warrior, often called a war leader, and planned against a specific enemy band or group. Such raids were carried out for singular purposes as well, including gaining new hunting lands at the expense of an enemy, acquiring honour among fellow tribesmen or as an act of vengeance for the death of another brave.

War leaders could come from any rank of a tribe's warriors. Such a brave outlined his strategy with fellow tribesmen and assumed responsibility for the raid's success. Before others agreed to follow him, they first had to feel that he was the possessor of Manitou. It was supernatural in nature but was considered to be a spiritual quality rather than a spirit itself. Both spiritual beings and humans could possess it, in much the same way that modern culture speaks of the human spirit. A war leader gained access to Manitou through a vision, and its possession was considered good for one military raid only. Any warrior who went on a raid did so by his own choice; no one could be forced to participate. Any volunteer warrior could abandon the expedition at any time of his choosing short of the actual raid itself.

Raids were often conducted far from the encampment, so the raiding party would spend several days in the forests making their way to the designated target. The advance was often slow, with warriors killing game along the way and storing the meat to consume on the way back. If a raiding party consisted of a couple of dozen braves, a sacred bundle was often taken to provide a measure of spiritual protection. With smaller parties, the war leader's personal bundle was considered adequate.

Once a raiding party located its enemy, the warriors usually made their assault as a surprise attack. If the raid was a success, the warrior who made the first kill led the group back. If the party had been defeated, the return was often disorganized, with every man for himself. During a raid, captives might be taken and brought back to the party's camp to serve as slaves. If a captive was old, he was usually killed on the trip back. When a successful war party returned to its people, a scalp dance was held, with a great feast for the returning warriors.

Algonquian Weaponry

As with many tribes in North America before the arrival of the Europeans, the chief weapon used by the Algonquins was the bow and arrow. A typical Algonquian bow was a straight, flat piece of wood measuring about five feet (1.5 metres) in length. The bow was about two inches (five centimetres) wide and half an inch (one centimetre) thick. The bow tapered on both ends where notches held the bowstring. Bows were often made from ash, hickory, red cedar and white oak. Bowstrings were made from deer sinew and other natural plant fibres. Some were even made from the neck skin of snapping turtles, a material prized in the making of bowstrings since it neither shrank nor stretched out of shape.

A warrior considered his bow to be an extension of himself and protected his weapon with extreme care. When carving a bow, a warrior first cut a piece of bow wood from a tree and then began working it, giving it its rudimentary shape. Then he rubbed bear grease on the unfinished piece and hung it inside his lodge, letting the wood season for several months. During those months, the warrior would periodically regrease it. When a bow was completed, it was handled with great respect. When not in use, bows were unstrung and kept in protective cases. Warriors continued to lubricate their bows with oil even when not in use. Long before they were of an age to be warriors, Algonquian boys carved small bows, learning, then perfecting their craft over their entire lifetimes. Warriors considered too old for the hunt or for warring raids often continued their work in making bows and also arrows.

Arrows were cut from several kinds of tree noted for their straight branches, including dogwood trees and the viburnum bush, which often went by the name of arrow-wood. Even branches that were not naturally straight were heated and bent into shape using a special tool designed for just such a purpose. Arrowheads were usually knapped from stone, but other materials were also used, including animal bone, slate, shell fragments and copper. Such arrowheads were carved to the appropriate shape and usually lashed on to the wooden shaft with sinew. Arrows were sometimes carved so that a bulbous portion of wood, called a bunt, was left on the end of the shaft, giving the arrow a natural head. These arrows were used to hunt birds and small game, and would stun the animal rather than cut through its body.

To give the arrow its trueness in flight, warriors cut strips of feathers and attached them to the opposite end of the wooden shaft. Most arrows featured three split feathers spaced evenly around the shaft's tail end. These were glued in place with spruce gum, the same material used to waterproof canoes. Arrows were kept in buckskin quivers hung behind a warrior's left shoulder blade. Accompanying the quiver was the warrior's bow case, which was generally decorated and fringed.

Algonquian Religion

The world of spirits and the supernatural was of great significance to the Algonquian tribes. As has already been stated, the concept central to the spirit life of Algonquins was that of Manitou. This was considered highly sacred, an abstract force that in some mysterious fashion determined whether a person's efforts were to be successful or not. Warriors tapped into the spirit world of Manitou by fasting, sometimes for several days, looking for some sign of the presence of the force, perhaps a visitation or vision from the spirit world. Even when one had the blessing of the Manitou, it was not permanent; one had to receive it over and over to continue to have spiritual confidence and to complete noteworthy tasks.

The Algonquins made medicine bundles for themselves, as was the custom with other regional culture groups. In such bundles the warrior kept items he had seen in his visions as symbols that helped him to make connection with the spirit world.

Kitshi Manitou and Wisagatcak

While Manitou was considered a spiritual quality that humans could achieve, the Algonquins recognized a great and powerful spirit that they called Kitshi, or Gitche Manitou. This being was the supreme god of the Algonquins. In addition, they recognized another god, named Wisagatcak, who was the creator of the world.

Stories abound about the trickster Wisagatcak, who built a pole fence across a river where he intended to trap the giant beaver. At the end of the day, Wisagatcak saw him swimming close by. As he prepared to spear the beaver, the muskrat bit Wisagatcak, causing his throw to go wild. Discouraged, Wisagatcak decided to give up on killing the giant beaver, so he began to tear down his wooden dam. As the dam came down, the river's waters poured out but the water level of the river did not recede. The giant beavers were causing the water to flow endlessly in torrents, flooding all the surrounding land.

To save himself and the nearby animals, Wisagatcak uprooted some trees and constructed himself a raft. He then collected many animals, rescuing them from the swirling waters. The giant beavers continued to make the waters flow, and Wisagatcak floated on his raft with his animals for two weeks. The muskrat then left the raft and dived under the water to see if he could find land. He couldn't and subsequently drowned. The raven was released from the raft to look for dry land, but could not find any. Wisagatcak then enlisted the help of the Wolf, who began running around the raft with a wad of moss in his mouth. While he ran, the moss began to grow, with clumps of earth attached. Wisagatcak then cast a powerful spell on the moss and it spread out until it became a new world. This story was common among the Cree Indians of the north.

Another spirit important in the Algonquin was the heroic figure Glooscap, who has already been mentioned (see page 16). Creation stores also credit him with making the world.

Nature and the Spiritual World

For the Algonquins, the natural and the spiritual or supernatural world were always inextricably linked. The sun and moon were Manitous, specifically the grandfather and grandmother of some tribes. The stars of the Milky Way formed a river in the sky, while other stars represented the dead and departed spirits of Algonquian ancestors. To the Algonquins, the four stars of the Big Dipper symbolized a bear, while the other three stars of the Dipper's handle represented three hunters chasing the bear through the otherwise black heavens. Each autumn the hunter spirits killed the bear. When his blood dripped down to earth, it turned the leaves of the trees red. This idea was part of a never-ending cycle of life and death in the spiritual world of the Algonquins.

Algonquian Witchcraft

Like many other North American tribes, the Algonquins believed in the presence of supernatural beings called witches. Witches were imagined as both male and female. Such spirits travelled about at night, making a hissing noise as they went along. Fire flashed from their mouths, lighting up the night sky. Witches performed acts of evil on both nature and humans, often receiving the black for any tragedy that befell an individual or his or her tribe which could not be explained otherwise. So, for example, unexplained deaths were blamed on witches, as were diseases and body swellings.

MYTHS AND LEGENDS
OF THE GREAT LAKES REGION

THE STAR-MAIDEN

Chippewa

A YOUNG WARRIOR NAMED ALGON was walking over the prairies. On his way, he discovered a circular pathway, worn as if by the tread of many feet, though there were no footmarks visible outside its bounds. The young hunter, who had never before encountered one of these 'fairy rings', was filled with surprise at the discovery, and hid himself in the long grass to see whether an explanation might not be forthcoming. He had not long to wait. In a little while he heard the sound of music, so faint and sweet that it surpassed anything he had ever dreamed of. The strains grew fuller and richer, and as they seemed to come from above he turned his eyes towards the sky. Far in the blue he could see a tiny white speck like a floating cloud. Nearer and nearer it came, and the astonished hunter saw that it was no cloud, but a dainty willow basket, in which were seated twelve beautiful maidens. The music he had heard was the sound of their voices as they sang strange and magical songs. Descending into the charmed ring, they danced round and round with such exquisite grace and abandon that it was a sheer delight to watch them. But after the first moments of dazzled surprise Algon had eyes only for the youngest of the group, a slight, vivacious creature, so fragile and delicate that it seemed to the stalwart hunter that a breath would blow her away.

He was, indeed, seized with a fierce passion for the dainty sprite, and he speedily decided to spring from the grass and carry her off. But the pretty creatures were too quick for him. The fairy of his choice skillfully eluded his grasp and rushed to the basket. The others followed, and in a moment they were soaring up in the air, singing a sweet, unearthly song. The disconsolate hunter returned to his lodge, but try as he might he could not get the thought of the Star-maiden out of his head, and next day, long before the hour of the fairies' arrival, he lay in the grass awaiting the sweet sounds that would herald their approach. At length the willow basket appeared. The twelve ethereal beings danced as before. Again Algon made a desperate attempt to seize the youngest, and again he as unsuccessful.

'Let us stay,' said one of the Star-maidens. 'Perhaps the mortal wishes to teach us his earthly dances.' But the youngest sister would not hear of it, and they all rose out of sight in their willow basket.

Poor Algon returned home more unhappy then ever. All night he lay awake dreaming of the pretty, elusive creature who had wound a chain of gossamer round his heart and brain, and early in the morning he repaired to the enchanted spot. Casting about for some means of gaining his end, he came upon the hollow trunk of a tree in which a number of mice played. With the aid of the charms in his sacred

Source

Lewis Spence, *North American Indians*, London: George G. Harrap & Co., 1914, pp. 152–6

bundle, he turned himself into one of these little animals, thinking the fair sisters would never pierce his disguise.

That day when the willow basket descended its occupants alighted and danced merrily as they were wont in the magic circle, till the youngest saw the hollow tree-trunk (which had not been there on the previous day) and turned to fly. Her sisters laughed at her fears, and tried to reassure her by overturning the tree trunk. The mice scampered in all directions, and were quickly pursued by the Star-maidens, who killed them all except Algon. The latter regained his own shape just as the youngest fairy raised her hand to strike him. Clasping her in his arms, he bore her to his village, while her frightened sisters ascended to their Star-country.

Arrived at his home, Algon married the maiden, and by his kindness and gentleness soon won her affection. However, her thoughts still dwelt on her own people, and though she indulged her sorrow only in secret, lest it should trouble her husband, she never ceased to lament her lost home.

One day while she was out with her little son she made a basket of willows, like the one in which she had first come to earth. Gathering together some flowers and gifts for the Star-people, she took the child with her into the basket, sang the magical songs she still remembered, and soon floated up to her own country, where she was welcomed by the king, her father.

Algon's grief was bitter indeed when he found that his wife and child had left him. But he had no means of following them. Every day he would go the magic circle on the prairie and give vent to his sorrow, but the years went past and there was no sign of his dear ones returning.

Meanwhile the woman and her son had almost forgotten Algon and the Earth-country. However, when the boy grew old enough to hear the story he wished to go and see his father. His mother consented, and arranged to go with him. While they were preparing to descent, the Star-people said, 'Bring Algon with you when you return, and ask him to being some feature from every beast and bird he has killed in the hunt.'

Algon, who had lately spent almost all his time at the charmed circle, was overjoyed to see his wife and son come back to him, and willingly agreed to go with them to the Star-country. He worked very hard to obtain a specimen of all the rare and curious birds and beasts in his land, and when at last he had gathered the relics – a claw of one, a feather of another, and so on – he piled them in the willow basket, climbed in himself with his wife and boy, and set off to the Star-country.

The people there were delighted with the curious gifts Algon had brought them, and, being permitted by their king to take one apiece, they did so. Those who took a tail or a claw of any beast at once became the quadruped represented by the fragment, and those who took the wings of birds became birds themselves. Algon and his wife and son took the feathers of a white falcon and flew down to the prairies, where their descendants may still be seen.

Descending into the charmed ring the fairies danced round and round with exquisite grace and abandon.

IOSCO, OR THE PRAIRIE BOY'S VISIT TO THE SUN AND MOON

Ottawa

ONE PLEASANT MORNING, five young men and a boy about ten years of age called Isoco went out a-shooting with their bows and arrows. They left their lodges with the first appearance of daylight and, having passed through a long reach of woods, had ascended a high hill before the sun arose. While standing there in a group, the sun suddenly burst forth in all its lory. The air was so clear that it appeared to be at no great distance.

'How very near it is,,' they all said.

'It cannot be far,' said the eldest, 'and if you will accompany me, we will see if we cannot reach it.'

A loud ascent burst from every lip. Even the boy, Iosco, said he would go. They told him he was too young, but he replied, 'If you do not permit me to go with you, I will tell your plan to each of your parents.' They then said to him, 'You shall also go with us, so be quiet.'

They then fell upon the following arrangement. It was resolved that each one should obtain from his parents as many pairs of moccasins as he could, and also new clothing of leather. They fixed on a spot where they would conceal all their articles, until they were ready to start on their journey, and which would serve, in the meantime, as a place of rendezvous, where they might secretly meet and consult. This being arranged, they returned home.

A long time passed before they could put their plan into execution. But they kept it a profound secret, even to the boy. They frequently met at the appointed place and discussed the subject. At length everything was in readiness and they decided on a day to set out. That morning the boy shed tears for a pair of new leather leggings.

'Don't you see,' said he to his parents, 'how my companions are dressed?' This appealed to their pride and envy prevailed. He obtained the leggings.

Artifices were also resorted to by the others, under the plea of going out on a special hunt. They said to one another, but in a tone that they might be overheard, 'We will see who will bring in the most game.' They went out in different directions, but soon met at the appointed place, where they had hidden the articles for their journey, with as many arrows as they had time to make. Each one took something on his back and they began their march.

They travelled day after day, through a thick forest, but the sun was always at the same distance.

'We must,' said they, 'travel towards Waubunong, the east, and we shall get to the object, some time or other.' No one was discouraged, although winter overtook them. They built a lodge and hunted till they obtained as much dried meat as they could carry and then continued on. This they did several times; season followed season. More than one winter overtook them. Yet none of them became discouraged' or expressed dissatisfaction.

One day the travellers came to the banks of a river whose waters ran towards the east. They followed it down many days. As they were walking one day, they came to rising ground, from which they saw something white or clear through the trees. They encamped on this elevation. Next morning they came, suddenly, in

Source
Henry R. Schoolcraft, *North American Indian Legends,* Philadelphia: J.B. Lippincott & Co., 1856, pp. 278–91

view of an immense body of water. No land could be seen as far as the eye could reach. One or two of them lay down on the beach to drink. As soon as they got the water in their mouths, they spat it out and exclaimed, with surprise, 'Shewetagon awbo! – salt water'. It was the sea.

While looking on the water, the sun arose as if from the deep, and went on its steady course through the heavens, enlivening the scene with its cheering and animating beams. They stood in admiration, but the object appeared to be as distant from them as ever. They thought it best to encamp and consult whether it were advisable to go on or return.

'We see,' said the leader, 'that the sun is still on the opposite side of this great water, but let us not be disheartened. We can walk around the shore.' To this they all assented.

Next morning they took the northerly shore, to walk around it, but had gone only a short distance when they came to a large river. They again encamped and, while sitting before the fire, the question was put, whether any one of them had ever dreamed of water, or of walking on it. After a long silence, the eldest said he had. Soon after, they lay down to sleep.

When they arose the following morning, the eldest addressed them: 'We have done wrong in coming north. Last night my spirit appeared to me and told me to go south, and that but a short distance beyond the spot we left yesterday, we should come to a river with high banks. That by looking off its mouth, we should see an island which would approach to us. He directed that we should all get on it. He then told me to cast my eyes towards the water. I did so, and I saw all he had declared. He then informed me that we must return south and wait at the river until the day after tomorrow. I believe all that was revealed to me in this dream and that wel shall do well to follow it.'

The party immediately retraced their footsteps in exact obedience to this dream. Towards the evening they came to the borders of the indicated river. It had high banks, behind which they encamped, and here they patiently awaited the fulfilment of the dream. The appointed day arrived. They said, 'We will see if that which has been said will be seen. Midday is the promised time.' Early in the morning two had gone to the shore to keep a look-out. They waited anxiously for the middle of the day, straining their eyes to see if they could discover anything. Suddenly they raised a shout, *'Ewaddee suh neen!'* – There it is! There it is!'

On rushing to the spot, they beheld something like an island steadily advancing towards the shore. As it approached, they could discover that something was moving on it in various directions. They said, 'It is a Manito, let us be off into the woods.'

'No, no,' cried the eldest, 'let us stay and watch.'

It now became stationary and lost much of its imagined height. They could see only three trees, as they thought, resembling trees in a pinery that had been burned. The wind, which had been off the sea, now died away into a perfect calm. They saw something leaving the fancied island and approaching the shore, throwing and flapping its wings, like a loon when he attempts to fly in calm weather. It entered the mouth of the river.

They were on the point of running away, but the eldest dissuaded them. 'Let us hide in this hollow,' he said, 'and we will see what it can be.' They did so. They soon heard the sounds of chopping, and quickly after they heard the falling of trees. Suddenly a man came up to the place of their concealment. He stood still and gazed at them. They did the same in utter amazement. After looking at them for some time, the person advanced and extended his hand towards them. The eldest took it and they shook hands. He then spoke, but they could not understand each other. He then credit out for his comrades. They came and examined very minutely the dress of the travellers.

They again tried to converse. Finding it impossible, the strangers then motioned to the *naubequon*, a small boat, wishing them to embark. They consulted with each other for a short time. The eldest then motioned that they should go on board. They embarked on board the boat, which they found to be loaded with wood. When they reached the side of the supposed island, they were surprised to see a great number of people, who all came to the side and looked at them with open mouths. One spoke out, above the others, and appeared to be the leader. He motioned them to get on board. He look at and examined them, and took them down into the cabin and set things before them to eat. He treated them very kindly.

When they came on deck again, all the sails were spread and they were fast losing sight of land. In the course of the night and the following day, they were sick at the stomach, but soon recovered. When they had been out at sea ten days, they became sorrowful, as they could not converse with the strangers – those who had hats on.

The following night Iosco dreamed that his spirit appeared to him. He told him not to be discouraged, that he would open his ears, so as to be able to understand the people with hats. 'I will not permit you to understand much,' said he, 'only sufficient to reveal your wants, and to know what is said to you.' Iosco repeated this dream to his friends, and they were satisfied and encouraged by it. When they had been out about thirty days, the master of the ship motioned them to change their dresses of leather for such as his people wore; for if they did not, his master would be displeased. It was on this occasion that the elder first understood a few words of the language. The first phrase he understood was *La Que notte*, and from one word to another he was soon able to speak it.

One day the men cried out, 'Land!' and soon after they heard a noise resembling thunder, in repeated peals. When they had got over their fears, they were shown the large guns which made this noise. Soon after, they saw a vessel smaller than their own, sailing out of a bay, in the direction towards them. She had flags on her masts, and when she came near she fired a gun. The large vessel also hoisted her flags, and the boat came alongside. The master told the person who came in it to tell his master or king that he had six travellers on board, such as had never been seen before, and that they were coming to visit him. It was some time after the departure of this messenger before the vessel got up to the town. It was then dark, but they could see people, and horses, and vehicles ashore. They were landed and placed in a covered vehicle, and driven off. When they stopped, they were taken into a large and splendid room. They were here told that the great chief wished to see them. They were shown into another large room, filled with men and women. All the room was of massive silver.

The chief asked them their business and the object of their journey. They told him where they were from, and where they were going, and the nature of the enterprise which they had undertaken. He tried to dissuade them from its execution, telling them of the many trials and difficulties they would have to undergo; that so many days' march from his country dwelt a bad spirit, or Manito, who foreknew and foretold the existence and arrival of all who entered his country. It is impossible, he said, my children, for you ever to arrive at the object you are in search of.

Iosco replied, '*Nosa,*' and they could see the chief blush in being called father, 'we have come so far on our way, and we will continue it; we have resolved firmly that we will do so. We think our lives are of no value, for we have given them up for this object. '*Nosa,*' he repeated, 'do not then prevent us from going on our journey.' The chief then dismissed them with valuable presents, after having appointed the next day to speak to them again, and provided everything that they needed or wished for.

Next day they were again summoned to appear before the king. He again tried to dissuade them. He said he would send them back to their country in one of his vessels; but all he said had no effect.

'Well,' said he, 'if you will go, I will furnish you all that is needed for your journey.' He had everything provided accordingly. He told them that three days before they reached the bad spirit he had warned them of, they would hear his rattle. He cautioned them to be wise, for he felt that he should never see them all again.

They resumed their journey and travelled sometimes through villages, but they soon left them behind and passed over a region of forests and plains, without inhabitants. They found that all the productions of the new country, trees, animals, birds, were entirely different from those they were accustomed to, on the other side of the great waters. They travelled and travelled, till they wore out all of the clothing that had been given to them, and had to take to their leather cloth-ing again.

The three days the chief spoke of meant three years, for it was only at the end of the third year that they came within the sound of the spirit's rattle. The sound appeared to be near, but they continued walking on, day after day, without apparently getting any nearer to it. Suddenly they came to a very extensive plain. They could see the blue ridges of distant mountains rising on the horizon beyond it. They pushed on, thinking to get over the plain before night, but they were overtaken by darkness. They were now on a stony part of the plain, covered by about a foot's depth of water. They were weary and fatigued.

Some of them said, 'Let us lie down.'

'No, no,' said the others, 'let us push on.'

Soon they stood on firm ground, but it was as much as they could do to stand, for they were very weary. They, however, made an effort to encamp, lighted a fire and refreshed themselves by eating. They then began conversing about the sound of the spirit's rattle, which they had heard for several days. Suddenly the noise began again; it sounded as if it was subterraneous, and it shook the ground. They tied up their bundles and went towards the spot. They soon came to a large building which was illuminated. As soon as they came to the door, they were met by a rather elderly man.

'How do ye do,' said he, 'my grandsons? Walk in, walk in; I am glad to see you; I knew when you started; I saw you encamp this evening. Sit down and tell me the news of the country you left, for I am interested in it.'

They complied with his wishes, and when they had concluded, each one presented him with a piece of tobacco. He then revealed to them things that would happen in their journey, and predicted its successful accomplishment.

'I do not say that all of you,' said he, 'will successfully go through it. You have passed over three-fourths of your way, and I will tell you how to proceed after you get to the edge of the earth. Soon after you leave this place, you will hear a deafening sound. It is the sky descending on the edge, but it keeps moving up and down. You will watch, and when it moves up, you will see a vacant space between it and the earth. You must not be afraid. A chasm of awful depth is there, which separates the unknown from this earth, and a veil of darkness conceals it. Fear not. You must leap through; and if you succeed, you will find yourselves on a beautiful plain, and in a soft and mild light emitted by the moon.'

They thanked him for his advice. A pause ensued.

'I have told you the way,' he said. 'Now tell me again of the country you have left, for I committed dreadful ravages while I was there. Does not the country show marks of it? And do not the inhabitants tell of me to their children? I came to this place to mourn over my bad actions and am trying, by my present course of life, to relieve my mind of the load that is on it.'

They told him that their fathers spoke often of a celebrated personage called Manabozho, who performed great exploits.

'I am he,' said the spirit. They gazed with astonishment and fear.

'Do you see this pointed house?' said he, pointing to one that resembled a sugar loaf. 'You can now each speak your wishes, and will be answered from that house. Speak out, and ask what each wants, and it shall be granted.'

One of them, who was vain, asked with presumption that he might live for ever, and never be in want. He was answered, 'Your wish shall be granted.' The second made the same request, and received the same answer. The third asked to live longer than common people, and to be always successful in his war excursions, never losing any of his young men. He was told, 'Your wishes are granted.' The fourth joined in the same request, and received the same reply. The fifth made a humble request, asking to live as long as men generally do, and that he might be crowned with such success in hunting as to be able to provide for his parents and relatives. The sixth made the same request, and it was granted to both, in pleasing tones, from the pointed house.

After hearing these responses they prepared to depart. They were told by Manabozho that they had been with him but one day, but they afterward found that they had remained there upward of a year.

When they were on the point of setting out, Manabozho exclaimed, 'Stop! You two, who asked me for eternal life, will receive the boon you wish immediately.' He spoke, and one was turned into a stone called Shin-gauba-wossin and the other into a cedar tree.

'Now,' said he to the others, 'you can go.'

The moon was happy to see them; she informed them that they were halfway to her brother's and that from the earth to her abode was half the distance.

They left him in fear, saying, 'We were fortunate to escape so, for the king told us he was wicked, and that we should not probably escape from him. 'They had not proceeded far when they began to hear the sound of the beating sky. It appeared to be near at hand, but they had a long interval to travel before they came near, and the sound was then stunning to their senses; for when the sky came down, its pressure would force gusts of wind from the opening, so strong that it was with difficulty they could keep their feet, and the sun passed but a short distance above their heads. They, however, approached boldly, but had to wait some time before they could muster courage enough to leap through the dark veil that covered the pasin want of the necessaries of life as long as you are permitted to live; and you will have the satisfaction of relating your journey to your friends, and also of telling them of me. Follow me, follow me,' he said, commencing his course again.

The ascent was now gradual, and they soon came to a level plain. After travelline some time he again sat down to rest, for he had arrived at the half-way line.

'You see,' said he, 'it is level at this place, but a short distance onward, my way descends gradually to my last resting place, for which there is an abrupt descent.' He repeated his assurance that they should be shielded from danger if they relied firmly on his power.

'Come here quickly,' he said, placing something before them on which they could descend. 'Keep firm,' said he, as they resumed the descent. They went downwards as if they had been let down by ropes.

In the meantime, the parents of these two young men dreamed that their sons were returning, and that they should soon see them. They placed the fullest confidence in their dreams. Early in the morning they left their lodges for a remote point in the forest, where they expected to meet them. They were not long at the place before they saw the adventurers returning, for they had descended not far from that place. The young men knew they were their fathers. They met and were happy. They related all that had befallen them. They did not conceal anything; and they expressed their gratitude to the different Manitous who had preserved them, by feasting and gifts, and particularly to the sun and moon, who had received them as their children.

Mon-daw-min, or the Origin of Indian Corn
Chippewa and Ojibwa

IN TIMES PAST, a poor Indian was living with his wife and children in a beautiful part of the country. He was not only poor but was not expert in procuring food for his family, and his children were all too young to give him assistance. Although poor, he was a men of a kind and contented disposition. He was always thankful to the Great Spirit for everything he received.

The same disposition was inherited by his eldest son, who had now arrived at the proper age to undertake the ceremony of the Ke-ig-uish-im-o-win, a fast to see what kind of spirit would be his guide and guardian through life. Wunzh, for this was his name, had been an obedient boy from his infancy, and was of a pensive, thoughtful and mild disposition, so that he was beloved by the whole family. As soon as the first indications of spring appeared, they built him the customary little lodge at a retired spot, some distance from their own, where he would not be disturbed during this solemn rite. In the meantime, he prepared himself, and immediately went into it and commenced his fast.

The first few days, he amused himself in the mornings by walking in the woods and over the mountains, examining the early plants and flowers, and in this way prepared himself to enjoy his sleep, and at the same time stored his mind with pleasant ideas for his dreams. While he rambled through the woods, he felt a strong desire to know how the plants, herbs and berries grew without any aid from man,

Source

Henry R. Schoolcraft, *North American Indian Legends,* Philadelphia: J.B. Lippincott & Co., 1856, pp. 99

and why it was that some species were good to eat and others possessed medicinal or poisonous juices. He recalled these thoughts to mind after he became too languid to walk about and had confined himself strictly to the lodge. He wishes he could dream of something that would prove a benefit to his father and family, and to all others.

'True,' he thought, 'the Great Spirit made all things, and it is to him that we owe our lives. But could he not make it easier for us to get our food than by hunting animals and taking fish? I must try to find this out in my visions.'

On the third day he became weak and faint, and kept to his bed. He fancied, while thus lying, that he saw a handsome young man coming down from the sky and advancing towards him. He was richly and gaily dressed, having on a great many garments of green and yellow colours, but differing in their deeper or lighter shades. He had a plume of waving feathers on his head, and all his motions were graceful.

'I am sent to you, my friend,' said the celestial visitor, 'by that Great Spirit who made all things in the sky and on the earth. He has seen and knows your motives in fasting. He sees that it is from a kind and benevolent wish to do good to your people, and to procure a benefit for them, and that you do not seek for strength in war or the praise of warriors. I am sent to instruct you, and show you how you can do your kindred good.' He then told the young man to arise, and prepare to wrestle with him, as it was only by this means that he could hope to succeed in his wishes.

Wunzh knew he was weak from fasting, but he felt his courage rising in his heart, and immediately got up, determined to die rather than fail. He commenced the trial and, after a protracted effort, was almost exhausted, when the beautiful stranger said, 'My friend, it is enough for once; I will come again to try you'; and smiling on him, he ascended in the air in the same direction from which he came.

The next day the celestial visitor reappeared at the same hour and renewed the trial. Wunzh felt that his strength was even less than the day before, but the courage of his mind seemed to increase in proportion as his body became weaker. Seeing this, the stranger again spoke to him in the same words he used before, adding, 'Tomorrow will be your last trial. Be strong, my friend, for this is the only way you can overcome me, and obtain the boon you seek.'

On the third day he again appeared at the same time and renewed the struggle. The poor youth was very faint in body, but grew stronger in mind at every contest, and was determined to prevail or perish in the attempt. He exerted his utmost powers, and after the contest had been continued the usual time, the stranger ceased his efforts and declared himself conquered. For the first time he entered the lodge and, sitting down beside the youth, he began to deliver his instructions to him, telling him in what manner he should proceed to take advantage of his victory.

The Celestial Visitor told the young man to arise and prepare to wrestle with him.

'You have won your desires of the Great Spirit,' said the stranger. 'You have wrestled manfully. Tomorrow will be the seventh day of your fasting. Your father will give you food to strengthen you, and as it is the last day of trial, you will prevail. I know this, and now tell you what you must do to benefit your family and your tribe. Tomorrow I shall meet you and wrestle with you for the last time; and as soon as you have prevailed against me, you will strip off my garments and throw me down, clean the earth of roots and weeds, make it soft and bury me in the spot.

When you have done this, leave my body in the earth, and do not disturb it, but come occasionally to visit the place to see whether I have come to life, and be careful never to let the grass or weeds grow on my grave. Once a month cover me with fresh earth. If you follow my instructions, you will accomplish your object of doing good to your fellow creatures by teaching them the knowledge I now teach you.' He then shook him by the hand and disappeared.

In the morning, the youth's father came with some light refreshments, saying, 'My son, you have fasted long enough. If the Great Spirit will favour you, he will do it now. It is seven days since you have tasted food and you must not sacrifice your life. The Master of Life does not require that.'

'My father,' replied the youth, 'wait till the sun goes down. I have a particular reason for extending my fast to that hour.'

'Very well,' said the old man, 'I shall wait till the hour arrives and you feel inclined to eat.'

At the usual hour of the day, the sky visitor returned and the trial of strength was renewed. Although the youth had not availed himself of his father's offer of food, he felt that new strength had been given to him, and that exertion had renewed his strength and fortified his courage. He grasped his angelic antagonist with supernatural strength, threw him down, took from him his beautiful garments and plume and, finding him dead, immediately buried him on the spot, taking all the precautions he had been told of, and being very confident, at the same time, that his friend would again come to life.

He then returned to his father's lodge and partook sparingly of the meal that had been prepared for him. But he never for a moment forgot the grave of his friend. He carefully visited it throughout the spring, and weeded out the grass, and kept the ground in a soft and pliant state. Very soon he saw the tops of the green plumes coming through the ground; and the more careful he was to obey his instructions in keeping the ground in order the faster they grew. He was, however, careful to conceal the exploit from his father. Days and weeks had passed in this way.

The summer was now drawing towards a close, when one day, after a long absence in hunting, Wunzh invited his father to follow him to the quiet and lonesome spot of his former fast. The lodge had been removed, and the weeds kept from growing on the circle where it stood, but in its place stood a tall and graceful plant, with bright-coloured silken hair, surmounted with nodding plumes and stately leaves, and golden clusters on each side.

'It is my friend,' shouted the lad. 'It is the friend of all mankind. It is Mon-daw-min. We need no longer rely on hunting alone, for as long as this gift of corn is cherished and taken care of, the ground itself will give us a living.'

He then pulled an ear. 'See, my father,' said he, 'this is what I fasted for. The Great Spirit has listened to my voice, and sent us something new, and henceforth our people will not alone depend upon the chase or upon the waters.'

He then told his father the instructions given him by the stranger. He told him that the broad husks must be torn away, as he had pulled off the garments in his wrestling. And having done this, directed him how the ear must be held before the fire till the outer skin became brown, while all the milk was retained in the grain. The whole family then united in a feast on the newly grown ears, expressing gratitude to the Merciful Spirit who gave it. So corn came into the world.

SHE WHO HAS A SOUL

Great Lakes Sioux

IT WAS A LONG TIME AGO, nearly two hundred years ago, that some of our people were living upon the shores of the Great Lake, Lake Superior. The chief of this band was called Tatankaota, Many Buffaloes.

One day the young son of Tatankaota led a war-party against the Ojibways, who occupied the country east of us, towards the rising sun. Whey they had gone a day's journey in the direction of Sault St Marie, in our language Skesketatanka, the warriors took up their position on the lake shore, at a point which the Ojibways were accustomed to pass in their canoes.

Long they gazed, and scanned the surface of the water, watching for the coming of the foe. The sun had risen above the dark pines, over the great ridge of woodland across the bay. It was the awakening of all living things. The birds were singing and shining fishes leaped out of the water as if at play. At last, far off, there came the warning cry of the loon to stir their expectant ears.

'Warriors, look close to the horizon! This brother of ours does not lie. The enemy comes!' exclaimed their leader. Presently upon the sparkling face of the water there appeared a moving canoe. There was but one, and it was coming directly towards them.

'Hahatonwan! Hahatonwan!' they exclaimed with one voice, and, grasping their weapons, they hastily concealed themselves in the bushes. 'Spare none – take no captives!' ordered the chief's son.

Nearer and nearer approached the strange canoe. The glistening blades of its paddles flashed as if it were the signal of good news or a welcome challenge. All impatiently waited until it should come within arrow-shot.

'Surely it is an Ojibway canoe,' one murmured. 'Yet look! The stroke is ungainly!' Now, among all the tribes only the Ojibway's art is perfect in paddling a birch canoe. This was a powerful stroke, but harsh and unsteady.

'See! There are no feathers on this man's head!' exclaimed the son of the chief. 'Hold, warriors, he wears a woman's dress, and I can see no weapon. No courage is needed to take his life, and therefore let it be spared! I command that only coups (blows) be counted on him, and he shall tell us from where he comes, and on what errand.'

The signal was given; the warriors sprang to their feet, and like wolves they sped from the forest, out upon the white, sandy beach and straight into the sparkling waters of the lake, giving the shrill war-cry, the warning of death! The solitary oarsman made no outcry – he offered no defence! Kneeling calmly in the prow of the little vessel, he merely ceased paddling and seemed to await with patience the deadly blow of the tomahawk.

The son of Tatankaota was foremost in the charge, but suddenly an impulse seized him to stop his warriors, lest one in the heat of excitement should do a mischief to the stranger. The canoe with its occupant was now very near, and it could be seen that the expression of his face was very gentle and even benignant. None could doubt his utter harmlessness; and the chief's son afterwards declared that at this moment he felt a premonition of some event, but whether good or evil he could not tell.

Source
Charles A. Eastman, (Ohiyesa). *Old Indian Days,* New York: McClure Company, 1907, pp. 208–18

No blows were struck – no coups counted. The young man bade his warriors take up the canoe and carry it to the shore; and although they murmured somewhat among themselves, they did as he commanded them. They seized the light bark and bore it dripping to a hill covered with tall pines and overlooking the waters of the Great Lake.

Then the warriors lifted their war-clubs over their heads and sang, standing around the canoe in which the black-robed stranger was still kneeling. Looking at him closely, they perceived that he was of a peculiar complexion, pale and inclined to red. He wore a necklace of beads, from which hung a cross bearing the form of a man. His garments were strange, and most like the robes of woman. All of these things perplexed them greatly.

Presently the Black Robe told them by signs, in response to their inquiries, that he came from the rising sun, even beyond the Great Salt Water, and he seemed to say that he formerly came from the sky. Upon this the warriors believed that he must be a prophet or mysterious man.

Their leader directed them to take up again the canoe with the man in it, and appointed the warriors to carry it by turns until they should reach his father's village. This was done according to the ancient custom, as a mark of respect and honour. They took it up forthwith, and travelled with all convenient speed along the lake shore, through forests and across streams to a place called the Maiden's Retreat, a short distance from the village.

Thence the chief's son sent a messenger to announce to his father that he was bringing home a stranger, and to ask whether or not he should be allowed to enter the village.

'His appearance,' declared the scout, 'is unlike that of any man we have ever seen and his ways are mysterious!'

When the chief heard these words, he immediately called his council-men together to decide what was to be done, for he feared by admitting the mysterious stranger to bring some disaster upon his people. Finally he went out with his wisest men to meet his son's war-party. They looked with astonishment upon the Black Robe.

'Dispatch him! Dispatch him! Show him no mercy!' cried some of the council-men.

'Let him go on his way unharmed. Trouble him not,' advised others.

'It is well known that the evil spirits sometimes take the form of a man or animal. From his strange appearance I judge this to be such a one. He should be put to death, least some harm befall our people,' an old man urged.

By this time several of the women of the village had reached the spot. Among them was She Who Has a Soul, the chief's youngest daughter, whom tradition says was a maiden of much beauty, and of a generous heart. The stranger was evidently footsore from much travel and weakened by fasting. When she saw that the poor man clasped his hands and looked skyward as he uttered words in an unknown tongue, she pleaded with her father that a stranger who has entered their midst unchallenged may claim the hospitality of the people, according to the ancient custom.

'Father, he is weary and in want of food. Hold him no longer! Delay your council until he is refreshed!' These were the words of She Who Has a Soul, and her father could not refuse her prayer. The Black Robe was released, and the Sioux maiden led him to her father's tepee.

She anointed the blistered feet of the holy man with perfumed otter oil.

Now the warriors had been surprised and indeed displeased to find him dressed after the fashion of a woman, and they looked upon him with suspicion. But from the moment that she first beheld him, the heart of the maiden had turned towards this strange and seemingly unfortunate man. It appeared to her that great rever-ence and meekness were in his face, and with it all she was struck by his utter fear-lessness, his apparent unconsciousness of danger.

The chief's daughter, having gained her father's permission, invited the Black Robe to his great buffalo-skin tent and, spreading a fine robe, she gently asked him to be seated. With the aid of her mother, she prepared wild rice sweetened with maple sugar and some broiled venison for his food. The youthful warriors were astonished to observe these attentions, but the maiden heeded them not. She anointed the blistered feet of the holy man with perfumed otter oil, and put upon him a pair of moccasins beautifully worked by her own hands.

It was only an act of charity on her part, but the young men were displeased, and again urged that the stranger should at once be turned away. Some even sug-gested harsher measures; but they were overruled by the chief, softened by the per-suasions of a well-beloved daughter.

During the few days that the Black Robe remained in the Sioux village he preached earnestly to the maiden, for she had been permitted to converse with him by signs, that she might try to ascertain what manner of man he was. He told her of the coming of a 'Great Prophet' from the sky, and of his words that he had left with the people. The cross with the figure of a man he explained as his totem which he had told them to carry. He also said that those who love him are commanded to go among strange peoples to tell the news, and that all who believe must be marked with holy water and accept the totem.

He asked by signs if She Who Has a Soul believed the story. To this she replied, 'It is a sweet story – a likely legend! I do believe!'

Then the good father took out a small cross and, having pressed it to his heart and crossed his forehead and breast, he gave it to her. Finally he dipped his finger in water and touched the forehead of the maiden, repeating meanwhile some words in an unknown tongue.

The mother was troubled, for she feared that the stranger was trying to bewitch her daughter, but the chief decided thus: 'This is a praying-man, and he is not of our people; his customs are different, but they are not evil. Warriors, take him back to the spot where you saw him first! It is my desire, and the good custom of our tribe requires that you free him without injury!'

Accordingly they formed a large party, and carried the Black Robe in his canoe back to the shore of the Great Lake, to the place where they had met him, and he was allowed to depart thence and go wherever he chose. He took his leave with signs of gratitude for their hospitality, and especially for the kindness of the beau-tiful Sioux maiden. She seemed to have understood his mission better than anyone else, and as long as she lived she kept his queer trinket – as it seemed to the others – and performed the strange acts that he had taught her.

Furthermore, it was through the pleadings of She Who Has a Soul that the chief Tatankaota advised his people in after days to befriend the white strangers, and though many of the other chiefs opposed him in this, his counsel prevailed. Hence it was that both the French and the English received much kindness from our peo-ple, mainly through the influence of this one woman!

Such was the first coming of the white man among us, as it is told in our traditions. Other praying-men came later, and many of the Sioux allowed themselves to be baptized. True, there have been Indian wars, but not without reason; and it is pleasant to remember that the Sioux were hospitable to the first white 'praying-man', and that it was a tender-hearted maiden of my people who first took in her hands the cross of the new religion.

STORIES OF WAK-CHUNG-KAKA AND WASH-CHING-GEKA

Winnebago

MA-O-NA, THE EARTH-MAKER, made the earth and everything on it. He made a man, but the man was not good. Ma-o-na did not want to burn him up, so he tossed him to one side and went on with his work. This man became Wa-cho-pi-ni-shi-shik, an evil spirit. He watched Ma-o-na at work, and everything that Ma-o-na made he copied; but whereas Ma-o-na's works were all good, those of Wa-cho-pi-ni-shi-shik were evil. Ma-o-na made the deer and elk and buffalo; Wa-cho-pi-ni-shi-shik made the huge animals, the monsters that devoured men. All bad things, evil spirits and the like, are the work of Wa-cho-pi-ni-shi-shik.

Ma-o-na sent his son, Wak-chung-kaka, the Foolish One, to kill the monsters and make the earth fit for man. But Wak-chung-kaka could not destroy all the works of the evil spirit. Then Ma-o-na sent another son, Ke-chung-geka, the Tortoise, but he was too fond of war. So, too, was Wuh-te-huk, the third son. Last of all Ma-o-na sent his youngest son, Wash-ching-geka, the Little Hare.

These are stories of Wak-chung-kaka and Wash-ching-geka.

STORIES OF WAK-CHUNG-KAKA, THE FOOLISH ONE

I

One day Wak-chung-kaka was walking over a hill and he looked down into a hollow where reeds grew tall, and he thought he saw a throng of people with feathers on their heads. The wind blew through the reeds, and Wak-chung-kaka thought that the people danced and hallooed, 'Wu-wu-wu!' So he put a feather on his head and went in among the people and danced and shouted, 'Wu-wu-wu!' He danced all day long, till at evening the wind dropped and everything was still; and then Wak-chung-kaka looked around him and found himself along among the reeds.

II

Wak-chung-kaka was walking one day beside the water when he saw a chief standing there dressed all in black with a shining disc on his breast, and the chief was pointing across the water. He stood quite still, and always pointed steadily cross the water. Wak-chung-kaka spoke to him, but the chief never moved or answered; he still pointed steadily across the water. Wak-chung-kaka spoke to him again, and still there was no answer. Four times he spoke to him, and then at last Wak-chung-kaka grew angry and said, 'I can point too, and I can point longer than you.'

Source
Natalie Curtis
Burlin, *The
Indians' Book,*
New York:
Harper and
Brothers, 1923,
pp. 244–50

So Wak-chung-kaka set down his bundle and opened it and dressed himself all in black like the chief, and hung a disc on his breast and stood there beside the chief, pointing across the water. But when he had stood thus for a great time without moving, Wak-chung-kaka began to be weary of this, and he looked around at the chief, and, behold, it was only the blackened stump of a burned tree with a white spot that the fire had not touched.

III

Another time Wak-chung-kaka was walking along the andy shore of a lake, and when he came to a point of the shore he heard a cry, 'Wu-wu-wu!' He looked over the point, but could see nobody, so he walked on till he heard the cry, 'Wu-wu-wu!' and saw a little cloud of flies fly up into the air. There was an elk's head lying on the shore, and a swarm of flies flew in at the neck-hole behind, and then flew out again all at once. Wak-chung-kaka stood and looked at them. 'That must be good sport,' he thought. 'I wish I could do that too.'

A little fly looked up at him and said, 'Wak-chung-kaka, you can!'

At once Wak-chung-kaka felt himself growing smaller and smaller, till he was no bigger than a fly, and then he easily went in at the hole in the head and flew out again, crying, 'Wu-wu-wu!' He thought it was fine sport to fly in and out, in and out, with the swarm of flies. So the flies let him play with them for a while, till all at once, when Wak-chung-kaka was just starting to go in, he grew to his own natural size, and as he already had his head within the elk's head, the neck-hole fitted him so closely that he could not get his head out again.

Wak-chung-kaka walked on, wearing the elk's head; and as he could not see very well, he walked into the lake. The water came up to the eye-holes of the head, and Wak-chung-kaka swam until he came near to a village that stood beside the lake, and when the people saw the elk-horns moving along the water they said, 'It is a water-spirit; let us offer him gifts.' For there are spirits in the ground, under the water, and in the great springs of the hills, and the spirits often look like elk or buffalo.

So the people brought tobacco and beads and laid them on the shore before Wak-chung-kaka, and he stayed in the water; and the young people prayed to him, 'Spirit, grant us long life!' and the old people prayed, 'Long life for our children!' and to every prayer Wak-chung-kaka answered, 'Ho! (yes)'. At length, when all the people were gathered before him, he said, 'My nephews and nieces, I will grant your prayers if you will do what I tell you. Let two strong men take hold of my horns, one on each side, and let another one split my head down the middle, carefully, carefully – he must be careful not to cut too deep.'

So two strong men took hold of his horns, one on each side, and pulled with all their might, while the third took a stone axe and very carefully chopped the elk's head down the middle, till, crack, the skull fell apart and there stood Wak-chung-kaka, and laughed, 'Haw, haw, haw!'

Wak-chung-kaka stayed in the water and the young people prayed to him, 'Spirit, grant us long life!'

STORIES OF WASH-CHING-GEKA, THE LITTLE HARE

I

Wash-ching-geka lived with his grandmother while he was doing his works. His grandmother was the earth, and she was very wise. She cooked for the Little Hare and nourished him and took care of him.

Now among the other evil things then in the world were eight blind men who lived in a wood; they went about with the help of long cords and spread webs among the trees, in which they caught people and killed them.

One day when the blind men were cooking their dinner of bear's meat, Wash-ching-geka went in among them. There was a piece of meat for each. Now the men could not see Wash-ching-geka, and he stepped softly to the pot and took out one portion of meat. When the blind men began to eat they quarrelled with one another over the missing portion, because each one thought another had taken his meat. As they were quarrelling, Wash-ching-geka slapped one of them, and then that one slapped his neighbour, and he slapped the next, and so they all fell to fighting.

Meanwhile, Wash-ching-geka ran home to his wise grandmother and took counsel with her.

Next day he went again to the blind men, and while they were cooking he took out the meat and put poison on it. So the blind men ate of the poisoned meat and were killed. They would never again spread webs among the trees to destroy the people. And now when they were dead, behold, Wash-ching-geka saw that really they were spiders.

II

In the early days there was a great hill that used to open and shut like a pair of jaws and devour men and animals. The hill would open in the middle and the sides would fall back till they lay flat upon the ground, and all the land looked like good smooth prairie.

Then herds of elk and deer and buffalo would come to graze, and when the place was full, the jaws of the hill would close and, crack, all the animals would be crushed and killed. This hill killed so much game that the Earth-maker feared that all the people would starve. So he sent his son, Wash-ching-geka, to destroy the hill.

When the Little Hare came there the hill opened and all the ground was smooth; and Wash-ching-geka made himself like a small stone and lay quite still. Then the elk and deer and buffalo came to graze, but as soon as the mouth began to close on them, see, Wash-ching-geka quickly changed himself into a great stone, and so, when the hill shut on him, hoo, the jaws were broken all to pieces. The hill lay shattered and never could devour men or animals any more.

Manabozho

Algonquin

A RED MOON RODE the windy sky. A great, dark, bat-like shadow screened it for the length of a heartbeat. An owl hooted eerily in the depth of the dark forest; then the shrill shrieks of a newborn man-child filled the air. All night noises ceased. Black clouds veiled the moon, and the sky was filled with the wings of many birds in wild flight. Forest animals fled in terror. Manabozho, transformer and trickster, had been born. Very little is told of his early boyhood. We take him up in the following legend at a period of advanced youth, when we find him living with his grandmother. And at this time he possessed, although he had not yet exercised, all the anomalous and contradictory powers of body and mind, of manship and divinity, which he afterwards evinced.

The timidity and rawness of the boy quickly gave way in the courageous developments of the man. He soon evinced the sagacity, cunning, perseverance and heroic courage which constitute the admiration of the Indians. And he relied largely upon these in the gratification of an ambitious, vainglorious and mischief-loving disposition. In wisdom and energy he was superior to anyone who had ever lived before. Yet he was simple when circumstances required it, and was ever the object of tricks and ridicule in others. He could transform himself into any animal he pleased, being man or Manito, as circumstances rendered necessary. He often conversed with animals, fowls, reptiles and fish. He deemed himself related to them, and invariably addressed them by the term 'my brother'; and one of his greatest resources, when hard-pressed, was to change himself into their shapes.

◆

Manabozho was living with his grandmother near the edge of a wide prairie. On this prairie he first saw animals and birds of every kind. He there also saw exhibitions of divine power in the seeping tempests, in the thunder and lightning, and the various shades of light and darkness, which form a never-ending scene of observation. Every new sight he beheld in the heavens was a subject of remark; every new animal or bird an object of deep interest; and every sound uttered by the animal creation a new lesson, which he was expected to learn. He often trembled at what he heard and saw.

To this scene his grandmother sent him at an early age to watch. The first sound he heard was that of the owl, at which he was greatly terrified, and quickly descending the tree he had climbed, he ran with alarm to the lodge. 'Noko! Noko!' he cried, 'I have heard a monedo (evil spirit).' She laughed at his fears, and asked hi what kind of noise it made. He answered, 'It makes a noise like this, Ko-ko-ko-ho.' She told him that he was young and foolish, that what he had heard was only a bird, deriving its name from the noise it made.

He went back and continued his watch. While there he thought to himself, 'It is singular that I am so simple, and my grandmother is so wise, and that I have neither father nor mother. I have never heard a word about them. I must ask and find out.' He went home and sat down silent and dejected.

At length his grandmother asked him, 'Manabozho, what is the matter with you?'

Source
Henry R. Schoolcraft, *North American Indian Legends*, Philadelphia: J.B. Lippincott & Co., 1856, pp. 33–47

He answered, 'I wish you would tell me whether I have any parents living, and who my relatives are.' Knowing that he was of a wicked and revengeful disposition, she dreaded telling him the story of his parentage, but he insisted on her compliance.

'Yes,' she said, 'you have a father and three brothers living. Your mother is dead. She was taken without the consent of her parents by your father, the West. Your brothers are the North, East and the South, and being older than yourself, your father has given them great power with the winds, according to their names. You are the youngest of his children. I have nourished you from your infancy, for your mother died in giving you birth, owing to the ill-treatment of your father. I have no relations besides you this side of the planet in which I was born, and from which I was precipitated by female jealousy. Your mother was my only child, and you are my only hope.'

He appeared to be rejoiced to hear that his father was living, for he had already thought in his heart to try and kill him. He told his grandmother his should set out in the morning to visit him. She said it was a long distance to the place where Ningabium, wind of the West, lived. But that did not stop him, for he had now attained manhood, possessed a giant's height, and was endowed by nature with a giant's strength and power. He set out and soon reached the place, for every step he took covered a large surface of ground. The meeting took place on a high mountain in the west. His father was very happy to see him. He also appeared pleased. They spent some days in talking with each other.

One evening Manabozho asked his father what he was most afraid of on earth. He replied, 'Nothing.'

'But is there not something you dread here? Tell me.'

At last his father said, yielding, 'Yes, there is a black stone found in such a place. It is the only thing earthly I am afraid of; for if it should hit me or any part of my body, it would injure me very much.'

He said this as a secret, and in return asked his son the same question. Knowing each other's power, although the son's was limited, the father feared him on account of his great strength. Manabozho answered, 'Nothing!' intending to avoid the question, or to refer to some harmless object as the one of which he was afraid. He was asked again and again, and answered, 'Nothing!' But the West said, 'There must be something you are afraid of.'

'Well! I will tell you,' said Manabozho, 'what it is.'

But before he would pronounce the word, he affected great pain. '*Ie-ee – Ie-ee –* it is – it is,' said he. '*Yeo! Yeo!* I cannot name it; I am seized with a dread.'

The West told him to banish his fears. He commenced again, in a strain of mock sensitiveness, repeating the same words. At last he cried out, 'It is the root of the bulrush.' He appeared to be exhausted by the effort of pronouncing the word, in all this skillfully acting a studied part.

Some time after he observed, 'I will get some of the black rock.'

The West said, 'Far be it from you; do not do so, my son.' He still persisted.

'Well,' said the father, 'I will also get the *apukwa* root.' Manabozho immediately cried out, 'No! No!' affecting, as before, to be in great dread of it, but really wishing, by this course, to urge on the West to procure it, that he might draw him into combat. He went out and got a large piece of the black root and brought it home. The West also took care to bring the dreaded root.

In the course of conversation, he asked his father whether he had been the cause of his mother's death. The answer was, 'Yes!' He then took up the rock and struck him. Blow led to blow, and here commenced an obstinate and furious combat, which continued several days. Fragments of the rock, broken off under Manabozho's blows, can be seen in various places to this day. The root did not prove as mortal a weapon as his well-acted fears had led his father to expect, although he suffered severely from the blows. This battle commenced on the mountains. The West was forced to give ground. Manabozho drove him across rivers, and over mountains and lakes, and at last he came to the brink of this world.

'Hold!' cried he. 'My son, you know my power, and that it is impossible to kill me. Desist, and I will also portion you out with as much power as your brothers. The four quarters of the globe are already occupied; but you can go forth and do a great deal of good to the people of this earth, which is infested with large serpents, beasts and monsters, who make great havoc among the inhabitants. Go and do good. You have the power now to do so, and your fame with the beings of this earth will last for ever. When you have finished your work, I will have a place provided for you. You will then go and sit with your brother Kabibboonocca in the north.'

Manabozho was pacified. He returned to his lodge, where he was confined by the wounds he had received. But from his grandmother's skill in medicines he was soon recovered.

◆

Some time after this he commenced making preparations for a war excursion against the Pearl Feather, the Manitou who lived on the opposite side of the great lake, who had killed his grandfather. The abode of his spirit was defended, first, by fiery serpents, who hissed fire so that no one could pass them; and second, by a large mass of gummy matter lying on the water, so soft and adhesive that whoever attempted to pass, or whatever came in contact with it, was sure to stick there.

He continued making bows and arrows without number, but he had no heads for his arrows. At last Noko told him that an old man who lived at some distance could make them. He sent her to get some. She soon returned with her *conaus*, her wrapper, full. Still he told her he had not enough, and sent her again. She returned with as much more. He thought to himself, 'I must find out the way of making these heads.' Cunning and curiosity prompted him to make the discovery. But he deemed it necessary to deceive his grandmother in so doing.

'Noko,' said he, 'while I take my drum and rattle, and sing my war-songs, go and try to get me some larger heads for my arrows, for those you brought me are all of the same size. Go and see whether the old man cannot make some a little larger.'

He followed her as she went, keeping at a distance, and saw the old artificer at work, and so discovered his process. He also beheld the old man's daughter, and perceived that she was very beautiful. He felt his breast beat with a new emotion, but said nothing. He took care to get home before his grandmother, and commenced singing as if he had never left his lodge. When the old woman came near, she heard his drum and rattle, without any suspicion that he had followed her. She delivered him the arrowheads.

One evening the old woman said, 'My son you ought to fast before you go to war, as your brothers frequently do, to find out whether you will be successful.' He said he had no objection, and immediately commenced a fast for several days. He would retire every day from the lodge so far as to be out of reach of his grandmother's voice. It seems she had indicated this spot, and was very anxious he should fast there, and not at another place. She had a secret motive, which she carefully hid from him. Deception always begets suspicion. After a while he thought to himself, 'I must find out why my grandmother is so anxious for me to fast at this spot.'

Next evening he went but a short distance. She cried out, 'A little farther off'; but he came nearer to the lodge, and called in a low voice, to make it appear that he was distant. She then replied, 'That is far enough.' He had go so near that he could see all that passed in the ledge. He had not been long in his place of concealment, when a man in the shape of a bear entered the lodge. He had very long hair. They commenced talking about him, and appeared to be improperly familiar. At that time people lived to a very great age, and he perceived, from the marked attentions of this visitor, that he did not think a grandmother too old to be pleased with such attentions.

He listened to their conversation some time. At last he determined to play on the visitor a trick. He took some fire and, when the bear had turned his back, touched his long hair. When the animal felt the flame, he jumped out, but the open air only made it burn the fiercer, and he was seen running off in a full blaze.

Manabozho ran to his customery place of fasting and, assuming a tone of simplicity, began to cry out, 'Noko! Noko! Is it time for me to come home?'

'Yes,' she cried. When he came in, she told him what had taken place, at which he appeared to be very much surprised.

After having finished his term of fasting and sung his war-song – from which the Indians of the present day derive the custom – he embarked in his canoe, fully prepared for war. In addition to the usual implements, he had a plentiful supply of oil. He travelled rapidly night and day, for he had only to will or speak, and the canoe went. At length he arrived in sight of the fiery serpents. He stopped to view them. He saw they were some distance apart, and that only the flame which issued from them reached across the water. He commenced talking as a friend to them; but they answered, 'We know you, Manabozho, you cannot pass.'

He then thought of some expedient to deceive them, and hit upon this. He pushed his canoe as near as possible. All at once he cried out, with a loud and terrified voice, 'What is that behind you?' The serpents instantly turned their heads, when, at a single word, he passed them.

'Well,' said he placidly, after he had got by, 'how do you like my exploit?' He then took up his bow and arrows, and with deliberate aim shot them, which was easily done, for the serpents were stationary and could not move beyond a certain spot. They were of enormous length and of a bright colour.

Having overcome the sentinel serpents, he went on in his magic canoe till he came to a soft gummy portion of the lake, called Pigiu-wagumee, Pitchwater. He took the oil and rubbed it on his canoe, and then pushed into it. The oil softened the surface and enabled him to slip through it with ease, although it required frequent rubbing and a constant reapplication of the oil. Just as his oil failed, he extricated himself, and was the first person who ever succeeded in overcoming it.

He now came in view of land, on which he disembarked in safety, and could see the lodge of the Shining Manitou, situated on a hill. He commenced preparing for the fight, putting his arrows and clubs in order, and just at the dawn of day began his attack, yelling and shouting, and crying with triple voices, 'Surround him! Surround him! Run up! Run up!' making it appear that he had many followers. He advanced, crying out, 'It was you that killed my grandfather,' and with this shot his arrows.

The combat continued all day. Manabozho's arrows had no effect, for his antagonist was clothed with pure wampum. He was now reduced to three arrows, and it was only by extraordinary agility that he could escape the blows which the Manitou kept making at him. At that moment a large woodpecker, the *ma-ma*, flew past, and alighted on a tree.

'Manabozho,' he cried, 'your adversary has a vulnerable point; shoot at the lock of hair on the crown of his head.' He shot his first arrow so as only to draw blood from that part. The Manitou made one or two unsteady steps, but recovered himself. He began to parley, but in the act received a second arrow, which brought him to his knees. But he again recovered. In so doing, however, he exposed his head, and gave his adversary a chance to fire his third arrow, which penetrated deep, and brought him, a lifeless corpse, to the ground.

Manabozho uttered his *saw-saw-quan*, his war-cry, and taking the scalp as a trophy, he called the woodpecker to come and receive a reward for his information. He took the blood of the Manitou and rubbed it on the woodpecker's head, the feathers of which are red to this day.

After this victory he returned home, singing songs of triumph and beating his drum. When his grandmother heard him, she came to the shore and welcomed him with songs and dancing. Glory fired his mind. He displayed the trophies he had brought in the most conspicuous manner, and felt an unconquerable desire for other adventures. He felt himself urged by the consciousness of his power to new trials of bravery, skill and necromantic prowess. He had destroyed the Manitou of Wealth, and killed his guardian serpents and eluded all his charms.

PART 4
THE GREAT PLAINS

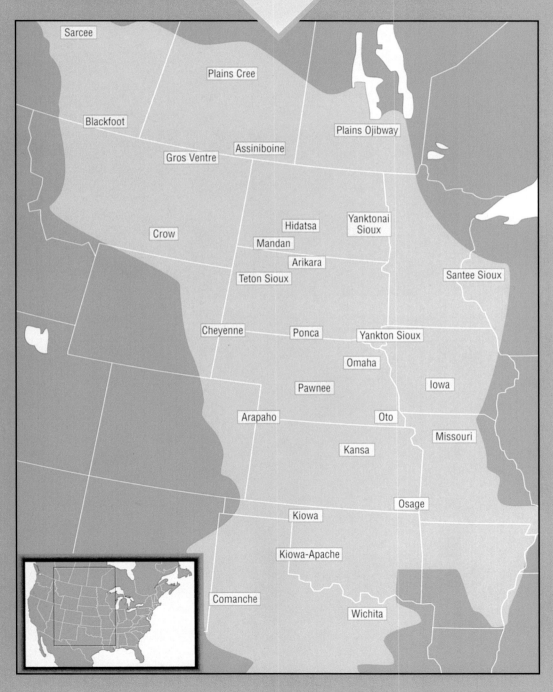

Sarcee

Plains Cree

Blackfoot

Plains Ojibway

Gros Ventre

Assiniboine

Crow

Hidatsa

Yanktonai Sioux

Mandan

Arikara

Santee Sioux

Teton Sioux

Cheyenne

Ponca

Yankton Sioux

Omaha

Pawnee

Iowa

Arapaho

Oto

Missouri

Kansa

Osage

Kiowa

Kiowa-Apache

Comanche

Wichita

TRIBES OF THE
GREAT PLAINS

The tribes of the Great Plains have become, thanks to the influence of Hollywood and countless television series, the North American cultural group that most people can call to mind. Generations of films, from the Howard Hawks–John Wayne cavalry epics, such as *She Wore a Yellow Ribbon,* to Arthur Penn's *Little Big Man* and Kevin Costner's *Dances with Wolves*, have presented the Plains tribes as the quintessential Indian groups of history, as well as cinematography. Conical tepees with their hide coverings, 'peace pipes', war bonnets of eagle feathers, fiercely painted warriors on their swift ponies, bows or rifles at the ready, chasing down lumbering buffalo: these are the typical images of the Native Americans of North America. Even our stock image of warfare between Native Americans and whites is generated from one battle between Plains tribes such as the Sioux and Northern Cheyenne and units of nineteenth-century US cavalry led by their flamboyant yet flawed commander, George Armstrong Custer: The Battle of the Little Bighorn.

While such images are potent and pervasive, they do not give a clear picture of life among the tribes of the Great Plains, much less an accurate view of Native Americans across the continent. And, perhaps ironically, the main elements of nineteenth-century Plains Indian culture – assumed to be the horse and the rifle – were not Native American in their origins but were derived from contact with white culture. In addition, the days of the Great Plains tribes' 'horse and buffalo' culture were, in the greater span of Indian history, relatively short lived, lasting about 150 years, depending on the tribe's first access to horses.

The history of the Native Americans of the Great Plains predates the arrival of Europeans on the North American continent by several thousand years. During those centuries, eastern Plains peoples lived in relatively permanent villages and practised a rudimentary agriculture, with food hunting being supplementary at best.

The Great Plains Region

The area of the Great Plains stretches across the borders of two nations today: the United States and Canada. From the vast, empty grasslands of Alberta, Manitoba and Saskatchewan to the souther brush lands of Texas, the Great Plains include all or portions of over a dozen states. The Mississippi River marks the region's furthest eastern edge, generally along the 97th meridian, while the foothills of the Rocky Mountains rise above the flatlands, serving as the boundary to the west. With little variation, the Plains form a steppe that rises gradually from east to west. There are breaks and disturbances in the landscape, however, including the Ozark Mountains of southern Missouri and northern Arkansas, the Wichita Mountains of Oklahoma and the Black Hills of South Dakota.

Average annual rainfall divides the Great Plains into two subregions, roughly along the 100th meridian, which runs north and south, bisecting the Dakotas and Nebraska, and separates the western thirds of Kansas, Oklahoma and Texas from their eastern parts. East of the line, the average rainfall is from twenty to forty inches (fifty to one hundred centimetres), while to the west the average precipitation is from ten to twenty inches (twenty five to fifty centimetres). Until recently, archaeologists and historians assumed that before the introduction of the horse North American tribes did not occupy the Plains, especially the drier western areas. However, it is now thought that the Plains have been inhabited for more than 11,000 years. Prehistoric studies reveal that nomadic groups occupied nearly all of the region between 10,000 and 7,000 years ago. These Neolithic groups hunted mammoths and bison. Then, between 7,000 and 4,500 years ago, the Plains groups nearly abandoned the region, due to a warming trend. The great Pleistocene animals left the area, and those people who remained were reduced to living on small game and gathering wild plants and berries.

About 4,500 years ago, the Great Plains experienced a repopulation. Many of those who found their way out on to the Plains came from the eastern woodlands. The resulting Plains Woodland period was firmly entrenched in the region between 500 BC and AD 1000. Between AD 200 and 400, a stable, semi-permanent village life existed in eastern Kansas, Nebraska, Colorado, northeastern Oklahoma and along the course of the Missouri River. Here, bands of Native Americans planted corn and beans for food, as well as relying on the hunt and gathering wild plants. Grave sites from this period reveal a culture that produced pottery, used tools and weapons of stone and bone and worked small amounts of copper into artefacts.

By AD 800, a generalized movement of bands from the woodlands east of the Mississippi River developed, bringing new settlements and villages to the eastern Plains. These peoples often built their villages along major rivers and streams. They raised the crops known as the Three Sisters – corn, beans and squash – as well as sunflowers. These Plains village bands constructed square or rectangular earthen lodges or mud-covered huts, which were often surrounded by protective palisades. Hunting was important to these tribes, with the man fanning out in search of bison, while the women did the farming, using digging sticks and hoes made from bison scapulae.

Around the year 1500 many of these farming-hunting villages of the western Plains were abandoned, probably as a result of drought. About this time, Plains cultural groups, separated from one another by hundreds of miles of empty, treeless land, began to move about, making contact with one another. Through interaction, the tribes of the northern and southern Plains developed a new culture, with larger villages and a greater reliance on agriculture. These new villages were increasingly permanent, leading to a more sedentary life. The earthen lodges were altered, becoming circular, for reasons that are not currently understood.

By the time the Europeans arrived on the Great Plains in the sixteenth and seventeenth centuries, several distinct subcultures were in place, located throughout the region. Scattered along the lower Missouri River basin were the Iowas, Kansas, Missouris, Omahas, Osages, Otos and Poncas. The Arikaras, Hidatsas and Mandans lived near the middle course of the Missouri River. To the south, across the modern-day state of Missouri, were the Pawnees. And south of them were the Wichitas. Each of these tribal groups lived in agricultural villages.

In all, twenty-six tribal groups have been identified by anthropologists as the nations of the Plains. They include those tribes mentioned above, plus the following: Sarcee, Blackfoot, Cree, Ojibway, Gros Ventre, Assiniboine, Crow, Shoshone, Arapaho, Cheyenne, Kiowa, Kiowa-Apache, Comanche and the wide-ranging group called the Sioux, also known as the Dakota or Lakota.

Great Plains Horse Culture

Once the peoples of the Plains experienced contact with the European explorers, trappers, traders and missionaries of the seventeenth and eighteenth centuries, they began to alter their culture. Perhaps no other regional group of Native Americans prior to 1800 was changed as much by white contact as the Plains tribes. Southwestern tribes were using the horse by the 1680s and 1690s. By 1750, most Plains tribes had horses, which had originally been brought by the Spanish in the 1500s. With the incorporation of the horse into their culture, Plains Indian groups came to rely less on systematic agriculture for their primary sources of food. By the eighteenth century, these tribes were developing the horse and buffalo culture by which they have come to be recognized. The horse provided hunters with greater mobility, allowing them to range considerable distances from their band's village in search of buffalo. Some tribes, particularly in the northern reaches of the Plains, were late or even slow to adopt the horse, and here farming remained paramount in the provision of food.

With the introduction of the horse, Plains tribes became, just as their ancestors hundreds of years before them, nomadic once again.

At the same time that Plains tribes were gaining access to the horse, other groups were being pushed on to the Plains by the ever-moving whites. Soon the Plains became populated by new tribes who had migrated from lands east of the Mississippi. Among them were the Arapaho, Cheyenne, Cree, Crow, Gros Ventre, Kiowa, Kiowa-Apache, Ojibway and Sioux. An extraordinary interaction developed between these tribes. They shared and adopted one another's customs, both new and old. They exchanged practices related to agriculture, horseback buffalo-hunting, methods of war and the newly developed shelter of lodge poles and buffalo-hide coverings called tepees. They also developed a hand-sign language in order to facilitate trade and communication between the leaders of different tribes.

While Plains dwellers identified themselves through tribal membership, their most immediate connection was to their individual band. Bands were made up of several families, both related and unrelated, with each generally boasting, at best, several hundred persons. Bands tended to live apart from one another throughout most of the year, but would come together during the summer months for joint buffalo hunts and religious rituals and ceremonies.

The Horse and Buffalo

Without a doubt, the adoption of the horse by the Native Americans of the Plains dramatically altered their culture, their means of transportation and their tribal economies. The horse – called Sacred Dog by some Plains tribes; Medicine Dog or Spirit Dog by others – became, in time, a symbol of wealth among the tribes.

These powerful animals were used in many ways by Plains tribes. Not only did they provide mobility for distant buffalo hunts, they also became a primary means of transport. Before the arrival of the horse on the North American continent, tribes relied on the dog as their beast of burden. They would attach two small poles, lashed together in a V-shape, to the dog's back, then stretch an animal hide between the poles to provide a carrier for the tribe's material goods. This device, called a travois, was small and limited by the dog's capacity to pull the dead weight behind it. With the coming of the horse, Plains Indians built larger travois that could carry greater weights, including ill or wounded adult men and women.

Great Plains peoples became very adept horsemen. Often they rode their animals bareback, using only one leather strap as a bridle. They rode their mounts skillfully into battle against neighbouring tribes, learning how to cling to a horse's flanks, protecting themselves from arrows and rifle balls. Sometimes they would fire their weapons from beneath the horse's neck.

Horses became important symbols for the Plains dwellers signifying wealth to fellow tribesmen. The more horses a warrior owned, the greater his status in the tribe. While most male tribal members owned fewer than ten horses, some warriors, especially tribal chiefs, might own hundreds and even as many as 1,000. Horses were used as a medium of exchange, usually having a value relative to buffalo robes, guns, steel knives and other Western trade goods. When a man chose a wife, he gave her family horses as a dowry. One tribe would often raid the horse reserves of a neighbouring tribe, adding the stolen animals to their own inventory. Stealing a horse was considered an act of bravery, skill and cunning.

Tribesmen decorated their horses in various ways, using paint, feathers and beadwork. Although most rode without the benefit of a saddle, some warriors fashioned small saddles of buffalo hide. Sometimes they might make wooden saddles sheathed in deer or antelope skin, decorating them with intricate patterns of beadwork. They also painted their ponies with their own personal symbols. Others decorated their steeds by dipping the ponies' tails in paint. Warriors took their small but powerfully swift ponies into battle on more than one occasion against each other and against units of the US army, where they usually outmanoeuvred the larger army mounts.

If the horse eventually became the Plains tribes' source of wealth, transport, warfare and mobility, the buffalo became their primary source of meat and other necessities. Before the

TRIBES OF THE GREAT PLAINS

adoption of the horse, Plains tribes could hunt only for buffalo that were located near a tribe's village. Warriors usually attempted to run a buffalo herd off a nearby cliff or into a ravine, where their quarry would either die from the fall or be trapped, allowing hunters to kill them with their arrows or rifles. Running a herd off a cliff usually resulted in great waste, as more buffalo died than the band of hunters could butcher and consume.

Once they began relying on the horse for mobility and speed in hunting, Plains tribes became equally dependent on the buffalo for food, clothing and shelter. Tribesmen prepared the animal's meat in a variety of ways, but usually roasted strips of flesh or ate them raw. Most tribes enjoyed the buffalo's hump and considered its meat to be quite tender. They also drank buffalo blood, which, it is said, has the taste of warm milk, and unborn calf foetus was considered a delicacy. They ate the buffalo's organs, including the intestines, and even the animal's bone marrow. Buffalo meat was also preserved for future meals, as well. Since refrigeration was non-existent in those days on the Plains, they cut buffalo meat into long strips and hung them over wooden frames to dry in the sum, creating jerky. To provide a ready food source in the winter when buffalo hunting was difficult or impossible, tribal women prepared a substance called pemmican. Pemmican was a mixture of pulverized buffalo meat, animal fat and wild berries. Once these foods were combined, the pemmican was placed in leather pouches and often buried. During snowy months, they would dig up their bags of stored food and were thus able to keep themselves alive thanks to forward planning.

Plains tribes not only utilized the buffalo meat but attempted to use nearly every other part of the animal in one way or another. They developed nearly a hundred uses for the parts of a buffalo, including robes, tepee coverings, shields and leather pouches, called parfleches. Women worked buffalo hides by scraping away the flesh and softening the animal covering into leather by applying ashes, animal fat and brains, and plant fibres. Tools were fashioned from the animal's bones. Thread for sewing clothing, as well as for stringing bows, was made from buffalo sinew. Ceremonial rattles were made from buffalo hoofs and horns. Skulls were used in Indian rituals as well. Even the dung of the buffalo, so-called 'buffalo chips', was used as fuel for campfires when trees and wood were not available in adequate quantities.

Plains Tepees

While not every Plains tribe lived in conical-shaped dwellings of wooden poles and buffalo hides called tepees, this means of shelter was typically used right across the Great Plains region. Generally, the men of a tribe were responsible for gathering the materials required to build a tepee. However, it was considered women's work to put a tepee together, to maintain the dwelling once erected, and to dismantle and transport it when the tribe moved to another site.

Most tepees followed the same basic construction design. Three or four poles were lashed together near their ends and placed upright to form the simple support structure. Other poles were then placed among them, forming a circle on the ground.

These poles provided the framework for the house. Women sewed buffalo hides together, the number of hides determined by the desired size of the tepee. Smaller tepees required as few as six or seven buffalo hides, while larger structures demanded up to twenty or thirty. Larger tepees indicated greater wealth and status for a warrior among his peers. Once the hides were stretched around the lodge pole framework, the women used wooden stakes, or lodge pins, to secure the hide to the ground all around the base. Lodge poles placed inside the tepee were used to open and close flaps located at the top of the structure. Such flaps could be opened to allow smoke to escape from the inside or closed to block out rain or snow. A buffalo hide was used as a door covering for the entrance. Generally, peoples on the Plains built their tepees with entrances facing out to the east, since the winds of the Plains often blow from the west. Plains tepees could be both cool in summer and warm in winter.

To the Plains tribes, such lodgings were not just places to live in. They were decorated with paintings of spirits, deceased ancestors and records of deeds carried out in battle. The tepee provided a series of symbols for Plains tribes. The rounded shape of the dwelling represented the interconnectedness of all parts of life. Most tepees featured an altar stone where warriors prayed while incense burned on the stone.

Earthen Lodges of the Mandan

Nearly every Plains tribe had come to live in tepees by the eighteenth century. A few, however, did not. One such northern Plains tribe was the Mandans. These people migrated on to the Plains around 1400 from the Great Lakes region and settled along the Missouri River in territory that is today North Dakota. When whites first made contact with the Mandans in the 1700s, they were living in the Big Bend region of the Missouri River.

The Mandans lived in permanent settlements and practised an extensive agriculture, which included the raising of corn, beans, squash, sunflowers and tobacco for ceremonial purposes. They built their homes in the form of earthen mounds rather than relying on the tepee design. To construct a typical Mandan dwelling involved digging a pit measuring one to four feet (thirty to 120 centimetres) in depth. This provided the floor for the lodge. A wooden frame was built up from the pit floor, with the poles lashed together and covered with several layers of willow branches, followed by a layer of prairie grass to provide insulation. Sod was then placed on top of the willow branches and grasses to provide the roof of the dwelling. These earthen houses had to provide warmth for the Mandan during the long winter months with temperatures far below freezing. The average Mandan village might feature from ten to a hundred earthen lodges.

These rounded lodges served as home to several families who lived together and often numbered as many as forty or fifty, if not more. Each family provided its own beds, which were placed around the wall of the lodge circle. In the centre of the lodge, a fire burned, providing warmth for the occupants and heat for cooking. In the centre of the lodge's roof, a hole allowed the fire's smoke to escape.

The Mandans were not the only northern Plains tribes to use the earthen lodge as a residence. In all, eight groups lived for at least for a majority of the year in such dwellings: in addition to the Mandan, these were the Arikaras, the Hidatsas, the Pawnees, the Omahas, the Caddos, the Wichitas and the Osages.

Plains Clothing

As with most people who live in temperate zones, the typical wardrobe of a Plains dweller varied according to the season. In summer, the men of the tribe wore leather breechclouts. The women wore sleeveless leather dresses. Both men and women wore moccasins. Children often went naked in summer, as well as barefoot. In winter, everyone wrapped themselves in buffalo robes, leggings and animal-skin shirts. The clothing of both men and women was frequently decorated with porcupine quills and beads.

Warriors wore their hair in a variety of styles and sported several different types of headdresses. Typically, braves wore eagle feathers attached directly to their hair. As they participated in battles and raids, warriors accumulated many honours, resulting in a head-dress brimming with eagle's feathers. These elaborate headpieces might include feathers, their tips dipped in black paint, which were attached to the skullcap of a buffalo, along with headbands embellished with fur, porcupine quills, beads and painted ribbons.

As to hairstyles, there was great variation. The men of some tribes shaved their heads entirely or left a centre strip of hair running to the back of the head, which might then be ornamented with a colourful fringe of stiffened deer-tail hair. Others left their hair unshorn, with a single forelock falling across the forehead. Regardless, nearly all warriors used feathers further to adorn their hairstyles.

Village Life

Within most Plains tribes, there were few authoritarian structures in place to govern the conduct of the tribe or its bands. Most bands operated independently of one another, selecting their own chiefs. Such men were chosen on the basis of their military successes, their leadership qualities and their perceived wisdom. Such men rarely gave strict orders to their people but were, rather, advisers. Discipline for each band often took the form of shunning members, shaming them or even forcing them out of the band.

When a tribe's bands came together, as they often did in summer, each band set up camp by erecting their tepees in a circle. Such villages, then, took on the shape of a series of circles adjacent to one another. At such times competitions were often held between bands, such as foot or horse races or gambling sessions. Certainly the bands shared the experiences of prescribed ceremonies, festivals and councils.

While life on the Plains for Native Americans could be filled with daily diversions, excitements and adventures, village life was often a matter of routine and pattern, generally determined by the passing of the seasons. Tribes people typically referred to their years as 'winters', indicating their awareness of seasonal differences. When winter approached, indicated by the first snowfall, the Plains tribes often carried out one last hunt, hoping to add to their stores or meat from the spring and summer forays. As the snows came and the temperatures dropped, village life for all members became sedentary. Often the camps established by the various bands of a tribe in November became permanent until the arrival of spring in early May.

A Plains winter could be a ferocious experience. Snows were often measured in feet rather than inches on the northern Plains and temperatures dropped sixty or seventy degrees Fahrenheit below freezing. Buffalo-hide tepees did, however, generally provide adequate warmth inside. Sleeping at night was done under small heaps of buffalo furs, with family members lying close to one another for warmth. Although winterbound, everyone had jobs to do. Men worked at repairing their hunting equipment, restringing bows and shaping new arrows. Women cooked and tended the children, as well as decorating hides and articles of clothing with beadwork and porcupine quills. Children had their own tasks to do, although they also spent much time playing games, often indoors. In the evenings, families came together to share stories and meals. Around a dancing fire, old men spun tales, young men and women paired off with one another, and children drifted off to sleep under heavy buffalo robes.

Despite the cold outdoor temperatures, activity did continue during winter camp beyond the warm interior of the tepees. Fighting between tribes was rare in winter, yet intrepid warriors did attempt an occasional horse-stealing raid against their neighbours. Braves patrolled their own encampments, always on the watch for the warriors of other tribes. If food stocks dwindled, small hunting parties might be sent out to try to replenish or supplement them.

With the long-awaited arrival of spring, the bands emerged from their relatively dormant lifestyle, ready for a move and new adventure. Springtime activities included the bands coming together for important ceremonies, such as those associated with planting, especially for the sedentary tribes. New chiefs might be selected, and a plan was laid out to determine each band's new encampment site.

Throughout much of the later spring and most of the summer, the nomadic tribal bands and clans scattered in all directions, becoming largely responsible for themselves. They each moved to a designated vicinity, yet they were free to move about at will and as often as they chose. Each band established its own pattern of hunting, warring and horse-stealing. By midsummer, the separated bands came together for the annual Sun Dance, the most significant series of annual ceremonies each tribe engaged in. Following the Sun Dance rituals, most Plains tribes engaged in a great buffalo hunt.

By autumn, the sedentary tribes began to reap the harvest of their agricultural endeavours, while nomadic bands continued to hunt, bartering with one another and dealing with white traders, and to work on their domestic and decorative crafts.

Plains Warfare

War was common among Plains tribes, as it would be in the nineteenth century between Native Americans and white soldiers and settlers. Plains warfare featured practices that were unique to the tribal culture. The warriors of many tribes belonged to military societies, typically entering them upon reaching a certain age, generally during their teen years. Such societies imposed a specific code of behaviour on their members and required specific dances, songs and insignia.

Some societies were intertribal, meaning their members could come from different tribes, although these were rare. Others were more closed, membership being 'by invitation only'. Invitation often hinged on the warrior's personal record of exploits and deeds in battle. One of the greatest acts of bravery a Plains warrior could carry out was the curious practice of 'counting coup'.

While most cultures who wage war expect their fighting men to kill the enemy, the Plains Indians had a custom of humiliating an enemy by merely touching him and perhaps allowing him to live. In such instances, a warrior carried a 'coup' stick into a skirmish, using it to tap or touch his opponent. (The word *coup* is French, meaning 'blow'). Counting coup was not limited to such official sticks, and using a bow, a lance, a club or even a hand was perfectly acceptable. A brave usually received an eagle feather for each successful coup. A coup might then be followed by a killing, then a scalping. All three acts committed together resulted in the warrior receiving three eagle feathers. Such acts of bravery, the mere touching of an armed opponent, were often recounted later around tribal fires, as warriors told of their exploits of the day and of days past. Warriors often embellished their stories, but any brave caught exaggerating his deeds might face the permanent shame of his fellow tribesmen.

Plains Religion

To the typical Native American of the Great Plains, the spirit world was a potent place, one that was interconnected with the natural world in which they found themselves. Their religion, as was true of all tribes in the Americas, was by nature animistic. All things – plants, animals, the stars and planets, water, even rocks – had spirits whose qualities could, at least in part, be passed on to warriors who performed certain deeds.

For many Great Plains tribes a practice called the 'vision quest' became an important avenue for making connection between the natural and the spirit world. Warriors sought visions through an involved series of rituals. A brave usually

attempted his first vision quest as a teenager. Normally, the process began with the building of a sweat lodge from tree saplings, something similar to a sauna, with the warrior sitting inside. Stones were heated inside the lodge and steam was created by pouring water over the hot rocks. This process 'purified' the brave. He then stripped off his clothing, painted his body with white clay and secluded himself outside the camp, fasting for several days.

After days without foot and water, plus continuous exposure to the elements, the warrior hoped to receive a vision – actually an induced hallucination. These visions were considered a window to the spirit world. If such a vision did not occur, the brave might then cut himself repeatedly, the resulting loss of blood often causing him to become semi-conscious, thus creating a trance-like state.

Once the vision came, it took on a variety of possible forms. The hallucinating brave might receive a visit from a deceased ancestor or have a conversation with an animal. Some visions involved rainstorms, visits to places unknown to the dreamer or a long list of other natural phenomena. During the course of the vision, the brave hoped to learn sacred songs and prayers, and receive instruction on behaviour. Once the vision had taken place, the warrior then often related his dream to a medicine man who would serve as the vision's interpreter. Whatever was considered to be the vision's most potent symbol – an animal, a tree or a natural element – was thought to be that warrior's guardian spirit. The brave then began collecting objects that he recalled from his vision to serve as charms. These were then placed in a sacred pouch called a medicine bundle.

Medicine Bundles

These leather pouches were considered powerful medicine to the Plains people who carried them. They included not only objects remembered from visions but other items considered sacred by members of the tribe. Medicine bundles were thought to possess magical powers and brought good fortune to the warrior and his family. While individuals usually carried their own medicine bundles, many Plains bands had medicine bundles of their own. Such bundles were held by tribal chiefs, medicine men or shamans, and their contents were considered sacred to the entire band or even to the whole tribe. Sacred items, such as smoking pipes, were often found among the potent inventory of tribal medicine bundles.

Sacred Pipes

Pipes were used in many of the sacred and ceremonial rituals of the Great Plains tribes. They were considered holy, sacred and spiritually powerful. Individuals often made their own pipes, but many bands and tribes had pipes that belonged to the entire group. Most pipes were made of wood, sometimes with the stem extending several feet in length. Other pipes were fashioned out of a soft, reddish rock called catlinite. The most famous catlinite quarry, located in Minnesota, was itself considered sacred, and braves from many different tribes came there. No warfare was to take place on this holy ground and enemies worked within sight of one another, carving out pieces of catlinite to fashion into pipe bowls and stems. Other Plains pipes were fashioned out of steatite, or soapstone. These were typically decorated with porcupine quills, feathers, beads and horsehair.

The tribes considered these pipes to be sacred, partly because of the tobacco burned in them, which was itself considered sacred. Although the common term used by Europeans for such pipes is 'peace pipes', these sacred objects were not used in peace councils. For those occasions, any pipe would do. Sacred pipes, on the other hand, served as the symbolic protection for the tribe, guarding the welfare and security of its people, whether an individual family, a band or the entire tribe.

The Sacred Sun Dance

While some vision quests were individually directed, the result of a lone warrior seeking his personal directive, most Plains tribes carried out a highly symbolic annual event, which was called by the Sioux the Sun Dance. While it went by other names – New Life Lodge among the Cheyennes; Mystery Dance among the Poncas –

the Sun Dance served as a yearly attempt by each tribe to make connection with the spiritual world.

Such connection was believed to be necessary for the good fortune of the tribe. It was needed to keep the buffalo abundant, to bring prosperity to the tribe, to bless marriages, to heal sick members and to ensure the renewing cycles of nature, such as the sun continuing its course through the sky each day.

The Sun Dance, and all its associated, peripheral activities, was held in the summertime, when a tribe's bands had joined together for extensive buffalo-hunting. Many special events took place, including horse races and interband competitions. Chief among the important events were the teaching of holy songs and the selection of a warrior to cut a tree for the sacred pole to serve as the centrepiece of the Sun Dance. Band chiefs met in councils to renew acquaintances, tell stories and re-create tribal unity. The apex of all this interaction was, however, the Sun Dance itself. It began during a full moon, usually in late summer, when the wild chokeberries were ripe for picking. The ceremony accompanying the Sun Dance lasted from eight to twelve days.

While the many rituals making up the Sun Dance were very involved, each one being highly symbolic, the dance itself took place around the freshly cut and painted pole, which had been carved out of a sacred tree trunk. Such poles were often as much as thirty feet (nine metres) in height. A wall was often raised around the pole, creating a sacred lodge. Those who danced around the pole did so in a simple repeated series of steps, which continued for days, with the participants denying themselves food and water. Just as with individual vision quests, these Sun Dance warriors were working themselves into a trance, in search of a vision.

Other Sun Dance rituals included a process of self-mutilation. Taking a knife, braves cut slits in their chests and ran wooden skewers through their skin. Rawhide straps were attached to the skewers, connected to the sacred pole. While drums beat out an endless rhythm, warriors danced back away from the pole, until the skewers ripped from their flesh. Other braves danced around with their skewers attached to bison skulls, dragging the skulls behind them. These self-mutilation exercises were designed to induce hallucination, and individual sacrifice was thought to bring good fortune to the entire tribe.

Mythology of the Plains Tribes

The Plains tribes as other Native Americans, believed in a supreme being, a rather vaguely defined presence called the Sky Father who was the guardian of all. Between his home in the sky and the earth below, Plains mythology continued, was a middle place, the home of not only distant planets, stars, the sun and moon, but beings closer to earth, such as eagles, clouds, lightning and thunder. Their lives between the sky and the earth were lived in much the same way as the tribes themselves lived: in tepees and earthen-lodge dwellings. These spirits frequently visited the earth and could take on human form, and could wreak havoc by causing droughts or floods, or making the buffalo herds disappear. Alternatively, they could bless individual warriors, as well as bands and whole tribes. Plains Indians believed that such spiritual beings could be appeased through self-mutilation and pain. This explains the importance of the Sun Dance rituals and individual vision quests.

Creation Myths of the Plains

Several different stories existed among the tribes of the Plains to explain the origins of the earth and how men and women came to be created. One such myth, as told by the Arikaras, related man's origins from beneath the earth's surface. In this myth, two ducks are enticed by two crea-tures named Wolf Man and Lucky Man to dive into a giant lake and retrieve mud from which the earth was fashioned. Once that was done, Wolf Man and Lucky Man went beneath the earth and convinced two spiders to give birth to a variety of animals and a race of giants.

Watching all this from his sky perch, the great Sky Spirit, Nesaru (the Sioux Indians gave him the name Wakonda), disliked the giants, because they did not worship him. In retaliation, he created corn. From the seeds of the corn,

Nesaru created a race of human beings similar to the tribes people themselves. He then sent the Corn Mother down to earth to fetch the newly created people to the surface. Once she appeared underground, the Corn Mother was soon sur-rounded by the people and their animals. Several animals began burrowing towards the earth's sur-face – the badger, the mole and the mouse – but the hole they created was not big enough. Thun-der shook the earth and loosened the soil, allowing the Corn Mother, the humans and the animals to emerge on the earth's surface.

Once they found themselves on the earth rather than under it, the human beings were directed by various birds – the kingfisher, the owl and the loon – to the places where they should live. In time, the humans began to fight and quarrel with one another. Nesaru and the Corn Mother finally appeared and each taught the humans everything they needed to know about planting and growing corn, about the gods of the sky, how to live at peace with one another and, when war became necessary, how to fight with honour. The Corn Mother explained to the human beings the magical properties of medicine bundles and the good fortune that they represented.

Before Nesaru and the Corn Mother left the humans, disease arrived, delivered by the Wind of the Southeast, one of the Gods of the Eight Directions of the Sky. To help the people, a dog appeared and it told them how to cure diseases and gave them medicine. As Nesaru prepared to leave, he left his personal medicine bundle with the humans, and the Corn Mother gave them a cedar tree as a symbol of her constantly present spirit. The two gods then ascended into the sky.

Myth of the Morning Star

A myth such as the preceding one places much emphasis on the power of the gods in the sky and of medicine bundles. Some Plains groups considered the gods in the heavens so important to their tribal mythology that they had tribal sky-watchers, men who served as astronomers, tracking the movements of the planets and the phases of the moon. They often decided when were the best times of the year to make offerings and to carry out sacred ceremonies. Such tribes recognized and worshipped the North Star, considering it to be the god of creation, identifying the South Star as a dark force, in command of the beings of the underworld. The star they called the Morning Star provided them with tribal comfort and security. The Evening Star was a dark power who sent his own daughter to diminish the powers of the Morning Star.

To ensure the continuation of the Morning Star in the sky, Plains tribes created a medicine bundle called the Morning Star bundle. A legend was developed and a ritual carried out every four years. A tribe's braves raided a neighbouring camp and kidnapped a young girl. After holding her prisoner and giving her messages for the gods in the sky, the braves stripped her naked and painted her half red and half black, these two colours symbolizing the Morning and Evening Stars. The young prisoner was then tied to a platform where the tribe's warriors killed her, shooting her body full of arrows. This human sacrifice and the shedding of her blood were intended as an offering to the Sky Father, who would then bless the tribe for another four years.

MYTHS AND LEGENDS
OF THE GREAT PLAINS

THE MADNESS OF BALD EAGLE

Sioux

'IT WAS MANY YEARS AGO, when I was only a child,' began White Ghost, the patriarchal old chief of the Yankton Sioux, 'that our band fought a hard battle with the Rees and the Mandans. The reason for the fight was an odd one. I will tell you the story'. And he laid aside his long-stemmed pipe and settled in for the telling.

'At that time the Yankton numbered a little over forty families. We were nicknamed by the other bands Shunkikcheka, or Domestic Dogs, because of our owning large numbers of these animals. My father was the head chief.

'Our favourite wintering place was a tract of timberland near the mouth of the Grand River (the Missouri), and it was here that we met with the Blackfoot Sioux for the annual fall hunt. Across the river, on the opposite bank, was the permanent village of the Rees and Mandans, whose houses were built partially underground of dirt and pols. For a hundred years before this time, they had planted great gardens, and we often traded them for corn, beans and pumpkins. Our peoples occasionally made treaties of peace between one another. Each Ree family had one or two buffalo boats – made from two or three skins – not rounded, as the Sioux made them. They carried their dried beans and other vegetables to us in these boats, and we traded buffalo meat jerky with them.

'It was a great time of celebration and hospitality. The Sioux braves were courting the Ree girls, and the Ree young men were courting the girls of our band. Meanwhile, the older people were busy trading with one another. It was a time of joy as the river came alive with canoes, trade and the laughter of the young men and maidens.

'My uncle – my father's younger brother – whose name was Big Whip, had a close friend named Bald Eagle. Both men were known for their ambition and daring. They had been following the Ree girls to their canoes each evening.

'Big Whip and his friend stood on the river's bank at sunset, one with a quiver full of arrows on his back while the other carried a gun underneath his blanket. Nearly all the village's people had crossed the river and the Ree chief, whose name was Bald Eagle, went home with his wife after everyone else was gone. It was about dusk as they entered their bull-hide boat. The two Sioux braves stood there watching them.

'Suddenly Big Whip exclaimed, 'Friend, let us kill the chief. I dare you to scalp him!'

'His friend answered, 'It shall be as you ask. I will stand by you through this and will die with you.'

Bald Eagle pulled out his gun and shot the Ree dead.

Source

Charles A. Eastman, (Ohiyesa). *Old Indian Days*, New York: McClure Company, 1907, pp. 68–75

'Then Bald Eagle pulled out his gun and shot the Ree dead. From that day on he took his name. The old chief fell back into his boat, and his wife screamed and cried as she rowed him across the river. The other young men shot an arrow or two at her, but she continued to row until she arrived on the opposite bank.

'There was great excitement on both sides of the river as soon as the people found out what had happened. There were two camps of Sioux, the Blackfoot Sioux and the Yankton, or our people. Naturally, the Mandans and Rees greatly outnumbered us. Their camp must have numbered at least two or three thousand, which was more than we had between our two camps put together.

'There was a Sioux whose name was Black Shield, who had a Ree wife. He came down to the river bank and shouted to us, "Of which one of your bands is the man who killed BAld Eagle?"

'One of the Blackfoot Sioux replied, "It is a man of the Yankton Sioux who killed Bald Eagle."

'Then he said, "The Rees desire to battle with the Yanktons. You had better separate from their camp."

'Accordingly the Blackfeet retired about a mile from our camp, upon the bluffs, and pitched their tents, while the Yankton remained on the prairie. The two bands had been great rivals in the practice of war, so we did not ask for help from them, but during the night we dug two trenches around our camp, the outer one for the men to battle and the inner one to provide protection for the women and children.

'The next morning at dawn the enemy crossed the river and approached our camp in great numbers. Some of their old men and women also came to watch the battle from the bluffs. The Blackfeet also came to watch from the bluffs. Just before the battle began, one Blackfoot came into our camp along with his wife. He intendded to fight alongside us. His name was Red Dog's Track, but after that day, he was called He Came Back. His wife was a Yankton and he had told her, "If I don't join your tribe today, my brothers-in-law will call me a coward."

'The Sioux were well entrenched and well armed with both guns and bows and arrows. Their aim was so deadly that the Rees crawled towards them slowly and picked off any Sioux who tried to show his head above the trenches. Similarly, every Ree who exposed himself was certain to die.

'Up to this time no one had seen the two braves responsible for this battle. There was a natural hollow in the river bank which was concealed by buffalo berry bushes, close to the spot where they stood when Bald Eagle shot the Ree.

'"Friend," said Big Whip, "It is likely that our own people will punish us for our deeds. They will hunt us down and punish us for our crime. No matter where we go, they will track us down. They have the right to do this, so the best think for us to do is to drop into the river and stay there until they stop looking for us."

'They did this, and remained hidden all through the night. But, after the fight began, Big Whip said, "Friend, we are the reason for these deaths today. We killed Bald Eagle to show how brave we are. We did this on a dare. We should now join our band and fight alongside them."

'Both braves stripped and, taking their weapons with them, ran towards their camp. They had to pass through the enemy's lines, yet they were not noticed until they had nearly passed through them. Then they found themselves between the two warring sides.

'Just as they nearly reached their entrenchment, they turned and faced the Rees, firing at them, while jumping about to avoid getting hit, as is the Indian custom. Bullets and arrows flew around them like hail. At last they dropped, unhurt, into the Sioux entrenchment. By these actions, the two braves saved their reputations for bravery. No one in the tribe ever openly criticized them for their actions on the previous day. Young men often carry out rash actions. However, they should not be criticized for an act of bravery or else they might become cowards.

'Many were killed in the battle, but more of the Rees than of our band. About mid-afternoon, a cold fall rain began, wetting the bow strings and the flints of the guns. It looked as if the fight might have to be carried on with knives.

'But the Rees were much dispirited. They had lost many of their warriors. As their women carried off the wounded, the Blackfoot Sioux watched from the bluffs. They turned and fled towards the river. The Sioux then followed like crazy wolves, using their tomahawks to kill the tired and the slow ones. Many were killed in their boats on the river and some of the boats were shot through and sank. That was the greatest battle ever fought by our band.' The old man concluded, with a deep sigh of both satisfaction and regret.

THE THREE TESTS

Sioux

THERE DWELT IN A CERTAIN VILLAGE a woman of remarkable grace and attractiveness. The fame of her beauty drew suitors from far and near, eager to display their prowess and win the love of this imperious creature – for, besides being beautiful, she was extremely hard to please, and set such tests for her lovers as none had ever been able to satisfy.

A certain young man who lived at a considerable distance had heard of her great charms, and made up his mind to woo and win her. The difficulty of the task did not daunt him and, full of hope, he set out on his mission.

As he travelled he came to a very high hill, and on the summit he saw a man rising and sitting down at short intervals. When the prospective suitor drew nearer he observed that the man was fastening large stones to his ankles. The youth approached him, saying, 'Why do you tie there great stones to your ankles?'

'Oh,' replied the other, 'I wish to chase buffaloes, and yet whenever I do so I go beyond them, so I am tying stones to my ankles that I may not run so fast.'

'My friend,' said the suitor, 'you can run some other time. In the meantime I am without a companion; come with me.'

The Swift One agreed, and they walked on their way together. Ere they had gone very far they saw two large lakes. By the side of one of them sat a man who frequently bowed his head to the water and drank. Surprised that his thirst was not quenched, they said to him, 'Why do you sit there drinking of the lake?'

'I can never get enough water. When I have finished this lake I shall start on the other.'

'My friend, said the suitor, 'do not trouble to drink it just now. Come and join us.'

Source

Lewis Spence, *North American Indians*, London: George G. Harrap & Co., 1914, pp. 275–8

The Thirsty One complied, and the three comrades journeyed on. When they had gone a little farther they noticed a man walking along with his face lifted to the sky. Curious to know why he acted thus, they addressed him.

'Why do you walk with your eyes turned skyward?' said they.

'I have shot an arrow,' he said, 'and I am waiting for it to reappear.'

'Never mind your arrow,' said the suitor. 'Come with us.'

'I will come,' said the Skillful Archer.

As the four companions journeyed through a forest they beheld a strange sight. A man was lying with his ear to the ground, and if he lifted his head for a moment he bowed it again, listening intently. The four approached him, saying, 'Friend, for what do you listen so earnestly?'

'I am listening,' said he, 'to the plants growing. This forest is full of plants, and I am listening to their breathing.'

'You can listen when the occasion arises,' they told him. 'Come and join us.'

He agreed, and so they travelled to the village where dwelt the beautiful maiden.

When they had reached their destination they were quickly surrounded by the villagers, who displayed no small curiosity as to who their visitors were and what object they had in coming so far. When they heard that one of the strangers desired to marry the village beauty they shook their heads over him. Did he not know the difficulties in the way? Finding that he would not be turned from his purpose, they led him to a huge rock which overshadowed the village, and described the first test he would be required to meet.

'If you wish to win the maiden,' they said, 'you must first of all push away that great stone. It is keeping the sunlight from us.'

'Alas!' said the youth, 'It is impossible.'

'Not so,' said his companion of the swift foot, 'nothing could be more easy.'

Saying this, he leaned his shoulder against the rock, and with a mighty crash it fell from its place. From the breaking up of it came the rocks and stones that are scattered over all the world.

The second test was of a different nature. The people brought the strangers a large quantity of food and water, and bade them eat and drink. Being very hungry, the succeeded in disposing of the foot, but the suitor sorrowfully regarded the great kettles of water.

'Alas!' said he, 'Who can drink up that?'

'I can,' said the Thirsty One, and in a twinkling he had drunk it all.

The people were amazed at the prowess of the visitors. However, they said, 'There is still another test,' and they brought out a woman who was a very swift runner, so swift that no one had ever outstripped her in a race.

'You must run a race with this woman,' said they. 'If you win you shall have the hand of the maiden you have come to seek.'

Naturally the suitor chose the Swift One for this test. When the runners were started the people hailed them as fairly matched, for they raced together will they were out of sight.

When they reached the turning point the woman said, 'Come let us rest for a little.'

The main agreed, but no sooner had he sat down than he fell asleep. The woman seized her opportunity. Making sure that her rival was sleeping soundly, she set off for the village, running as hard as she could.

'If you wish to win the maiden, you must first of all push away that great stone.'

Meanwhile, the four comrades were anxiously awaiting the return of the competitors, and great was their disappointment when the woman came in sight, while there was yet no sign of their champion.

The main who could hear the plants growing bent his ear to the ground.

'He is asleep,' said he, 'I can hear him snoring.'

The Skillful Archer came forward, and as he bit the point off an arrow he said, 'I will soon wake him.'

He shot an arrow from the bowstring with such a wonderful aim that it wounded the sleeper's nose, and roused him from his slumbers. The runner started to his feet and looked round for the woman. She was gone. Knowing that he had been tricked, the Swift One put all his energy into an effort to overtake her. She was within a few yards of the winning post when he passed her. It was a narrow margin, but nevertheless the Swift One had gained the race for his comrade.

The youth was then married to the damsel, whom he found to be all that her admirers had claimed, and more.

THE SNAKE OGRE

Sioux

ONE DAY A YOUNG BRAVE, feeling at variance with the world in general, and wishing to rid himself of the mood, left the lodges of his people and journeyed into the forest. By and by he came to an open space, in the centre of which was a high hill. Thinking he would climb to the top and reconnoitre, he directed his footsteps thither, and as he went he observed a man coming in the opposite direction and making for the same spot. The two met on the summit, and stood for a few moments silently regarding each other. The stranger was the first to speak, gravely inviting the young brave to accompany him to his lodge and to sup with him. The other accepted the invitation, and they proceeded in the direction the stranger indicated.

On approaching the lodge the youth saw with some surprise that there was a large heap of bones in front of the door. Within sat a very old woman tending a pot. When the young man learned that the feast was to be a cannibal one, however, he declined to partake of it. The woman then boiled some corn for him, and while doing so told him that his host was nothing more nor less than a Snake Man, a sort of ogre who killed and ate human beings. Because the brave was young and very handsome the old woman took pity on him, bemoaning the fate that would surely befall him unless he could escape from the wiles of the Snake Man.

'Listen,' said she, 'I will tell you what to do. Here are some moccasins. When the morning comes put them on your feet, take one step, and you will find yourself on that headland you see in the distance. Give this paper to the man you will meet there, and he will direct you farther. But remember that however far you may go, in the evening the Snake will overtake you. When you have finished with the moccasins take them off, place them on the ground facing this way, and they will return.'

'Is that all?' said the youth.

'No,' she replied. 'Before you go you must kill me and put a robe over my bones.'

Source

Lewis Spence, *Myths of the American Indians*, London: George G. Harrap & Co., 1914, pp. 278–82

The young brave forthwith proceeded to carry these instructions into effect. First of all, he killed the old woman, and disposed of her remains in accordance with her bidding.

In the morning, he put on the magic moccasins which she had provided for him, and with one great step he reached the distant headland. Here he met an old man, who received the paper from him, and then, giving him another pair of moccasins, directed him to a far-off point where he was to deliver another piece of paper to a man who would await him there. Turning the first moccasins homeward, the young brave put the second pair to use, and took another gigantic step. Arrived at the second stage of his journey from the Snake's lodge, he found it a repetition of the first. He was directed to another distant spot, and from that to yet another. But when he delivered his message for the fourth time he was treated somewhat differently.

'Down there in the hollow,' said the recipient of the paper, 'there is a stream. Go towards it, and walk straight on, but do not look at the water.'

The youth did as he was bidden, and shortly found himself on the opposite bank of the stream. He journeyed up the creek, and as evening fell he came upon a place where the river widened to a lake. Skirting its shores, he suddenly found himself face to face with the Snake. Only then did he remember the words of the old woman, who had warned him that in the evening the Snake would overtake him. So he turned himself into a little fish with red fins, lazily moving in the lake.

The Snake, high on the bank, saw the little creature, and cried, 'Little Fish! Have you seen the person I am looking for? If a bird had flown over the lake you must have seen it, the water is so still, and surely you have seen the man I am seeking?'

'Not so,' replied the little fish. 'I have seen no one. But if he passes this way, I will tell you.'

So the Snake continued downstream, and as he went there was little grey Toad right in his path.

'Little Road,' said he. 'Have you seen him for whom I am seeking? Even if only a shadow were here you must have seen it.'

'Yes,' said the little toad, 'I have seen him, but I cannot tell you which way he has gone.'

The Snake doubled and came back on his trail. Seeing a very large fish in shallow water, he said, 'Have you seen the man I am looking for?'

'That is he with whom you have just been talking,' said the fish, and the Snake turned homeward. Meeting a muskrat, he stopped.

'Have you seen the person I am looking for?' he said. Then, having his suspicions aroused, he added craftily, 'I think that you are he.'

But the muskrat began a bitter complaint.

'Just now,' said he, 'the person you seek passed over my lodge and broke it.'

So the Snake passed on and encountered a red-breasted Turtle. He repeated his query, and the turtle told him that the object of his search was to be met with farther on.

'But beware,' he added, 'for if you do not recognize him, he will kill you.'

Following the stream, the Snake came upon a large green frog floating in shallow water.

'I have been seeking a person since morning,' he said. 'I think that you are he.'

The frog allayed his suspicions saying, 'You will meet him farther down the stream.'

The Snake next found a large turtle floating among the green sum on a lake. Getting on the turtle's back, he said, 'You must be the person I seek,' and his head rose higher and higher as he prepared to strike.

'I am not,' replied the turtle. 'The next person you meet will be he. But beware, for if you do not recognize him he will kill you.'

When he had gone a little farther down the Snake attempted to cross the stream.In the middle was an eddy. Crafty as he was, the Snake failed to recognize his enemy, and the eddy drew him down into the water and drowned him. So the youth succeeded in slaying the Snake who had sought throughout the day to kill him.

CREATION TALE

Cheyenne

THE CREATION STORY of the Cheyennes tells of a being who was floating on the surface of the water. Water-birds – swans, geese, ducks and other birds that swim – already existed, and these were all about him. The person called to these birds and asked them to bring him some earth. They were glad to do so, and agreed one after another to dive down through the water and see if they could find earth at the bottom. The larger birds dived in vain. They came up without anything, for they could not reach the bottom, but at last one small duck came to the surface with a little mud in its bill. The bird swam to the being and put the mud in his hand, and he took it and worked it with his fingers until it was dry, when he placed it in little piles on the surface of the water,and each little pile became land,and grew and grew and spread, until, as far as one could see, solid land was everywhere. Thus was created the earth we walk on.

After there was firm ground the Creator took from his right side a rib and from it made a man. From the man's left side he took a rib and from that made a woman. These two persons were made at the same place, but after they had been made they were separated by the Creator, and the woman was put in the north, and the man in the south.

The Creator said to them, 'In that direction –' pointing to the south – 'you will find many sorts of animals and birds different from those which you will find in that direction –' pointing to the north, where the woman stood. 'The birds that live in the south will go to the north in summer. Where the woman is it will be cold and the grass and trees will not grow well. There will be hardly any of them, but where the man is everything will grow: trees, bushes, grass.'

The woman in the north, though she was grey-haired, was not old. She never seemed to grow any older. The man in the south was young. He never seemed to grow any older.

In the north lives Ho-im'-a-ha, the Winter Man, the power that brings cold and snow, and also brings sickness and death. He obeys the woman in the north. He is often spoken of in the stories and is said to have declared at a meeting of the super-natural beings that he would 'take pity on no one'. when at this meeting he spoke

The Creator made man and woman at the same place, but then they were separated,and the woman was put far in the north, and the man in the south.

Source
George Bird Grinnell, *By Cheyenne Campfires*, New Haven, Conn.: Yale University Press, 1926, pp. 16–18

in this way, the Thunder, who represents the power of the south, declared that it would not do to let Ho-im'-a-ha have everything to say; so, with the help of the buffalo, the Thunder made fire and taught one of the culture heroes how to do the same thing.

He said to Sweet Medicine, 'Get a stick and I will teach you something by which your people can warm themselves,can cook food and with which they can burn things'. He showed Sweet Medicine how to rest the point of the stick in the middle of a dried buffalo chip, and then to rub it between his hands and twirl it fast. The young man did so, and after a time the chip caught fire. Thus, by the help of the Thunder the people were given something to use against the cold, something that would warm them.

The man and woman in the south and in the north appear to typify summer and winter,the man representing the sun or the Thunder, while the woman represents the power that wars against the sun.

Twice a year there is a conflict between the Thunder and the Winter Man. At the end of summer when the streams get low and the grass becomes yellow and dry, Ho-im'-a-ha comes down from the north and says to the Thunder, 'Move back, move back,to the place from which you came. I want to spread all over the earth and freeze things and cover everything with snow.' Then the Thunder moves back. Towards spring,when the days begin to grow longer,the Thunder comes back from the south and says to Ho-im'-a-ha, 'Go back, go back, to the place from which you cam; I wish to warm the earth and to make the grass grow, and all things to turn green.' Then the Winter Man moves back and the Thunder comes, bringing the rain; the grass grows and all the earth is green. So there is a struggle between these two powers. They follow each other back and forth.

The two first people, the man in the south and the woman in the north,never came together, but later other people were created and from them the earth was populated.

ORIGIN OF THE MEDICINE PIPE

Blackfoot

Source
George Bird Grinnell, *Blackfoot Lodge Tales: The Story of a Prairie People*, New York: Charles Scribner's Sons, 1892 pp. 113–16

THUNDER – YOU HAVE HEARD HIM, he is everywhere. He roars in the mountains, he shouts far out on the prairie. He strikes the high rocks, and they fall to pieces. He hits a tree, and it is broken in slivers. He strikes the people, and they die. He is bad. He does not like the towering cliff, the standing tree, or living man. He likes to strike and crush them to the ground. Yes! Yes! Of all he is most powerful; he is the one most strong. But I have not told you the worst: he sometimes steals women.

Long ago, almost in the beginning, a man and his wife were sitting in their lodge, when Thunder came and struck them. The man was not killed. At first he was as if dead, but after a while he lived again,and rising looked about him. His wife was not there.

'Oh, well,' he thought, 'she has gone to get some water or wood'.

He sat a while; but when the sun had under-disappeared, he went out and inquired about her of the people. No one had seen her. He searched throughout the camp, but did not find her. Then he knew that Thunder had stolen her, and he went out on the hills alone and mourned. When morning came, he rose and wandered far away, and he asked al the animals he met if they knew where Thunder lived. They laughed, and would not answer.

The Wolf said, 'Do you think we would seek the home of the only one we fear? He is our only danger. From all others we can run away; but from him there is no running. He strikes, and there we lie. Turn back! Go home! Do not look for the dwelling place of that dreadful one.'

But the man kept on, and travelled far away. Now he came to a lodge – a queer lodge, for it was made of stone. It was just like any other lodge, only it was made of stone. Here lived the Raven chief. The man entered.

'Welcome, my friend,' said the chief of Ravens. 'Sit down, sit down.' And food was placed before him.

Then when he had finished eating, the Raven said, 'Why have you come?'

'Thunder has stolen my wife,' replied the man. 'I seek his dwelling place that I may find her.'

'Would you dare enter the lodge of that dreadful person?' asked the Raven. 'He lives close by here. His lodge is of stone, like this,and hanging there, within, are eyes – the eyes of those he has killed or stolen. He has taken out their eyes and hung them in his lodge. Now, then, dare you enter there?'

'No,' replied the man. 'I am afraid. What man could look at such dreadful things and live?'

'No person can,' said the Raven. 'There is but one old Thunder fears. There is but one he cannot kill. It is I, it is the Ravens. Now I will give you medicine, and he shall not harm you. You shall enter there, and seek among those eyes your wife's, and if you find them, tell that Thunder why you came, and make him give them to you. Here,now, is a raven's wing. Just point it at him,and he will start back quick. But if that fail, take this. It is an arrow, and the shaft is made of elk-horn. Take this, I say, and shoot it through the lodge.'

'Why make a fool of me?' the poor man asked. 'My heart is sad. I am crying.' And he covered his head with his robe and wept.

'Oh,' said the Raven, 'you do not believe me. Come out, come out, and I will make you believe.' When they stood outside, the Raven asked, 'Is the home of your people far?'

'A great distance,' said the man.

'Can you tell how many days you have travelled?'

'No,' he replied, 'my heart is sad. I did not count the days. The berries have grown and ripened since I left.'

'Can you see your camp from here?' asked the Raven.

The man did not speak. Then the Raven rubbed some medicine on his eyes and said, 'Look!' The man looked, and saw the camp. It was close. He saw the people. He saw the smoke rising from the lodges.

'Now you will believe,' said the Raven. 'Take now the arrow and the wing,and go and get your wife.'

So the man took these things, and went to Thunder's lodge. He entered and sat down by the doorway. The Thunder sat within and looked at him with awful eyes. But the man looked above,and saw those many pairs of eyes. Among them were those of his wife.

'Why have you come?' said the Thunder in a fearful voice.

'I seek my wife,' the man replied, 'whom you have stolen. There hand her eyes.'

'No man can enter my lodge and live,' said the Thunder, and he rose to strike him. Then the man pointed the raven wing at the Thunder, and he fell back on his couch and shivered. But he soon recovered and rose again. Then the man fitted the elk-horn arrow to his bow, and shot it through the lodge of rock. Right through the lodge of rock it pierced a jagged hole, and let the sunlight in.

'Hold,' said the Thunder. 'Stop, you are the stronger. Yours is the great medicine. You shall have your wife. Take down her eyes.' Then the man cut the string that held them, and immediately his wife stood beside him.

'Now,' said the Thunder, 'you know me. I am of great power. I live here in summer, but when winter comes, I go far south. I go south with the birds. Here is my pipe. It is medicine. Take it and keep it. Now, when I first come in the spring, you shall fill and light this pipe, and you shall pray to me, you and the people, for I bring the rain which makes the berries large and ripe. I bring the rain which makes all things grow, and for this you shall pray to me, you and all the people.'

Thus the people got the first medicine pipe. It was long ago.

> 'When I first come in the spring, fill and light this pipe,' said the Thunder, 'for I bring the rain which makes all things grow.'

The Fast Runners
Pawnee

O NCE, LONG AGO, the antelope and the deer met on the prairie. At this time both of them had galls and both dew claws. The began to talk together, and each was telling the other what he could do. Each one told how fast he could run, and before long they were disputing as to which could run the faster. Neither would allow that the other could beat him, so they agreed that they would have a race to decide which was the swifter, and they bet their galls on the race. When they ran, the antelope proved the faster runner, and beat the deer and took his gall.

Then the deer said, 'Yes, you have beaten me on the prairie, but that is not where I live. I only go out there sometimes to feet, or when I am travelling around. We ought to have another race in the timber. That is my home, and there I can run faster than you can.'

The antelope felt very big because he had beaten the deer in the race, and he thought wherever they might be, he could run faster than the deer. So he agreed to race to the timber, and on this race they bet their dew claws.

They ran through the thick timber, among the brush and over fallen logs, and this time the antelope ran slowly, because he was not used to this kind of travelling, and the deer easily beat him, and took his dew claws.

Since then the deer has had no gall, and the antelope no dew claws.

Source
George Bird Grinnell, *Blackfoot Lodge Tales: The Story of a Prairie People*, New York: Charles Scribner's Sons, 1892, p. 81

THE WOLF MAN

Blackfoot

THERE WAS ONCE A MAN who had two bad wives. They had no shame. the man thought if he moved away where there were no other people, he might teach these women to become good, so he moved his lodge away off on the prairie. Near where they camped was a high butte, and every evening about sundown, the man would go up on top of it, and look all over the country to see where the buffalo were feeding, and if any enemies were approaching. There was a buffalo skull on the hill, which he used to sit on.

'This is very lonesome,' said one woman to the other, one day. 'We have no one to talk with nor to visit.'

'Let us kill our husband,' said the other. 'Then we will go back to our relations and have a good time.'

Early in the morning, the man went out to hunt, and as soon as he was out of sight, his wives went up on top of the butte. There they dug a deep pit, and covered it over with light sticks, grass and dirt, and placed the buffalo skull on top.

In the afternoon they saw their husband coming home, loaded down with meat he had killed. So they hurried to cook for him. After eating, he went upon the butte and sat down on the skull. The slender sticks gave way, and he fell into the it. His wives were watching him, and when they saw him disappear, they took down the lodge, packed everything on the dog travois, and moved off, going towards the main camp. When they got near it, so that the people could hear them, they began to cry and mourn.

'Why is this?' they were asked. 'Why are you mourning? Where is your husband?'

'He is dead,' they replied. 'Five days ago he went out to hunt, and he never came back.' And they cried and mourned again.

◆

When the man fell into the pit, he was hurt. After a while he tried to get out, but he was so badly bruised he could not climb up. A wolf, travelling along, came to the pit and saw him and pitied him.

'Ah-h-w-o-o-o-o! Ah-h-w-o-o-o-o! he howled, and when the other wolves heard him they all came running to see what was the matter. There came also many coyotes, badgers and kit-foxes.

'In this hole,' said the wolf, 'is my find. Here is a fallen-in man. Let us dig him out, and we will have him for our brother.'

They all thought the wolf spoke well, and began to dig. In a little while they had a hole close to the man. Then the wolf who found him said, 'Hold on, I want to speak a few words to you.'

All the animals listening, he continued, 'We will all have this man for our brother, but I found him, so I think he ought to live with us big wolves.'

All the others agreed, so the wolf went into the hole and, tearing down the rest of the dirt, dragged the almost dead man out. They gave him a kidney to eat, and when he was able to walk a little, the big wolves took him to their home. Here there was a very old blind wolf, who had powerful medicine. He cured the man

Source
George Bird Grinnell, *Blackfoot Lodge Tales: The Story of a Prairie People*, New York: Charles Scribner's Sons, 1892, pp. 78–80

and made his head and hands look like those of a wolf. The rest of his body was not changed.

In those days the people used to make holes in the pis'kun walls (built from the foot of a cliff or canyon) and set snares,and when wolves and other animals came to steal meat, they were caught by the neck. One night the wolves all went down to the pis'kun to steal meat, and when they got close to it, the man-wolf said, 'Stand here a little while. I will go down and fix the places, so you will not be caught.'

He went on and sprang all the snares. Then he went back and called the wolves and others – the coyotes, badgers and foxes – and they all went in the pis'kun and feasted, and took meat to carry home.

In the morning the people were surprised to find the meat gone, and their nooses all drawn out. They wondered how it could have been done. For many nights the nooses were drawn and the meat stolen. But once,when the wolves went there to steal, they found only the meat of a scabby bull, and the man-wolf was angry, and cried out, 'Bad-you-give-us-o-o-o! Bad-you-give-us-o-o-o!'

The people heard him, and said, 'It is a man-wolf who has done all this. We will catch him.' So they put pemmican and nice back fat in the pis'kun, and many hid close by. After dark the wolves came again, and when the man-wolf saw the good food, he ran to it and began eating. Then the people rushed in and caught him with ropes and took him to a lodge. When they got inside to the light of the fire, they knew at once who it was. They said, 'This is the man who was lost.'

'No,' said the man, 'I was not lost. My wives tried to kill me. They dug a deep hole, and I fell into it, and I was hurt so badly that I could not get out. But the wolves took pity on me and helped me, or I would have died there.'

When the people heard this, they were angry, and they told the man to do something.

'You say well,' he replied. 'I give those women to the I-kun-uh'-kah-tsi (warrior society who punished crimes against the tribe). They know what to do.'

After that night the two women were never seen again.

THE SACRED BUNDLE

Pawnee

A CERTAIN YOUNG MAN was very vain of his personal appearance, and always wore the finest clothes and richest adornments he could procure. Among other possessions he had a down feather of an eagle, which he wore on his head when he went to war, and which possessed magical properties. He was unmarried, and cared nothing for women, though doubtless there was more than one maiden of the village who would not have disdained the hand of the young hunter, for he was as brave and good-natured as he was handsome.

One day while he was out hunting with his companions – the Indians hunted on foot in those days – he got separated from the others, and followed some buffaloes for a considerable distance. The animals managed to escape, with the exception of a young cow, which had become stranded in a mud-hole. The youth fitted

Source

Lewis Spence, *North American Indians*, London: George G. Harrap & Co., 1914, pp. 304–8

an arrow to his bow, and was about to fire, when he saw that the buffalo had vanished and only a young and pretty woman were in sight. The hunter was rather perplexed,for he could not understand where the animal had gone to, nor where the woman had come from. However, he talked to the maiden, and found her so agreeable that he proposed to marry her and return with her to his tribe. She consented to marry him, but only on condition that they remained where they were. To this he agreed,and gave her as a wedding gift a string of blue and white beads he wore round his neck.

One evening when he returned home after a day's hunting he found that his camp was gone and that all round about were the marks of many hoofs. No trace of his wife's body could he discover, and at last, mourning her bitterly, he returned to his tribe.

Years elapsed, and one summer morning as he was playing the stick game with his friends a little boy came towards him, wearing round his neck a string of blue and white beads.

'Father,' he said, 'mother wants you.'

The hunter was annoyed at the interruption.

'I am not your father,' he replied. 'Go away.'

The boy went away, and the man's companions laughed at him when they heard him addressed as 'father', for they knew that he was a woman-hater and that he was unmarried.

However, the boy returned in a little while. He was sent away again by the angry hunter, but one of the players now suggested that he should accompany the child and see what he wanted. All the time the hunter had been wondering where he had seen the beads before. As he reflected he saw a buffalo cow and calf running across the prairie, and suddenly he remembered.

Taking his bow and arrows, he followed the buffaloes, whom he now recognized as his wife and child. A long and wearisome journey they had. The woman was angry with her husband, and dried up every creek they came to, so that he feared he would die of thirst, but the strategy of his son obtained food and drink for him until they arrived at the home of the buffaloes. The big bulls, the leaders of the herd, were very angry, and threatened to kill him. First, however, they gave him a test, telling him that if he accomplished it he should live. Six cows, all exactly alike, were placed in a row, and he was told that if he could point out his wife his life would be spared. His son helped him secretly, and he succeeded. The old bulls were surprised, and much annoyed, for they had not expected him to distinguish his wife from the other cows. They gave him another test. He was requested to pick out his son from among several calves. Again the young buffalo helped him to perform the feat. Not yet satisfied, they decreed that he must run a race. If he should win they would let him go. They chose their fastest runners,but on the day set for the race a thin coating of ice covered the ground, and the buffaloes could not run at all, while the young Indian ran swiftly and steadily, and won with ease.

The chief bulls were still angry, however,and determined that they would kill him, even though he had passed their tests. so they made him sit on the ground, all the strongest and fiercest bulls round him. Together they rushed at him, and in a little while his feather was seen floating in the air. The chief bulls called on the others to stop, for they were sure that he must be trampled to pieces by this time.

The strongest and fiercest bulls rushed at the indian, but when they drew back there he sat in the centre of the circle with his feather in his hair.

But when they drew back there sat the Indian in the centre of the circle, with his feather in his hair.

It was, in fact, his magic feather to which he owed his escape, and a second rush which the buffaloes made had as little effect on him. Seeing that he was possessed of magical powers,the buffaloes made the best of matters and welcomed him into their camp, on condition that he would bring them gifts from his tribe. This he agreed to do.

When the Indian returned with his wife and son to the village people, they found that there was no food to be had. But the buffalo-wife produced some meat from under her robe,and they ate of it. afterwards they went back to the herd with gifts, which pleased the buffaloes greatly. The chief bulls, knowing that the people were in want of food, offered to return with the hunter. His son, who also wished to return, arranged to accompany the herd in the form of a buffalo, while his parents went ahead in human shape. The father warmed the people that they must not kill his son when they went to hunt buffaloes, for, he said,the yellow calf would always return leading more buffaloes.

By and by the child came to his father saying that he would no more visit the camp in the form of a boy, as he was about the lead the herd eastward. Ere he went he told his father than when the hunters sought the chase they should kill the yellow calf and sacrifice it to Atius Tirawa, tan its hide,and wrap in the skin an ear of the corn and other sacred things. Every year they should look out for another yellow calf, sacrifice it and keep a piece of its fat to add to the bundle. Then when food was scarce and famine threatened the tribe, the chiefs should gather in council and pray a friendly visit to the young buffalo, and he would tell Tirawa of their need, so that another yellow calf might be sent to lead the herd to the people.

When he had said this the boy left the camp. All was done as he had ordered. Food became plentiful, and the father became a chief, greatly respected by his people. His buffalo-wife, however, he almost forget, and one night she vanished. So distressed was the chief, and so remorseful for his neglect of her, that he never recovered, but withered away and died. But the sacred bundle was long preserved in the tribe as a magic charm to bring the buffalo.

THE ADVENTURES OF ICTINIKE

Iowa

Source
Lewis Spence,
*North American
Indians*,
London: George
G. Harrap &
Co., 1914,
pp. 266–71

MANY TALES ARE TOLD by the Iowa Indians regarding Ictinike, the son of the sun god, who had offended his father, and was consequently expelled from the celestial regions. He possessed a very bad reputation among the Indians for deceit and trickery. They say that he taught them all the evil things they know, and they seem to regard him as a Father of Lies.

I

One day Ictinike encountered the Rabbit, and hailed him in a friendly manner, calling him 'grandchild', and requesting him to do him a service. The Rabbit expressed his willingness to assist the god to the best of his ability, and inquired what he wished him to do.

'Oh, grandchild,' said the crafty one, pointing upwards to where a bird circled in the blue vault above them, 'take your bow and arrow and bring down yonder bird.'

The Rabbit fitted an arrow to his bow, and the shaft transfixed the bird, which fell like a stone and lodged in the branches of a great tree.

'Now, grandchild,' said Ictinike, 'go into the tree and fetch me the game.'

This, however, the Rabbit at first refused to do,but at length he took off his clothes and climbed into the tree, where he stuck fast among the tortuous branches.

Ictinike, seeing that he could not make his way down, donned the unfortunate Rabbit's garments, and,highly amused at the animal's predicament, betook him-self to the nearest village. There he encountered a chief who had two beautiful daughters,the elder of whom he married. The younger daughter, regarding this as an affront to her personal attractions, wandered off into the forest in a fit of the sulks.

As she paced angrily up and down she heard someone calling to her from above, and, looking upwards, she beheld the unfortunate Rabbit, whose fur was adhering to the natural gum that exuded from the bark of the tree. The girl cut down the tree and lit a fire near it, which melted the gum and freed the Rabbit. The Rabbit and the chief's daughter, after discussing things, discovered that the being who had tricked the one and affronted the other was the same. Together they proceeded to the chief's lodge, where the girl was laughed at because of the strange companion she had brought back with her.

Suddenly an eagle appeared in the air above them. Ictinike shot at and missed it, but the Rabbit loosed an arrow with great force and brought it to earth. Each morning a feather of the bird became another eagle, and each morning Ictinike shot at and missed this newly created bird,which the Rabbit invariably succeeded in killing. This went on until Ictinike had quite worn out the Rabbit's clothing and was wearing a very old piece of tent skin; but the Rabbit returned to him the garments he had been forced to don when Ictinike had stolen his. Then the Rabbit commanded the Indians to beat the drums, and each time they were beaten Ictinike jumped so high that every bone in his body was shaken. At length, after a more than usually loud series of beats,he leapt to such a height that when he came down it was found that the fall had broken his neck. The Rabbit was avenged.

II

One day Ictinike, footsore and weary, encountered a buzzard, which he asked to oblige him by carrying him on its back part of the way. The crafty bird immediately consented, and, seating Ictinike between its wings, flew off with him.

They had not gone far when they passed above a hollow tree,and Ictinike began to shift uneasily in his seat as he observed the buzzard hovering over it. He requested the bird to fly onward, but for answer it cast him headlong into the tree trunk, where he found himself a prisoner. For a long time he lay there in want and wretchedness, until at last a large hunting party struck camp at the spot. Ictinike chanced to be wearing some racoon skins, and he thrust the tails of these through the cracks in the tree. Three women who were standing near imagined that a number of racoons had become imprisoned in the hollow trunk, and they made a large hole in it for the purpose of capturing them. Ictinike at once merged, whereupon the women fled. Ictinike lay on the ground pretending to be dead,and as he was covered with the racoon skins the birds of prey, the eagle, the rook and the magpie, came to devour him. While they pecked at him the buzzard made his appearance for the purpose of joining in the feast, but Ictinike, rising quickly, tore the feathers from its scalp. That is why the buzzard has no feathers on its head.

THE GHOST BRIDE

Pawnee

IN A PLACE WHERE WE USED to have a village, a young woman died just before the tribe started on the hunt. When she died they dressed her up in her finest clothes and buried her, and soon after this the tribe started on the hunt.

A party of young men had gone off to visit another tribe, and they did not get back until after this girl had died and the tribe had left the village. Most of this party did not go back to the village, but met the tribe and went with them on the hunt. Among the young men who had been away was one who had loved this girl who had died. He went back alone to the village. It was empty and silent, but before he reached it, he could see, far off, someone sitting on top of a lodge. When he came near, he saw that it was the girl he loved. He did not know that she had died, and he wondered to see her there alone, for the time was coming when he would be her husband and she his wife. When she saw him coming, she came down from the top of the lodge and went inside. When he came close to her, he spoke and said, 'Why are you here alone in the village?'

She answered him, 'They have gone off on the hunt. I was sulky with my relations, and they went off and left me behind.'

The man wanted her now to be his wife, but the girl said to him, 'No, not yet, but later we will be married.' She said to him, 'You must not be afraid. Tonight there will be dances here; the ghosts will dance.'

This is an old custom of the Pawnees. When they danced they used to from one lodge to another, singing, dancing and hallooing. so now, then the tribe had gone and the village was deserted, the ghosts did this. He could hear them coming along the empty streets and going from one lodge to another. They came into the lodge where he was, and danced about, and whooped and sang, and sometimes they almost touched him, and he came pretty near being scared.

The next day, the young man persuaded the girl to go on with him and follow the tribe, to join it on the hunt. They started to travel together, and she promised him that she would surely be his wife, but not until the time came. They overtook the tribe; but before they got to the camp, the girl stopped.

She said, 'Now we have arrived, but you must go first to the village, and prepare a place for me. Where I sleep, let it be behind a curtain. For four days and four nights I must remain behind this curtain. Do not speak of me. Do not mention my name to anyone.'

The young man left here there and went into the camp. When he got to his lodge,he told a woman, one of his relations, to go out to a certain place and bring in a woman who was waiting there for him.

His relative asked him, 'Who is the woman?'

The ghosts came into the lodge where the man was, and danced about and whooped and sang.

Source
George Bird Grinnell, *Pawnee Hero Stories and Folk Tales*, New York: Forest and Stream Publishing Company, 1889, pp. 143–6

And to avoid speaking her name, he told who were her father and mother.

His relation, in surprise, said, 'It cannot be that girl, for she died some days before we started on the hunt.'

When the woman went to look for the girl she could not find her. The girl had disappeared. The young man had disobeyed her, and had told who she was. She had told him that she must stay behind a curtain for four days, and that no one must know who she was. Instead of doing what she had said, he told who she was, and the girl disappeared because she was a ghost. If he had obeyed the girl, she would have lived a second time upon earth. That same night this young man died in sleep.

Then the people were convinced that there must be a life after this one.

OLD MAN AND THE LYNX

Blackfoot

OLD MAN WAS TRAVELLING round over the prairie when he saw a lot of prairie dogs sitting in a circle. They had built a fire and were sitting around it. Old Man went towards them, and when he got near them, he began to cry and said, 'Let me, too, sit by that fire.' The prairie dogs said, 'All right, Old Man. Don't cry. Come and sit by the fire.' Old Man sat down, and saw that the prairie dogs were playing a game. They would put one of their number in the fire and cover him up with the hot ashes; and then, after he had been there a little while, he would say *sk, sk,* and they would push the ashes off him and pull him out.

Old Man said, 'Teach me how to do that'; and they told him what to do, and put him in the fire, and covered him up with the ashes, and after a little while he said *sk, sk,* like a prairie dog, and they pulled him out again. Then he did it to the prairie dogs. At first he put them in one at a time, but there were many of them, and pretty soon he got tired and said, 'Come, I will put you all in at once.' They said, 'Very well, Old Man,' and all got in the ashes; but just as Old Man was about to cover them up, one of them, a female heavy with young, said, 'Do not cover me up; the heat may hurt my children, which are about to be born.' Old Man sad, 'Very well. If you do not want to be covered up, you can sit over by the fire and watch the rest.' Then he covered up all the others.

At length the prairie dogs said sk, sk, but Old Man did not sweep the ashes off and pull them out of the fire. He let them stay there and die. The old she one ran off to a hole and, as she went down in it, said sk, sk. Old Man chased her, but he got to the hole too late to catch her. So he said, Oh, well, you can go. There will be more prairie dogs by and by.'

When the prairie dogs were roasted, Old Man cut a lot of red willow brush to lay them on, and then sat down and began to eat. He ate until he was full, and then felt sleepy. He said to his nose, 'I am going to sleep now. Watch for me and wake me up in case anything comes near.' Then the Old Man slept. Pretty soon his nose snored, and he woke up and said, 'What is it?' The nose said, 'A raven is flying over there.' Old Man said, 'That is nothing,' and went to sleep again. Soon his nose snored again. Old Man said, 'What is it now?' The nose said, 'There is a coyote over there, coming this way.' Old Man said, 'A coyote is nothing,' and again went to

Source
George Bird Grinnell, *Blackfoot Lodge Tales: The Story of a Prairie People,* New York: Charles Scribner's Sons, 1892, pp. 171–3

sleep. Presently his nose snored again, but Old Man did not wake up. Again it snored, and called out, 'Wake up, a bob cat is coming.' Old Man paid no attention. He slept on.

The bob cat crept up to where the fire was and ate up all the roast prairie dogs, and then went off and lay down on a flat rock, and went to sleep. All this time the nose kept trying to wake Old Man up, and at last he awoke,and the nose said, 'A bob cat is over there on a flat rock. He as eaten all your food.' Then Old Man called out loud, he was so angry. He went softly over to where the bob cat lay and seized it, before it could wake up to bite or scratch him. The bob cat cried out, 'Hold on, let me speak a word or two.' But Old Man would not listen; he said, 'I will teach you to steal my food.' He pulled off the lynx's tail, pounded his head against the rock so as to make his face flat, pulled him long, so as to make him small-bellied, and then threw him away into the brush. As he went sneaking off, Old Man said, 'There, that is the way you bob cats shall always be.' That is the reason the lynxes look so today.

PART 5
THE SOUTHWEST

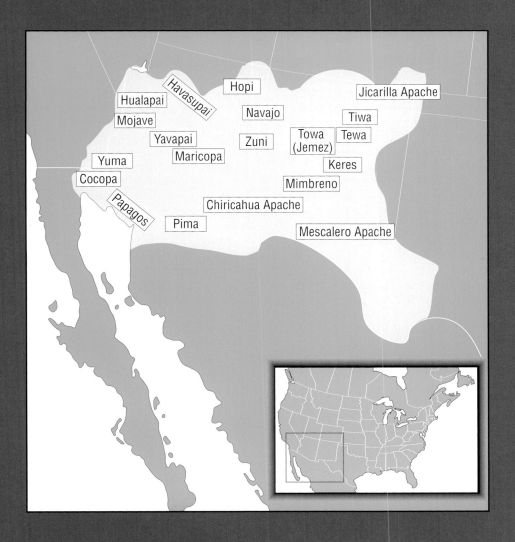

Hopi

Jicarilla Apache

Havasupai

Hualapai

Mojave

Navajo

Tiwa

Yavapai

Zuni

Towa
(Jemez)

Tewa

Maricopa

Keres

Yuma

Cocopa

Mimbreno

Papagos

Chiricahua Apache

Pima

Mescalero Apache

TRIBES OF THE SOUTHWEST

Largely determined by their regional geography, topography and climate, the Native Americans of the American Southwest have produced a unique set of cultures, as well as a unique history. The Southwest is a vast region of mostly desert lands, which stretch across the entire states of Arizona and New Mexico, spread north into the southern half of Utah, the southwestern third of Colorado and a portion of western Texas, as well as slivers of southeastern Nevada and California.

This region is noted for its rugged landscape. Perhaps more so than any other region in the American West, the Southwest provides modern observers with those topographical images which have become the popular stereotypes of Western geography. These are the lands of painted deserts dotted with scattered stands of saguaro cacti, of snow-capped mountain ranges, and of rocky canyons of yellow, brown and red sandstone. It is the location of countless Hollywood-produced Western films – a place of awe-inspiring land formations, from Arizona's Grand Canyon to the erosive monoliths of Utah's Monument Valley. The deserts of the American Southwest generally receive only 50–125mm (2–5in) of rain per year.

Despite the aridity of the Southwest, it has been occupied for thousands of years. Modern anthropology cannot pinpoint a date of first occupation for Southwestern peoples. However, archaeological sites such as Tule Springs, Nevada, indicate the presence of primitive hunters by approximately 9000 BC. Other sites, including Sandia and Clovis, New Mexico, have yielded spear-points (named after the places of their discovery as Sandia and Clovis projectiles) which point to big-game hunting forays dating to, perhaps, 20,000 years ago. These elusive hunters may have stalked, using stone-tipped spears, great Pleistocene animals, including horses, bison, camels, mammoths and mastodons.

By 7000 BC, the great Ice Age mammals began to decline and the prehistoric peoples of the Southwest began to develop the Desert Culture. These early inhabitants began collecting wild plants for food and gathering seeds for planting and cultivation, while continuing their hunting and trapping activities. As the large Pleistocene creatures began to die out, they were replaced as quarry by small game such as deer, rabbits, lizards, snakes, rodents, desert birds and even insects. Piñon nuts, the fruit of the yucca plant, berries and mesquite beans were all gathered. This food-gathering provided a subsistence standard of living for the Native Americans of the Southwest.

These hunter-gatherers, referred to by anthropologists as the Cochise People, lived in small, scattered encampments, taking up residence in caves or dome-shaped grass huts called wickiups. Their culture continued for thousands of years with little change or improvement. Their women used millstones to grind seeds and nuts, creating a coarse flour for baking. It was not until around 2500 BC that the Native Americans of the Southwest began cultivating maize. This early corn plant was primitive, growing in pods, and did not threaten to supplant wild foods in the Southwestern diet until around 2500 BC, when a drought-resistant variety was introduced, from Pre-Columbian Mexico. This food spread rapidly throughout the Southwest and in just a few centuries became the primary crop food of these Native Americans.

By the same time, the Native Americans of the final stage of the Cochise People, the San Pedro Culture Group, were developing other plants, especially beans and squash, which soon became, along with corn, the mainstays of Southwestern agriculture. In time, Native Americans referred to this trio of staple crops as the Three Sisters. Cotton was also beginning to be cultivated. Planting these crops was rudimentary, with Native American farmers using simple drilling sticks, boring individual holes in the ground and dropping in the seeds. Because of the limited rainfall, these agriculturalists built irrigation ditches and attempted to reroute floodwaters and the runoff from nearby gulleys and arroyos.

While their agriculture was undergoing extreme change, the San Pedro Culture was creating semi-permanent villages, with established garden and farming tracts. By 300 BC, their homes were changing, designed for a longer period of occupation. They built pit houses, usually circular in shape, dug into the ground and bearing a roof of log beams covered over with brush and dirt. Each such lodge included a fire pit for cooking and warmth, as well as storage areas and sleeping space. By 100 BC, such people were making pottery, an art form which continues among Native American cultures of today. A new culture – the Mogollon Culture – was soon to emerge in the Southwest, based on these improvements in housing and agriculture, and the use of pottery. This culture group was located in the southern half of New Mexico and southeastern Arizona. Mogollon peoples could also be found in the Mexican provinces of Chihuahua and Sonora.

The 'Mountain People'

These are probably the descendants of the ancient Cochise people. The Mogollons – the name is taken from a short, twisted range of mountains on the southern border between Arizona and New Mexico – are considered to have been the first Southwestern people to adopt a culture which included sustained agriculture, the building of permanent housing and the making of pottery. Their farming included raising the Three Sisters, as well as cotton and tobacco. They continued to be small-game hunters and wild-plant gatherers as well.

The difference between these people and their predecessors lay in their permanent encampments. While they built their sunken, circular homes just as the Cochise people had, including larger structures called 'kivas', which served as religious, social and ceremonial centres, the Mogollons also developed a new type of

housing. Around AD 1100, they began constructing adobe structures above ground. Such housing, called 'pueblos' by the Spanish four centuries later, became the dwelling of choice among the Mogollons. Some Mogollon villages featured as many as 20 to 30 pueblos.

Through the growing of cotton, Mogollon women became skilled weavers, creating intricate blankets and clothing which sported feathers and animal furs. Other domestic arts – including pottery and basketry – were developed by the Mogollons. Their early pots were made by laying coils of brown clay one on another, then smoothing them out and firing them. A later Mogollon subculture, the Mimbres group, developed a style of painted pottery which featured black paint on white clay.

By AD 1400, the Mogollon culture had given way to another, more advanced group to the north – the Anasazi. Despite this cultural absorption, the modern Zuni Native Americans consider themselves to be the descendants of the ancient Mogollons.

The 'Vanished Ones'

At the same time as the Mogollons were flourishing, the Southwest region could boast another significant culture group living to the west – the Hohokam. The name comes from the Pima tribe of later centuries which referred to these ancient people as 'hohokam', 'the vanished ones'. These Southwest dwellers were located in south-central Arizona, in the valleys of the San Pedro, Salt and Gila rivers. They, too, were noted for their sustained agriculture, subterranean houses and pottery. Owing to the hostile desert environs of southern Arizona, the lands of the Hohokam did not support adequate small game or wild plants to provide this ancient people with food. Therefore, they relied almost totally on agriculture for their survival, unlike the hunter-gatherer Mogollons.

For this reason, the Hohokam were among the best irrigation engineers in the region. They not only built water canals and ditches to divert precious water to their fields, but they also constructed dams on neighbouring rivers. They used woven grass mats to open and close their diversion ditches to the fields which needed water. Their irrigation operations were so extensive that some Hohokam canals ran nearly 16km (10 miles) in length.

Beginning to develop as a distinct culture group as early as a century before Christ, the Hohokam cultural development is now divided into four stages: Pioneer (c. AD 1–600); Colonial (c. 600–900); Sedentary (c. 900–1100); and Classic (c. 1100–1400). These stages are marked by differences in how advanced the people of each stage are considered by archaeologists to have been.

The centre of the Hohokam culture was a village called Snaketown. This site was home for the Hohokam for 1,500 years. Located south of modern-day Phoenix, Snaketown included 100 underground pit dwellings, scattered over 120ha (300 acres). Their homes were similar to those of the Mogollons, but the Hohokam houses were larger.

Artistically, the Hohokam were in advance of their Mogollon neighbours. This was due, possibly, to their closer proximity to Meso-America (modern Mexico) to the south, where advanced cultures such as the Aztec may have had trade connections with the Hohokam people. As a result of this outside influence, the Hohokam were skilled with textiles, clay, metals and stone. These skills were acquired by the Hohokam of the Colonial Stage. Their red-on-buff pottery included clay human figures. They were excellent weavers. Among the artefacts uncovered by modern archaeologists in Hohokam settlements are copper items, mosaics, stoneware and even mirrors made of iron pyrites. Near their pit homes, the Hohokam played ball games on large courts using crude rubber balls. As a proof of trade between the American Southwest and the Meso-Americans, archaeologists have unearthed the skeletons of macaws, colourful birds indigenous to South and Central America. Apparently, the Hohokam kept them as pets.

The Sedentary Stage of the Hohokam featured more elaborate pottery with greater intricacy of design, using repeated geometric patterns. Ornamental items made from shells, which had made their way to the Southwest from the Pacific through trade, are counted among those of the Sedentary period. The Hohokam also developed the art of etching. Their artisans painted shells with pitch, then carved a design on the shell itself. Next, they washed the shell with an acid produced from the fermented fruit of the saguaro cactus. This 'etched' the shell. The pitch was then removed, leaving behind the permanent pattern of artwork. Also during the Sedentary Stage, the Hohokam began building above-ground pueblos similar to those of their neighbours.

By 1400 the Hohokam culture was in decline. Within a century, these people abandoned their primary settlement at Snaketown for reasons which remain unclear. Probably, anthropologists tell us, the region may have experienced an extensive drought, making sustained agriculture impossible. Although the Hohokam culture dwindled and died in around 1500, people remained in the region, and these people are today identified as the ancestors of the more modern Pima and Papago tribes.

The 'Ancient Ones'

A third cultural group to develop in the region of the ancient Southwest were the Anasazi, meaning 'ancient ones' in the Navajo language. The Anasazi culture began taking on its individual identity around 100 BC. These people lived in the region known as the 'four corners' plateau, where the states of Colorado, Utah, Arizona and New Mexico meet.

As with the Mogollons and the Hohokam, the Anasazi culture developed through a series of stages. The first stage is known as the Basket Maker. Spanning the four centuries prior to AD 400, this stage features many examples of finely woven baskets and sandals, made from available plants including straw, rushes and yucca. As with other contemporary cultures, the Anasazi lived in rounded pit houses, practised agriculture, hunted and gathered. They used spears, snares and a device called an 'atlatl' – a spear-throwing, hand-held catapult – for their hunting. These Anasazi lived in small villages.

The second phase of Anasazi culture is called the Modified Basket Maker Culture (c. AD 400–700). In this era, they lived in pit homes lined with flat stones and covered with wooden timbers and brush. The bow and arrow came into use, stone axes were developed and farming advanced to include the domestication of turkeys. Corn, beans, squash and cotton were grown. In the later years of the Modified Basket Maker

Culture, the Anasazi progressed in the decorative arts, creating turquoise bracelets, shell jewellery and clay effigies of human figures. By AD 750, they were also living in pueblos.

Over the next few centuries, during the third stage of cultural development called the Developmental Pueblo Period (c. AD 700–1100), the Anasazi developed more elaborate pueblo systems, building units which grouped rooms together and were multi-storeyed. The upper-storey apartments in such pueblos were reached by using wooden-pole ladders. Several such sites have been examined by modern archaeologists. Around AD 900, one of the most elaborate Anasazi pueblo systems was being developed. Today called Pueblo Bonito, the site is located in Chaco Canyon in northwestern New Mexico. Pueblo Bonito was an intricate complex of 800 rooms built in the shape of a semicircle. The pueblo rose from the desert floor to a height of five storeys. Additional structures dot the landscape near Pueblo Bonito, such as elaborate kivas and the remains of fire-beacon towers. Such a site may have supported over 1,000 people at one time. Pueblo Bonito is only one of the sites built by the Anasazi during the Developmental Pueblo Period.

Such pueblo-based culture reached its zenith during the period known as the Great Pueblo (c. AD 1100–1300). By this time, the Anasazi had clearly delineated divisions of labour among their workers, who included pueblo-builders, weavers, agriculturalists, potters and other craftsmen. Their artwork featured intricate pottery, turquoise jewellery, mosaics and brilliantly dyed textiles of cotton and feathers. Many of the elaborate pueblos, such as Pueblo Bonito, were abandoned during this stage, and other sites, especially cliff dwellings, were occupied. These structures were built into the cool shade of canyon walls; examples can be found in Mesa Verde in the southwestern corner of Colorado and Canyon de Chelly in northeastern Arizona.

Although the Anasazi were able to carve out a culture in the harsh landscape of the American Southwest with little technology at their service, still, ultimately, the environment proved too difficult. By the end of the thirteenth century, the Anasazi were abandoning their villages, cliff dwellings and pueblos and moving to other sites, many along major rivers in the Southwest,

including the Colorado and Rio Grande. The reason was, once again, drought. Anthropologists today have strong evidence pointing to a drought for the years 1276–99, which may have driven the Anasazi to river locales where water was more available. Other factors which may have driven the Anasazi from their homes include raids by nomads such as the Apaches or Utes, or something as simple as a lack of available wood for kiva timbers, pueblo support beams and the hundreds of campfires which lit up the night sky at Anasazi pueblo sites.

During the following 250 years (1300–1550) – the Regressive Pueblo Period – the Anasazi became the Native Americans of the Southwest, known today as the Pueblos. They continued to live in pueblo dwellings at sites which include the Verde Valley, the Tonto Basin and the river basin of the upper Salt. By 1450, many of those pueblos had been abandoned, so that when the Spaniards arrived in the Southwest in 1540 there were few Native Americans living in such apartment systems. When the Spanish explorer Francisco Coronado arrived in the Southwest in that year, the Pueblos were living in approximately 80 villages and numbered nearly 16,000 people. They were spread out from the Arizona settlements of the Hopi and Zuni to the eastern Pueblos found along the Rio Grande valley.

Modern Tribes of the Southwest

Anthropologists and historians know very few specifics concerning the history of the Native Americans known today as the Pueblos prior to the arrival of the Spaniards in the Southwest in 1540. Yet, after 1540, the record is a written one and the information becomes more abundant.

The Spanish dubbed these Southwestern people 'Pueblo' after the Spanish word for 'village', and this name is still used today. The term is a general one, and includes the tribes known as the Hopi and Zuni of the Colorado Plateau region. The Hopis lived in what is now the state of Arizona, while the Zunis lived in the western part of New Mexico. Other 'Pueblo' groups include those who have historically lived along a stretch, over 100 miles (150 km) in length, of the Rio Grande. These tribal groups include the Tiwa (or Tigua), the Tewa, the Towa (or Jemez) and the Keres. Each of these speaks a different language, but they are all descendants of the Anasazi and Mogollon peoples.

Other recorded Southwestern tribes were the Hualapai, Havasupai and Yavapai groups, known to be desert agriculturalists residing in central and northern Arizona; the River Yumans (the Yuma, Mojave, Cocopa and Maricopa), located in the southwestern quarter of Arizona; the Pimas and Papagos; and the Athapascans, a broad group which includes the Navajos and the Chiricahua, Mimbreno and Mescalero Apache groups.

The permanent communities of the Pueblos were the homes of a close-knit group of Native Americans, considered to have been peaceful and non-aggressive. The name for the Hopi, in fact, means 'peaceful ones'. The apartment-like pueblos provided the inhabitants of the village with their homes, but the real centres of life in the pueblo were the kivas.

Leadership in the Pueblo Communities

Unlike other North American tribes, such as the Great Plains Sioux who were directed by various warrior bands and societies, the Pueblo people were led by various religious societies. Each society met in a kiva in the village, and had responsibility for a specific task, such as hunting, military defence, political leadership or medicinal cures for tribal diseases. The societies were led by their own priests, each of whom was a member of a village council which handed down important decisions on behalf of the tribe. The council usually had a membership ranging from 10 to 30, and served as the tribal court, trying those accused of everything from tribal treason to witchcraft.

The Kachina

Perhaps the most important religious society of the Pueblos was the Kachina cult. All male members of a tribe served in this society, which was split into six divisions, representing north, south, east, west, 'up' and 'down'. Each had its own kiva or ceremonial chamber.

Kachina priests were responsible for everything to do with the tribal masked dances. In most tribes, each Kachina kiva group sponsored three dances per year. Kachina priests were considered to be representations or symbols of either the tribe's gods or the spirits of the dead. They donned masks and elaborate costumes for use during tribal ceremonies. A mask was made of painted leather, adorned with feathers, and covered the entire head of its wearer. Tribal members took the Kachina priests so seriously that they often considered the wearer of a Kachina mask actually to be the embodiment of the spirit or deity he represented. The Kachina mask was considered so potent a symbol that each one was burned after the death of its wearer.

Kachina priests often roamed within the village, making their presence known to all. They were extremely well respected, and were believed to have the power to bring rain, cause crops to grow and provide fertility to tribal women. Each had his own songs, poems and distinctive cry. Yet the Kachina priests were also often at work within the kivas, performing in secret rituals and ceremonies.

Mystical Centres

Kivas were usually circular religious centres, built in the ground as sunken chambers. The walls were stone-lined, and covered over with branches and earth, supported by cut log beams. The kivas were very symbolic places, shrouded in mystery, where women and children were not welcome. Boys between the ages of five and nine were initiated into the various cults which operated the kivas. During their first visit to a kiva, the boys were confronted by a tribal Kachina priest, who took initiates in hand and whipped them, ostensibly to drive out evil spirits and evil personal habits.

Later, when a youth reached puberty, he was returned to the kiva, again receiving a beating. This was followed by the Kachina priests removing their masks and revealing themselves to the young initiate. At this point, the youth was to vow he would keep the secrets of the Kachina and of the kiva, under the threat of extreme punishment. The boys were then instructed to scourge the Kachinas themselves. Over the intervening months, such young men were given instruction in the secrets of the kiva, while they learned the rites and ceremonies which went with Kachina membership. However, such men had to marry before they could be considered full members of the society and become Kachinas themselves.

Domestic Life Among the Pueblos

Pueblo men and women were often skilled in crafts, producing a variety of goods including baskets, pottery and clothing. Textile manufacture was a well-developed art form among these tribes. Although clothing manufacture was generally considered to be women's work by other tribes in North America, many Pueblo tribes considered it to be men's work. Cotton products were woven by men, who prepared the cotton by carding and spinning it into thread. They worked the thread on large looms which could be found in either their personal apartments or in a kiva. The cloth produced by Pueblo men was often dyed in a variety of colours, including red, yellow, brown, green, orange and black. A rainbow of coloured threads was used by the men to produce brilliantly coloured blankets, shirts, kilts and sashes. Women might also have woven on looms, but generally they only produced rabbitskin blankets.

Pueblo women wore simple cotton dresses, brush sandals or boots, and often deerskin and rabbitskin clothing as well. They wore their hair in a variety of styles, some of which indicated the marital status of a young girl. Girls wore their hair long and unbraided until they reached puberty, after which a young girl experienced the Girls' Adolescent Ceremony. Then unmarried Zuni and Hopi women wove their hair into large coils located just above their ears. This style was referred to as 'squash blossoms' or 'butterfly wings'. Once married, women normally let their hair hang down in braids behind the shoulders.

In general, Pueblo men wore cotton kilts over a loincloth and leather sandals. The men might also have worn 'shirts', made by cutting a head-hole in the middle of a piece of rectangular cotton cloth. They wore their hair long and kept it tied up at the back in a knot. They also kept their fringes long in front, letting the hair fall over their foreheads.

Basketry and pottery were considered women's work among the Pueblos. Basket styles and adornments varied from tribe to tribe. Baskets were often woven into shallow containers and coloured with vegetable dyes of yellow, purple, green, blue and black, often in geometric patterns for artistic emphasis. Some pottery was considered merely utilitarian and consisted of unadorned pots for cooking and food storage. Other pieces of pottery were highly decorated for ceremonial use or for their aesthetic beauty. Pottery was made from local clay deposits, using the coiling and firing method.

The cooking was done by the women. Most Southwestern tribes who practised sustained agriculture relied greatly on maize, or corn, as their main food crop. Among the Hopi, for example, three types were grown: flint, flour and sweet. The flint variety had a tough grain and stored well over long periods of time, but was difficult to grind. The most popular type was the flour variety, which grew in several strains such as white and blue (although 20 different varieties of flour existed among the Southwestern tribes), and was used for making cornflour. Small amounts of sweetcorn were grown to supplement the Native American diet.

Dozens of dishes were prepared in the Southwest using corn as the basis. Cornflour was made into gruel, bread, corn soup and dumplings. The Pueblos also boiled corn into hominy. Corn-on-the-cob was considered an excellent food, and popcorn was popular. Another food, which resembled popcorn, involved soaking the corn kernels in salt water and cooking them in heated sand. Pueblo women baked a corn-based bread called 'piki', which was cooked on a specially prepared stone slab over a fire.

Although the centrepiece of the Pueblo diet was corn (it was, in fact, their symbol of life) in its various forms, many other foods were also available. Prior to contact with the Spanish in the sixteenth century, Southwestern Native Americans relied on primary crops such as kidney and tepary beans, maize and squash, but other crops which might have been grown then include gourds, sunflowers, and lima and Aztec beans. Additional foods introduced by the Spanish were wheat, onions, peaches, watermelons and the now ever-present food symbol of the Southwest – the chilli. As well as these domesticated plants, grains and crops, the Southwestern people ate as many as 60 different wild plants and greens. Other plants, including tobacco, were grown and harvested for ceremonial and medicinal purposes.

Hunting by the Pueblo men supplemented the diets of their villagers. Antelopes were sometimes chased down by hunters and suffocated. Deer were hunted with bows and arrows. Rabbits and coyotes were often surrounded by parties of men, who formed a circle and then closed in, killing their quarry with clubs and boomerangs. The men returned from the hunt and gave their catches to a wife, mother, sister or aunt, who would cook the meat, often preparing an offering to the God of the Hunt by adding an animal's gall to a cake of piki bread, and throwing the offering into a fire pit.

Prepared for Battle

The Pueblo Native Americans were a peaceful, even gentle, people who did not tend to wage offensive war. However, they would defend their pueblos from outside attack, and warrior societies did exist among the Pueblos. Membership was required of all males, who were divided by various military ranks. Boys were trained at an early age, being put through a preparation regime which included extensive practice with the bow and arrow, foot races and early morning cold baths.

In combat, Pueblo warriors did not wear special clothing except for caps fashioned from mountain-lion skin adorned with eagle feathers. Pueblo weaponry included bows and arrows, as well as spears, boomerangs and stone-headed clubs. Prior to a battle, the warriors participated in rituals which included praying, smoking and singing. When a foe was vanquished, Pueblo warriors scalped the victims, while chanting a scalping song. Warriors returned to their villages carrying their enemies' scalps on poles. Apache and Ute scalps were highly prized, whereas the hair lock of a Navajo was considered insignificant.

Marriage and Family Life

Pueblo men and women practised monogamy, generally keeping a spouse for life. Their courtship practices were few and generally sexually unrestricted. A boy interested in a Pueblo girl showed his interest by visiting her at night in her own lodge, covered in a blanket. If the girl was willing, the two engaged in sexual intercourse. This ritual, called the 'dumaiya', did not restrict the number of sexual partners a boy or girl might have. Often, such activity led to a girl's pregnancy, in which case she picked the boy she most wanted to marry, declaring the child to be his.

Divorce was not unheard of among the Pueblos, and was simple to accomplish. Any woman who wished to divorce her husband had only to take her spouse's belongings and place them outside the door of their dwelling. By this act, she declared her divorce from her husband, and he had little choice in the matter, except to gather his personal goods up and return to the pueblo of his mother.

As their divorce process indicates, the Pueblos lived in a society where households were dominated by a matrilineal structure. The women – including the grandmother, her daughters and her granddaughters – comprised the core of the family unit, with husbands and unmarried sons rounding out the unit's identity.

Navajos and Apaches

Compared to the Pueblo Native Americans, the Navajos and the Apaches, both Athapascan-speaking peoples, arrived in the Southwest much later than the Pueblos. Archaeological evidence indicates that the first Apache arrivals settled in the Southwest around AD 825 and that another 200 years would pass before the coming of the Navajo. Both these groups survived for generations as nomadic bands of hunters and gatherers. They frequently launched offensive raids against their neighbours, the sedentary Pueblos, capturing food, women, domestic items and slaves.

In time, however, the nomadic Navajos became much like their Pueblo neighbours, adapting their culture to include sustained agriculture. They acquired such domestic skills as pottery and basket-weaving. After making contact with the Spanish, Navajo men began acquiring herds of sheep and goats. These domesticated animals provided the Navajo with meat, milk and wool for clothing and blankets. Not until the late seventeenth century did the Navajo acquire horses, which they then used in their continuing raids on their enemies, a practice that had not ended with their increasingly agriculture-based culture.

By the late 1700s and early 1800s, the Navajos were counted among the enemies of the Spanish, and raided their villages in a regular cycle of violence. In part, this raid-and-counter-raid cycle of the Navajos was provoked by the Spanish and, later, Mexican practice of kidnapping Navajo children.

Just as the Navajo had been when they entered the American Southwest, the Apaches remained primarily a nomadic hunter-gatherer society. They migrated south around the ninth century, coming from as far north as Canada. Their diet consisted of rabbit, antelope and deer meat, together with supplements of elk and mountain sheep, and wild plants, including cactus and mesquite seeds. Apache women gathered local wild produce such as wild onions, acorns, piñon nuts, juniper berries, mescal cactus fruit and mesquite beans. When food sources did not provide an adequate diet, the Apaches attacked neighbouring tribes of farmers such as the Pueblos, and later the Spanish, Mexicans and, eventually, the Anglo-Americans.

The Apaches lived in primitive huts called 'wickiups', which were conical lodges featuring a wooden-pole framework covered with branches, twigs and grasses. These lodges were small, squat homes that provided shelter for four or five people, with little room for anything else. Animal skins were used in cold weather to cover the wickiups, helping to insulate the hut. Some Apaches, notably the Jicarilla and Kiowa groups, lived in tepees similar to those of the Plains tribes.

Apache Clothing and Crafts

The Apaches did not generally grow cotton or raise sheep for wool, and they tended to wear leather clothing, although they did acquire cotton and woollen clothes from their neighbours through continuous raids. They also acquired sheep, which they chose to eat rather than tend. The men wore their hair long, without braids, as did the women. Women wore two-piece dresses made of animal hide, and both sexes wore high-topped moccasins. Jewellery was common among both men and women, with each wearing earrings, bracelets and necklaces. They rarely used feathers for outer ornamentation.

Pottery was not a noted craft, but basket-weaving was a fine art among Apache craftsmen, who wove intricate baskets featuring elaborate designs. By the time of white contact in the Southwest, Apache basket-weavers were producing a musical instrument called the Apache fiddle. It consisted of a round and hollowed musical tube, woven from a yucca stalk, and a single string attached to a knob which could be turned for tuning. Apache musicians used a sinew and wood bow to play this musical instrument.

Apache Political and Religious Practices

The Apaches operated in bands, as subdivisions of their tribes. Each band consisted of several extended families and was led by a warrior known for his courage and military experience.

The Apache men belonged to societies, similar to the Pueblo Kachinas, and dressed up to imitate the mountain gods, known as the Gans. Their costumes included tall, wooden headdresses and black masks, as well as elaborate body paint. The Apaches recognized some Gans as evil, others as good, and they created elaborate dance rituals to recognize these gods and their power.

Religion and Mythology

Navajo beliefs included a reliance on powerful shamans or great medicine men who were considered to have direct connections to the spirit world. In that hidden and distant realm resided the spirits of Navajo ancestors and the gods of the tribe, who represented entities important to the tribe such as the sun, thunder, the rainbow and maize. A powerful and well-connected shaman (connected with the spirit world) was believed to have the gift of prophecy, the power to ensure a bountiful harvest and the ability to cure the sick.

To become a shaman, a boy of usually 12 years of age would be sent out of the village for several days, with the goal of discovering a spirit protector. During his quest, he denied himself food and offered up many prayers. Ultimately, he sought a vision in which he might receive a revelation. Such visions might feature a talking animal or, with even greater significance, a god promising to serve as the spiritual connection for the young shaman initiate. Upon returning to his village, the young man would relate his vision to his people and they would decide if his contacts were powerful enough to ensure him a role as spiritual leader of the tribal unit.

Shamans engaged in many ceremonial rituals. To illustrate their beliefs, they created elaborate sand paintings, 'drawings' made from sands of various colours, each of which carried a special power and purpose. As they created such works of art, the shamans would chant and sing special songs.

The colours used in sand paintings were highly symbolic. The Navajo divided the earth into four parts (the cardinal points of the compass), each identified by a specific colour: white, symbolizing the dawn, for the east; blue, for the sky, representing the south; the colour of the sunset, yellow, for the west; and black, symbol of the night sky, for the north. To keep the colour code consistent, shamans used white shells in the 'eastern' portion of sand paintings; turquoise for the south; haliotis shells for the west; and black cannel-coal for the north. Other colours symbolized the inclusion of animals, birds or corn in the sand paintings.

Many of the myths of the Navajo reflect the general themes found among traditional Native American stories. They include tales of the creation of the earth and of the first man and woman. Many of their stories serve as poetic expressions of interactions between men and their gods, much in the same way as classical Greek mythology brought mortals and immortals into transworld interplay. A recurring character in several Southwestern myths is Coyote, a talking animal who represents the trickster motif common to stories found in other Native American regions of North America.

Gods and Goddesses

Southwestern tribal deities include a broad pantheon of spirits. Greatest among them is Awonawilona, as called by the Zuni, who represented the supreme power in the universe and the creator of life. This deity was not recognized as either male or female, but was referred to as He-She. Chief among the other gods are Father Sun and Mother Earth. Each is known by a variety of names in Southwestern myths. The Hopi refer to the sun as Heart of the Sky, and mother earth as Old Woman, Spider Woman, Corn Maiden, Goddess of Growth and Mother of Germs or Seed.

Other deities worthy of attention among the Southwestern tribes are the Moon Mother and the Morning and Evening Stars, as well as the deities of several of the constellations, including the Pleiades, Orion, Ursa Major and Ursa Minor.

Creatures and monsters also inhabit the Southwestern pantheon. A great god-monster of the Zuni was one called Achiyalatopa. The Zuni and the Hopi both acknowledge a being known as the Plumed Serpent, called Koloowisi by the Zuni and Palulukon by the Hopi. The Plumed Serpent was symbolized by lightning and associated with fertility. The serpent and its shifting movements were considered to be connected to the zigzag of the lightning, which brought the rain to the desert and mesa lands, giving life to the fields of the Native Americans of the Southwest. One group of gods included the Anaye, or Alien Gods, who are known in the mythology as powerful destroyers of humans. This category included monsters, menacing giants and frightening bogeys. Other destructive and evil gods included the Tshindi, the Devils of the Southwest. Key among them is the Corpse Spirit which accompanied a deceased human's soul on its way to the underworld.

To provide comfort to the Navajo, and to counter the threat of the Alien Gods, the tribe recognized a pair of brothers, Nayanezgani, the Slayer of the Alien Gods, and Thobadzistshini, Child of the Waters. Some stories refer to them as the Sun-Carrier and Estsanatlehi. The task of these two deities was to battle against the Alien Gods and overthrow this menacing force, thus neutralizing them for all time. Just as Mount Olympus was regarded as the home of the Greek gods, the Navajo believed that these two brother deities lived in the mountains in the midst of Navajo country. Navajo warriors often approached these mountains with reverence and looked for guidance through prayer and chant from the powerful pair who dwelled in the mountainous peaks.

MYTHS AND LEGENDS
OF THE SOUTHWEST

THE CREATION

Navajo

NEAR THE PLACE-WHERE-THEY-CAME-UP were two buttes which looked alike, and over the top of one, when the First People emerged, there was always a cloud. In this cloud there was a light like a lot of rainbows tied up together. The First People had a man who was their scout and they sent him to see what caused the cloud. He came back and told them there was a big pool of water under the cloud with beautiful flowers all around it, and the mud of the shore was formed of sacred corn pollen. They would not believe the scout, so he went back and brought down a little pinch of the corn pollen. When the people saw that it was the sacred pollen, they held a council and decided to make something which should be perfect and eternal, something which would rule over them and tell them what to do, something they could pray to and sing to.

So first, they went out and ran down 12 big deer which they killed with their bare hands, so there would be no mark of arrows on them, and tanned the 12 perfect skins. Then they laid them down and all the people (or the elements) gathered together to make 'The Something'! The right leg was made first. Its skeleton was made of white shell, the common white beads that the Indians wear; the flesh was made of the sacred corn pollen, but the foot was very rough and had no toes. Then the heat-lightning, which flashes up in the clouds at nights, said, 'I will make the toes – I will make them just right – you can leave it all to me.' Then with a flash he split out one toe after the other, but the foot and the leg up to the knee still had no joint.

Then the Sun's rays that shine so bright at midday and blind people, said, 'I will make the joints – I will make them right – I will do it all myself.' So with his rays he broke the leg and made all the joints, but they came apart and would not stay together.

Then the Dawn took its long rays and bound the joints together tight, but the foot could not move. So the Eternal Wind said, 'I will go down into the leg – I will tell it which way to go – you can leave it all to me!'

The Something was formed as far up as the knee, but there were no veins and no blood. Then the Red Corn said, 'I will go down into the leg.' And it formed the veins and the blood.

Now the body was built up as far as the waist and they had a big Council whether to make The Something a man or a woman. At last they decided to make it a woman, but they had nothing to make the big arteries around the groin. Then the Striped Corn went down into the body and made those arteries and The

Source

Mary Roberts Coolidge, *The Rain-Makers: Indians of Arizona and New Mexico*, Boston: Houghton Mifflin Co., 1929, pp. 182–85

When the Goddess was formed they put a beautiful feather in her hair and on top of her head they put a round crystal like a turquoise.

Something was a woman. The intestines were made from the long sun-dogs or rays of the Sun, the ribs were made from white shell, the floating ribs that protect the stomach were made from two abalone shells, the heart was made from solid turquoise, the liver from ground corn and the lungs from ground corn, which is why they are so white.

Now the body was formed up to the neck and they made the two arms in the same way as the two legs. When it came to the windpipe, the Eternal Wind said, 'I will go down – I will make it right – you can leave it all to me!'

So he went down into the throat and lungs and formed them; the collar bones were made from the little half-rainbows that you see in the clouds and the jaw was made from another half-rainbow. The teeth and bones were made from white shell, the nose was formed by the Wind and the eyes were made by the Moon and the Sun. The Moon formed the ball of the eyes and the Sun said, 'I will go into it – I will give her light to look around and see!' The pupil of the eye is the Sun and the ball of the eye is the Moon. The ears were formed by the Wind, the way it makes patterns in the sand. Then the Wind went into her ears to make her hear.

Now the Goddess was all made but her hair, which was formed by Night and Dark Cloud together. That is why the Indians' hair is so black, but when it was formed the Rainbow combed it down as far as the Goddess's knees, which is what gives their hair such a sheen when it is wet.

Now the Goddess was all formed, but she could not move nor talk. The Wind said, 'I will go down into her – I will make her walk.' So he did and she could stand up and walk. When she stood up, they put a beautiful feather straight up in her hair behind, and on top of her head they put a round crystal like a turquoise. When this was there, a Bluebird flew and lit on the crystal and began to sing and the words went down into the Goddess's mouth, so that she talks as the Bluebird sings. Only the people who have learned to talk like the Bluebird have any great happiness. If they will not listen and learn her song, they are always having trouble and lose everything.

Now the Goddess was all formed, but she did not talk nor have anything to say and the Dark Cloud said, 'I will go down into her – I will make her talk – you can leave it all to me!' So he went down into her mouth and she talked.

At this time she was very small, only about three feet high, but they put her on the 12 medicine buckskins and in four days she grew up to be a woman. When she had her first flow of blood, the people sang over her for four days, which is the origin of the ceremonial at puberty. (It was prophesied that this song would always be sung over the girls of the Navajos as long as they lived in the world.)

When the Goddess was finished, the people said, 'Everybody has helped to make her except the Earth and the Blue Sky.'

'I will be under her feet and support her,' said the Earth. 'I will feed and take care of her.'

'I will look down on the Earth and make her fertile,' said the Blue Sky. 'I will send the rain to make things grow.' So they all had a part in the creation.

THE MAIDEN HUNTRESS

Zuni

NEAR K'YANAWE, in the days of the ancients, there lived a poor maiden with her feeble old father and her aged mother. Her brothers had all been killed in the wars, so the family lived there helplessly.

It is true that they had a small garden – a little planting of beans, pumpkins, squashes, melons and corn – and the maiden was able to take care of this very well, and it was because of this that the family had food. Sometimes, however, they wished for meat, and, as there was no man to go to the hunt and bring back the deer and rabbits for them, they had no way in which to get it.

Long before the family had had plenty, the house had been great, for there were many brave and strong young men who had lived in it; but the rooms were empty now, and only relics of the past remained.

One autumn day, near winter time, snow fell and it became very cold. The maiden had gathered a great pile of brush and firewood, and, as she went to get an armful in the early morning, she saw the young men leaving the village in great numbers. Their feet were protected by long stockings of deerskin, the fur turned inward, and they carried stone axes and rabbit-sticks on their shoulders and stuck in their belts. And as she watched them from the roof of her house, she said to herself, 'O, how I wish that I were a man and could go out and hunt for rabbits as these young men do. Then my poor old mother and father would not lack for meat.'

That night she saw the same young men coming in, some of them bringing long strings of rabbits, others short ones, but none of them empty-handed. Then she decided that, even though she was a maiden, she would set forth the next morning to try what luck she might find in the killing of rabbits herself.

It may seem strange that although this maiden was beautiful and young, the youths did not give her some of their rabbits. But their feelings were not friendly, for one after another these young men had offered themselves for marriage, and she would not accept any of them for a husband. So they went past the poor girl on the house-top, never lifting their eyes in her direction.

That evening the maiden sat down by the fireplace, and, turning toward her old parents, said, 'Dear mother and father, I see that the snow has fallen, and rabbits are easily tracked. The young men of the village who went out this morning returned carrying heavy strings of this game. In the other rooms of our house many rabbit-sticks and stone axes hang on the walls. If I take one of the rabbit-sticks I might strike down a rabbit, or, if he ran into a log, an axe would split it, and I could dig him out. I have thought during this whole day, and I have decided to go out in the early morning and hunt, as do the youths of our people.'

'Naiya, my daughter,' quavered the old mother. 'You would surely be very cold, or you would lose your way, or grow so tired that you could not return before night. Remember that you are a maiden, and it is not right that you should go out and hunt rabbits.'

'Why, certainly not,' insisted the old man, rubbing his lean knees, and shaking his grey head over the days that were gone. 'No, no; let us live in poverty rather than you should run such risks as these, my dear daughter.'

Source
Aileen
Nusbaum, *Zuni
Indian Tales*,
New York: G.P.
Putnam's Sons,
1926, pp. 27–36

But, say what they would, the girl was determined. And the old man said at last, 'Very well! You will not be turned from your course; therefore I will help you.' He hobbled into another room, and found there some old deerskins covered with fur. He drew them out, and, after moistening them, he carefully softened them, and cut out long stockings for the maiden, which he sewed up with sinew and the fibre of the yucca leaf. Then he selected for her from the old possessions of his brothers and sons a number of rabbit-sticks and a fine heavy stone axe. Meanwhile the old mother busied herself in preparing food for the girl. There were little cakes of corn-meal, spiced with pepper and wild onions, pierced through the middle and baked in the ashes. And when she had made a long string of these by threading them like beads on a rope of yucca fibre, she laid them down on a little bench with the rabbit-sticks, the stone axe and the deerskin stockings.

Early the next morning, long before the young men were about, the maiden was up. She put on a short-skirted dress, knotted a mantle over her shoulder, and threw another and larger one over her back. She drew on her deerskin stockings, and, sticking the rabbit-sticks in her belt, she tied the corn-cakes to the knot of her mantle. Taking the stone axe in her hand, she went out. She walked eastward toward the plain and into the valley called the Burnt River, on account of the black, roasted-looking rocks along some parts of its sides.

Dazzlingly white, the snow stretched out before her, and when she came near the cliffs with many little canyons in them she saw the trails of rabbits running in and out among the rocks and bushes.

Warm and excited by her exercises, she did not heed a coming snowstorm, but ran about from one place to another, following the trails of the rabbits, sometimes up into canyons, where the forest of piñon and cedar stood. She had the good fortune to run two, three or four rabbits into a single log. It was not hard to split these logs with her stone axe, and after killing each rabbit she raised it carefully and breathed the prayer of thanksgiving upon it. Then she tied their legs together and placed them on the string which after a while, because of her success, began to grow heavy on her shoulders.

She kept on, little heeding the snow which was falling fast, nor did she notice that it was growing darker and darker. The poor girl was so happy to think that she, a maiden, could kill game as the youths did; and from now on she could supply her old parents with fresh meat. 'How strong my poor dear ones will grow now,' she cried, and she ran on faster than ever.

At last the twilight came, and, looking around, she found that the snow had fallen deeply, there was no trail, and she had lost her way. She turned about and started in the direction of her home, as she supposed, walking as fast as she could through the soft, deep snow. But she went southward, and, as it grew dark, she thought it best to find a shelter among the rocks, and there to spend the night, and wait the coming of the morning.

'By light I shall know my way,' she said.

Fortunately, among the rocks which appeared black and dim was a cave. She soon came to it, and, looking into the black hole, she saw far in the back a little glow-light.

'Ah!' thought she. 'Some rabbit-hunters like myself must have passed the night here, and left the fire burning. This is greater good fortune than I could have looked for.'

Each of the
War-Gods hit
the Demon
a terrific blow
with his
war-club.

So, lowering the string of rabbits which she carried on her shoulder, she crawled in, peering well into the darkness for fear of wild beasts, then, returning, she drew in the string of rabbits.

The girl found a bed of hot coals buried under the ashes in the very middle of the cave, and piled up on one side were pieces of broken wood. She gathered more wood from the cliff side, and, by bringing them in in little armfuls, she finally succeeded in gathering a store that would keep the fire burning brightly all the night through. Then she drew off the snow-covered stockings of deerskin and the bedraggled mantles, and, hanging them up in front of the fire to dry, she sat down to rest herself. The fire burned up and glowed so that the whole cave was as light as a room at night when a dance is being celebrated.

After her clothing had dried, the maiden spread a mantle on the floor of the cave by the side of the fire, and, sitting down, dressed one of her rabbits and roasted it. She untied the string of corn-cakes her mother had given her, and she feasted on the roasted meat and the cakes.

She had just finished eating and was about to lie down by the side of the fire, when she heard away off in the distance a long, low cry of distress.

'Ah!' thought the maiden, 'Someone like myself is lost in the storm.' She got up and went nearer to the entrance of the cavern.

'Ho-o-o-o!' sounded the cry, nearer this time. She ran out and cried as loudly as possible, 'Here! Here!'

The cry was repeated, and presently the maiden, listening first and then shouting, and listening again, heard the clatter of an enormous rattle. In terror she threw her hands into the air, and, crouching down, rushed into the cavern. She tried to hide in the darkest corner, and she trembled for fear as she knew that one of the dreadful Cannibal Demons had seen the light of her fire through the cave entrance; and, pretending to be a lost hunter, had cried out for help and been led to her cave.

On came the Demon, snapping the twigs under his feet and shouting in a hoarse, loud voice now, 'Ho! So you are in there, are you?' He clanged his rattle, while, almost fainting from fear, closer to the rock crouched the poor girl.

The old Demon came to the entrance of the cave and bawled out, 'I am cold, I am hungry. Let me in.' And he tried to get in, but the entrance was too small for his giant shoulders to pass, so he said, 'Come out, and bring me something to eat.'

'I have nothing for you,' cried the maiden.

'Have you no rabbits?' asked the Demon.

'Yes,' answered the maiden faintly.

'Then come out and bring me some of them.'

But the maiden was so terrified that she dared not move toward the entrance.

'Throw me a rabbit!' shouted the old Demon.

The maiden threw him one of her precious rabbits.

'Throw me another,' he yelled, and so on until at last the maiden said, 'I have no more.'

'Then throw me your overshoes,' he cried.

And the maiden threw out the stockings of deerskin; and these, like the rabbits, he swallowed. Then he called for her moccasins, and she threw them; for her belt, and she threw it; and finally she was forced to throw him her mantles and her overdress, and she had hardly anything left.

'Come out yourself,' shouted the Demon, but the girl would not, so, becoming very angry, he lifted his great flint axe and began to shatter the rock about the entrance of the cave.

In the distance the two War-Gods were sitting in their home on To'yallanne, and they heard the pounding of the Demon's hammer-axe against the rocks.

They knew at once that the poor maiden, for the sake of her father and mother, had been out hunting. They knew that she had lost her way and had crawled into the little cave, and that the light of her fire had attracted the Demon. So, catching up their wonderful weapons, these two War-Gods flew away into the darkness and they arrived at the cave just as the Demon was about to enter it. Each one hit him a terrific blow with his war-club, killing him. They flung the huge body of the giant Demon down into the depths of the Canyon, and, turning, called out gentle words to the maiden.

She looked out, and, seeing the two handsome youths, was greatly comforted. But she crouched low with shame, for the Demon had eaten her garments, and she dared not come out from the shelter. The Gods, understanding this, made from their magic beautiful clothing, and gave them to her, and then, spreading their mantles by the door of the cave, they slept there that night in order to protect the maiden.

On the morrow they wakened her, and, speaking kindly, they told her that a maiden should marry, and that she must return to her people, and look with favour upon the youth that would court her that day.

Then the two Gods threw their sticks into the yucca plants nearby, and at once there appeared two great strings of rabbits. When the sun burned clear in the sky, they each took a string of the rabbits, and then, laying hold of the maiden's hands, they led her out of the cave, and down into the valley and to the very outskirts of the village. Then the two War-Gods turned to her and said, 'Forget not the words of Ahaiyuta the Elder and Matsailema the Young.'

The maiden bent low and breathed on their hands, and, dropping the strings of rabbits which they carried, they swiftly disappeared in a whirlwind.

Thinking much of all she had learned, the maiden continued her way to the home of her father and mother. She went through the town, dressed in the beautiful robes the Gods had given her, and dragging the strings of rabbits behind her.

The young men and the older men and the women and the children beheld her in wonder. No hunter in all of Cibola could compare himself with the maiden huntress.

And, when she arrived at her home, her old father and mother received her joyfully. She told them of her adventure, and of the two wonderful youths, and of what they had told her.

Then, that evening, while they were sitting around their fire, the most splendid youth in the village presented himself with a bundle. The maiden, smilingly and delightedly, accepted him, and there was great happiness.

THE GIANT CACTUS

Papagos

IN A CERTAIN VILLAGE there lived a girl who did not wish to marry. This girl would never listen to the women when they tried to teach her things. All she wanted was to play taw-kah all day long. Taw-kah is a game very much like shinny or hockey, played by women. And this girl was a very swift runner and such a good player that the people who bet on her would always win.

Finally the girl's father and mother grew tired of her playing taw-kah all the time. So they married their daughter to a good man. And they made her a fine new house where she and her husband went to live.

But very soon the new house was dirty. There were never any beans ready for the husband when he came from the fields. Again the young woman was spending all her time playing taw-kah.

At last the young woman's husband grew tired of the dirty house and of having to work all day and then prepare his own supper. So he went away and left her.

After a while the woman had a son. The older women of the village thought that surely now this young mother would stop running about playing her favourite game. But the young mother filled a big gourd with milk and put it beside her baby. Then she fixed her hair with a bright feather and put beads around her neck and went out to play taw-kah just as she had always done.

But the women of the village did not like to play taw-kah with anyone who always won. And they did not like to think of this young woman's baby alone, crying. So the women of the kee-him – village – would not play with this young mother. And she went over the mountain to another village where the people did not know her. She played taw-kah with the women of this kee-him, and went to a more distant village where she continued to win.

Now, when this woman's child was left alone he began to grow. He looked around the room and saw all the beads and feathers and baskets which his mother had won playing taw-kah. He saw the gourd full of milk. He drank the milk and grew larger and larger.

Then he arose and put a feather in his hair and took all the bright things which his mother had won and went outside the house.

When the women of the kee-him saw the boy they said, 'Here is the boy without a mother.'

But the boy said, 'No, I have a mother but she is playing taw-kah somewhere. Can you tell me where?'

The women could only tell the boy that his mother had gone away over the mountains.

So the boy started after his mother. He carried all the things which his mother had won from the other women. And as he travelled he gave these things to the people who gave him food. But the way was very long.

After a time the boy came to some cultivated fields which belonged to a man who had a great deal of wheat and was busy clearing out the weeds. And the boy asked his question again: where could he find his mother?

And the man answered that he knew the boy's mother well. He said she was always playing taw-kah and always winning; that she always wore a bright

Source
Harold Bell Wright, *Long Ago Told: Legends of The Papago Indians*, New York: D. Appleton & Co., 1929, pp. 109–22

Crow gathered the fruit as Chief had told him to do, and flew slowly back to the village.

feather in her hair; and that she was in a kee-him on the other side of a black mountain.

So the boy started up the black mountain. The trail was long. Sometimes Hoo-e-chut – a lizard – would stop long enough to laugh at him. Sometimes Oo-oo-fick – the birds – would fly very near and tell him not to be troubled.

Finally the boy reached the top of the black mountain and saw the village which lay below. There were some women playing taw-kah. And as the boy watched he saw a young woman who always won. And in this one's hair there was a bright feather.

The boy went on down the mountain to the village. But he did not go into the kee-him. He stopped in an arroyo near where there were children playing. And the boy asked one of the children to go to the woman who was playing taw-kah – the woman who had a bright feather in her hair and who always won – and tell her that her son had come and wanted to see his mother.

The child carried the boy's message.

But the woman answered, 'I will come as soon as I win this game.'

The boy waited some time. Then he sent another child with a message to his mother.

But the boy's mother had not yet won that game of taw-kah, so she sent the same message back that she would surely come when she had won.

Again the boy waited. And the boy was hungry. So he sent the third child to his mother begging her to please come soon because he wanted to see her.

But this game of taw-kah was very long and the boy's mother had to run very swiftly. So she answered the messenger, 'Yes, yes, tell him I will come when I win this game.'

When the third messenger returned the boy was angry. And he asked the children to help him find the hole of Hee-ah-e – a tarantula.

When they had found a tarantula's hole the boy asked the children to help him sing. So ah-ah-lee – the children – formed a ring around the boy and began to dance and sing. And as the boy and the children danced and sang the boy sank into the tarantula's hole. With the first song he sank as far as his knees. He asked the children to sing louder and to dance harder. And as they circled around him singing and dancing he kept on sinking into the ground.

When only the boy's shoulders were above ground one of the children ran to his mother, who was still playing taw-kah, and told her she must come quickly because the boy was almost buried in a tarantula's hole.

The mother dropped her taw-kah stick and ran as fast as she could. But the sun was in the mother's eyes and she could not see to go very swiftly. And when she reached the arroyo there was nothing to be seen but a bright feather sticking out of a tarantula hole. And the sand was closing around the feather.

Then the woman began to cry.

And Pahn – the coyote – who was passing, came to see what all the noise was about.

The mother told Pahn that her son had just been buried in the tarantula's hole, and she asked him to help her dig her son out of the ground.

Pahn told the woman he thought he could get her son out. And he began to dig, and found that the boy was not very deep in the ground.

Now, Pahn was hungry with all his work, and he didn't see why he should take

this boy to a mother who had never done anything for her son. So he ate the boy. When the bones were well cleaned Pahn took them out of the hole and gave them to the woman with the bright feather. And Pahn said to the woman, 'Someone must have eaten your son. This is all I could find.'

The woman with the bright feather looked at the bones. But the bones of her son were not very bright and so she had no use for them. She told Pahn to bury them again, which he did.

Four days later something green came out of the ground on the spot where the boy's bones were buried. In four more days this green thing was ah-lee-choom hah-shahn – a baby saguaro. And this was the first saguaro, or giant cactus, in all the world.

This giant cactus was a very strange thing. It was just a tall, thick, soft, green thing growing out of the ground.

All the Indians and all the animals came to look at it. Ah-ah-lee – the children – played around it and stuck sticks into it. This hurt Hah-shahn and he put out long sharp needles for protection so the children could not touch him. Then ah-ah-lee took their bows and arrows and shot at Hah-shahn. This made Hah-shahn very angry. He sank into the ground and went away where no one could find him and he could live in peace.

After Hah-shahn disappeared the people were sorry and began looking for him. They hunted over all the mountains near the village. They asked all the animals and birds to help them.

After a very long time Ha-vahn-e – the crow – wandered over Kee-ho Toahk, which means Burden Basket Mountain. And Crow told the people that he had seen a very large cactus where there was nothing but rocks and where no animals nor Indians ever hunted.

Kooh – the chief – called a council of all the animals and the people. And Kooh told the people to prepare four large round baskets. Then Chief gave Crow orders to fly back to the giant cactus, and told him what he should do when he arrived.

When Crow reached the giant cactus he found the top covered with fruit. The fruit was red and large and full of juice and sugar. Crow gathered the fruit as Chief had told him to do, and flew slowly back to the village.

The people were waiting.

And Crow put Hah-shahn pah-hee-tahch – the cactus fruit – into ollas, which are large jars, and which were filled with water. Chief placed the ollas on the fire and from sunrise to sunset the fruit was kept boiling.

For four days this see-toe-ly – syrup – was cooked. Then Kooh – the chief – told all the people to prepare for a nah-vite ee – special feast – which is wine feast, or wine drinking. They were to have a wine which they had never had before.

Oo-oo-fick – the birds – were the quickest to get ready for the feast. They came dressed in red and black and yellow. Some of the smaller ones were all in blue. Then Kaw-koy – the rattlesnake – came crawling in. And Kaw-koy was all painted in very brilliant colours.

The birds did not like it because Kaw-koy was painted so bright. They gossiped and scolded and were jealous. Kaw-koy heard Oo-oo-fick talking and rolled himself in some ashes. And that is why, even in these days, you will find the skin of Kaw-koy marked with grey. The grey markings are where the ashes were caked onto his new paint.

Choo-ah-tuck – the Gila monster – gathered bright pebbles and made himself a very beautiful coat. And the Gila monster's beautiful coat was very hard. You can see it today because he is still wearing it.

So all the people and animals and birds gathered around and drank nah-vite, the wine. And nah-vite was very strong. It made some sing. Others it put to sleep. Others were sick.

Choo-hoo Neu-putt – the night-hawk – who was dressed up in grey and yellow, did not wish to spoil his breast feathers so he brought a stick of cane to drink through.

All the girls thought this very wonderful of Choo-hoo Neu-putt, and he received a great deal of attention. And Saw-aw – the grasshopper – who had borrowed Tawk-e-toot – the spider's web – and with it had made himself beautiful new wings, was very jealous to see the attention given the night-hawk. Saw-aw felt he must do something to make the people notice him. So he pulled off one of his hind legs and stuck it on his head.

When Night-hawk saw Saw-aw with his new headdress he laughed and laughed and laughed until he could not stop laughing. He laughed so hard he split his mouth. And it is that way even to this very day. That is why the night-hawk never flies in the daytime. His mouth is so big and white and ugly that he had to fly at night so people will not see hm. And that is why he darts past you so quickly in the evening.

Often in these days, too, you will see Saw-aw – the grasshopper – jumping around without a leg.

After a while, as they kept on drinking nah-vite, the birds all began to fight. They pulled each other's feathers. And some had bloody heads – just as you see them today.

When Kooh – the chief – saw the fighting and the bloody feathers, he decided that there should be no more wine feasts or wine drinking like that. So, when the wine was gone, Kooh very carefully gathered all the seeds of the giant cactus fruit and he called a messenger to take the seeds away off toward the rising sun.

The people watched Kooh's messenger take the seeds away off into a strange country and they did not like it. So they held a council. And Pahn – the coyote – said he would go after Kooh's messenger.

Pahn travelled very fast. He circled around the one who was carrying the seed and came back so that when he met the messenger it appeared that he was coming from the opposite direction. Pahn greeted Messenger and asked what it was that Messenger carried in his hands.

The one who had the saguaro seed answered, 'It is something Kooh wants me to carry a way off.'

Pahn said, 'Let me see.'

Messenger said, 'No, that is impossible.'

But Pahn begged, 'Just one little look.'

At last, after much coaxing, Pahn persuaded Messenger to open one finger of the hand which held the seed.

Then Pahn complained that he could not see enough and begged Messenger to open one more finger.

And so, little by little, Messenger's hand was opened.

Then, suddenly, Pahn struck Messenger's hand and the seeds of Hah-shahn – the giant cactus – flew into the air.

Huh-wuh-le – the wind – was coming from the north, and caught up the seeds and carried them high over the mountaintops and scattered them all over the south side of the mountains.

And this is why the saguaro, or giant cactus, still grows in the Land of the Desert People. This is why Hah-shahn is always on the southern slopes of the mountains.

Ever since that time, once each year, the Indians have held nah-vite ee – the feast of the cactus wine.

HOW FIRE WAS BROUGHT FROM THE SUN

Papagos

FOR SOME TIME AFTER Ee-e-toy had made everything and fixed Tahs – the sun – in his road, the days were warm and every day was just the same. And that was good for making hoon – the corn – and pee-lee-kahn – the wheat – ripen. But sometimes the nights were cold.

So the Indians thought about it. And they decided it would be nice to have more warmth when they wanted it. They tried to tell Ee-e-toy but Big Brother was too busy to listen.

Then the Taw-haw-no Aw-o-tahm – the Desert People – said they would have to help themselves.

And this is how tie – which is fire – was brought from the sun.

Early one morning before Tahs started on his journey across the world, Oofe – a woman – was sent with a basket to get some of Tahs's heat so that the people might keep it.

But Oofe was too late. When she reached the east, where Tahs has his home, he was already well on his journey, very high in the sky, and very hot. He was so hot that when the people asked Oofe to go again the next day she refused.

The people said Oofe was always slow anyway. So they sent Vee-ah-poy – a boy.

When Boy came back he said he was almost there in time but Sun was so hot he could not see.

The Indians thought this was just an excuse. But they decided it would be better to get the heat when Tahs came down at the end of his day's journey. They wanted the heat for the night anyway.

Koor-lee Aw-o-tahm – an old man – said he would go this time. And Koor-lee Aw-o-tahm ran all day to get to the place where Tahs goes at night.

But when the old man returned the next day he did not have any heat. He said that Tahs, at the end of his journey, jumped into a big hole and the Indians would have to send some of the flying people to bring the fire.

An oriole who was listening said he would like to go. So next morning Oriole started off toward the east.

Oriole did not return home until it was very late. And he was all changed. Some of his feathers had turned to the colour of the sun, and some were black. Oriole told the people that he had gone so close to Sun that his feathers began to burn and so he turned back and flew until he saw some water and dropped in.

And now you know why, even in these days, some of Oriole's feathers are yellow and some are black.

Source
Harold Bell Wright, *Long Ago Told: Legends of The Papago Indians*, New York: D. Appleton & Co., 1929, pp. 37–42

Then several other birds were sent. But none could bring the heat. At last the Indians said the small birds were too weak. They must find a large one.

Neu-fee – a buzzard – was floating around in the sky and the people called him and told him he flew so well that it would be a small thing for him to go to Tahs and bring back some fire. Neu-fee thought it would be very easy. So the next morning he started.

All the people felt sure this time. And they stopped work to watch for the return of Neu-fee with the heat.

It was about noon when they saw the black speck in the sky a great distance away. When he came nearer, the people saw that the buzzard's feathers, which had been brown were now all black. And when Neu-fee came down among them they saw that his head had no feathers at all and was all covered with blood.

Neu-fee told the people how he had flown straight into the sun and how when he went to take some of it his head was so burned the feathers fell off, and all his other feathers were burned black.

The Indians did what they could for poor Neu-fee. But that is the way he is even to this day.

Then, for a while, the people did not know what to do. But the nights were cold and they wanted the heat. And the stories told by those who had tried to bring the fire only made them want it more. At last they thought if they could find a bird who could fly at night perhaps he might slip through the hole into which Tahs jumps at the end of his day's journey and catch him asleep or not so hot.

They looked around and saw Nah-kuh-muh-lee – the bat. They called Nah-kuh-muh-lee and asked him if he would try to slip through the hole and get some of Tahs's fire. Bat said he would try. And about sunset he started on his journey to the west.

Now the bat, when he went to bring heat from the sun, was covered with nice grey feathers. When he flew up in the sky no one could see him. So the people knew that this time they would surely have the fire.

And the Indians all stayed awake to watch for Nah-kuh-muh-lee to return with the heat. It was very dark that night. Suddenly they saw a light coming. As the light came down toward the earth it flashed far from side to side. And there was a great roar. And when the light reached the earth there was a bang.

Some of the people were frightened. Others said, 'It is tie – the fire – it flashes like the sun.' And these ran as fast as they could to the place where the grass was burning, and a tree. And one of the men who ran to the fire took a stick that was burning and waved it up and down – east and west – so that the others would know what it was and not be afraid.

There was still much noise and the Indians called this noise pu-putck, which is thunder. The light they call wuh-pu-kuh, which is lightning.

And no one thought of Nah-kuh-muh-lee, who brought the fire, until next day. Then they began to look for him. They looked all around.

At last they found him hanging all limp to a tree. He had not one feather left on his body. He was burned down to the skin. And he was so very much ashamed that no one could coax him to come out in the daytime.

Even to this day Nah-kuh-muh-lee – the bat – will not fly in the light because he has no feathers.

THE YELLOW HAND

Papagos

ALONG TIME AGO there was a large village where San Xavier Mission is now. In those days before the Mission was built a man who lived in this village had fields and worked very hard. He was always managing to get fields from someone else who did not work so hard.

Sometimes the man's wife scolded a little. She would say it was nothing but work for both of them. She would say they already had more than they needed. They had more than their only child, a girl, would need.

But the man kept on working and trading until he had the very best land in all the valley. He had the best horses. He had the greatest number of cattle.

Then this man began collecting yellow stones.

His wife scolded more and more. She said it was time to choose a husband for their daughter. She said he was always too busy to go with the other Indians on hunts or to the feasts. She said the people of the village did not like him and were afraid of him.

Then, one day, a strange man appeared from the south. Stranger rode a burro. He went to the place where the man was working and emptied a sack of rocks. Then Stranger and the man pounded some of these rocks and washed them and burned them.

This took a long time. So the man brought Stranger to his house for food.

The wife and daughter served them. The mother was very cross and scolded a great deal. Stranger watched the girl.

When Stranger left the woman asked her husband what he had traded this time.

The man only laughed and showed her a handful of yellow stones.

Now the woman had decided upon a husband for her girl. But the man would not listen to her. He would not pay attention to anything she said. She was very sad. She went about her work worried and quiet.

And then, one morning, the woman looked far to the south and saw something moving. She watched.

What she saw was a number of burros with big baskets on their sides. The burros with the baskets came to the house. The stranger who had been there before was driving the burros.

Stranger asked the woman for her husband.

The man came from his fields.

Stranger was emptying the baskets which were filled with rocks.

Source

Harold Bell
Wright, *Long
Ago Told: Legends
of The Papago
Indians,*
New York:
D. Appleton &
Co., 1929,
pp. 277–90

When the baskets were all unloaded the man came to the house. He told his wife he had a husband for their girl. He said the girl must get her things together and go with Stranger.

The mother wept and begged. She did not want to give up her girl to a stranger from a strange land.

But her husband was already pounding the rocks which Stranger had brought and paid no attention to her.

The next day the girl started south with her husband.

The father was pounding the rocks which Stranger had brought to him. The mother went scolding about her work. She felt very heavy and queer inside.

Time passed. The man no longer worked in his fields. He spent all his time pounding his rocks and washing them and burning them.

The stranger came again with his burros loaded with rock. He emptied the baskets of rock and went away. And all the people in the village knew now that the man had traded his girl for a pile of rocks. They laughed at him and left him alone.

The woman was very sad these days. She complained that her husband was turning to rock.

When the man had almost finished one pile of rock Stranger would arrive from the south with more. This would make the man work harder than ever. The woman did not know what her husband did with the small yellow stones which he got out of the rock. She thought he put them in a hole in the ground.

Often the woman had to carry her husband's meals out to the place where he was working. All day long he would pound, pound at the rocks. The pile of the rocks he had crushed was larger than three houses.

And the woman noticed that the man's hands were always covered with yellow dust.

After a time the wife became old and very tired. She refused to work in the fields. The man did nothing but pound rocks. So others ploughed and planted the fields and gave the man and his wife a certain portion.

The summer rains came. The man refused to leave his rocks. He worked all day. He worked at night by the light of a big fire. He was wet with the rain many times. He began to cough very hard. His wife begged him to rest. She said, 'If you do not rest the deer will come.'

The woman said this to her husband because the belief was that a certain sickness was brought by a deer. When one who is sick in this way coughs, there is no hope for that one to get well. The deer that brings this sickness is a blacktail deer. And when the Desert People eat blacktail deermeat they are very careful. If you cough when you are eating the meat of this deer you will cough until you die.

But even the fear that the deer would come did not stop this man from working at his rocks. Day after day he sat in the rain and pounded and pounded the rocks for which he had traded his daughter.

And the woman noticed that even the rain had not washed the yellow dust from one of his hands.

Then, one morning, when the woman looked out, her husband was not pounding rocks. She went to him and found that he was dead.

The woman called the people living nearest and they began preparing for the burial ceremony. The woman brought out all the blankets and things which the man had.

While they were wrapping the dead man in the blankets his right hand fell off. The woman picked up the hand and it was very yellow and heavy and hard, just like a rock.

When all was ready the body was taken to the burial hill. The hand was placed beside the body and everything was covered with the brush and stones as the custom is.

And that night some kind women stayed with the woman in her house because she was now all alone. The woman and her friends had been sleeping for some time when they heard a sound of pounding. It was near the house.

The wife of the dead man was very tired and very sleepy. She was only half

As the woman sat there some Little People, who work day and night in the summer, passed by.

awake. She said, 'It is only the old man at his rocks,' and went to sleep again.

But the other women were frightened and could not sleep. The pounding continued until morning.

In the morning the woman was awake enough to know that her dead husband could not be working at his rocks. So she went out to find who had made the sound of pounding. She found no one and came back to the house puzzled.

The next night the sound was heard again. The next night it was heard again. And the sound of pounding seemed to be growing louder. The people of the village began to whisper. They began to keep away from the woman.

This made the woman angry. She made up her mind to find out who was making the noise. So when night came and she heard the pound, pound, pound, she went to the rocks which her husband had been breaking up when he died.

As she went near the pile of rocks the sounds grew fainter. When she moved farther away the pounding grew louder. Then the woman decided to visit her husband's grave.

It was very dark. As she came nearer the burial mound the sound of the pounding became louder. It was too dark to see. She decided to go home and wait until it was day.

Early the next morning the woman and some friends went to the place where Man-Who-Pounded-Rocks was buried. There was no noise. But there was a very restless spirit around. The woman could not understand it. She walked all around the mound of brush and rocks looking at it and wondering. Then she saw something bright. She stooped and looked carefully. It was the yellow hand of her husband which had broken off.

The woman's friends who were with her thought the coyotes had been after the hand. But she knew better. They took the yellow hand to the house. One of the woman's friends kept watching the yellow hand. She picked up the hand and several little pieces of yellow rock fell out. The woman quickly slipped the pieces of yellow rock out of sight. She thought no one saw her.

But the wife of the dead man had seen.

The woman and her friends talked about what they should do. They decided to put the yellow hand in the ground. They went out not far from the house and dug a hole and put the hand in it and covered it. That night the woman was very tired and went to sleep early.

But she did not sleep long. She heard a sound: tap, tap, tap!

She went to the door. There was no one there. She came back into the house and thought she must have been mistaken.

In a few minutes the sound was repeated. This time the woman felt sure it was the yellow hand. She started to go to the place where they had buried the hand. She had only gone a little way when she stumbled over something. She felt in the dark to see what she had stumbled over. It was the yellow hand. The woman sat down to think. She did not know what to do. There seemed to be no one for her to ask.

Then, as the woman sat there, some Little People, who work day and night in the summer, passed by. The woman called. And the message was carried quickly to all the Little People that a human being wanted their help.

The woman sat on the ground waiting. She was very still in the dark, with her ears keen for the word which would come. The Little People will not always help, but when they are willing the advice is always very good.

After a time, in the darkness, the woman heard, or felt, or understood what she was to do. She knew now that her dead husband's yellow hand had returned for the little pieces of yellow rock it had loved so much. The sound of pounding in the night was the yellow hand working at the rocks as the man was working when he died. The woman knew that if this yellow hand was left where others could find it, those who found it would feel that same love for these little pieces of yellow rock. So the woman must hide the yellow hand far away where no one would ever find it. And she must find all the pieces of yellow rock which the hand wanted, so it would never come back again.

When it was morning the woman went to her friend who had kept the pieces of rock which fell from the yellow hand and asked for them. At first the friend said she had not taken the pieces of yellow rock. But later she gave them up.

Then the woman went to the place where her husband had broken so many rocks. She hunted until she found all of the little yellow pieces.

When it was late in the day the woman took the yellow hand and the pieces of rock she had taken from her friend, and those she had found where her husband had worked, and put them all in her blanket. Then she started up the steep side of the mountain. The way was very rough and very steep and very hard. The woman was old and tired.

She sat down in the dusk to rest. She thought she would rather throw the yellow hand far from her and go back to her house and her supper. As the woman sat there thinking and feeling tired, Taw-tawn-ye – an ant – ran over her hand. And Taw-tawn-ye, the ant, stopped. So the woman thought the ant might have a message for her. And she was very still and listened very hard. She listened with the inside ears.

Taw-tawn-ye reminded the woman of the advice his people had given her. He told her to remember what troubles would happen if she left this yellow hand where the people could find it.

Then the woman thought of all her lonely years. She thought of her only daughter traded for rocks. And she knew she could not let any one else live this way. She wrapped her blanket around her and slept until the morning light made things clear. Then she took up the yellow hand and the pieces of yellow rock and hid them somewhere on the mountain. When she had done this the woman returned to her home and lived in peace and happiness with all the people. She never again heard the sound of the yellow hand pounding rocks.

Now this mountain where the woman hid the yellow hand and pieces of yellow rock, is called Schook Toahk, which means Black Mountain. It is not far from San Xavier Mission. But you need not try to find this golden hand and the gold that is hidden with it. Many people have looked for the place where this gold is hidden. But the gold has never been found.

The Indians are afraid to look for the yellow hand. They know that to do so would bring trouble and sickness and death.

And this is why Taw-haw-no Aw-o-tahm – the Desert People – will not tell you if they know where there is gold. They would rather die before they would tell. Gold has always brought trouble for the Indians. This was the very first that the Indians knew about gold.

This was the beginning of all their trouble.

Hah-pah-mah-sah-mah huh-mooch – it is the same now.

THE ORIGIN OF ANIMALS

Jicarilla Apache

WHEN THE APACHES EMERGED from the underworld, they travelled southward on foot for four days. They had no other food than the seeds of the two plants, k'atl'-tai-i and k'atl'-tai-il-tsu-yo, from which they made a sort of flour by grinding between stones. When they camped for the fourth time, one of their tepees stood somewhat apart from the others. While the owner and his wife were absent from this lodge, a Raven brought a bow and a quiver of arrows, and hung them upon the lodge poles. The couple's children took down the quiver, and found some meat in it. They ate the meat and immediately became very fat. When their mother returned, she saw the grease on the hands and cheeks of her children. The woman hastened to her husband with the tale. Marvelling at the appearance of the children, the people gathered to await the reappearance of the Raven, which subsisted upon such remarkable food. When the Raven found the food had been stolen from the quiver, he flew away toward the east. His destination was a mountain just beyond the range of vision of the Indians. A bat, however, followed the flight of the Raven, and informed them where the Raven had alighted.

That night, a council of the whole tribe was held, and it was decided that they should go to the home of the Raven, and try to obtain from him the food which had wrought such a miraculous change in those who had partaken of it. At the end of four days, they came to a place where a large number of logs were lying in irregular heaps. Many ravens were seen, but they avoided the Indians, and no information could be obtained from them. At one point they discovered a great circle of ashes where the ravens were accustomed to cook their meals.

Again a council was held, and they talked over the problem of how to spy upon the ravens, and learn where they obtained the precious animal food. That night the medicine men transformed a boy into a puppy, and concealed him in the bushes near the camp. After the Indians had departed, next morning the ravens came, as is their habit, to examine the abandoned camp. One of the young ravens found the puppy, and was so pleased with it that he exclaimed, 'This shall be my puppy.' When he carried home his prize his parents told him to throw it away. He begged permission to keep it, but agreed to give it up if the puppy winked when a splinter of burning wood was waved before its eyes. As the puppy possessed much more than canine intelligence, it stared during the test without the quiver of an eyelid. So the young raven won consent to keep the puppy, which he placed under his own blanket, where it remained until evening. At sunset the puppy peeped from his cover, and saw an old raven brush aside the ashes of the fireplace, and take up a large flat stone which disclosed an opening beneath; through this he disappeared, but arose again with a buffalo, which was killed and eaten by the ravens.

For four days the puppy remained at the camp of the ravens, and each evening he saw a buffalo brought up from the depths and devoured. Satisfied that he had discovered the source from which the ravens derived their food, the puppy resumed the form of a boy on the morning of the fifth day, and, with a white eagle feather in one hand and a black one in the other, descended through the opening beneath the fireplace, as he had seen the ravens do.

In the underworld in which he found himself he saw four buffaloes. He placed the white eagle-feather in the mouth of the nearest buffalo, and commanded it to

Source
Frank Russell, 'Myth of the Jicarilla Apache', *JAFL*, 11 (1898), pp. 253–71

follow him, but the buffalo told him to go on to the last of the four and take it. This the boy tried to do, but the fourth buffalo sent him back to the first, in whose mouth the boy again thrust the feather, declaring it to be the king of animals. He then returned to the world above, followed by all the animals at present upon the surface of the earth, except those specially created later, such, for example, as the horse and aquatic animals. As the large herd of animals passed through the hole, one of the ravens awoke, and hastened to clap down the stone covering the opening, but he was too late to prevent their escape. Seeing that they had passed from his control into that of man, he exclaimed, 'When you kill any of these animals you must at least leave their eyes for me.'

Attended by the troop of beasts of many species, the boy followed the track made by the departing Apaches. On the site of their first camp he found a firestick or poker, of which he inquired, 'When did my people leave here?'

'Three days ago,' was the reply. At the next camping-place was an abandoned ladder of which he asked, 'When did my people leave here?'

'Two days ago,' replied the ladder. Continuing his journey the boy soon reached the third camping-place, where he questioned a second firestick, and learned that the people had been gone but one day. At the fourth camp another ladder answered his question, with the news that the Indians had left there that morning. That evening he overtook them and entered the camp, the herd of animals following him like a flock of sheep. One old woman who lived in a brush lodge became vexed at the deer which ate the covering of her rude shelter. Snatching up a stick from the fire, she struck the deer over the nose, to which the white ashes adhered, causing the white mark which we see on the nose of that animal today.

'Hereafter you shall avoid mankind; your nose will tell you when you are near them,' said she.

Thus terminated the brief period of harmony between man and the beast: they left the camp at once, going farther each day, until on the fourth they disappeared from sight. That night the Apaches prayed for the return of the animals, that they might use them for food, and that is why animals approach nearer the camps now at night than at any other time. They never come very close, because the old woman told them to be guided by their noses and avoid the Indians.

The Story of the
Flint Knife Boys and the Great Warrior of Aztec

Navajo

Source

Aileen O'Bryan,
'The Dine:
Origin Myths of
the Navajo
Indians', *Bulletin
of the Bureau of
Ethnology*, 163
(1956),
pp. 126–31

BEYOND DEBENSA, La Plata Mountains, there is a yellowish coloured mountain and near it there is a mountain with shiny rocks on it; this mountain is called Dessos. Now the man who was formed inside the first mountain is called Tso y natlaye, and the man who was formed in Dessos is named Klay ya ne'yan, One Who Was Raised inside the Earth.

The first man had no children. The second man had twin boys. These boys were given the names of the First Holy Twin Brothers: the elder was called Na'yei na' zone, but the younger was called La'chee na'yana, He Who Grew in One Day, as well as To ba'ches chini. Both boys grew up in one day.

The Journey of the Elder Brother

The Elder Brother took a long journey. He covered the whole country – mountains, plains and all. When he was on the side of La Plata Mountains he saw a fire on the mesa, which is a part of Mesa Verde. He saw this fire at night. Now this boy knew of three strong medicines, so when he got to the place where he had seen the fire, and found people living there, he was not afraid, for he had a plan.

Among these people there were two beautiful maidens who turned away many suitors from all parts of the country. The reason was that it was believed that only young men with superpower were to marry the two maidens, and there were no such young men to be found. Their father decided that whoever could shoot an arrow into a little hole far up in the side of the cliff would be the persons to marry his daughters.

All the hunters and warriors gathered there with their bows and arrows. They all tried, but no one could shoot into the hole in the cliff. Then there came two old men; one was the Bear and the other was the Big Snake. The warriors asked, 'Where do you come from?' And when all the other men saw the two old men with their bows and arrows they all laughed and said, 'Whoever heard of old men shooting that far?' But one shot at the hole far up on the side of the cliff and the arrow went into the hole. It was decided, however, that they were too old to have the maidens. The father said, 'Whoever shoots an arrow over the cliff will have my daughters.' All the other men tried and failed; but the two old men shot at the same time and their arrows went, side by side, clear over the cliff. But it was again decided that they were too old to have the maidens.

Now at that time there was a strong people living at the place now called Aztec. For their chief they had a tall, strong warrior whom everyone in the country feared. He was a great warrior and whatever he said was law.

The uncle of the maidens said, 'Whoever kills the Great Warrior of Aztec will have my two nieces.' He said that it would be three days from that time before they would start the war against the Great Warrior.

At the end of the third day the Elder Brother joined these people. He gathered together a party of warriors and they started out for Aztec. The two old men followed behind them. The people tried to persuade the old men to go back. They said that the two were too old to fight; but the old men would not listen to them.

The first night the two old men camped not far behind the warriors. One slept on one side of the fire and the other on the opposite side. And on this first night an old woman came in sight of the warriors. She had with her a group of boys. They camped near the warriors, and they made a frightful noise all the night long. The warriors could hear them, but they could not pass them for they sang the chants against the enemy. The second night the camp was again made and the old woman and her boys camped nearby, and the boys made a fearful racket. The two old men also camped near; and one slept on the one side of the fire and the other on the other side. On the third night the old woman and her boys camped just opposite the warriors, and the boys played and fought and yelled all the night long. The two old men camped nearby as before, and they slept peacefully.

On the fourth night the Elder Brother and his warriors made their camp, and the old woman and the boys camped just ahead of them. That night one of the boys broke a bough from a cedar tree toward the east side, and he laid it down and said,

'May I kill the Great Warrior!' Another boy broke a bough from a piñon tree on the west side, and he laid it across the cedar branch and said, 'May I kill the Great Warrior!' Then all the rest of the boys jumped up and taking stones piled them on the two boughs, and each said, as had the first two, 'May I kill the Great Warrior!' There was a very great pile of stones.

The Elder Brother was angry. He said, 'Go kill one of those boys.'

But these were Holy Beings, the grandsons of the old Hard Flint Woman, and the boys were the Flint Knife Boys. They came from the land of the Flint Mountain near Dulce.

The next morning the young boys bathed themselves in mud. They jumped off a cliff, rolled down the slopes and had a fine time. Then the boys went to the Elder Brother and said, 'Now kill us all.' And there was lightning flashing from their toes, knees, sides of the body, arms, heads and tongues. When the Elder Brother saw this he begged them, saying, 'I was only teasing. It is all right for a grandfather to tease his grandchildren.' So they turned and went away.

Soon they were approaching Kin teel, Aztec. The Flint Knife Boys were striking their flint knives and the flashes shot up into the sky. The Elder Brother went against the town and the enemy came out.

The Flint Knife Boys and the Elder Brother and his warriors killed all the enemies and took their scalps. The old woman filled her basket full of scalps before they marched away. As they neared home they made camp and they lined up all the scalps, but the Great Warrior's scalp was not to be found, nor was the scalp of the warrior chief next in rank among those that they had with them.

Now the two old men had drawn the two great warriors and they had killed them. Soon they joined the others and they brought out their two scalps. Everyone knew that they were the scalps of the Great Warrior and of his chief. They returned home, but still the uncle of the two maidens refused to let the two old men take the two girls.

The people held the Great Scalp Dance. While this was going on the uncle of the two maidens said to them, 'Go to where the young men are singing and choose whichever young men you would like to be your husbands.' So the maidens went to where the young men were singing and they got in the middle of the group.

Now the two old men were camped in a brush shelter; one lay on one side of the fire and the other on the other side. Toward nightfall they got up and the old man Bear said to the old man Snake, 'Our two young girls are in the pot.' So the Bear rolled a cigarette made of a certain herb, and he drew the smoke from it and blew it in the direction of the singing where the maidens were dancing among the young men. The Snake did the same thing. When the two maidens smelled the smoke the elder said, 'Let us go and see where it comes from.' When they got to the place from which the sweet odour had come they found two handsome young men, one on one side of the fire and the other on the other side. Each youth wore a beautiful robe which covered him. The two sisters thought that these handsome young men were their husbands, so the elder maiden went to the Bear and the younger went to the Snake.

In the morning, when the elder sister awakened, she had her arm around the Bear's neck, and his arm was around the girl. He was still asleep and all his ugly teeth showed. She awakened her sister. A great Snake was coiled around the body of the young girl; their heads were together, and her hand was on the Snake.

The two sisters went through the singing to the four directions, and they went to the river.

After the two young women had crossed the river (the Mancos River) they climbed to the top of La Plata Mountains. They went to the Bear People who lived there. The Bear People said, 'Where are you from, sister-in-law?' As the young women were ashamed of their acts they said nothing and left. They travelled on and on until they came to the mountain called Tse dzil. A community of big snakes lived there. They asked the two young women, 'Where are you going, sister-in-law?' Again they were ashamed and they left that place also. From there they went to a mountain called Dzil se'he'dzil et. There also lived another branch of the Bear People; and again they were called 'sister-in-law'.

Now the two old men followed their brides. They used the smoke from their magic cigarettes to tell them which way the young women had gone. Whichever way the smoke drifted, that way they followed.

The sisters travelled to the mountain called Tso dzil, Mount Taylor, and they were called 'sister-in-law' by the Big Snake People who lived there. They left the place because of their shame and they went to the mountain called Tschosh gaeye, above Tqo hache, and there they were greeted as 'sister-in-law' by members of the Bear family. It was after this that they decided to part. One went one way, the other went the other way. The old man Bear followed the elder sister, and the old man Snake followed the younger one.

The Story of the Younger Sister

The younger sister reached a people called Nat at tsele, and there were some members of the Big Snake People living with them who called out, 'Where are you going, sister-in-law?' Hearing this, the girl left them and fled to the Lukaichukai Mountains. But members of the Big Snake family lived there also, and they called after her as before.

By this time the younger sister was very tired. Her moccasins were worn and her garments nothing but rags. She could see the smoke from the Great Snake's cigarette close behind her. She went on to a place called Tsel tiel, Sage Canyon. She was running along when she noticed a slender young man lying on a rock. The young man's face was painted with a bluish paint called tlish do chee. Now this young man was the Racer Snake, and he asked her where she was going.

She said, 'I am being chased by the Big Snake.'

'No big snake comes here,' said the young man. 'Take off your clothing and come with me.'

So she took off her clothing and put it behind a rock, and she went to the young man naked. In the rocks there was a tiny hole. The young man blew into the hole four times, and it was large enough for the young woman to enter. When the Big Snake came to the place he grabbed her clothing and said, 'Oh, my wife!'

By his power the young man sent the Big Snake away. After he had departed the two young people started out. They passed through great fields of corn. The young woman had her monthly period, so she made an apron out of the corn husks. That is why some husks are red.

Soon they came to the home of the young man. The maidens there were dressed beautifully. That night the young man was dressed in a beautiful dress, the

skin of a snake. But that night the younger sister wished to go out. She started to go forward but there was a throng of snakes ahead of her. She tried again, but there were snakes on all sides of her, so she threw herself on the ground. The next morning the snake people told what she had done when they had coiled and stretched.

One snake said, 'The sister-in-law is not kind. She stepped on my neck.' Another said, 'She stepped on my leg.'

Another complained of his arm, and still another said that she had crossed his body.

Later she had a pain in her abdomen. They gave her medicine and she was quiet. Then came her children. The boy was called Male Snake, and the girl was called Female Snake.

And so whenever the Navajo see these snakes they call them by their names and send them away. They do not kill snakes.

The boys went to the Elder Brother and there was lightning flashing from their toes, knees, sides of the body, arms, heads and tongues.

THE STORY OF THE MAIDEN AND THE BEAR

Navajo

THERE WERE 12 YOUNG MEN and two young women. The men went hunting and they killed two of the Eagle Dancers of Wide Ruin. The Cliff Dwellers were angered over this and they chased the 12 young men to the top of a flat mesa. Now the 12 hunters rode on sun dogs; but the Great Warrior of the Cliff Dwellers and his chief, through their power, took the sun dogs from them. Soon the flat mesa was surrounded by warriors, and the 12 young men knew that they must make a plan. They cut down a tall cedar tree, and, after trimming off the branches and making it a straight pole, they tied eagle feathers to the top of it. When it was ready the two youngest brothers climbed to its top, and the ten other brothers dropped it over the side of the cliff. The two young men landed safely. They gave the call of the owl, which told the others that they were safe. Now the owl heard this and said, 'But the ten on the mesa top must die.' And it was so. The Great Warrior of the Cliff Dwellers killed the ten young men. Before they died these brothers gave the coyote call, and the two who had been saved knew that they would have to kill the Great Warrior of the Cliff Dwellers and his chief.

Now these two warriors of the Cliff Dwellers lived under the ground. They wore strings of shell and turquoise around their necks and their arms and their legs. On their heads they wore large caps shaped like shells with turquoise and white shell beads tied to the middle of them. They would crawl through a little hole in their dwelling and come to top of the ground only when the Cliff Dwellers were at war. After the latter were successful the warriors would crawl back under the earth.

The two brothers travelled far to the great ocean of the West, to the home of the Woman Who Changes. She told the brothers that they must get help of the Flint Knife Woman who lived on the mountain called Tso dzil, that the Flint Knife People were great warriors and would help the two brothers fight the Cliff Dweller People. The brothers journeyed to the home of the Flint Knife People, and they promised to give their two sisters, who were beautiful maidens, to the two warriors who would kill the Great Warrior and his chief.

Source

Aileen O'Bryan, 'The Dine: Origin Myths of the Navajo Indians', *Bulletin of the Bureau of Ethnology*, 163 (1956), pp. 131–37

The brothers and Flint Knife Warriors started out for Kin teel. It was night when they arrived near it. The Flint Knife Men made a fire and held a Fire Dance. They used sticks that made a curious whirring sound.

'The enemy will see this,' said the brothers.

'No, for they will believe it to be stars,' said the Flint Knife Warriors. The next morning they still danced, and the huge fire sent a great smoke cloud into the sky.

Again the brothers said, 'The Cliff Dwellers will see this.'

But the Flint Knife Warriors answered, 'They will think that they see a storm cloud.'

Then the two brothers and the Flint Knife Warriors went near Kin teel and they fought the Cliff Dwellers. They took many scalps the first day. That night they looked them over, but the scalps of the two great chiefs were not among them. They waited three days and they again fought the Cliff Dwellers. Then they waited for five days. At this time two old men appeared. They were the Turtle and the Frog.

These two old men went to the water hole, or spring, where the women came for water. They took stone axes and they killed all the people who came for water. They took their scalps and they tied them to a pole. (This is the origin of the pole in the Scalp or Squaw Dance which now has branches representing scalps tied to it.) When the Cliff Dwellers learned of the killings at the spring they rushed there and prepared to kill the Turtle and the Frog with their stone axes.

'Now they will kill us,' said the Frog.

The Turtle said, 'Be not afraid. Come, get under me.'

So the Cliff Dwellers struck the Turtle, but their blows glanced off his shell, and they were not harmed.

The Cliff Dwellers said, 'Now we will burn them.'

The Turtle said, 'This time they will kill us.'

But the Frog answered, 'Be not afraid.' And after they were thrown into the fire the Frog made water and put it out.

'We will boil them,' said the Cliff Dwellers. They brought out a huge pot and filled it with water. This time it was the Frog who was frightened, but the Turtle reassured him. And when they were thrown into the pot the Turtle expanded his shell and cracked the pot and they were free. Finally the Cliff Dwellers decided to drown them. They threw them into the river, where they swam off to the opposite shore.

Now when the Brothers and the Flint Knife Warriors counted the scalps on the pole which the Frog and the Turtle had made, they did not find those of the Great Warrior and his chief among them. So on the seventh day they prepared to attack again.

Then two old men came and sat on a rock. One was the old man Bear and the other was the old man Snake.

'Where do you come from?' the Flint Knife Warriors asked.

'I come from the mountains,' said the Bear.

'I come from the plains,' said the Snake.

While the warriors were fighting, the Bear said to the Snake, 'Let us look around.' So they climbed into the cliff dwelling. Presently they saw coming toward them two creatures crawling on their hands and knees. Taking up a stone, the Bear struck them and killed them. The Snake split their skins and took them, covered as they were with turquoise and shell beads. Then the two old men went back to the rock and waited.

Again when the Flint Knife Warriors and the Brothers returned and counted the scalps they did not find those of the Great Warrior and his chief. Then the Bear and the Snake threw the two skins on the ground, and the others saw what they were. They asked who had killed them.

'You killed them,' said the Bear indicating the Snake.

'No, you killed them,' returned the Snake.

The Cliff Dwellers cried aloud and wept, as they knew that now they would all die.

The two brothers were greatly troubled when they thought that they must give their two beautiful sisters to the two old men, the Bear and the Snake, so they stopped many times on their journey to their home and held games. Each time they held the games they promised that the winners would have their sisters, and each time the Bear and the Snake won.

At last they came to the place where the two maidens waited. They prepared to give a great Scalp and Squaw Dance. The two maidens were dressed in ceremonial robes; and the warriors of the Flint Knife People were also dressed in ceremonial attire. The brothers said, 'Now we will let the maidens choose their own husbands.' Soon the dance began and the maidens danced and danced with the young warriors.

Now the two old men, the Bear and the Snake, climbed to the top of a nearby mountain. They bathed and clothed themselves, and they appeared as two handsome young men. They took their pipes and filled them with certain herbs from their medicine bags and began to smoke quietly.

About this same time the maidens grew weary and were covered with sweat. The elder sister said, 'Come, let us go apart and bathe.' And they went to a little stream, and the elder maiden took the water in her hand and threw it into her mouth, and the younger sister cupped her hand and so drank. After they had bathed and drunk and were refreshed. The older sister said, 'I smell a sweet odour.'

'Let us find out what it is,' said the younger maiden. And they went in search of the origin of this sweet smoke. They had no idea that it came from the pipes of the Bear and the Snake.

The maidens climbed the mountain, and when they reached the summit they saw the two beautiful youths there smoking.

'Where did you come from?' asked the elder maiden.

'I came from the mountain,' said the Bear.

'And I came from the plain,' said the Snake.

'Give us also something sweet to smoke,' said the younger sister. The two youths gave them their pipes, and after a few puffs the maidens fell asleep.

When they awoke they found that they had slept with a Bear and a Snake, for the two creatures lay there beside them.

Being very frightened, the two sisters started to run down the mountain path.

'Wait,' said the Bear. 'If you return your brothers will kill you.' So the Bear and the Snake gave the sisters each a basket with feathers tied to the outer rim.

'Place the basket on the ground and step into it if you are in trouble or in danger,' said the Bear, and the Snake repeated this advice. And so they let the sisters go on their way.

When the sisters came to the place where their two brothers and the Flint Knife people waited, they saw at once that they would be killed. The warriors tied their hands behind them and prepared to beat them to death. The elder sister said, 'If we are to die we should be allowed to stand in our baskets.' And as soon as they stepped in the baskets they disappeared.

Now the two sisters landed on the summit of a mountain. And, as soon as they stepped from their baskets, they sent them back to the Bear and the Snake by the Wind. Almost at once they saw the Bear and the Snake coming towards them.

'We must separate,' they said. The elder sister stayed in the mountain, and the younger sister ran down to the plain. On and on they travelled. They became thin and almost without clothing.

The elder sister came to a great cave, and, being very weary, she wished to enter it. She saw two bears guarding the entrance. They were fierce and she knew that she could not pass. Just then she heard a whistling and she saw a chipmunk. He said, 'Follow me.' She did this, and he whistled so lively a tune that the two bears listened to him and let her pass. Next they came to a second cave, and guarding the entrance were two dlo'ee [animals with faces like dogs]; one was white and one was yellow. The chipmunk whistled his tune again, and again they passed unharmed. The entrance of the third cave was guarded by two cranes, male and female. From there the elder sister and the chipmunk went into the big kiva of the Yei-bichai.

Four men and four women in ceremonial robes came forward to meet her. The women took her aside and bathed her; they rubbed her first with cornmeal and then with pollen and she was beautiful. They dressed her in ceremonial robes and led her into a room lined with fur. And there her baby girl was born. The child had little tufts of hair back of its ears and downy hair on its arms and legs.

After the child was born the people all gave the Mountain Chant.

HOW A BEAUTIFUL MAIDEN CHANGED INTO A FROG

Various

IN THE BEGINNING THERE WERE two suns who were brothers. They lived in a beautiful valley beyond the western mountains. One would fly through the heavens by day, the other by night. Then, however, there was no night for the face and hair of one brother was as dazzling as the face and hair of the other. In the days not long after The People had come down from the north, they could change themselves into animals, and the animals could change themselves into people, and they could understand one another, for they were brothers.

There was a young girl who was a maiden. She was exceedingly beautiful, and she loved the young Sun-brother. When the older one had finished his flight in the sky and veiled his face from the mountains, then the maid would bare her bosom, and, turning her face and hands to the sky, would beseech the one she loved to come to her. But he heeded not her love, nor her cries. One day as she stood alone upon the prairie, imploring her beloved, the Coyote came and asked what troubled her.

'O Coyote!,' said she, 'you are wise and cunning beyond all The People: tell me how I shall win the sun, for I love him and long to sleep in his tepee.'

'Foolish maid,' said the Coyote. 'You do not know what you say. The love of the sun will kill you. Forget it.'

Source

Charles Erskine Scott Wood, *A Book of Tales: Being Some Myths of the North American Indians*, New York: Vanguard Press, 1929, pp. 13–19

But she gave the Coyote no peace till he promised to get her the sun as a hus-band. So they set out upon the journey. For many days they journeyed to the southward and westward until the maid was held captive by a chief. But the Coyote told her to seem glad. Then he went to the river and caught some fish.

'When he visits you in your tepee, fill your bosom with these fish.'

When the chief visited her, he saw her breast was shining like silver, and, putting out his hand, he found her colder than the dead. 'Away with you – witch!'

Then they fled, still to the southward and westward, till they came to a great river, too wide for the maid to swim. But the Coyote called on the otters and they carried her over. To some, the Coyote said she was his sister; to some that she was the daughter of the sun. So they were afraid to molest her.

At last, after a weary time, through many seasons, by the lies and cunning of the Coyote they came through all adventures to the foot of the mountains beyond which lay the Beautiful Valley of the Sun. But the pass was guarded by a sorcerer bear who sat in the way so none might enter.

Then the maid, by order of the Coyote, changed herself into a fox and crept towards the gateway. The Coyote drew to one side and in a little bare spot com-menced to circle after his own tail. Around and around he went, and the bear looked wonderingly. Faster and faster turned the Coyote, till no one could tell what it was that was whirling in the dust. The bear could not resist any longer, but ran over to see what this thing was. Then the fox and the Coyote flew through the pass toward the Valley.

'Now,' said the Coyote, 'you must go to yonder spring and wash yourself and make yourself beautiful, for if the sun does not like you he will slay you. I can go no further. Go to him, but do not look at his uncovered face, or you will die.'

The maid did as she was told, and walked alone toward the great lodge of the sun, her eyes cast down, a necklace of shell upon her breast, gold shining on her wrists and ankles and her hair about her like a veil. The birds followed her and sang, the fawns came to look at her; there were rivers and forests and herds of deer and buffalo; there was no winter in this place. So she came to the lodge and the sun looked upon her and loved her and set her apart from his other wives in a bower of her own.

He visited her there, and, when he left for his journey across the sky, he hur-ried back to put his head in her lap. They were happy for they loved each other, but always his face was covered when he came to her. More and more she begged him to show her his naked face, but he refused, saying, 'You cannot look upon my face and live.' But ever she insisted, even weeping.

At last he said, 'I will show you my face and hair, bare and uncovered, but you must change yourself into a frog and get beneath the water of the crystal spring and look at me through the water. Otherwise you will surely be burned to a cinder.'

Therefore, she changed herself into a frog and got beneath the water. The sun came and stood before her and bared his face and his hair. When she saw the glory of his face she loved him the more, and, forgetful that she was a frog, she sprang from the water to embrace him. She leaped upon his face and instantly she was withered to a ghost. And there she remains to this day. But the sun's glory was quenched so that now he is the cold pale moon. When he turns his face full upon the earth, anyone may see like a shadow upon it his wife, in the shape of a frog.

The Coyote was so starved and frightened on his long journey home that he became the lean little animal that he is now. He prefers the moon to the sun, the night to the day. When the moon is full he will talk to it all night long.

THE MAN WHO MARRIED THE MOON

Pueblo

LONG BEFORE THE FIRST Spaniards came to New Mexico, Isleta stood where it stands today – on a lava ridge that defies the gnawing current of the Rio Grande. In those far-off days, Nah-chu-ru-chu dwelt in Isleta, and was a leader of his people. A weaver by trade, his rude loom hung from the dark rafters of his room; and in it he wove the strong black 'mantas' which are the dress of Pueblo women to this day.

Besides being very wise in medicine, Nah-chu-ru-chu was young, and tall, and strong, and handsome; and all the girls of the village thought it a shame that he did not care to take a wife. For him the shyest dimples played, for him the whitest teeth flashed out, as the owners passed him in the village, but he had no eyes for them. Then, bashful fingers worked wondrous fringed shirts of buckskin, or gay awl-sheaths, which found their way to his house by unknown messengers – each as much as to say, 'She who made this is yours, if you will have her.' But Nah-chu-ru-chu paid no more attention to the gifts than to the smiles, and just kept weaving and weaving – such mantas as were never seen in the land before or since.

The most persistent of his admirers were two sisters who were called the Yellow Corn Maidens. They were both young and pretty, but they were possessed of a magic power which they always used for ill. When all the other girls gave up, discouraged at Nah-chu-ru-chu's indifference, the Yellow Corn Maidens kept coming day after day, trying to attract him. At last the matter became such a nuisance to Nah-chu-ru-chu that he hired a deep-voiced town-crier to go through all the village and announce that in four days he would choose a wife.

For dippers, to take water from the big earthen containers, the villagers used then, as they use today, queer little ladles made of gourd. But Nah-chu-ru-chu, being a great medicine man and very rich, had a dipper of pure pearl, shaped like the gourds, but wonderfully precious.

'On the fourth day,' proclaimed the crier, 'Nah-chu-ru-chu will hand his pearl dipper at his door, where every girl who will may throw a handful of cornmeal at it. And she whose meal is so well ground that it sticks to the dipper, she shall be the wife of Nah-chu-ru-chu!'

When the strange news came rolling down the still evening air, there was a great scampering of little moccasined feet. The girls ran out from hundreds of grey adobe houses to catch every word; and, when the crier had passed on, they ran back into the storerooms and began to ransack the corn bins for the biggest, evenest and most perfect ears. Shelling the choicest, each took her few handfuls of kernels to the sloping handmill and with the mano, or handstone, scrubbed the grist up and down and up and down, till the hard corn was a soft, blue meal. All the next day, and the next, and the next, they ground it over and over again, until it grew

Source
Charles F. Lummis, *The Man Who Married the Moon and Other Pueblo Indian Folk Stories*, New York: Century Co., 1894, pp. 53–70

finer than ever flour was before; and every girl felt sure that her meal would stick to the dipper of the handsome young weaver. The Yellow Corn Maidens worked hardest of all; day and night for four days they ground and ground, with all the magic spells they knew.

Now in those far-off days, the Moon had not gone up into the sky to live, but was a maiden of Shee-eh-whib-bak. And a very beautiful girl she was, though blind in one eye. She had long admired Nah-chu-ru-chu, but was always too maidenly to try to attract his attention as other girls had done; and, at the time when the crier made his proclamation, she happened to be away at her father's village. It was only upon the fourth day that she returned to town, and, in a few moments, the girls were to go with their meal to test it upon the magic dipper. The two Yellow Corn Maidens were just coming from their house as she passed, and told her of what was to be done. They were very confident of success and told the Moon girl only to pain her; and laughed derisively as she went running to her home.

By this time a long file of girls was coming to Nah-chu-ru-chu's house, outside whose door hung the pearl dipper. Each girl carried in her left hand a little jar of meal, and, as they passed the door one by one, each took from the jar a handful and threw it against the magic dipper, but each time the meal dropped to the ground, and left the pure pearl undimmed and radiant as ever.

At last came the Yellow Corn Maidens, who had waited to watch the failure of the others. As they came where they could see Nah-chu-ru-chu sitting at his loom, they called, 'Ah! Here we have the meal that will stick!' and each threw a handful at the dipper. But it did not stick at all; and still from his seat Nah-chu-ru-chu could see, in that mirror-like surface, all that went on outside.

The Yellow Corn Maidens were very angry, and, instead of passing on as the others had done, they stood there and kept throwing and throwing at the dipper, which smiled back at them with undiminished lustre.

Just then, last of all, came the Moon, with a single handful of meal which she had hastily ground. The two sisters were in a fine rage by this time, and mocked her, saying, 'Hoh! Moon, you poor thing, we are very sorry for you! Here we have been grinding our meal for four days and still it will not stick, and you we did not tell until today. How, then, can you ever hope to win Nah-chu-ru-chu? You are a silly little thing!' But the Moon paid no attention whatever to their taunts. Drawing back her little dimpled hand, she threw the meal gently against the pearl dipper, and so fine was it ground that every tiniest bit of it clung to the polished shell, and not a particle fell to the ground.

When Nah-chu-ru-chu saw that, he rose up quickly from his loom and came and took the Moon by the hand, saying, 'You are she who shall be my wife. You shall never want for anything, since I have very much.' And he gave her many beautiful mantas, and cotton wraps, and fat boots of buckskin that wrap round and round, that she might dress as the wife of a rich chief. But the Yellow Corn Maidens, who had seen it all, went away vowing vengeance on the Moon.

Nah-chu-ru-chu and his sweet Moon Wife were very happy together. There was no other such housekeeper in all the pueblo as she, and no other hunter brought home so much buffalo-meat from the vast plains to the east, nor so many antelopes, and blacktailed deer, and jackrabbits from the Manzanos, as did Nah-chu-ru-chu. But he constantly was saying to her, 'Moon Wife, beware of the Yellow Corn Maidens, for they have the evil road and will try to do you harm, but you

The Moon
threw the meal
gently against
the pearl dipper,
and so fine was
it ground that
every tiniest bit
of it clung to the
polished shell.

must always refuse to do whatever they propose.' And always the young wife promised.

One day the Yellow Corn Maidens came to the house and said, 'Friend Nah-chu-ru-chu, we are going to the plain to gather the root of the palmilla. Will you not let your wife go with us?'

'Oh, yes, she may go,' said Nah-chu-ru-chu; but, taking her aside, he said, 'Now be sure that you refuse whatever they may propose.'

The Moon promised, and started away with the Yellow Corn Maidens.

In those days there was only a thick forest of cottonwoods where are now the vineyards and gardens and orchards of Isleta, and to reach the Ilano Plain the three women had to go through this forest. In the very centre of it they came to a deep well, with steps at one side leading down to the water's edge.

'Ay!' said the Yellow Corn Maidens. 'How hot and thirsty is our walk! Come, let us get a drink of water.'

But the Moon, remembering her husband's words, said politely that she did not wish to drink. They urged in vain, but at last, looking down into the well, called, 'Oh, Moon Friend! Come and look in this still water, and see how pretty you are!'

The Moon, you must know, has always been just as fond of looking at herself in the water as she is to this very day, and, forgetting Nah-chu-ru-chu's warning, she came to the brink, and looked down upon her fair reflection. But, at that very moment, the two witch sisters pushed her head foremost into the well and drowned her; and then filled the well with earth and went away as happy as wicked hearts can be.

Nah-chu-ru-chu began to look often from his loom to the door as the sun crept along the adobe floor, closer and closer to his seat; and, when the shadows were very long, he sprang suddenly to his feet, and walked to the house of the Yellow Corn Maidens with long, strong strides.

'Where is my little wife?' he said, very sternly.

'Why, isn't she at home?' asked the wicked sisters as if in great surprise. 'She got enough amole long before we did, and started home with it. We supposed she had come long ago.'

'Ah,' groaned Nah-chu-ru-chu within himself. 'It is as I thought – they have done her ill.' But without a word to them he turned on his heel and went away.

From that hour all went ill with Isleta, for Nah-chu-ru-chu held the well-being of all his people, even unto life and death. Paying no attention to what was going on about him, he sat motionless upon the highest point in the village, the top rung of a pueblo ladder, with his head bowed upon his hands. There he sat for days, never speaking, never moving. The children that played along the streets looked up to the motionless figure, and ceased their boisterous play. The old men shook their heads gravely, and muttered, 'We are in evil times, for Nah-chu-ru-chu is mourning, and will not be comforted. And there is no more rain, so that our crops are drying in the fields. What shall we do?'

At last all the village leaders met together, and decided that there must be another effort made to find the lost wife. It was true that the great Nah-chu-ru-chu had searched for her in vain, and the people had helped him; but perhaps someone else might be more fortunate. So they took some of the sacred smoking weed wrapped in a corn husk and went to Shee-wid-deh, who has the sharpest eyes in

all the world. Giving him the sacred gift, they said, 'Eagle Friend, we see Nah-chu-ru-chu in great trouble, for he has lost his Moon Wife. Come, search for her, we pray you, if she be alive or dead.'

So the Eagle took the offering and smoked the smoke prayer and then he went winging upward into the very sky. Higher and higher he rose, in great upward circles, while his keen eyes noted every stick, and stone, and animal on the face of all the world. But, with all his eyes, he could see nothing of the lost wife; and at last he came back sadly, and said, 'People Friends, I went up to where I could see the whole world, but I could not find her.'

Then the people went with an offering to the Coyote, whose nose is sharpest in all the world; and asked him to try to find the Moon. The Coyote smoked the smoke prayer and started off with his nose to the ground, trying to find her tracks. He trotted all over the earth; but at last he too came back without finding what he sought.

Then the troubled people got the Badger to search, for he is best of all the beast at digging – and he it was whom the village employed to dig the caves in which the people first dwelt when they came to this world. The Badger trotted and pawed, and dug everywhere, but he could not find the Moon; and he came home very sad.

Then they asked the Osprey, who can see farthest under water, and he sailed high above all the lakes and rivers in the world until he could count the pebbles and the fish in them, but he too failed to discover the lost Moon.

By now the crops were dead and dried up in the fields, and thirsty animals walked crying along the dry river bed. Scarcely could the people themselves dig deep enough to find so much water as would keep them alive. They were at a loss which way to turn, but, at last, they thought, 'We will go to P'ah-ku-ee-teh-ay-deh, who can find the dead – for surely she is dead, or the others would have found her.'

So they went to him and begged him. The Turkey Buzzard wept when he saw Nah-chu-ru-chu still sitting there upon the ladder, and said, 'Truly it is sad for our great friend, but, for me, I am afraid to go, since they who are more mighty than I have already failed; but I will try.' And spreading his broad wings he went climbing up the spiral ladder of the sky. Higher he wheeled, and higher, till at last not even the Eagle could see him. Up and up, till the hot sun began to singe his head and not even the Eagle had ever been so high. he cried with pain, but still he kept mounting – until he was so close to the sun that all the feathers were burned from his head and neck. But he could see nothing; and at last, frantic with the burning, he came wheeling downward. When he got back to the village where all the people were waiting, they saw that his head and neck had been burnt bare of feathers – and from that day to this the feathers would never grow out again.

'And did you see nothing?' they all asked, after they had bathed his burns.

'Nothing,' he answered, 'except that when I was half-way down I saw in the middle of a cottonwood forest a little mound covered with all the beautiful flowers in the world.'

'Oh!' cried Nah-chu-ru-chu, speaking for the first time. 'Go, friend, and bring me one flower from the very middle of that mound.'

Off flew the Buzzard, and in a few minutes returned with a little white flower. Nah-chu-ru-chu took it, and, descending from the ladder in silence, walked to his house, while all the wondering people followed.

When Nah-chu-ru-chu came inside his home once more, he took a new manta and spread it in the middle of the room; and, laying the small white flower tenderly in its centre, he put another new manta above it. Then, dressing himself in the splendid buckskin suit the lost wife had made him, and taking in his right hand the sacred rattle, he seated himself at the head of the mantas and sang:

Shu-nah, shu-nah! Ai-ay-ay, ai-ay-ay, ai-ay-ay!
(Seeking her, seeking her! There away, there away!)

When he had finished the song, all could see that the flower had begun to grow, so that it lifted the upper manta a little. Again he sang, shaking his gourd; and still the flower kept growing. Again and again he sang; and when he had finished for the fourth time, it was plain to all that a human form lay between the two mantas. And when he sang his song the fifth time, the form sat up and moved. Tenderly he lifted away the overcloth, and there sat his sweet Moon Wife, fairer than ever, and alive as before!

For four days the people danced and sang in the centre of the village. Nah-chu-ru-chu was happy again; and now the rain began to fall. The choked earth drank and was glad and green, and the dead crops came to life.

When his wife told him what the witch-sisters had done, he was very angry; and that very day he made a beautiful hoop. He painted it, and put strings across it, decorated with beaded buckskin.

'Now,' said he, 'the wicked Yellow Corn Maidens will come to congratulate you and will pretend not to know where you were. You must not speak of that, but invite them to go out and play a game with you.'

In a day or two, the witch-sisters did come, with deceitful words; and the Moon invited them to go out and play a game. They went up to the edge of the Ilano and there she let them get a glimpse of the pretty hoop.

'Oh, give us that, Moon Friend,' they teased, but she refused. At last, however, she said, 'Well, we will play the hoop game. I will stand here, and you there; and if, when I roll it to you, you catch it before it falls upon its side, you may have it.'

So the witch-sisters stood a little way down the hill, and she rolled the bright hoop. As it came trundling to them, both grasped it at the same instant, and lo! Instead of the Yellow Corn Maidens, there were two great snakes, with tears rolling down ugly faces. The Moon came and put upon their heads a little of the pollen of the corn blossom, still used by Pueblo snake charmers to tame them, and a pinch of the sacred meal for their food.

'Now,' said she, 'you have the reward of treacherous friends. Here shall be your home among these rocks and cliffs forever, but you must never be found upon the prairie; and you must never bite a person. Remember you are women and must be gentle.'

And then the Moon went home to her husband and they were very happy together. As for the snakes, they still dwell where she bade them and never venture away; though sometimes the people bring them to their houses to catch the mice, for these snakes never hurt a person.

PART 6
THE WESTERN RANGE

Shuswap

Ntlakyapamuk

Okanagan

Sanpoil

Spokane · Kalispel

Yakima · Palouse · Cœur D'Alene

Nez Perce · Flathead

Cayuse

Northern Paiute
(Paviotso)

Bannock

Northern Shoshone
(Wind River)

Washo

Western Shoshone

Mono

Gosiute

Owens Valley

Paiute

Ute

TRIBES OF THE
WESTERN RANGE

Lying across a vast stretch of the continental United States and Canada is a wide, open territory called the Western Range. Its geographical position makes it a place filled with contradictions. Great mountain ranges define the region on its western and eastern borders – the Cascade Range and Sierra Nevadas on the west, and the massive Rocky Mountains on the east; but it is also a land of deep valleys. The Native Americans who lived in this great wilderness found themselves either in fruitful pockets of forested abundance or in scraggly desert brush. For its inhabitants, life in the Western Range could be one of feast and famine. This was a region where northern riverine settlements lived off the abundance of salmon, while occupants of the southern part grubbed for worms in an arid, hostile landscape.

The Western Range may be divided into two subregions: the Plateau in the north, and the Great Basin in the south. The Great Basin was the homeland for tribes such as the Shoshone and Paiute. While the Plateau is usually considered to be a more hospitable region than the Great Basin, owing to a higher level of annual rainfall and a greater abundance of forests and meadowlands, a line of distinction between the two is not clear. Portions of the Plateau, such as the lowlands of central Washington and Oregon, are very arid, while the generally hostile world of the Great Basin is broken occasionally by fertile mountain country such as the Humboldt Range of Nevada and Utah's Wasatch Range.

Just as the land of the Western Range is varied, so are the Native Americans who have lived there for thousands of years. The tribes of the Western Range comprise a collection of identities that have survived the vicissitudes of time and of the natural world in which they live.

The Land of the Great Basin

The Great Basin is a region surrounded by vast mountain ranges, including various lower ranges. Since the area is at a lower elevation than its surroundings, it forms a natural 'basin' for the region's rainfall. Water has no natural outlet by which to flow out of the Great Basin, so it collects in myriad lakes within the mountain-locked system. Rivers and streams also drain from the snow-capped mountains into these lakes. With no means of escape, the lake water evaporates and then falls as rain once more. This cycle produces lakes of a higher than normal salt content, as salt leached from the rocks remains in the lake when the water evaporates. The greatest example of a high-saline lake is the Great Salt Lake of Utah.

Thousands of years ago, the Great Basin was the home of vast glaciers which created as many as 68 massive lakes in the region, including Lake Bonneville and Lake Lahontan. Portions of these lakes remain today. In addition to the Great Salt Lake, formerly a part of Lake Bonneville, there are Utah Lake and Sevier Lake. Other remaining natural lakes are Pyramid Lake, Walker Lake and Winnemucca Lake, all of which are remnants of Lake Lahontan.

Other former lakes are today dry salt beds. Perhaps the most famous is Death Valley, the lowest point on the map in the continental United States. This dry lake basin represents an extremely hostile environment, where summer temperatures have been recorded at 72°C (140°F). In addition, the Bonneville Salt Flats extend over a broad, level plain east of Wendover, Utah, in a portion of the Great Salt Lake desert. This site has been made famous as a test site for land-speed records as high-performance cars, specially designed for speed, have raced along the barren, level Flats at velocities of hundreds of miles an hour.

The Great Basin is not without its interior mountains as well. Historically, these inner mountains often served to separate rival tribes from one another. Ranges divided the Shoshone and Northern Paiute in Nevada, as well as the Shoshone and the Ute in Utah. The Great Basin mountain ranges vary in elevation from 2,000m to 4,000m (6,500–13,000ft), with the majority standing at less than 3,000m (10,000ft) above sea level. Even 'valley floors' are elevated, with many located between 1,200m and 1,800m (4,000–6,000ft) above sea level.

Native American inhabitants of the Great Basin often faced a hostile environment. Since much of the region is arid, plant forms tend to be sparse. It is a place dominated by juniper trees, scrub oaks, piñon trees (prized by Native Americans for their pine-nuts which have a nutty flavour) and sagebrush. Some Native Americans in the area had no choice but to work as foragers and gatherers, searching for any food they could find, including berries, roots, pine-nuts, seeds, rodents, snakes, lizards and even insects.

Earliest Occupation of the Great Basin

Although they were generally scattered over vast distances, Native Americans have occupied the Great Basin lands for thousands of years. The region has experienced little change over the past 10,000 years. Plagued by aridity and sometimes scorching summer heat, the Native Americans who lived there in prehistoric times practised subsistence lifestyles.

Little remains of these earliest inhabitants of the Great Basin. Evidence dating from 10,000 to perhaps 11,500 years ago reveals a hunter-gatherer society which used stone spears to kill big-game animals. Archaeologists have unearthed examples of Cascade point spears – the spear-heads were narrow, tapered to a point on both ends and somewhat leaf-shaped – and scattered findings, which include the use of Clovis and Folsom spear points which were fluted.

In about 7,000 BC, the region was home to the Desert Culture, which relied on small-game hunting, since the large Pleistocene animals had

died out by that time. The Native Americans located in the Great Basin during the Desert Culture era lived in caves and underneath rock cliffs for protection from the hot climate. In these caves and cliff dwellings, the inhabitants used stone and wooden tools and weapons, including digging sticks, wooden clubs, milling stones and stone scrapping tools. Archaeologists have unearthed the first evidence of basket-weaving in the Great Basin in Danger Cave in western Utah. This discovery dates from 7,000–9,000 years ago. Around 6,000 years ago, early Shoshonean-speaking arrivals entered the Great Basin and their descendants remained there into historic times. This new migration did little to change the lifestyles of those living in the Great Basin, however.

Between 2000 BC and AD 1 the Basin population had developed villages which were situated near the lakes of the region. Their culture was adapted to their lake environment and archaeologists have unearthed evidence of the use of fish-hooks and fishing nets, as well as early duck decoys, woven out of local grasses. Hunting was still practised, and acorns and pine-nuts had become an important part of the local diet.

For these Native Americans, agriculture remained non-existent. Gathering parties regularly foraged through the greener lower valleys near their villages, collecting pine-nuts, seeds and berries in woven baskets. They used digging sticks to dig up edible roots. When white men entered the area and witnessed this foraging practice, they dubbed the Native Americans there 'Digger Indians'. Tribes practised regular 'roundups' as their men scattered over a field and drove out rabbits, antelopes and even grasshoppers for eating. Fires were sometimes started in order to force animals from their homes and into the waiting nets and brush corrals of the tribesmen.

Reliance on Hunting

When a village participated in an animal drive, it was an event which required much organization. Often, before such a drive, ceremonies were held to bless the event, during which shamans or tribal medicine men would speak charms to cause the animal to co-operate. Northern Paiute and Shoshone antelope hunts, for example, centred around a medicine man's ability to attract a herd of antelopes by singing a song. Men would drive antelopes into a designated site, encircling their prey and closing in for the kill.

Since antelopes did not reproduce in adequate numbers to allow for frequent hunts by Great Basin tribes, rabbits – especially quick-moving, black-eared jackrabbits – were one of the primary meat animals of the region. Roundups of rabbits generally took place when the rabbit population was plentiful. The numbers of rabbits fluctuated generally in two-year cycles, with the region experiencing either an abundance of the creatures or almost none.

Rabbit drives often took place during the late autumn. The rabbit hunters used a net, in which they caught their unsuspecting quarry. Such a hunting net was so important in some bands of hunters that it was passed down from one generation to the next, and was carefully maintained. Nets were woven from the long fibres of milk-weeds. Women performed the net-weaving art, creating lengthy strands of fibres by twisting and rubbing them on their bare thighs. Such nets, when opened up for use, stood barely over 30cm (1ft) tall, but they were extremely long. Some even stretched for nearly 1.6km (1 mile).

Once the hunting group had gathered for the rabbit roundup, the chief of the drive determined the location of the long nets. Then the band split up, with some of the hunters walking across an open piece of prairie, often walking for miles along a valley, herding the rabbits in front of them towards the waiting nets. While some hunters did the herding, others manned the nets, killing all the rabbits which were trapped in the net as soon as possible, to avoid the nets being damaged by their frightened captives. When the hunt was over, the rabbits were divided between all participants. The chief of the drive and the net owners were usually given extra portions. The rabbits were then cleaned and dressed; their hides were cut into strips of fur, later woven into blankets; and the meat was dried for later consumption.

The Land of the Plateau

The Plateau lies between the Rocky Mountains and the Cascade Mountains of Oregon and Washington states. These mountain ranges run nearly parallel to one another from north to south. Several additional ranges within the region cause the land to be marked by many peaks and valleys, with great rivers flowing throughout the Plateau. The region is drained by two vast river systems – the Fraser and the Columbia. The great northern bend of the Fraser system, located in the Canadian province of British Columbia, forms the northern boundary of the Plateau. Important rivers which flow either into the Columbia or the Fraser are the Deschutes, Umatilla, Okanagan, Thompson, Snake and Willamette.

The region is an incredibly rich one. Today it comprises portions of eastern Washington and Oregon, as well as the entire state of Idaho, a sliver of northern California, and much of Canadian British Columbia. The land is thick with forests, which gave rise to a massive lumbering industry during the twentieth century. For many years these forests have been the home to different kinds of fur-bearing animals, from grizzly bears to beavers, as well as great antler-bearing creatures, ranging from deer and antelope to elk and moose. The rivers of the region teem with fish, including trout and sturgeon, and especially salmon, which has been a primary food source for the Native Americans in the region for thousands of years.

Because of the abundance of natural resources throughout the Plateau region, there were many diverse tribes, speaking various languages and often isolated by the mountainous geography. Although these northern tribes did not densely populate the region, approximately two dozen tribes have been historically located in the Plateau for centuries. In the southern part of the region were the Penutian speakers, which included the Klamath, Modoc, Chinook, Nez Perce, Cayuse and Palouse. In the lands north of the Columbia river, which flows east to west where it drains into the Pacific Ocean, were the Salish speakers, such as the Flathead, Kalispel, Spokane, Coeur d'Alene, Shuswap and Ntylakya-pamuk. Of the two Plateau groups, those of the southern region were the earliest arrivals, their ancestors having migrated to the mountainous country as early as 4000 BC, while those of the northern region date from around 1500 BC.

Ancient Inhabitants

Archaeologists have done much work over the last 50 years in an attempt to find out more about the origins of Native American culture in the Plateau region. Remnants of the earliest occupants of the region have been dated to approximately 9000 BC. These hunters, fishermen and gatherers of wild plants and roots travelled south from Alaska along the western side of the Rocky Mountains. The culture they established has been identified as the Old Cordilleran Culture. Most of the artefacts discovered to date – mostly stone and bone implements and tools – have been connected to the Old Cordilleran period, and are dated between 7,500 and 9,500 years ago.

These ancient arrivals to the region practised large-game hunting and used a double-pointed, narrow spearhead called the Cascade point. Archaeologists have discovered some sites in the Plateau which have been occupied without interruption for the past 10,000 years. One such site is located near The Dalles on the Columbia river, and is called the Five Mile Rapids site. There is evidence here that the early Native Americans used spears for salmon fishing, and that they hunted the big-game animals found in America during the most recent ice age, known as the Wisconsin Glaciation.

The region experienced a dry, warming trend, beginning about 7,000 years ago, which caused the extinction of the large Pleistocene animals, resulting in a new phase of life in the Plateau, called the Desert Culture. Although this climatic change is more often identified with the Great Basin region, it caused alterations in the Native American lifestyles found in the Plateau. Hunters had to rely on smaller animals such as rabbits for their food. Milling stones were common, and basketry was practised.

Around 2000 BC the region once again experienced a shift in temperature patterns, which brought an end to the warm Desert Culture period and ushered in a cooler climate. During this period, the mountains were more highly snow-covered, causing a greater flow of rivers in the region as well as increased annual rainfall. Native Americans began to settle permanently along rivers, and fishing developed as a chief means of sustenance. By 1000 BC the Northern Forest Culture had taken root in the Plateau. This culture introduced the region to highly polished stone tools and implements, highly stylized stone carvings, and some metal working, primarily with copper. In addition, the Plateau inhabitants developed more elaborate funerary rites, including significant burial mounds and the use of effigy figures. In some important respects, the Native Americans of this cultural period appeared similar to their contemporary counterparts residing in the Northeastern Woodland Culture groups. Some archaeologists have theorized that the Native Americans of the Northeast influenced the peoples of the Plateau region, and helped them develop their culture.

By the time of Christ, the peoples of the Plateau had developed a culture called the Plateau Culture, which varied slightly between groups found within the region, with each still relying heavily on fishing, hunting and gathering wild foods. Change came slowly through these years as various culture pockets developed and adapted their primitive technologies to their environment. By about AD 500 the tribes of the interior were seriously trading with the nations of the Pacific Coast and with the tribes located on the Great Plains. Five hundred years later, the Plateau culture developed distinct social patterns which continued despite the arrival of Europeans on the continent.

Post-contact Villages and Leaders

Europeans did not make contact with the interior tribes of the Plateau until the eighteenth century, and then only in piecemeal fashion through French and British fur-traders and trappers. By the early nineteenth century, white people made more permanent contact with the Native Americans, who they found living in fishing villages along major river systems and their tributaries. These villages were semi-autonomous settlements, each administered by a group of chiefs who served as both civil and military leaders and who were selected for their successes at war, their wisdom and their general abilities to lead. These men led their own people and co-operated with the leaders of other bands and villages by meeting with them to enact trade, to carry out a communal hunt, to go to war against a shared enemy, to carry on council, or simply just to socialize.

Plateau tribes and bands not only kept up contact with one another, but they were also directly influenced by tribes and peoples living outside their region. Several groups of Native Americans living in the Pacific Northwest brought cultural adaptations to their Plateau neighbours in the west. These included the tradition of head-flattening (a practice carried out among Pacific tribes such as the Clatsop, who flattened the foreheads of their infants in specially designed cradle boards), nose-piercing and the wearing of cedar-slat protective gear for fighting, as well as the shredded wood clothing found along the coast. Interior Plateau tribes made their connections with Pacific Coast tribes by canoe travel along the western Rocky rivers, such as the Snake and Columbia watershed, which took them into the vicinity of their western neighbours.

By the 1700s, the Native Americans of the Plateau had been introduced to horses, which had made their way from the south through Spanish settlements in modern-day New Mexico. Horses thrived in impressive and wild herds which found sustenance in the lush grasslands of the highlands of the region. The Cayuse, Nez Perce and Yakima gained the earliest access to horses in their region and soon other tribes became horse-bound as well. With the introduction of the horse, life changed significantly for the Native Americans of the Plateau. They gained a new mobility which they adapted to their buffalo-hunting techniques, allowing tribal hunting bands to roam in even greater circles outside the Plateau and onto the Great Plains. Here they made contact with Plains Native Americans, which influenced the clothing styles, ornamentation and housing habits of the Plateau tribes. By the late eighteenth century, Plateau tribes were in regular contact with French-Canadian fur-traders, not to mention the British and eventually the Americans. All such contacts and influences from outside the Plateau region worked to change the lives of those native peoples in dramatic and permanent ways.

Change Comes to the Great Basin

Through contact with white people, the tribes of the Great Basin gained access to new goods for trade, new technologies and, perhaps most significantly, the horse. Tribes such as the Shoshone gained access to their first horses from the herds of the Spanish to the south, and traded for their first rifles from American fur-trappers. These additions to their culture provided tribes with interior mobility and a new capacity to hunt the bison in ways unthinkable earlier. The horse came to the Rockies in around 1700, and the tribes of the Plateau were soon able to carry out horseback bison hunts on the High Plains of eastern Wyoming. Other tribes were riding into Idaho to fish for salmon, and added to their food supply smoked and dried fish, as well as greater amounts of dried buffalo meat. This increased mobility brought tribes together more regularly, and bonded the Shoshone and Northern Paiutes into virtually a single tribal unit.

Village Life on the Plateau

Although village life varied somewhat from tribe to tribe, the Native Americans of the Plateau shared many common domestic elements. Typically, a Plateau village might feature a people living together throughout the winter months, taking residence in circular earthen lodges which were partially underground. Such housing was generally fairly warm and cosy during the winter months. Some tribes constructed homes reminiscent of the longhouses found in the Northeast. These houses consisted of a bark-covered dwelling which might extend for 30m (100ft) or more in length. Several families would take up residence in such a house. The occupants of these bark houses usually slept along the inside walls, with their various family fires centred in the longhouse's interior, the smoke drifting out of the lodge through roof openings situated along the central ridgepoles.

In summer, the villagers might live in open-air houses, built of wooden poles and covered with bark, reeds or rushes. These summer homes were typically single-family dwellings and less communally based than those occupied during the harsh winter months. Another summer-home style involved using planks; those tribes which lived in the western part of the Plateau copied the Pacific tribes who constructed plank homes out of cedar and other woods. These homes were often built in the fishing camps which a band might construct along a river or a lake during the summer months, to catch a large supply of fish for winter eating. Such houses were built in close proximity to one another, often along a 'street' facing the river or other body of water. They were often open on the river side, with the daily catches of trout and other fish hung on the backs of the houses to dry.

Methods of Catching Fish

Plateau tribes relied principally on spearing and trapping to catch fish. The chosen method determined where a fishing village might be built and how much co-operation had to take place between the band's members to make the fishing season a success for the entire group.

Spearing was a means of fishing carried out by one person, but still required much communal effort before it could be practised with productive results. To prepare a river site for spearers, the village might set up camp near rapids which naturally forced fish to swim in a narrow channel, one which could serve as the site for a spearing station. The village worked communally, setting up a diverted channel for the fish, lining the bottom of the manmade watercourse with white stones to allow the spear-bearer to see the trout or salmon clearly. The men took turns manning the spear site, usually using a three-pronged spear crafted from a deer antler. Once a spear fisherman caught a fish with his weapon, he then gave his position to the next man, and so on.

Spearing, although it could be efficiently done, was not as effective as trapping. Some tribes throughout the Plateau, including the Sanpoil peoples, used nets and fish seines, but such devices could only be used when the river was at an appropriate level and was not too swift. Fish-traps, called weirs, were more commonly used. These were usually placed at the mouth of a narrow river or stream where salmon spawned. A weir included a barrier built in the stream, much like a fence, which allowed the fish to pass

through breaks in the fence, only to find themselves being guided into specially set traps located along a second fence. Once the fish had passed through the first fence, they had no option but to follow the fenced paths set for them in the water. The fish entered the trap, often fashioned in the form of willow baskets. Such an elaborate fishing technique demanded co-operation by a band's members. However, one family might be large enough to organize a weir system on its own. A typical Plateau Native American might consume as many as 180kg (400lb) of fish annually, so the fishing season was important as a primary food source to the members of these Western tribes.

Spearing and catching fish was considered a man's job. The cleaning of the catch and its subsequent drying was the task of the women of the village. In summer fishing villages, special racks were set up for drying the fish. Those salmon captured during the autumn were typically smoked inside the lodges. Once dried, the prepared fish was placed in storage bags and kept on raised platforms or in storehouses.

Hunting

By autumn's end, generally the month of October, the village fishing season was complete. Soon the men were heading out on great hunting expeditions, while the women and children worked as gatherers, picking berries in season, as well as other plants, roots and seeds.

Hunting was a specialized activity steeped in ritual and tradition. Before a hunting party set out on the trail, each member of the party experienced a sweat in a specially constructed lodge where steam was produced by dropping cold water on rocks heated in a fire. The sweating process might be repeated over a period of days, sometimes as many as ten. The men of the hunt were careful not to participate in sexual activities during these days, as they were purifying themselves for the task ahead. Songs about the hunt were chanted, as blessings for the hunt.

Each organized hunt required a hunt leader, with his spirit bearing the responsibility of giving direction to the hunt itself. During the hunt, the men often herded unsuspecting deer into a narrow canyon where hunters waited with their bows and arrows. Sometimes, in more mountainous and rugged terrain, deer were herded over cliffs, falling to their deaths. In the autumn, a hunting party might search near berry patches for bears, both black bears and the larger grizzlies. Sometimes such quarry was smoked out of a cave and shot with arrows. Once a bear or other animal was shot by a party, ceremonies followed, including ceremonial songs and blessings. While the bow and arrow was widely used on a hunt, other means of capturing animals were also used. Traps might be set, and fallen trees were prepared as deadfalls, in which a trunk was caused to fall on an animal and crush it.

The fur of the animal – whether a bear, deer, antelope, wolf, fox or rabbit – was usually considered as important as its meat. Rabbit fur was used to make caps and warm gloves and mittens, as well as the comfortable rabbitskin blankets.

Gathering Food

Although meat procured by hunting was a mainstay of the Western Range peoples' diet, the practice of gathering provided food rich in other essential nutrients. Owing to the wide variations in the topography of this vast region, and the differences of elevation in the landscape, the women of the tribes were able to harvest a natural abundance of hundreds of varieties of plants, roots, berries and nuts. Those tribes which lived in mountainous parts of the region found the same plants and berries maturing at different times of the year, allowing them to harvest a plant in a valley perhaps weeks before it was ready for consumption at a higher level. This gave the Native American in such locales many different 'seasons' for plants compared to other regions.

There was an abundant variety of harvestable plants. Many berries were available, including currants, elderberries, buffalo berries, choke-cherries and service berries. Each of these ripened at a different time of the summer, since they thrived at different elevations. Plants such as bulrushes and tules were picked during a short season; at other times they were considered too hard to chew and were therefore inedible. Tender shoots of watercress, clover, squaw and even thistle were included in Native American diets. In the Great Basin, various forms of cactus were

harvested for both their fruit and spines. Some cactus fruit was considered sweet and delectable. Cactus needles were roasted for consumption.

During the summer months, women foraged for roots and bulbs, using a sharpened digging stick, often hewn from a wood hardened by fire and fashioned with antler prong. They dug for bitterroot, sego, yampa and wild carrots, plus many others unique to some more limited regions. Native Americans also dug up camas bulbs, which were not easily digested but considered tasty. One white missionary described the taste of camas as a combination of chestnuts and prunes. If too many camas bulbs were ingested, the victim might suffer an attack of diarrhoea or severe flatulence. Natives often ate camas along with wild onions or fennel, which helped neutralize the bulbs' harsh effects.

Some native foods helped break the monotony of greens, bulbs and roots. In the forested regions, Native Americans gathered pine sap, a sugary substance, similar to maple syrup, which was siphoned out of the trees. Cat-tail seeds were plucked in autumn and roasted to provide the base for a hearty, brown and pasty sauce, considered a delicacy by some tribes. The Washo people gathered wild strawberries along the banks of Lake Tahoe, and sometimes pulverized them into a sweet berry drink.

Other plants were less a treat and used more for medicinal purposes. The Native Americans had a natural pharmacy of cures including using skullcap for the heart, Canadian violet for lung problems and geranium petals for ulcer treatment. Prior to labour, pregnant women gathered and stored snowberries, as these contained properties considered important in reducing the pain of childbirth.

Not only did Native American women have the responsibility of gathering these naturally produced foods, but they also processed them for consumption. Many of the roots and bulbs were dried in the sun or even baked over fires to give them a longer storage life. They were then placed in nearly airtight baskets, buried inside a lining of grasses. While winter winds blew all around their snug lodges, the women dug up their summer's bounty, and boiled their plants along with pieces of dried or fresh meat, seasoning the stew with dried pine moss collected during the summer harvest. Cooking was often done in tightly woven, watertight baskets, with women heating stones and dropping them into the soup to heat the mixture.

Gumbasbai: the Annual Nut Harvest

One of the most important natural products gathered by Western Range tribes was the piñon nut. The Washoes called the annual harvest of piñon nuts Gumbasbai, which meant 'big time'. This event carried as much importance to many tribes as did white frontier activities such as husking bees (in which people gathered socially to take the husks off their corn crop). The harvest provided an opportunity for the members of a tribe to come together for the purposes of gathering a large amount of food and for socialization. It was a grand celebration. All tribal members, both young and old, participated in the harvest. Often the tribe's council elders met during the autumnal event. Special dances were performed, such as the Round Dances of the Paiutes and Shoshones, celebrating the harvest and a spirit of unity within the tribe. Washoes prayed for a good harvest early in the season, a rite symbolized by the ritualistic burial of cone-laden branches by a river or stream.

Once a ritual leader determined the exact day on which his tribe's people should begin to harvest the piñon nuts, the four-day process began. While the men of the tribe hunted, the women began gathering the nuts. Before going out, women took sacred baths to purify themselves. To gather in the crop, the women used long poles with hooked tips to shake the tree branches, collecting their bounty in baskets. The ritual leader fasted during the four-day harvest, continually praying for an abundance of piñon nuts. The women and children of one family, working hard, could easily gather over 450kg (1,000lb) of piñon nuts in a seasonal harvest.

Once the harvest was completed, the ritual leader divided the nuts, and the game killed by the men on their hunt, among the families of the tribe equally. After each family had received their portion, however, they then gave away their share to another family, while receiving an equal amount from another. A great feast was then laid out – a thanksgiving celebration for the tribes of the Western Range.

Piñon nuts were prepared similarly to other foods on the Plateau and Great Basin. The women roasted them until they could prise open the outer shell of the nut. Inside were seeds, which were then shelled. The inner kernels were eaten raw or ground into a flour meal. Water was added to the meal to make a piñon mush. In winter, piñon mush might be placed outside the lodge and then eaten as an Native American version of ice cream.

The Art of War as a Native

Just as hunting and gathering parties required a level of organization and hierarchy, so did the practice of war. War parties were often formed among Plateau tribes, typically with all warriors participating on a volunteer basis. Warriors generally joined war parties led by leaders recognized for their skill in battle and their bravery. A war party leader was not necessarily a chief of a band or tribe. Typically, war parties numbered 20 to 30, and they were motivated in their actions by a variety of circumstances. A war party might be formed for revenge, in response to a previous attack by another tribe to retaliate for the death of a kinsman or for the taking of a captive by the attacking tribe. Some tribes fought their neighbours for the spoils of war, or to gain property, including horses or human slaves.

War parties relied primarily on surprise attacks against their enemies. Once a party attacked, however, there was usually great noise, with much whooping and screaming designed to frighten the enemy and to heighten an attacker's bravery. Women sometimes accompanied a war party, not to participate in the fight but to add to the vocal noise of the attack. Bows and arrows were the main weapons of the day, prior to contact with whites and the introduction of the gun. Spears were common and war clubs were brandished by the warriors of virtually every tribe in the region.

Once an opponent was killed, he was usually scalped, and, among some tribes, even dismembered, with the scalp lock and the body parts being taken back to camp for the glory of those who had participated in the battle. Scalping was done thoroughly, for Plateau warriors often took off the entire top of an enemy's head, from the eyebrows to the back of the neck and laterally from ear to ear. After a successful battle, the war party returned to camp and celebrated their victory with a scalp dance, which might last several days.

Among the tribes of the Great Basin, the art of war was little different from that practised by the tribes of the Plateau. Inter-tribal rivalry dominated in the region and wars occurred as a result. One record (Edward Curtis, *The North American Indian*, vol. 15, New York: Johnson Reprint Corporation, 1970, pp. 77–78) relates how two Basin tribes, the Paviotso and the Bannocks, went to war against a neighbouring tribe, the Saii:

> The [Paviotso] war-chief called for all men from the Paviotso bands. They went along the range of hills east of the lake, and were met by a party of Bannock, armed with spears. They camped together . . . and the two parties travelled together northward as far as the site of Lakeview, Oregon, and there chose a Bannock and Paviotso scout . . . After a time they saw a fire, toward which they travelled, and by daylight they were close to it. The Saii had been dancing for a menstruating girl, and were sleeping soundly. The Paviotso crossed a stream, attacked the camp, and killed many. They liberated some Paviotso young women who had been captured by the Saii as little girls, and captured two Saii women.

With the arrival of horses in the Western Range, tribal warfare became more frequent and covered greater distances. Tribes which had not previously come in contact with one another, owing to their separation over vast distances, found themselves making contact on horseback. Plateau peoples, such as the Flatheads, Nez Perce and Kootenai, once they acquired the horse, generally in around 1700, began extensive raids out on the Plains for war and hunting buffalo.

Perhaps the best example of this new mobility may be seen in the Utes of the Great Basin. On horseback, they travelled out onto the Great Plains in hunting parties and war forays. Their horses took them west as well, raiding into modern-day Nevada, battling with Shoshones and Paiutes, taking prisoners as slaves. Some warring tribes simply killed all captives. The Flatheads usually killed their prisoners before the victors returned to camp. Those victims who were brought back to the Flathead village were subjected to the anger and violence of the women of the tribe who might have lost a husband or family member in a raid or battle, resulting in the prisoners' eventual death. An exception to this rule involved the female captives, who were often allowed to live and were absorbed into the tribe.

Trading in slaves was practised by several tribes found in the Western Range. On the Plateau, tribes traded their captives with coastal peoples, who often had goods they had acquired from white trading ships, which the tribes of the interior coveted. The Klamaths, located in southern Oregon, organized raiding expeditions into California and east into the Great Basin to capture slaves. Once they had acquired several, they transported them to the northwest. Here the captives were traded to the Chinooks, who frequently served as middlemen in the slave trade, selling them to Northwestern Coastal tribes. Others, such as the northern tribes of the Plateau, the Thompson and Lillooet, battled with their neighbours, the Athapaskan-speaking tribes. Some tribes, including the Yakima and the Klickitat, did not participate in the slave trade.

Religion

The religious acts of prayer, experiencing visions and curing the sick dominated the spiritual lives of many of the Native Americans of the Western Range. Chief among the religious leaders of many of these tribes were the specially designated spiritualists called shamans. These tribal and band medicine men bore the responsibility of curing the sick members of the group. Healing the sick began with a vision which was intended to guide the shaman in his efforts.

Many shamans practised healing in the same manner. Typically, a shaman danced and shook rattles over a sick tribal member, while chanting incantations. This practice symbolized the shaman 'sucking' the 'poison blood' out of a physical sufferer. Herbs were often used, many of which actually had medicinal properties. Western

Range shamans were always male, and their female counterparts, usually considered witches, were discouraged by Western Range tribes.

Great Basin religion relied heavily on the tribal concepts of the spirits which might influence their lives of the tribe members, as well as a reliance on the powers of shamans and ritualistic dances and ceremonies. Just as with Plateau tribes, shamans were essential for curing the sick. Both men and women could be shamans among the Great Basin tribes, although most were male. Not only could shamans heal, but they could also curse. Shaman spirits could be cast on a human being, causing physical and mental illness, even delirium.

Because of the perception that shamans were capable of great powers, they were both respected and feared. Historian Robert Spencer, in his book *The Native Americans: Prehistory and Ethnology of the North American Indians* (New York: Harper & Row Publishers, 1965), describes the power of a Plateau shaman:

> As is frequently the case in societies admitting shamanism, the Sanpoil [Plateau tribes] being no exception, the shaman was feared. He who could cure illness could also cause it. Although sorcery could be practised by anyone, accusations of witchcraft were often made against shamans, with care, of course, since it did not do to invite the enmity of a shaman. A chief took care to keep a shaman 'on his side', giving him gifts, as did others in the community. Shamans were thus regarded as wealthy, even if wealth among the Sanpoil was not a highly developed concept.

While cures and blessings from a shaman were greatly valued among Great Basin tribes, another important aspect of an individual's religion hinged on the quest for a guardian spirit. Such a quest did not typically involve a shaman, but was a highly individual experience. All males of a tribe were required to engage in such a quest, but it was not an activity closed to women.

The quest was similar to the vision quest practised by Great Plains tribes. A prepubescent boy was encouraged to make a series of one-night quests, wandering away from his band's encampment, seeking contact with a spirit. The sought spirit was to appear to the youth in a dream or vision. Such spirits usually visited the seeker in animal form, appearing as every creature from a bear to an insect.

Such a visitation by a spirit bonded it with the young boy for the rest of his life. Implicit in this union was the spirit's assurance that it would protect the youth, promising to make the young warrior impervious to an enemy's weapons. Spirits might also guarantee skill in any gambling the youth might engage in, or even power over the weather.

Despite the importance which Western Range tribes placed on the guardian-spirit quest, once the spirit and human had made contact with one another the human was expected to begin immediately 'forgetting' the experience. He was to move through life understanding the presence of his spirit but without calling frequently on his guardian. Such a spirit could be recalled by the warrior later in life, when circumstances began to change, but typically the spirit was intended to keep a low profile in his daily life.

Religious Dances

Many tribes of the Western Range practised a host of religious dances, each of which had a special spiritual purpose. Perhaps the most important dance for several Great Basin tribes – among them the Shoshone and Paiute – was the Round Dance. Although there were variations from tribe to tribe, the Round Dance consisted of the participants forming a circle around a sacred tree or prepared pole. Men and women joined the circle, alternating male and female dancers. As the participants faced into the circle, they linked arms and danced clockwise around the centre pole. Such a dance might continue for several days. Round Dances might be held to bless the tribe with an abundance of piñon nuts or other gathered foods. Others were held to pray for a bountiful fish harvest or hunt; to bring health to the tribe; or to bless individuals. The Lemhi Shoshone practised a Round Dance variation called the Nuakin. This springtime dance was performed to bless the tribe with a great salmon catch.

MYTHS AND LEGENDS OF THE WESTERN RANGE

THE LOST TRAIL

Ute

ACANTOW, ONE OF THE CHIEFS of his tribe, usually placed his lodge beside the spring that bubbled from a thicket of wild roses in the place where Rosita, Colorado, stands today. He left his wife – Manetabee (Rosebud) – in the lodge while he went across the mountains to attend a council, and was gone four sleeps. On his return he found neither wife nor lodge, but footprints and hoofprints in the ground showed to his keen eye that it was the Arapahoes who had been there.

Getting on their trail he rode over it furiously, and at night had reached Oak Canyon, along which he travelled until he saw the gleam of a small fire ahead. A squall was coming up, and the noise of it might have enabled him to gallop fairly into the group that he saw huddled about the glow; but instead he tied up his horse and began to crawl forward.

The Arapahoes were gambling to decide the ownership of Manetabee.

There were 15 of the Arapahoes, and they were gambling to decide the ownership of Manetabee, who sat bound beneath a willow near them. So engrossed were the savages in the contest that the snake-like approach of Acantow was unnoticed until he had cut the thongs that bound Manetabee's wrists and ankles – she did not cry out, for she had expected rescue – and both imperceptibly slid away from them. Then, with a yell, one of the gamblers pointed to the receding forms, and straightaway the 15 made an onset.

Swinging his wife lightly to his shoulders Acantow set off at a run and he had almost reached his horse when his foot caught in a root and he fell headlong. The pursuers were almost upon him when the storm burst in fury. A flood of fire rushed from the clouds and struck the earth with an appalling roar. Trees were snapped, rocks were splintered, and a whirlwind passed. Acantow was nearly insensible for a time – then he felt the touch of the Rosebud's hand on his cheek, and together they arose and looked about them. A huge block of riven granite lay in the canyon, dripping blood. Their enemies were not to be seen.

'The trail is gone,' said Acantow. 'Manitou has broken it, that the Arapahoes may never cross it more. He would not allow them to take you. Let us thank the Manitou.' So they went back to where the spring burst amid the rose bushes.

Source

Charles Skinner, *Myths and Legends of Our Own Land*, vol. 2, Philadelphia: J.B. Lippincott & Co., 1896; reprinted by Singing Tree Press, 1969, pp. 135–36

THE LOVE OF RED BEAR AND FEATHER CLOUD

Paiute

A LONG TIME AGO, before [the American explorer and army officer John C.] Fremont or any white man came to this country, my people, the Paiutes, held all the land from the Columbia to below the Humboldt; all Nevada, California and southern Oregon. There was plenty of food and furs and they were happy. But our enemies conquered, so that at last the Paiutes just had a little desert land in the Humboldt Valley. The chief of the Paiute nation was my father's ancestor, but this is so long ago I cannot tell you how long. The daughter of this chief was a beautiful maiden. Her name was Feather Cloud, because of the small white cloud seen at her birth. She was smooth-armed, her eyes were very bright, but she always looked modestly down when in camp or among the men or the elders. She could sew with the deer sinew and tan buckskin, and kept her father's moccasins always soft and dry. No one could make such fine baskets of the hazel and the willow twigs, or of the rye grass and the maiden-hair fern stems. She could make mats from the inner bark of trees and of the tules. She was very neat and clean and her hair was as glossy as the blackbird's back. Her father had many ponies, but he was offered many more for the pretty Feather Cloud. 'No,' said he. 'She shall make her bed where she chooses.' She was 18 years old.

In the tribe, but living in another band, was a young man named Red Bear. He was tall, straight and braver than an eagle. He held his head up and looked every one in the face as an eagle does. He was not afraid of any one. He had no father, no mother, no squaw. His tribe had brought him up till he could hunt for himself, and he did not seem to care to get horses or robes or any riches. What he killed more than he needed he gave with the hides to the old people, and sometimes he asked an old woman to make him a new robe or pair of leggings. So everybody liked Red Bear and everyone was afraid of him. Red Bear had seen Feather Cloud for the first time at the Wreath Feast to celebrate her coming to womanhood. The feast was in the springtime, as it always is.

The day was warm; the birds played through the branches and sang in the tree-tops. The pine squirrels and the gophers ran about chirping; everything was glad to live. That morning Feather Cloud with all her companions, young girls of 16 or 18, had gone into the forest to gather flowers and make wreaths. They found the most flowers in the edge of the woods, in the open places where the sun was, and here they sat them down and made wreaths of violets, purple and yellow using anemones, yellow lilies, and purple iris, lupin and larkspur, the wild currant so pink, and strawberry blossoms.

Source

Charles Erskine Scott Wood, *A Book of Tales: Being Some Myths of the North American Indians*, New York: Vanguard Press, 1929, pp. 51–71

When the time had run and the shadow had reached the mark, the wreaths were counted; and as Feather Cloud had the most, she was crowned queen. She was clothed with flower wreaths. The others were ornamented also with wreaths. No one today could dispute her will; what she ordered was law. Every one laughed and was very happy. She decreed foot-races, and the maidens ran like frightened fawns, and wreaths were given as prizes. She decreed dances, and they took hold of hands and danced in a circle, sometimes very slowly. She ordered many games and moved about like a queen.

Red Bear had been hunting that day. He had killed a black bear coming out of a large hollow tree. The hide was on his arm as he came through the woods. Suddenly, he was near to the maidens as they were dancing. Feather Cloud was in the centre, her teeth and her eyes and her feet were all laughing, she was so happy and excited. Red Bear looked on her and loved her. She was very beautiful to him, the most beautiful in all the earth. But he said nothing, for men are not allowed at the wreath games. He stood still like a pine, but when the dance was done he walked forward and laid the bearskin at her feet and walked away. She said nothing and he said nothing. Only he looked into her eyes as boldly as a hawk and she looked into his and was ashamed.

In the evening the great campfires were lighted and the meat and the nuts were roasted, and the tribe sat around to see Feather Cloud and the maidens dance and celebrate the end of the feast. None but the relatives of Feather Cloud could take part. But Red Bear stood in the ring of onlookers and watched Feather Cloud. The more he watched, the more his heart seemed to go out to her hands and feet and the more hungry he became to take her for his wife; and he said to himself, I have found the one I want.

So all evening, while Feather Cloud and her companions chanted and danced and celebrated the end of the feast, Red Bear sat in the shadows of the fire and let love eat into his heart. The next night, after the custom of his people, Red Bear went to the lodge of Feather Cloud's father and sat at her feet like a statue. He did not speak, nor she nor any one; for no one at such a time must speak inside the lodge. Feather Cloud was awake; for all day she had wondered if Red Bear would come to her lodge as he now was. After he had sat a long time, she arose and moved to the other side of the tent and lay down again, and Red Bear moved and sat at her feet as before. Then after a time he went away. It would have been wrong to have offered him any hospitality.

The old chief, the father of Feather Cloud, did not like that he should come wooing his daughter; and outside the lodge, in the daytime when he could talk, he said to Red Bear, 'Red Bear, the beaver seeks a mate in its own village, the wolf in its own band; you are not of my band, and Wounded Elk is to be my son. He has horses and a skin lodge. He has relatives who will give rich presents and who will fight for him. You have nothing and are alone.'

Then Red Bear said, 'Skins for a lodge are easily killed, and beaver and mink for her to wear, instead of a robe of rabbit skins. Bears are in the mountains. They will be glad to lend their skins for us to sleep on. Do you not know I kill more than two others, or even three? Horses can be taken from the enemy. But all these things are nothing. What you need is a strong heart which will fight your battles, drive away your enemies, widen your hunting ground, make your name feared. You cannot get this with presents. Wounded Elk is a dandy; he is very lazy. I will drive him away as you drive a dog from the fire. You must not drive him away, you must go away yourself. If I go, I shall come back for Feather Cloud and to be chief.'

That night Red Bear sat at the feet of Feather Cloud in the lodge, as before, and the next day he spoke to her and said, 'By the law, I cannot speak to you in the lodge, but now I can tell you that you are dearer to me than my own hand. Your father is not pleased that I have nothing. Does he think you would ever go hungry? Does he think you would not be warm in the furs of the otter and sable? You are my eyes and like my very blood. You shall dry my moccasins and keep the fire burning and make soft buckskin and bring children to my tent. And does he think

Feather Cloud had made the most flower wreaths, and she was crowned Queen. No one today could dispute her will.

you shall not always have meat and skins? You shall put the sinew on my bow-back and make my warbonnet. Does he think you shall be given to our enemies? These things your father wants are easy to get. Will you wait for me?'

Then Feather Cloud put her eyes on the ground and said in a whisper, 'I will wait.'

That night again Red Bear sat at her feet, without speaking as is the law. Then he was gone. More than a moon passed, and Red Bear was not heard of. No one knew whither he had gone. Then came Wounded Elk, who had been far to the north, to the Great River. And he came to the lodge after all had lain down for the night. and sat at the feet of Feather Cloud. But she slept or pretended to sleep. Thus it went on until the thin edge of the moon had cut through the sky three times and three times had slid back again behind the sky. And the heart of Feather Cloud was very heavy, for she knew naught of Red Bear and her breast was empty for him. Then her father began to upbraid her, saying, 'See how patient is Wounded Elk. He needs you for his lodge. He is young and strong. He has many horses. He will be good to you. If you are sick he will take care of you. You are waiting for Red Bear, who has forgotten you. This must stop; you must take Wounded Elk.' Then Feather Cloud would look at the ground and say, 'I do not love Wounded Elk. Tell me what it is that I do not do right for you, that you turn me away from your fire.'

And her father would say, 'You shall not marry him if you do not love him; I shall not force you.'

And so three more moons crept out of the sky and back into it again. Then came Wounded Elk with his father and his relatives; and they brought many fine horses and robes and offered them all for Feather Cloud. Then her father said, 'Now I will give you to Wounded Elk whether you like it or not.'

But Feather Cloud sat down in the dust and put dust on her head and cried; and again she asked, 'What have I done that you like horses better than me?' Her father answered, 'Very well, you need not go to him if you do not love him. But now listen; this is the Feast of the Autumn; you may keep it with the maidens. If Red Bear returns before the Midwinter Festival and wants you, you may go to him. But if he does not return, you shall belong to Wounded Elk.' This comforted her a little, and she told every one that went away from the tribe to tell Red Bear to hurry back. But after they traced Red Bear as far north as the Bannocks, or to the Blackfoot country, they lost him. No one knew where he was. Feather Cloud's heart was too heavy for the Autumn Festival; but she also gathered the nuts and the seeds, pine-nuts, hazel nuts, sweet acorns, grass – and the roots, wild anise roots and camas and many others. For five days they gathered; then the women brought all these to the great fires, bearing them on their heads in the close-woven stiff baskets like buckets, the maidens walking behind the older women and all chanting the song of thankfulness to the Earth as they walked. Then, around the fires, they ground up the seeds in the stone mortars. Also they roasted the nuts and roots in the fire. They cooked all that had been gathered in the five days, and they sang songs and danced and made a great feast to celebrate the Autumn Season and to thank the Earth. They cooked no meat of any kind, because meat they had all the year round. When the winter had well begun and all the lodges were hidden among the willows in the little valleys, the camp was attacked one morning by the Snakes, enemies from the North. They were beaten off, but a few were killed on each side and many were wounded. Feather Cloud's father got an arrow in his side, but not too deep. He pulled it out

and stopped the hole with fresh pitch from the pine and with owl feathers. There was a young Snake taken prisoner, and they were getting ready to torture him, but he commenced laughing and calling the Paiutes women and liars. He said they had been coaxed to come on this expedition by Wounded Elk, who wanted his chief killed; then he would be chief and would marry the daughter. While he was telling this tale and jeering at such a people, Wounded Elk rushed forward to where the prisoner was bound, and brained him with a war club. The old men and women were angry that he should have done just what the captive wanted and released him from their torture. Wounded Elk was sorry, and gave dried venison for a feast. But Feather Cloud believed what the captive had said. The Midwinter Festival is for three days, to celebrate the sun's getting stronger and climbing higher into the sky. For in winter the sun is sick. The night before the first day of the feast, Feather Cloud did not sleep at all, for she had given up all hope of seeing Red Bear, and snow lay on the ground too deep for good travelling. When the day came, all began to gather in the great medicine lodge. The fires were built higher and the drumming of the drums and the whistling of the flutes began. So they kept up the dancing and the chanting all day. When one was tired another would take his place. The young men would dance and tell what they had done. The day and the night ended, and the old chief said to Feather Cloud, 'Tomorrow you must have Wounded Elk.'

'He called the Snakes to kill you,' said she.

'That is a lie told by a captive to madden him,' said her father quietly. 'Tomorrow you shall marry him. I am old.'

Feather Cloud wept all night. Her eyes were like fire. She ran into the woods and hid. That day they did not find her, but the next day they found her and brought her to her father, who said, 'Why do you do this? Is marriage like death? You can leave him if you do not like him. I shall give you to him. That is all I can do.'

So Feather Cloud made herself clean and put on her feather-trimmed white tunic, and braided her hair very smooth, and sat very sorrowful in the medicine lodge with her eyes cast down. In the evening the fires were built very high. It was the last hours of the feast. The pipes were sending out blue smoke and the fluters were whistling and the drummers drumming. Wounded Elk stepped into the circle, and, slowly twisting and stepping, began to chant. He was telling of his life and what he had done. He told how a wounded elk had nearly killed him, but he had stabbed it. He told how he had brained the captive. These were the most honourable things he had to tell.

When he had finished, a young man with only his loincloth on and a great warbonnet of eagle feathers which hid his face, stepped into the circle and began to dance. He was beautiful as a cougar. When he began to recite, then the heart of Feather Cloud gave a jump.

'I am a Paiute,' he said, 'and I have the heart of a man. I do not talk of killing elk. What is that? That is to get food; a boy does that. I have gone across the mountains to where the land runs to meet the sky, and there is the end of the world.'

'I found a party of Crows on the warpath. They were coming here. I crept among them at night like a snake and stabbed seven of them. This is the way they died. I was not afraid, I laughed at them. I followed them again for a week. I made no fire, I ate raw meat and I was cold, but I am not a baby. Then I crept among them again and killed five. It is hard to kill five men in the dark. You must strike just right and hold your hand on their mouths. Again I got away and hid in the rocks.'

'They were now afraid. They considered together and determined to turn back. Each man had two horses for travel and three war-horses. To steal these horses from a war party one must be brave as a grizzly and sly as a coyote. I slipped among them and cut their lariats. I tied them together, and, going back, I stabbed one of our enemies; but my hand slipped a little and he made much noise. Then I jumped on the back of one of the horses and gave our war cry and drove them off. They followed a little, but were afraid. They did not know how many there were. I laughed at them and was not afraid.'

'I had 20 horses, and for three days and nights I only stopped a little. Then I found buffalo in a large valley, and I rode to the head of the herd and killed the best cows as they ran, until I had more meat and robes than I wanted. Then I hid my horses and went among the Blackfeet and traded for some fine blankets, made from the wild goat's hair.'

'Then I loaded my herd with jerked buffalo and robes and blankets and some fine bows and many things and came among the Snakes. No one knew me to be a Paiute. No Paiute has ever done what I have done. There among the Snakes I heard of the messages from Wounded Elk. He asked them to come slay his own blood, to kill his own chief. I say it is true. I say I have stayed behind the rocks three days keeping off the Crows who wanted my blood. I say I have fought hand to hand with Spotted Hawk, a Crow chief, and fell upon him so tired I could hardly kill him; but I have not killed a captive. That is for the women. I say Wounded Elk is a Snake, a liar, a coward; he is worse than the dirt beneath my feet.'

Then the stranger, who had been dancing and singing faster and louder, stopped in front of Wounded Elk and threw his warbonnet far from him; and there was Red Bear, his eyes shining like a snake's. Wounded Elk leaped to his feet as if a snake had bitten him and looked for a way to escape. Then quickly he grabbed a hatchet pipe from an old man squatting near, but before he could use it Red Bear had grasped him by the waist and hurled him clear over into the fire, leaping upon him instantly like a wild cat and fastening his fingers on his throat. No one interfered, and presently the body of Wounded Elk was carried out.

Then Red Bear went to where Feather Cloud sat with her head hanging down, and said, 'I have horses and robes and a skin lodge, more than another could give, though he had many relatives, and from your relatives I ask nothing.'

Then spoke the old chief and said, 'I will give you my war-bow and you shall be my son.' A bowl was put in the hands of Feather Cloud, filled with roasted acorns. She offered this, standing, to Red Bear; but instead of taking it from her he took her by the wrist and drew her to him. Then he took the bowl from her and handed her some of the acorns to eat, then he ate some, and thus they were married.

He became the great war chief of the Paiutes and drove back their enemies till again they wandered over what is now California, Nevada, and part of Oregon. Feather Cloud was happy, for she had waited for him a long time, and a marriage feast was made, and the old people gave much advice to them how they should live, and at the end they went to live in their own lodge.

HOW THE NEZ PERCES GOT FIRE

Nez Perce

THERE WAS A TIME when the Chu-te-pa-lus had no fire. They tore raw flesh as the wolf does and ate the raw camas as the bear does; and in the winter they were very cold. Fire belonged to the Great Spirit. He kept it in the sky in the fire bags, which were black clouds. When the great bags bumped against each other there was terrible thunder, and through the rent made in the cloud the fire inside could be seen. All the tribe cried out for fire; and especially the little children who were cold, and the women, who were sorry to see their children freezing to death. The medicine men drummed the great drum and tried to get even a spark of fire; but they could not, and the people were very angry.

Then a young boy, only about 16 years old, said, 'I will get the fire for you.'

And the medicine men abused him and the people laughed. Nevertheless, when the great black fire clouds were drifting overhead, the lad made ready to steal the fire and the whole people stood around at a distance to watch him. He had bathed and made himself very clean. He was naked and very handsome. In his left hand he held his bow and in his right an arrow, wrapped about at the head with the dry inside bark of the cedar. He took from his neck the abalone shell of pearly white and placed it before him on the ground. Then he held up his hands and prayed.

The medicine men were telling the people to kill him, before he made the Great Spirit angry, but they said, 'Wait; if he does not steal fire for us, then we will kill him.'

When the largest fire cloud rolled above him, growling, suddenly he fitted his arrow to the string and shot straight up into the sky. The people, watching, could not follow the arrow; but there came quickly a terrible crash. Takoshahyokhot flashed through the sky; and then, falling like a star, the blazing arrow came back to earth. It struck exactly in the abalone shell and a small flame rose from the pearl shell – to-tegpkh.

The people with a shout rushed forward; some lighted sticks, some mats; some ran about laughing. But when they looked for the boy, he had gone; only there lay on the ground the shell, burned so that it showed all the colours of the fire, as it does to this day. When the strongest tried to bend the bow, they could not; and no man could ever bend it. The boy was never seen again. Thus the Great Spirit gave fire; of all blessings it is the best.

> When the largest fire cloud rolled above him, growling, he fitted his arrow to the string and shot straight up into the sky.

Source

Charles Erskine Scott Wood, *A Book of Tales: Being Some Myths of the North American Indians*, New York: Vanguard Press, 1929, pp. 47–50

HOW THE TE-TAW-KEN CAME TO BE

Nez Perce

THE NAME OF THE NEZ PERCES is Te-taw-ken – We the people. Once upon a time there were four giants and their giant sister who lived in the Salmon River and Palouse country. The sister wanted some otter liver to make big medicine. The great otter lived in the Palouse, which was a smooth river at that time, from the Snake to its head. So the four brothers took their spears and bows and went to hunt him.

They stationed themselves along the river; and the lowest, seeing the great beast asleep, shot an arrow into him. At this the otter fell into the water and

Source

Charles Erskine Scott Wood, *A Book of Tales: Being Some Myths of the North American Indians*, New York: Vanguard Press, 1929, pp. 81–83

shivered. This made the first rapids of the Palouse. As the otter swam upstream, the next brother also shot an arrow into him; again he shivered, and this made the second rapids. Still he swam upstream, lashing the water into foam with his tail; and the third brother shot him. At this he made some tremendous struggles, and thus came the rapids just below the falls. at this time the last giant ran down and thrust his spear through the otter; and the dying animal tore up the earth and rocks, and threw them about like sand. This made the falls of the Palouse.

Then the sister cut the beast into pieces, and threw some here, some there; where a piece fell there was made a band of the Chu-te-pa-lus or Ne-me-pus nation, Cayuses, Spokanes, Okanokanes, Umatillas, Walla Wallas. But the Nez Perces themselves – the Te-taw-ken, who are truly the people – they came from the strong heart of the otter. Then, when the giants saw the earth was filled with brave men (homonick), they took stations to watch over them; and, standing so long on guard, they were turned into mountains. There they still stand, white snow mountains above the earth.

ORIGIN OF PINE-NUTS AND DEATH

Paviotso

COYOTE SMELLED PINE-NUTS in the east, and blood gushed from his nose. He travelled all day toward the odour; but he did not find the place, and returned. The next day he tried again, and discovered a place where there were many people. The chief was directing them to make the pine-nut mush very thin, for he did not want Coyote to carry it away. The children were holding mush tightly grasped in their little hands, and Coyote made them drop it by thumping their hands. But when he attempted to hold it in his mouth in order to carry it back to his people, it was so thin that he swallowed it. Then he went home again.

His brother Wolf was making a speech to the assembled animal people, and Coyote stood beside him. Then all started out to obtain the pine-nuts, leaving behind only Sanaki [a small bird] to watch for their return. On the way they teased one another. Wildcat scratched the others, and, when they complained, he showed his hands and rubbed them together to prove that he had no claws.

The pine-nuts were concealed in the wrapping of a bow. All night they searched, and it was near morning when Louse found them and Woodpecker picked them out. Then they all ran westward, and the pine-nut people pursued them.

Coyote said, 'Let me be killed first.'

But Wolf said, 'No, I will be the one.' So he remained behind and was killed.

Blackbird had on his leg a sore, in which they hid the nuts so that the pursuers would not be able to find them. When the people overtook them and searched in vain for the nuts, they killed all except Blackbird, who, pretending to be dead, flew onward after they had gone. When he arrived home, Sanaki helped him build a fire to parch the nuts.

The eastern people made a great wall of ice between the dead western people

Source
Edward Curtis, *The North American Indian*, vol. 15, New York: Johnson Reprint Corporation, 1970, pp. 148–49

and their home; but after a while Wolf came to life and revived his people, who broke through the ice wall and returned home.

Wolf wanted the nuts to be like acorns, but Coyote said they should be in cones. And so it was. They discussed how many months should be in the year. Coyote placed his hands beside his forehead and said, 'Perhaps there will be this many.' Nobody replied.

They sent him to another house for tobacco, and while he was absent they arranged that there should be three months in the summer, three in the winter, three in the spring, and three in the autumn. Wolf proposed that people should live forever, but Coyote returned just then and changed this. He said, 'We will grow old and die.'

'No,' answered Wolf, 'you insisted that we die, and so it shall be.' Coyote's son was the first person to die.

THE DIVISION OF TWO TRIBES

Shoshone

WHEN WHITE MEN FIRST penetrated the Western wilderness of America they found the tribes of Shoshone and Comanche at odds. These tribes met one another in a hollow of the foothills in the shadow of the noble peak of Pike, a common meeting-ground for several tribes. Councils were held in safety there, for no Indian dared provoke the wrath of the manitou whose breath sparkled in the medicine waters there; except for one.

Hundreds of moons ago, a Shoshone and a Comanche stopped here on their return from a hunt to drink. The Shoshone had been successful; the Comanche was empty-handed and ill-tempered, jealous of the other's skill and fortune. Flinging down the fat deer that he was bearing homeward on his shoulders, the Shoshone bent over the spring of sweet water, and, after pouring a handful of it on the ground, as an offering to the spirit of the place, he put his lips to the surface. The Comanche took the opportunity to begin a quarrel with the Shoshone, asking him, 'Why does a stranger drink at the spring-head when one of the owners of the fountain contents himself with its overflow? How does a Shoshone dare to drink above me?'

The other replied, 'The Great Spirit places the water at the spring that his children may drink it undefiled. I am Ausaqua, chief of Shoshones, and I drink at the head-water. Shoshone and Comanche are brothers. Let them drink together.'

'No, the Shoshone pays tribute to the Comanche, and Wacomish leads that nation to war. He is the chief of the Shoshone as he is of his own people.'

'Wacomish lies,' said the Shoshone. 'His tongue is forked, like the snake's. His heart is black. When the Great Spirit made his children he said not to one, "Drink here", and to another, "Drink there", but gave water that all might drink.'

The other made no answer, but as Ausaqua stooped toward the bubbling surface Wacomish crept behind him, flung himself against the hunter, forced his head beneath the water, and held him there until he was drowned.

As he pulled the dead body from the spring the water became agitated, and from the bubbles arose a vapour that gradually assumed the form of a venerable

Source
Charles Skinner, *Myths and Legends of Our Own Land*, vol. 3, Philadelphia: J.B. Lippincott & Co., 1896; reprinted by Singing Tree Press, 1969, pp. 200–202

Indian, with long white locks, in whom the murderer recognized Waukauga, father of the Shoshone and Comanche nation, and a man whose heroism and goodness made his name revered in both these tribes.

The face of the old chief was dark with wrath, and he cried, in terrible tones, 'Cursed of my race! This day you have severed the mightiest nation in the world. The blood of the brave Shoshone appeals for vengeance. May the water of your tribe be rank and bitter in their throats.'

Then, whirling up an elk-horn club, he brought it full on the head of the wretched man, who cringed before him. The murderer's head was burst open and he tumbled lifeless into the spring, that to this day is nauseous, while, to perpetuate the memory of Ausaqua, the manitou struck a neighbouring rock, and from it gushed a fountain of delicious water. The bodies were found, and the warriors of the tribes of both hunters began on that day a long and destructive warfare, in which other tribes became involved until mountaineers were arrayed against plainsmen through all that region.

> The face of the old chief was dark with wrath, and he cried in terrible tones, 'Cursed of my race! The blood of the brave Shoshone appeals for vengeance.'

How the Coyote Got His Cunning

Klamath-Karok

KHARAIA, THE MAN IN THE SKY, told the Earth Man, the father of the Klamaths, to call together all the animals, that each might receive a bow. Whoever got the longest bow was to be chief and most powerful among the animals; and so on, according to the lengths of the bows. In those days animals could act like men and could use bows; animals and men could talk together.

On the day appointed, all the animals met together, and Kharaia gave to the Man the great sheaf of bows; but the Man said he would not give them out till the next morning, so that all could have a chance to come in that day. Then the Coyote determined he would sit up all night, so as to be first in the line next morning and get the largest bow; for it was very much in the heart of the Coyote to be the lord of beasts. He sat there all night watching the stars. But in the morning, just before the dawn came, he fell asleep. The sun rose, and all the animals walked past the Coyote, who slept as if he was dead. When all had got their bows and only the shortest was left, the Coyote woke up. He was very much ashamed, but when the animals laughed he laughed too, to pretend he did not care. But his laugh was not good.

The Man felt sorry for the Coyote, and he begged Kharaia to give a long bow to him. But Kharaia said, 'No, I will not break my word. But I will order that he shall be the smartest and most cunning of all. That is why he sits up all night now, and laughs in such a sorry way, and that is why he is the most knowing of all animals.'

Source
Charles Erskine Scott Wood, *A Book of Tales: Being Some Myths of the North American Indians*, New York: Vanguard Press, 1929, pp. 84–86

HOW SALMON GOT INTO THE KLAMATH RIVER

Klamath-Karok

ONE TIME, LONG AGO, all the salmon were in the sea. Klamath river had a great big rock across it, and no salmon could get into the river. The Klamath Indians could not go down to the sea. Moreover, nobody could catch the salmon in the sea. So, the Indians lived on nuts and roots and grass seeds. They pounded the seeds fine between stones and made cakes. But in the springtime, when the winter stock was eaten up, and before new roots and seeds were come, the Indians got very hungry.

The little children cried very much for food. This made everybody very sorry. The Coyote was a good friend to the Indian, because they were cousins, and the Indian one time was a very good friend to the Coyote. So the Coyote said, 'Why don't you go unlock the rock gate and let the salmon come up the river? Then you can eat till you burst.'

The Indian said, 'How can we unlock the great rock? You know the key is kept by the two sisters of the devil.'

'Well,' said the Coyote, 'you do your part, and I'll fill the river forever with salmon.' 'What must I do?' said the Man.

'Come with me,' said the Coyote, 'to the lodge of the witches. I will get close to the lodge hole. Then you make a noise, and when they rush out at you, you run away. That is all for you to do.'

So the Man and the Coyote journeyed along together, till they came to the sea. There they saw the great rock wall across the river, and there was the vast lodge of the witch sisters. The Coyote crept close to the lodge hole, so silently that not even the moon could hear him. Then the Man came up and shook the lodge a little. Out rushed the two sisters, snapping their jaws like huge owls. The Man ran like an antelope, and in between the witches rushed the Coyote, biting their legs and tripping them up. Before they knew what they must do, the Coyote had carried off the key of the dam. When the old devil-women saw this, they turned and ran after the Coyote, but he was far ahead. The key was heavy, and he was panting and nearly tired out when he reached the great dam. Quickly he got the key into its place, and pulled with all his strength. The old women were almost on him, when just then the key turned and the rock dam opened to the sea. The waters rushed together and the salmon crowded from the sea up the river. The old women, when they saw this, changed into two white-headed fish eagles and followed the salmon, screaming and calling. Ever since then, the Indians, even in the springtime, had plenty of food.

Source

Charles Erskine Scott Wood, *A Book of Tales: Being Some Myths of the North American Indians,* New York: Vanguard Press, 1929, pp. 87–90

HOW THE COYOTE STOLE FIRE FOR THE KLAMATHS

Klamath

IN THE BEGINNING THE KLAMATHS had no fire. The only fire in the world was guarded by two very bad-hearted, old devil-women, not the same as those who barred out the salmon, but two different ones. They lived in their great lodges, which are now the white-topped twin mountain. The fire was inside the mountain.

Again the Coyote came to the Man and said, 'Why do you not get some fire for yourself and your children?'

The Man said, 'I cannot, the devil-women have it.'

Then the Coyote said, 'I will get it for you, because you were good to me. Wait, I shall be back.'

The Coyote went to all the animals and told them they must do as he said, and help steal fire from the witches. Then he put them in a long line, from the Fire Mountain to the home of the Klamaths, each one about as far from the next as he could make a good run. The swiftest and strongest he placed nearest the devil-women's lodges. The eagle was first, just a little way off. Then, a long way down the mountain was the cougar; then the bear; then the elk and deer; then, across the open prairie, the antelope, the swiftest animal; then the rabbit, with his long bushy white tail; and all the animals down to the squirrel, and last of all the frog.

The frog was not then so small as he is now. He was a large animal and could give great leaps, but he was the slowest. He was put at the edge of the river, where the Klamaths lived.

The Coyote, when he had got all the animals ready, came for the Man, and together they went to the fire lodges of the old women. When they were there, the Coyote made the Man wound him a little bit in the skin of one leg, but not much. The Man cut himself, too, and smeared plenty of blood over the Coyote. Then the Coyote went limping on three legs to the lodge, and crept in, whining and crying.

'What is the matter?' said the devil-women, cracking their great teeth together as cranes clash their bills, only louder.

'The Man has tried to kill me,' said the Coyote, and showed his wounds. 'But I have bitten him so he will die. Smell; some of this blood is his.'

Then the old women sniffed the blood and gnashed their teeth more than ever, and laughed so the mountain shook, and down in the mountain you could hear the rumble of their laughter.

'Lie down by the sacred fire,' said they to the Coyote.

He lay down and commenced to lick his leg. After a time he pretended to fall asleep, and stretched himself out before the fire and snored. Presently the devil-women dropped their chins on their breasts and dozed. Then, like the dart of a salmon, the Coyote seized a brand and fled. The hags followed after him, screaming and gnashing their teeth.

They were nearly on him, when he handed the brand to the eagle. Away flew the great bird, his wings hitting the air like a tempest in the pines. But the old women followed fast and never grew tired. The eagle was glad to give the fire to the cougar, And so it went down the line, the devil-women just missing it each time, and shrieking with anger as they pursued each new fire-bearer. They were so close to the rabbit that, just as he gave it to the bat, one old woman seized his tail

Source

Charles Erskine Scott Wood, *A Book of Tales: Being Some Myths of the North American Indians*, New York: Vanguard Press, 1929, pp. 91–96

and pulled it off. That is why rabbits are stump-tailed. The bat took the fire. He could not fly very fast, but always, just as the old women thought they had him, he would dodge. They could not touch him, for he dodged this way and that, and brought the fire safe to the squirrel.

When the fire got to the squirrel, it was much smaller than it had been, but it had been fanned into a blaze, and in carrying it he scorched his back, so that his tail was drawn clear over his back, and the brown is still on his fur to this day.

At last it came to the frog, but he, knowing he could not outrun the old women, swallowed the fire and jumped into the river. Then, with yells of rage, the devil-women gave up the chase and went back to their lodges. Their fire went out, and there they stand today, cold and white. When they had gone, the frog came up and spat the fire out into a log, which is why it can be got by twirling one stick of wood very fast on another. The fire had burned the frog inside so badly that he shrank to the little fellow he is now, and his eyes nearly popped out of his head with pain.

The coyote seized a brand and fled. The hags followed after him, screaming and gnashing their teeth.

How the Spirit Coyote Passed from Earth

Klamath

In those days the Coyote was a spirit Coyote. He was a friend of the Man. They were cousins and they talked together. The Coyote loved the night. All night long he would sit and watch the stars. There was one large star, more beautiful than the moon or the sun. He was in love with the star, and would talk to her, night after night, and all night long. But the star would not answer him. She walked across the sky, looking at him, but saying nothing.

The Coyote grew more and more crazy for the star. He noticed that always, as she walked through the sky, she passed very close to a certain mountain peak, so close it would be easy to touch her. The Coyote travelled as fast as he could, a long, long way, until, very tired, he stood on this mountain, at the place the star always touched. He would not sleep for fear of missing her, so he sat and waited.

In the evening he saw her coming. She was very beautiful. He could see not that she and the other stars were dancing as they moved through the sky. The Coyote waited, his heart nearly bursting through his skin. But he kept very quiet.

The star danced nearer and nearer. At last she was on the mountain. He reached up as high as he could, but he could not quite touch her. Then, he begged her to reach her hand down to him. She did so, and took his paws into her hand. Slowly, she danced with him, up from the mountain, far up into the sky, over the earth. The Coyote got very dizzy and his heart became afraid. They went higher into the sky, among all the stars. It was bitter cold and silent. None of the stars spoke. The Coyote looked down, and fear made his heart very cold. He begged the star to take him back to the earth.

When they were at the very top of the sky, the star let go of the Coyote. He was one whole moon falling, and, when he struck the earth, he knocked a great hole in it. His blood turned to water and made a lake. This is Crater Lake, in Klamath County. When the Coyotes talk to the stars at night, they are scolding the star that killed their father.

Source

Charles Erskine Scott Wood, *A Book of Tales: Being Some Myths of the North American Indians*, New York: Vanguard Press, 1929, pp. 97–99

CREATION OF THE WORLD AND THE ANIMAL PEOPLE

Owens Valley Mono

THERE WAS NOTHING but water. In a boat were Wolf, the elder brother, and Coyote, the younger. They poured sand on the water, and it spread out and formed land.

'Brother, put more sand into the water,' said Coyote. More sand was poured out.

'Add more sand. I want to go out on it. I want to travel.'

Wolf added more sand.

'Add more sand,' said Coyote. 'I want to go farther.' So more and more land was created, until it was in its present form.

Then Wolf travelled and created mountains, trees, lakes and rivers, and all the food-bearing plants. He also made the animals, but these were really people. He gave the power of medicine men. At first he said there would be no medicine men, but Coyote insisted that they were necessary and Wolf yielded. In all things Coyote opposed his brother, and thus all the evil customs were established.

After their creation the people all raced to Coso springs. At that place was a large fire, and if Coyote won the race he was to toss a certain living thing into the fire. After the first day's race the people all stopped to sleep, and in the morning they all went on and left coyote sleeping. Frog urinated on him and covered his eyes so that he could not see; but he awoke and shook it off and ran on, and he won the race.

Now Wolf did not want him to burn the creature, yet he insisted, 'If you had won, I would not have asked you to let me roast this thing.'

So Wolf gave in. 'Go on and roast it, but wait until we reach our house,' he said.

The fire keeper was Snipe. His eyes were red from the smoke. Coyote made the movement of tossing the creature into the fire, and when he drew it back a great storm arose. While the rain fell he looked for the door of the house into which Wolf had gone. He threw the creature into the fire, and Snipe held it down with a stick. Now the rain fell all the harder. Coyote could not see. It was very dark. He said, 'Where is the house? Where is the house?' Nobody answered. He could not find the door.

Then he went about howling like a coyote. All winter long he did this. When spring came, Wolf told his people in the house to answer Coyote. So they called to him, and he came into the house. He was wet to the skin, and smelled like a coyote.

While he was drying, he thought about things, and decided to consult two medicine men to see if they could not bring light into the world. But they did not accept his offer of payment. So he spoke to Mallard and Great-horned Owl, who accepted his offer. They began to sing, and a faint light appeared. He told them to keep it up.

'The songs are not long enough, the light is not strong enough,' he said. He was going about gathering food, and when darkness came he was lost. They called him in and Mallard and Owl started again to sing. The light became stronger. Then all the people went out seeking food. This house was at Tugwebu [Black Rock].

Wolf had the deer penned up in the foothills and would kill one whenever he needed food. One day he said to Coyote, 'Go and kill one. Kill the one next to the first one.'

Source

Edward Curtis, *The North American Indian*, vol. 15, New York: Johnson Reprint Corporation, 1970, pp. 123–28

Coyote went to the place and said, 'What are these? Can you not smell?' He attempted to insert his member into the nose of a deer, and they began to sniff. They could smell. They became wild and ran about in the pen and broke out and scattered in the hills. He tried to hold them together, but could not.

When Wolf saw what his brother had done, he was angry and started eastward. At Ozabaiya [Deep Spring, south of Oasis] he stopped and gathered about him another tribe of people. He said he was going to hunt deer. Ishaa and his people came to Ozabaiya and lived.

In his house Wolf would hang his arrows on the sunbeams that poured through the cracks. Coyote, the pretender, said, 'I see my brother is trying to do what I used to do.' He tried to hang his arrow on the sunbeams, but they fell down.

When the men came back from the hunt, Wolf said, 'Now skin them and tan the hides. Then we will get some women.'

So they prepared to go to Tovowa where the women lived. The husbands of the women were hunting. From his house to the women's house Wolf extended a long tube, and through it they passed. The house was empty.

Outside one said to the youngest sister, 'Go and see what is in our house. It seems heavy.'

The youngest sister went in. To her Wolf said, 'Bring water for your husbands.'

She went back and said, 'Sisters, there is a man who said, "Bring water for your husbands." '

'Who are those men? Is Roadrunner there?'

'No, he is not there. A handsome young man is sitting in the corner.'

'Oh, that is Coyote. Is Wolf there?'

'There is a man in the back of the room, lying down.'

'Yes, that is Wolf. You can give them water.' Then she, the eldest, told all her sisters to gather around a pot and urinate into it. This the youngest sister took into the house.

'This is not good,' said Wolf. 'Take it out and throw it away. Bring good water to your husbands.'

So she took it out and repeated what Topi had said. The eldest said, 'Well, take them good water.' She sent in a very small cup.

Wolf said to the man sitting at the north side of the door, 'Drink, and pass it around. Drink all you want.' The cup came last to Coyote. He drank, and vomited vile-smelling stuff. Then a small quantity of food in the same kind of cup was sent in. It was passed around and everybody ate all he could hold. When night fell, the women came in and lay with the men.

Everyone had a woman except Coyote. The youngest sister was the one who should have been his, but the other women hid her. A very old woman came and started to prepare a bed beside him. He said, 'We will not lie together, because we are nanawakashi [the relation of a man and his child's parents-in-law].' He kept pushing her away, and she started to go out. At that moment she became a beautiful young woman, and she ran away. He exclaimed, 'What! Was I pushing away a young woman?' He ran after her. At the fire outside sat an old woman, the mother of the absent hunters.

'Old woman, where is that young woman who ran away?'

'I did not see her. Perhaps she went away.' She continued to repeat her words, and he said, 'Oh, you talk too much!' He put his member into her ear. She broke away after he had finished, and ran into the mountains, where her sons were. Along the way she built signal fires, and when they saw the smoke they made a fire to guide her to them.

When she reached their camp, she said, 'My sons, all your wives are sleeping with strange men.' They were angry and decided to make war. They started homeward, and set upon Wolf and his people. That was the beginning of warfare. All except two were killed, Wolf and Sagehen, who was one of the deer hunters. These two agreed to have a contest, and then Sagehen lost his life, being caught by the neck and strangled.

Wolf was now alone with all the women. Every day he killed a deer and told the mother of the women where it was. In an instant she would be gone and would return with the deer. Each night he slept between two different women, but he did not touch them. He would say, 'Lie quiet! Do not disturb me!' Each day the deer he killed was a little farther away than before, but each time the old woman was back almost instantly. While she was away Wolf would begin to look for the young girl who had been hidden, but there never was time enough.

At last one day the old woman's pack-rope broke, and while she was repairing it Wolf found the youngest sister and cut off her head. Then he started away. He had wanted to marry this girl, and because she was kept from him he killed her. While the old woman was repairing her pack-rope, she from time to time would look back to see it Wolf was still sitting outside the house where she had left him. But he had placed there something that resembled him, and so she was not troubled and went on with her work. When she came home and saw what had happened, she said, 'You cannot get away!'

She pursued him and caught him before he had gone far. She had an instrument which she would throw with a great whizzing sound. When it struck anyone it cut him asunder. She had also an obsidian knife, which she used in the same way. These she kept throwing at Wolf, but the weapon always passed over him and the knife beside him. She pursued him to the house of Roadrunner. Round and round the house she chased him, while Wolf kept crying, 'Where is your door? Where is your door?'

At last Roadrunner said, 'The door is in the top.' Then Wolf ran up on the roof and leaped down inside. Roadrunner was cooking something. The old woman smelled it and said, 'Throw out what you are cooking!'

'Hold your mouth up!' said Roadrunner. He threw out a red-hot stone, and it fell down her throat into her stomach. She went home with the stone in her stomach. Then Roadrunner told his sons to go and see if she reached home safely: if they saw smoke coming out of her head they would know she would soon die.

Wolf had left Roadrunner behind when he had gone to visit the house of the women, because he had feared that the youngest, whom he desired for himself, would fall in love with him. He had turned Roadrunner into a small worm and concealed him in a cocoon, and cautioned his sister, who lived there in the house, not to attempt to look into the cocoon. Thinking herself all alone, the girl would lie on the floor naked, with her legs apart; and Roadrunner, seeing her, would spit on her vulva. She would say, 'What can that be that is spitting on me? I wonder why my brother told me not to look into that little box?' Then one day she looked into it and drew out the small worm. It grew larger and larger, and at last became a man.

She said, 'Is it my brother's son? No, it is not.' So she named all the various relationships, but when she came to husband, she could go no further. Then Roadrunner lay with her, and she was his wife. They had a child.

Wolf lay about the house for a long time, resting after his hard race. His sister said to her child, 'That is your uncle.'

Roadrunner said, 'No, that is your stepfather.'

'Why are you disputing?' asked Wolf. 'I am his stepfather.'

Then she became sad, that he should renounce her as his sister.

Topi went back to where his men had been killed, struck them with his arrows, and awoke them to life, and brought them to the house. He decided to go hunting, and Roadrunner accompanied him and his men. Every night after they had killed something and camped, Roadrunner would bring back some meat to his family. They were proceeding eastward, and as they went farther and further, still Roadrunner kept returning home each night.

Grey hair began to show on the cheeks of Wolf. He no longer said to Roadrunner, 'Take this meat home to your wife.'

One night Roadrunner said to his wife, 'I am afraid of Wolf. He is becoming hairy all over his body.' The next morning when he returned to the hunters' camp he found the fire, and all the bows and arrows piled up, but nobody was to be seen. In the distance he heard something howling. Wolf and his men had become animals of various kinds.

Then Roadrunner returned home and said to his wife, 'Everything is changed. You are going to become an edible plant. I shall be Roadrunner. I shall be able to move about, but you will remain in one place.'

TAMALILI AND GOJI

Washo

TAMALILI WAS A SMALL BOY. He was always looking about, searching the distance. One day he saw something on a distant snowy mountain, and asked the people to help him observe it. They watched for a long time. Gradually it became larger. It was approaching. After a long time it came to the camp, and they saw that it was a small boy. His name was Goji. He remained with Tamalili that night.

The next morning Tamalili said, 'I am going to keep you with me. Let us go across the western mountains. Goji said nothing, but sat there. Tamalili had a bow and some arrows. He said, 'My bow and arrows, I know it, wish to go around and look for another country. These arrows are for killing game as we go along. They will kill anything, and we will have plenty of food.'

So they started. They ran all day. They started at the Valley of the Pine-Nuts. They ran southward and stopped at Waller Spring. Tamalili wished to camp there, but Goji said, 'No! We will not remain here. Let us go to the summit and camp.'

Before arriving at the summit they shot some chipmunks, and on the summit they roasted them. While the chipmunks were roasting, Goji fell asleep. Tamalili was constantly walking about. He had said to Goji, 'You must watch the fire. Something may come up out of it.' When he came back he found Goji asleep, and in the edge of the fire he saw Spider. He said, 'Who are you?'

'I do not belong to any people,' answered Spider.

Source

Edward Curtis, *The North American Indian*, vol. 15, New York: Johnson Reprint Corporation, 1970, pp. 151–54

'Have you no family?'

'No, I do not know who are my people. I am always alone.'

'Well, you are a strange fellow. You ought to know your parents.'

'I do not know who is my mother nor who is my father. I have no relations.'

'Well, then, how were you born?'

'I do not know. Nobody fed me and cared for me. I just grew up by myself. I think I will go with you.'

'No, I do not want you,' said Tamalili. 'You do not tell me about your people. I do not want to take you.'

'But I will go with you.'

'How can you keep up with me?' asked Tamalili. 'I run always. I can run to the top of this hill and jump to the bottom. Can you follow me all day?'

'Yes, I am a good runner. I am a strong man.'

'Well, then, let us go.' Tamalili started off, leaving Goji asleep. He ran swiftly, but Spider remained at his side. He ran up and down the hills, trying to outrun Spider and lose him in the mountains, but he could not.

In the middle of the afternoon Spider became angry. He demanded, 'What are you trying to do? I can tell what you are going to do.'

'What is it?'

'I know it. You want to kill me. You want to take me into the mountains and lose me.' They ran on, and he said, 'What is the matter? I am sweating.'

'I do not know,' answered Tamalili.

'Well, I can tell you,' said Spider. 'It is caused by my finding a bad man today. If he were a good man, he would sit down and talk to me; but he is a bad man, who tried to run away from me. I do not know where he is going nor where his home is. He runs all the time and visits nobody.' Then Tamalili was fearful. Spider went on, 'I know you are a good runner, but if you do not stop troubling me I will kill you.'

He was very angry. He struck Tamalili many times and each time a swarm of young spiders was planted in the eyes, or the ears, or the nose of Tamalili. He was nearly killed, and he ran back to Goji. He shook his friend and exclaimed, 'I! I am nearly killed, brother. Wake up!' He shook him and called him again and again, but Goji only snored on. Then Tamalili fell down dead, and after a while Goji awoke. He called his brother, 'My brother, where are you? Come, these chipmunks are cooked! Let us eat!' He walked about and found his brother's tracks, and the tracks of Spider. Then he feared. He kept on searching, wandering about the mountains, and always following the trail. But he could not find his brother.

He went into the sky and talked to the Sun. 'Friend, did you see my brother yesterday?'

'No,' answered the Sun. 'Go to the other house.'

Goji went to the Moon's house. 'Well,' said Moon, 'I do not look about in the daytime, because my eyes hurt. But at night I look over the whole world. That other man looks in the daytime. He can tell you.'

'Perhaps he does not wish me to come again.'

'If he does not wish you to come again, take this along.' The Moon gave him Porcupine. 'This will wake him up,' he said. 'If the Sun will not talk to you, let this Porcupine help you.'

When Goji returned to the Sun's house, he looked in and saw the Sun sitting there with his back to the door. He drew Porcupine out from under his arm and said, 'What is the matter with you? If you do not talk to me, this will hurt you.' Porcupine waved his tail, and the house was filled with sharp quills. Then the Sun looked around and asked, 'What is it?'

'Did you see my brother yesterday? If you do not tell me, this will hurt you.'

'Put him back, that Porcupine! I do not want to see him. But I will tell you.' Then the Sun told him about Tamalili and Spider, and added, 'Your brother is in a hole near the fire where you were roasting chipmunks. Spider dragged him in after he died.'

So Goji returned to the fire and scraped away the ashes, and there he saw the feet of his brother. He drew out the body and laid it beside the fire and stepped across it, and Tamalili sat up alive. Goji took him to the spring and washed him, and leaving the roasted chipmunks they went on.

In the afternoon Goji found a great buck. Tamalili said, 'You cannot shoot. Let me shoot him.'

'No, I am a good shot,' said Goji. He shot from a great distance and struck the deer, but did not kill it. The buck ran down along the American River and they followed. Goji became exhausted and Tamalili continued the chase alone. Near the trail he saw a great sweat-house. A watchman on the roof called his fellows, and out came more than a hundred Miwok. Tamalili said nothing to them, but continued on the deer's trail, and several men with bows and arrows followed him, headed off the buck, and killed it. When Tamalili came up he found them standing beside the dead animal. Each of them took a small piece of venison, and they sent a messenger to the sweat-house; and every man came and took a piece of the deer, until only the skin and bones were left. Then they killed Tamalili.

Goji, sleeping beside the fire, dreamed that his brother was in trouble. So he followed the tracks. On the way he found a little boy, who had a jug of water on his back. He took the boy along, and again he restored life to his brother. Then these two with the little boy went along westward. They came to the ocean. The people there wore wildcat skins. They were dancing. As the travellers sat watching, a girl approached and asked, 'Whence come you?'

'We came a long way. We cannot tell you all about it. You would be frightened.'

'Where are you camping?'

They told her, and she said, 'When anyone comes here, we treat him well. We feed him and give him a place to sleep. I will bring a friend and visit your camp tomorrow.'

Then Goji, Tamalili, and the little boy returned to their camp. The next morning two girls visited them, and proposed to remain; but Goji and Tamalili urged them to go home and not cause their parents sorrow. 'Well, we will go home, but tomorrow we will bring another girl,' said one of them. The following morning a number of girls came, and thereafter more and more. They proposed to take Tamalili and Goji hunting, for these girls hunted like men.

After remaining in that place for a time, Goji said, 'I do not like so many women around our camp. We had better go home tomorrow.' They left the little boy with the water-jug and travelled eastward.

THE WOMEN WHO MARRIED STARS

Washo

AN OLD MAN HAD TWO GRANDDAUGHTERS. They lived in Pau [Carson Valley]. He had a fishing hut at the edge of the river, where he speared fish. The two girls remained always in the camp. One of them said, 'I think my grandfather has been eating fish every day, and he must be tired of fish. We will grind some seed and take mush to him.' They ground some seeds and made mush, which they took to him, but he refused to eat it. They took pine-mush and other foods, but he would not eat. So much food they carried that the bits of mush and flour they spilled made a trail from the camp to the fishing hut. Then they were angry.

'What can we do? Can we go somewhere and find something good for our grandfather? Perhaps he will become angry with us and kill us. You can tell how this old man is feeling, because when we give him food he throws it away. This shows that he does not like us. Perhaps we had better leave him and go away by ourselves.' That is what they said.

So that very evening they started westward. They passed the night on the summit, and as it was very cold they slept close together. They laughed and joked. 'Well, if we find a good man on the trail or in a camp, let us get married.' So they talked. The younger sister said, 'See those large stars. You marry that red one, and I will marry the white one.'

Now the stars heard this and came down and carried the girls into the air and married them. In the upper world the girls learned that the red star was the Sun and the white star the Moon.

One day the younger went to her sister's camp, and said, 'What kind of meat have you? Have you good venison?'

'Yes, I have good meat, fat and juicy.'

'I think that man does not shoot with bow and arrows. It seems that he bites with his mouth, like a coyote. If he does not give me better meat, I will not stay much longer.'

'Do not say that! If we leave, I do not know where we shall go. We have no home. We have no friends. We must stay here another year. If you do not get the right kind of meat, feed your husband and then come here and eat with me.'

This the younger sister promised to do. She said, 'I am going to gather roots and seeds.'

'Well, I will go with you,' said her sister. So they went together to the younger sister's camp. The elder saw that the meat was bad. She said, 'Do not eat more. I think this is the flesh of a dog or a coyote. My meat at home is good venison. Your meat is bad. Let your man eat alone, and you come and eat my good meat.'

They went out to dig roots. As they worked, the younger sister's stick struck an anthill. It seemed to be hollow. She said, 'Let us dig here. I think we will find a hole.' When they thrust a heavy stick into the nest, the ground gave way and they looked down upon the earth. There they beheld their grandfather going about as if searching for a trail, and the younger sister was sorry. She said, 'My poor grandfather! He has nobody to care for him. I think I will go to him.' So they agreed to try to escape.

The end of the rope reached the earth, and the women started to climb down.

Source

Edward Curtis, *The North American Indian*, vol. 15, New York: Johnson Reprint Corporation, 1970, pp. 154–56

The elder sister had a baby. She said to her husband, 'My baby will not eat this venison. Whenever he sees sinew he cries. I think you had better get sinew for him.' By this deception she gradually secured a store of sinew, and each day she would go away from the camp and twist cord. They told their husbands that they wished to go to the valley and camp alone and make some fine baskets, which they did not wish the men to see until completed. The younger sister thought it best to leave the child, because otherwise its father might be angry and pursue them to the earth. The mother was unwilling to give it up; yet she consented. They tied the sinew rope to a log and dropped it through the hole. The end reached the earth, and they prepared to climb down. Meanwhile the baby was growing rapidly. As the women started down the rope, the child cried, 'Mother, where are you going?'

'Oh, I am going down for water.'

'I think you are going to leave me,' said the child. He ran home and told his father that his mother and his aunt had been spending all their time in making rope, and now were climbing down to the earth. Then the Sun and his child came running to the hole. He cut the rope, and the women fell to the earth and were killed.

The old man, their grandfather, was the one who taught the people how to make sinew nets and lines, bone fish-hooks and spoons, bows and arrows, and all the implements used by them. Had the two girls not run away and been killed, he would have been able to do much better for the people. For it was on these things that he was working and studying when the girls tried to induce him to eat.

ORIGIN OF THE BELT OF ORION

Walker River Paviotso

A MAN WITH HIS WIFE, his son, and his younger brother, had a camp at Tugwunusonii. Each day the woman, starting out to harvest seed, would say to her husband, 'Give me your best sinew, so that when the child cries I can roast a piece and give it to him to chew.' And he would give her a piece of sinew from the leg of a deer or a mountain-sheep.

While the woman gathered seed, the men hunted mountain-sheep. They were having bad luck: each day they chased the same sheep round and round the mountain, but they could not kill it.

Then the elder brother said, 'You had better sit down here beside the trail and watch. I wonder why that mountain-sheep never tires.' Crouching beside the trail, the man saw the sheep coming and his brother in pursuit. As the sheep passed, he saw that his brother's little boy was tied between its horns. The child was covered with foam, like the lather between the legs of a horse. Then he knew that the sheep was his sister-in-law. His brother came running up and stopped. He sat down, and when he had recovered his breath he asked, 'Did you see that sheep pass?'

The other did not answer at once. Then he said, 'Yes, the sheep! And your little child was tied between its horns!' The elder brother said nothing, but he was enraged that his wife had been causing them to hunt fruitlessly. The two men went home.

Source

Edward Curtis, *The North American Indian,* vol. 15, New York: Johnson Reprint Corporation, 1970, pp. 147–48

The next morning the woman asked for sinew, but her husband said, 'No! Leave that child at home and gather seeds by yourself. We are going to remain at home and mend our moccasins. We will take care of the child.' So the woman went to harvest seeds.

The men placed certain sticks of wood in the bed and arranged the blankets and some moccasins so that it appeared there were two men and a baby lying there. Then they transformed themselves and the baby into mountain-sheep and went and stood at the spring. At noon the woman came home. She was thirsty, but there was no water. She kicked the empty water-basket and said, 'Where is the water? Where is the water?' She took the basket to the spring. There she saw three mountain-sheep standing in the water, and she ran back to the house and cried, 'Get up, you lazy men! Do not sleep all day! There are three sheep in the spring.' She seized the blankets and threw them off. In the bed was nothing but sticks of wood. She ran to the spring, but the others had already gone.

The elder brother said to the younger and to his son, 'Do not look back, my brother; do not look back, my son! She has long hair on her vulva and she might catch you with it.' So the three ran on, the elder brother first, the boy second, and the younger brother last. The woman pursued them as she ran, she shook her breasts, calling to the child, 'Here is your milk, my child!' With the other hand she shook her vulva, calling to her husband. But neither would look back. As they ran along they encountered Coyote, who killed the three. While they lay there, the woman came up. She raised them to life and said, 'You must not turn yourselves into mountain-sheep.' She tore the flesh from the front of her pelvis and threw it at them. It struck the back of their necks and remained there. That is why the mountain-sheep has a lump on the back of the neck. She said, 'Go along the way you were. I will follow behind.' They became stars, forming the Belt of Orion, travelling behind the Pleiades.

PART 7
THE PACIFIC NORTHWEST

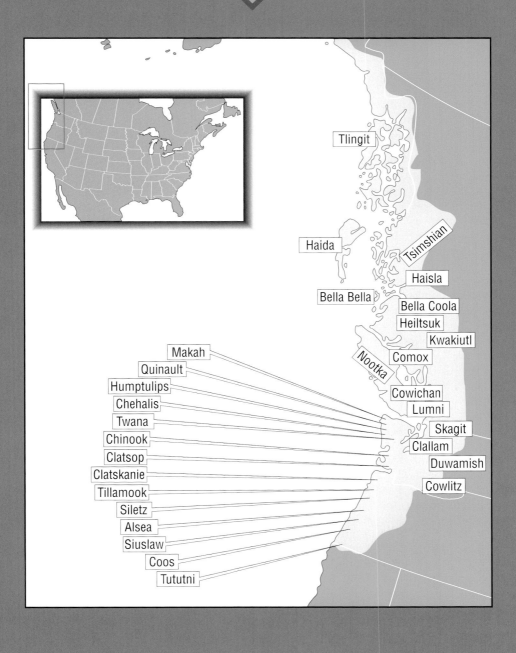

Tlingit

Haida

Tsimshian

Haisla

Bella Bella

Bella Coola

Heiltsuk

Kwakiutl

Comox

Nootka

Cowichan

Lumni

Makah

Quinault

Humptulips

Chehalis

Twana

Chinook

Clatsop

Clatskanie

Tillamook

Siletz

Alsea

Siuslaw

Coos

Tututni

Skagit

Clallam

Duwamish

Cowlitz

TRIBES OF THE PACIFIC NORTHWEST

The Northwest Coastal culture group occupies the smallest region of all the tribes of North America. These people are found along an elongated strip of coastland, rarely wider than 160km (100 miles) east to west, which extends from the border between the modern states of Oregon and California to Prince William Sound on the Alaskan coast. The region includes western portions of Oregon and Washington, and the Canadian province of British Columbia. Additional lands of the region include major island groups, including Vancouver Island, the Queen Charlotte Islands and the Alexander Archipelago, plus scores of smaller island chains which dot the Northwestern coastline.

Despite the region's relatively small size, the Northwest culture group comprised many tribes. They created a culture which adapted to the region's high rainfall (over 2.5m/100in annually), the abundant forests and the coastal waters and rivers that teemed with fish and other aquatic life. Most of these tribal groups centred their lives around wealthy villages, made possible through a combination of such natural factors.

The tribes of the Northwest were not a cohesive group. They spoke several different and distinct dialects, including Athapascan, Nadene, Penutian, Salishan and Wakashan. Among the Athapascan-speakers were the Clatskanie and Tututni, who lived in northern and southern coastal Oregon, respectively. The Nadene-language tribes were the Eyak, Haida and Tlingit groups. Penutian speakers included the Alsea, Chinook, Clatsop, Coos, Kalapuya, Siuslaw, Takelma and Tsimshian. The Salishan-language groups were the Bella Coola, Chehalis, Clallam, Comox, Cowichan, Cowlitz, Duwamish, Humptulips, Lumni, Quinault, Siletz, Skagit, Tillamook and Twana. Nearly all these tribes ranged from Washington state, north into British Columbia. Those tribes speaking Wakashan were the Bella Bella, Haisla, Heiltsuk, Kwakiutl, Makah and Nootka. Many additional tribes were also located in the Northwest, most of which were smaller in number.

Ancient Roots of the Northwest Peoples

Dating the earliest arrivals of Native Americans to the Northwest region is difficult. To date groups, archaeologists have traditionally relied on various stages of pottery created by a particular people or by their use of stone tools and weapon points. However, the tribes of the Northwest did not rely on pottery, and there is scant evidence of flaked stone tools and weapons left for archaeological examination.

Owing to their geographical location, the Northwest tribes were isolated, and thus generally developed without any contact with other tribal and regional cultures. Evidence is limited, however, concerning when, and even how, they arrived in their traditional homelands. Archaeological evidence points to an initial period of occupation, often referred to as the Coastal Land Hunting period, which dates from around 6000 BC. Hunters of that period appear to have used flaked stone-tipped implements of the Clovis variety.

A 5,000-year gap in the archaeological record leaves little evidence of a culture in the Northwest of any distinguishable extent, and it is not until 1000 BC that archaeologists and anthropologists pick up the historical scent again. The culture of that period, known as Early Maritime, was a coastal-based, sea-oriented culture. The Northwest inhabitants of 3,000 years ago used harpoons to hunt sea mammals, and slate to make their stone points and tools. Such practices suggest a strong connection between these peoples and the Eskimos further north.

Following the Early Maritime period, archaeologists identify eras of cultural advancement through the integration of hunting practices on both land and sea, as well as other ways of life, which, progressively, produced a finely tuned maritime culture. By the time of Christ, Northwestern cultural practices and values were based on hunting, fishing and gathering wild plants. Like their predecessors, these people were not known for their systematic agriculture. Over the past seven centuries, Northwestern Native Americans have developed their intricate social systems and have become extraordinary craftsmen, hewing the various woods of the region into a variety of art forms, tools and hunting objects.

Capitalist Native Americans

By the time of white contact, and throughout the past three centuries, many of the Northwest tribes have developed an extraordinarily rich economy. In a modern sense, these Native Americans have become known as 'capitalists', having created a well-defined system of monetary worth, based partly on an obsession with property and the financially based social prestige, which often comes with being a possessor. Historian Sidney Fletcher, in his book *The American Indian* (New York: Grosset & Dunlap Publishers, 1954, pp. 101–102), describes this Northwestern cultural tendency to accumulate wealth:

> Blankets woven from the hair of dogs and mountain goats were their equivalent of one, or five, or ten, dollar bills. A rich man had thousands and thousands of blankets that he stored away in cedar chests or loaned out at interest. Instead of gold and silver coins, he was likely to have strings of a rare seashell called dentalium. Instead of stocks and bonds, he prided himself on big plates of copper, each one worth possibly three, four, or even six thousand blankets in his money. A wealthy man might also invest in slaves, but his biggest investment was in names. He was

a nobody unless he could boast at least one expensive name.

Fletcher's reference to 'one expensive name' may seem an odd one; however, it goes to point out how extraordinarily different the tribes of the Northwest could be from their contemporaries in other regions of North America. Their conspicuous wealth caused them to create a social system based on material possessions and titles of honour and prestige.

Honour within the tribe was based not on the exploits of a warrior, as with many other tribes outside the region, but rather on the names he might possess. A Northwestern tribesman who wanted to marry into the family of a nobleman was expected to 'buy' into the family. A would-be suitor had to bargain for his prospective wife, generally paying a high price for her and her name. Once they were married, the husband did not stop paying, either. He was expected to continue paying for her annually, as long as he expected to have her as his wife and keep her in his house.

This approach to prestige and family honour spawned a unique social system in North America. A reasonable comparison to this approach to tribal honour might be made with the system of heraldry developed in Europe during the Middle Ages. Just as the social structure of that time and place relied on the existence of a nobility, represented by coats-of-arms and other symbols of heraldry, so did the social class system of the Northwestern tribes.

To this end, families possessed a collection of hereditary titles which only members of that family might use, and then only in reference to one person at a time. But these names were not merely handed out. They were often bought at a cost of thousands of blankets by an individual from his family or his wife's family. Even the names which were sought indicated the wealth of its recipient, including names such as 'Too-Rich', 'Throwing-Away-Property' and 'Always-Giving-Away-Blankets-While-Talking'.

All this social finagling caused a stratification of rank based on chiefs, nobles, commoners and slaves. Slaves were captives of war, and their descendants, whose rank was not negotiable, remained ever at the bottom of the social heap.

The other ranks were hardly part of a caste system, however. One could move up from one to another by circumstances of birth or marriage, or through some conspicuous validation of wealth. Such acts might include simple bartering, exchanges of labour and gifts, food gifts and special feasts; but the grandest act of the wealthy person seeking rank was a ceremony called the potlatch.

The Potlatch

The word 'potlatch' comes from the Chinook term meaning 'to give'. It was a highly ritualized event designed to celebrate the raising of a house or a totem-pole, the birth of a child, a marriage or a death. Potlatches were also used as a means of receiving or purchasing rank in the tribe. The ceremony validated the status of an individual. Such status was essential to establishing rank among one's peers.

The potlatch offers an explanation for the drive among Northwestern tribes to accumulate wealth. Having done so, a tribe member could, in turn, bestow a part of his wealth on others, thereby demonstrating a validation of his right to a particular title, rank or name. The famed American anthropologist Franz Boas observed such a potlatch ritual in the 1920s, and presented this interpretation (*Ethnology of the Kwakiutl*, Washington DC: Government Printing Office, 1921, p. 844) of the actions taken by a Kwakiutl nobleman:

> Now he gave away the four sea otter blankets, ten marten blankets, seven black bear blankets, thirty-five mink blankets, and fifty deerskin blankets . . . . As soon as he had finished his potlatch, he told the [guests] that he had changed his name. You will call me Lalelit . . . . Thus [he] said to his guests. Therefore, I am full of names and privileges. And therefore I have many chiefs as ancestors all over the world; and therefore I feel like laughing at what is said by the lower chiefs, when they claim to belong to the chief, my ancestor.

Great potlatches might take years to plan. A chief or any other man with title in the tribe arranged for contributions to the potlatch from his relatives. He would inform them of when the potlatch was to be held and what their contribution was to be, for potlatches were considered important for the reputation of an entire clan. Invitations were sent out to the guests of the potlatch. Even rivals and enemies of an individual were invited. No one receiving an invitation could refuse to attend without being disgraced.

Potlatches were not simply lively, boisterous parties. Rival guests of the host had to sit and endure long, egotistical pronouncements made by their host about his wealth that amounted to little more than bragging. Much food was served, and all guests had to eat whatever they were given, regardless of how much they might want or not want. Following various dances and the grand meal, the centrepiece of the potlatch followed: the giving of the gifts. The giving spirit of a potlatch was a warped one, however – one which demanded that the host pile the largest number of presents on his most despised guest. This was because a secondary purpose of the potlatch, in addition to showing off one's wealth, was to obligate others financially to the host. These 'gifts' were not gifts at all, but merely loans. Each recipient of a potlatch gift was expected to repay the gift within a year at 100 per cent interest! In other words, for every blanket heaped on a guest, the host expected two in return within 12 months. To fail to repay a potlatch gift was an absolute disgrace which might require a chief or nobleman to sell himself into slavery to pay off the debt. By this tactic, the chief of one village might force the chief of another into a debt so deep he might not be able to get out, bringing about personal bankruptcy.

Such a practice could, therefore, be highly destructive economically. To give greater emphasis to his amassed wealth during a potlatch, a chief might opt not to give away his material goods but to destroy them instead, by throwing items into the ocean or by pouring crates of whale oil onto a fire. Many Northwestern potlatches included a chief tearing up blankets, punching holes in canoes, and even killing his own slaves or burning down his house.

Totem-Pole: Symbol of Prestige

As an extension of the powerful drive of Northwestern tribesmen to accumulate status, rank and honour among their peers, they created an art form which has come to be known as the totem-pole. Such a pole was typically carved from cedar and served several purposes, depending on the type of pole it was. The most common totem-pole was the memorial pole, which natives erected along the shore of their village's inlet or river. Such poles were intended to note the assumption of a chief's heir to his new position. Another pole type, the mortuary pole, was often placed near the grave of a deceased tribal leader. Often such poles had a container at the top which housed the cremated remains of a chief. Other poles were raised as potlatch poles, and were carved to further the prestige of a family after they had hosted a potlatch ceremony. Whereas most poles were carved and erected in order to commemorate some prestige gained by a tribesman, the ridicule pole served to shame someone for a lack of honour, such as not repaying a potlatch.

The most pervasive of all totem-poles was the type called the house pole. These symbolic poles were erected either outside the front door or inside the home, and proclaimed the family's status to all who passed by or entered. Once inside, visitors might encounter a further post, often serving as the primary support crossbeam for the house, which further trumpeted, in the fashion of a medieval coat-of-arms, the owner's familial pedigree.

Totem-poles featured a variety of animal-spirit creatures, stacked on top of one another. Many incorporated figures of Eagle, Killer Whale, Wolf, Raven and mythical beasts such as Thunderbird and the greatly feared Hokhokw, a monstrous bird which sported a lengthy beak powerful enough to crush a warrior's skull. By including a particular animal in a totem-pole, the carver was paying his respects to the spirit of the animal and wished for that spirit to grace his family.

Although the purposes of totem-poles were to recognize one's honour and to connect one with the spirits of the carvings, totem-poles were not venerated themselves. In fact, once such a pole was erected, it was largely ignored. Most Northwestern tribes did not maintain their poles, attaching no real importance to them once they had been raised, a process that served as an end in itself. If a pole began to deteriorate, rotting in the region's rainy environment, nothing was done to save it. They did not even bother to restraighten a pole that had leaned out of position. Such poles were allowed to decay and were simply replaced by another pole, adding further to the household's prestige. As a result, since few totem-poles have been raised since 1900, historical totem-poles are extremely rare, typically found at museums, local parks and national monuments.

An Economy Based on Salmon

What allowed the Native Americans of the Northwest to live such extravagant lives? How could they have amassed such conspicuous wealth? The answers lie with the abundance of nature which surrounded them. Unlike tribes found elsewhere in North America, many of whom faced the constant problem of hunting, raising and gathering enough food to provide adequate sustenance all year round, the Northwestern tribes never lacked for food sources. Chief among these sources was salmon, a fish which could be found by the million in the icy waters of the Northwest.

The salmon was, and remains, a creature of habit and instinct. Annually, during the warmer months of the year, salmon made spawning runs up every available water source in the Northwest. During those runs, whole villages were abandoned, and sites erected along various rivers for the fishing season. Salmon were caught by a variety of methods. The traditional hook and line was common, but other means might yield greater results. Net systems were set up which might enable a single fisherman to catch 100 salmon a day, trapping them in his net and clubbing them to death. Other methods of salmon-fishing included long basket traps and elaborate weirs, or fences placed in the water of a stream which diverted the course of the salmon to where waiting fisherman could more easily club their prey. Through the abundance of the salmon, a man might be able, in just a few weeks, to catch enough food to feed his family for an entire year. As a result, Northwestern people did not have to spend most of their days searching for food. This gave them a freedom to pursue elaborate crafts which helped create their wealth.

Beyond the natural abundance of fish, the Northwestern tribes relied on another bounty – immense red cedar trees which, due to the high rainfall of the region, grew to great heights. These tall, majestic trees provided the raw material for many of the material goods of the Northwest. Tribes made their houses out of cedar planks, creating some of the roomiest dwellings built by Native Americans. Cedar wood is a finely grained material, which is easy to work using simple tools. They carved cedar canoes, tools, weapons, baskets and domestic items such as dishes, bowls and great chests to hold the abundance of blankets accumulated by a wealthy chief. With a enormous reliance on the abundance of salmon and cedar, the tribes of the Northwest became the wealthiest, best fed and best housed of North America.

Hunters of Whale

Although salmon was a mainstay of the diet of the Northwestern tribes, other foods were also important. Despite their general reliance on seafood and river fish, these Native Americans also hunted elk, deer, caribou, bears and other woodland animals for food, fur, sinew and bone. Because of their unique location along the Pacific Coast, however, they could also hunt whales.

Native American whale hunts were not much different from those of the Yankee whalers of New England. Large wooden canoes were built for just such a purpose. Building a whaling canoe was a vast undertaking. Generally, they were carved from the trunk of a single giant red cedar tree, a process which took two to three years to complete. Without the benefit of large saws, the craftsmen felled such a tree by burning a girdle around its trunk, achieved by holding heated stones against the outer wood. Once they had the tree they needed, it was floated to the village site and placed on shore. Carpenters spent many

months chipping away at the log, forming the hollow of the boat, and carving the outside of the craft. As the hull of the canoe deepened, a craftsman drilled test holes to examine the thickness of the vessel's side and bottom. After drilling, he plugged the holes up again.

To widen the shape of the boat's hull, the newly carved boat was filled with water, and hot rocks were placed in the bottom of the craft. This procedure made the wood more pliable and allowed the craftsmen to wedge open the hull's sides. Cross-braces were placed in the widened hull, and the boat was allowed to dry. Decorations were added, including elaborate carvings and a high prow, often in the shape of an animal. The whole canoe was sanded down with sharkskin.

The result of many months of work, only such a craft could have played host to its wealthy patron and provided the vessel needed to catch an elusive whale. A typical 'crew' consisted of eight or nine men. Such crews were often 'hired' by a rich man of the village, who went along on the hunt dressed in his finest bearskin or sea-otter robe, but did little of the work of the hunt. His role was one of honour.

The whalers relied on harpoons to spear their prey, with lines attached to the harpoon head rather than the shaft. This ensured that, even when a harpoon broke, the head would usually remain in the wounded animal, and the line remained attached to the kill. Prior to copying this technique from Pacific whalers in around the mid-nineteenth century, New England whalers always attached their lines to the harpoon shaft, resulting in many a splintered harpoon and lost whale. Once a whale was speared, the sea-bound hunters attached inflated sealskins to the line; this floated on the water, marking the location of the harpooned whale and making it difficult for the animal to submerge and escape.

Once killed, the whale was towed to shore, and the entire village participated in the removal of whale blubber from the carcass. The rich sponsor of the whale hunt usually paid his workers in blubber. Ceremonies and prayers were performed, to pay the village's respects to the spirit of the whale. Such a ritual went on for four days, culminating in a great feast with the villagers gorging themselves on whale blubber. In addition to the blubber, whales provided the Northwestern tribes with valuable oil, which was used for a variety of purposes.

Plank Houses

The natives of the Northwest were not only master craftsmen but also skilled carpenters. They constructed their homes out of cedar, which they felled from the thick forests and split into planks. In building a cedar house, carpenters set two heavy tree trunks upright, extending about 3.6m (12ft) high and set approximately 1.8m (6ft) apart. A pair of support posts was planted upright opposite the first two, at a distance of around 18m (60ft). The dimensions varied according to the size of house required. Two great support beams were placed parallel to one another, resting on the four support posts. These provided support for the gabled, plank roof. As the building progressed, feasts and ceremonies were often held to commemorate each stage. Such rituals paid homage to the trees themselves, which were considered to have souls. The Kwakiutl referred to these as nawalak, the 'soul of the living wood'.

Once the primary posts and beams were set in place, additional corner posts were put up, along with cross-beams. Interlocking planking was used to form the frame of the house. The planking was pegged together using cedar-bark withes or wooden pegs. Despite the solid nature of these heavy-beamed plank homes, the carpenters might also place heavy stones on the roof of such a dwelling to keep the roof planks from blowing off in strong winds.

The inside configuration of such a house varied from tribe to tribe. While most measured in the neighbourhood of 15m (50ft) square, some were gigantic, providing shelter for an entire village. One such house was noted by a European explorer in 1808 as measuring 18m (60ft) in width and stretching on for a length of 200m (650ft)!

A variety of familial activities took place inside a Northwestern plank house. The typical household chores, such as food preparation, took place around a centrally located fire pit. Most homes were left open inside, with no rooms dividing up the space. If spaces were divided off, movable screens provided the distinction. Such 'rooms' provided some privacy for individual families, for these homes were the residences of extended family units which might include several generations. Although their homes were often communal in nature, the Northwestern people were so bound by the law of ownership that each family unit living in such a dwelling considered itself the owners of the planks which made up their portion of the house.

The contents of such a home might be considerable. Cedar-bark sleeping mats lined the perimeter, flanked by large cedar chests containing clothes as well as furs and blankets for freezing winter nights. Baskets filled with dried fish and tubs of whale blubber might also be placed around the house. Cooking utensils, tools and weapons also had their place inside these snug homes. After contact with white traders, the typical Northwest home might feature iron pots and skillets, oil lamps, cooking stoves, which replaced the central fire pit, and manufactured furniture such as rocking chairs, armoires and chests of drawers.

Since their livelihood and wealth came from the inlets and coastal waters of the Pacific, most Northwest tribes built their villages right on the shoreline, often in the quiet waters of ocean harbours or the banks of cold, mountain-fed streams. A village might boast as few as 50 residents, while many numbered several hundred. Often the houses were built in one of two rows, allowing for one main 'street' for the village. The buildings of the community included not only family dwellings but also houses for smoking fish, as well as sweat-lodges, storage barns and special huts for women to occupy when giving birth or menstruating. Several of these wooden-plank villages stretched along for up to a mile along the placid waters of a Pacific inlet. They were home to their tribes and clans throughout the cold winter months and for a portion of the summer, between foraging and fishing expeditions. Otherwise, a village was often abandoned during food-gathering months, with its inhabitants actually dismantling and taking their buildings with them, only to return later to the original site to reassemble their wooden community.

Warfare

The capitalistic drive of the region's Native Americans led them to practise the art of war and raiding to gain material wealth. Most warrior raiding parties were carried out to gain slaves. Frequently, slaves accounted for a large portion of a village's population, sometimes representing one-third of the people living there.

Men preparing for battle carved sturdy wooden helmets and cedar slat armour. Their personal arsenal might have included bows and arrows, clubs, daggers and spears. The chief means of mobility for war was the war canoe, in which warriors travelled to an enemy's village. Such vessels were large enough to hold several warriors. Often measuring 15–18m (50–60ft) in length, the war canoes were fierce-looking crafts. Each craft might have carried 30 or 40 men into battle. These canoes were often also used for whale hunts.

Wooden Clothing

Despite their general emphasis on wealth and material possessions, the clothing worn by the tribes of the Northwest Coastal region tended toward the basic and simple. As with many North American regions, the season of the year often determined the type of clothing worn. During the warmer summer months, men wore either a loincloth or simply went naked. Women, on the other hand, always wore something, regardless of the season; they made some clothes out of shredded cedar bark, and wove skirts and vests from plant fibres. In colder weather, people wore fur robes and cloaks made from animal skins. Nearly everyone went barefoot on land, and moccasins were extremely rare. Due to the heavy annual rainfall, Northwestern peoples wore conical basket hats made of spruce root, headgear resembling that traditionally found in China.

Body decorating was done by the Northwestern tribes. The males used pieces of wood and shell to pierce their noses, in order to sport decorations. Beards and moustaches, usually rare among North American tribes, were common in the Northwest, as was tattooing, done by drawing blackened thread through the skin. Among some Northwestern tribes, infants were kept in their cradleboards, their heads wedged between the cradleboard and a slat which was bound over their foreheads. As they developed, their heads were flattened, a look considered noble and attractive. Slave babies' foreheads were not flattened, making them easy to identify during social interaction.

Marriage and Family Life

When a child was born, the mother usually named him or her a few days after having given birth. The name of a dead ancestor was generally selected, bestowing honour on the child. Women nursed their children for at least their first two years, sometimes for a year or two longer. Cradleboards were used to carry an infant from place to place.

At the age of ten, boys often left their homes and went to live with an uncle and aunt. This was a sign of honour to the uncle, and the young boy was supposed to work for the uncle. This removal from the parental home marked the last days he would spend in that house. Before leaving home, the youth might experience the first potlatch held in his honour.

Girls continued to live with their mothers. When a girl reached puberty, she underwent the puberty rite, a ritual common in many forms among many North American tribes. Her advancement into young adulthood was noted by her aunts who became her advisers, giving her instructions and helping her in ritualistic piercings of her ears and lips. Such acts were symbolic of status.

When young boys and girls reached the age of sexual activity, there were few prohibitions against premarital escapades. Children were cautioned, however, not to have relations with someone far below their own social and material status, and incest was an act punishable by death. Young men, depending on the tribe, might have sexual relations with the wife of his brother or with the wife of his mother's brother.

When two young people married, they did so with the understanding that ultimately such a match had much to do with the social and material status of their respective families. When couples became 'engaged', gifts were exchanged between the families. Prior to the marriage, the young fiancé might work for the parents of his bride-to-be. Marriage conferred complete adult status on both the man and the woman. Women, even when married, retained ownership of their own property.

When an aged person of the tribe was near to death, relatives paid their respects by visiting the dying one, while the immediate family gathered his or her property around the bed. A family – often a male cousin – had the task of carving a grave box for the remains of the dying member. After death, the body was dressed and ceremoniously painted, then propped up near the fire pit or stove in the house. There it remained for four days, after which it was removed and placed in the grave box, perhaps after cremation. Mourning rituals involved feasts for the remaining family members, and went on for many days.

Mythology and Religion

As with the tribes of all other regions of North America, the mythology of the Northwestern peoples was one based on animism. Nature held many powers, some of which could be tapped by humans who paid a spirit the appropriate homage and respect. Animals are presented as heroic figures. The totem creatures of heroic tales had the capacity to change from animal to human form, and vice versa. Such stories sometimes included a group of beings called the Sky People, a vaguely drawn cast of characters who wielded power beyond that of ordinary spirits.

There are few gods and goddesses in Northwestern mythology. Among those found are a Sky Being or Lord of the Sky, something akin to the Great Spirit of legends from other regions of North America. This being had great power, which could include causing storms, earthquakes and other forms of natural destruction. Other deities were the Sun and Moon, and a mischievous creature – a trickster – the Raven. This trickster character has a counterpart in the myths of other regional tribes, for example the Coyote of the Southwest and the rabbit Glooscap of the Northeast.

The animals commonly included in totem-poles are present in the Northwestern mythology, and are often depicted as creatures which are not entirely animal or human, but a strangely morphing combination of both. These animals were the objects of tribal rituals and ceremonies.

The supernatural beings found in Northwestern mythology are a combination of both helping spirits and evil-doers or mischief-makers. Most tribes practised rituals designed to transform the actions of a would-be evil spirit into those of a helper. Tribesmen and women called on the spirits to give them blessings in nearly everything they did, from hunting and going to war, to carving a canoe or making a basket. Those seeking help from the gods approached them in a variety of ways, including prayers, incantations and charms, and pilgrimages to sacred spots such as lakes, rivers, mountains and valleys. Rituals often accompanied these other religiously motivated acts. For example, a warrior might take a saltwater bath to gain strength and courage, for the sea was the home of powerful sharks. Shamans, or tribal holy men, were also approached as intercessors, since they were seen as the tribal members with the most direct connections to the spirit world.

The search for a connection between the spirit world and the physical may be seen in the theology surrounding such native activities as fishing and hunting. A Northwestern hunter practised a different ritual for each hunt. A Nootka whaler painted his face, rubbed his body all over with sacred herbs, and took a bath, careful to swim anticlockwise while making whale noises. A Nootka seal-hunter might perform a four-night ritual which included rubbing himself over with seaweed, praying aloud and taking a dip in the ocean. This ritual was repeated as many as ten times each night.

Salmon-fishing required an involved set of rituals. Some Northwestern peoples believed that salmon, except during their spawning season, appeared and lived as humans, and actually lived in houses. During a single season, however, they transformed into the appearance of a fish, and took to the streams and rivers, sacrificing themselves for the upriver humans. According to the theology, the natives could capture the animal but not its soul. A village and its fishermen also had to be worthy of a salmon's sacrifice. A village was expected to practise good ecology by keeping its river clean. Menstruating women were always cautioned to stay out of a fishing stream since they made the water impure.

The first salmon caught in a season, or the first forest animal killed, was to be treated with great respect. This practice could set the pattern of success or failure for the entire season. The first salmon catch was taken to a village chief, where the leader of the clan sprinkled the fish body with eagle down and offered a prayer of thanks to the sacrificed prey: 'We are glad you have come to visit us. We have been saving these feathers for you for a long time. We hope you will return to visit us soon.' A meal followed, with the first salmon cooked and eaten during a large feast. Once consumed, the bones of the first catch were strewn in the river. This completed the cycle and the salmon season continued with abundance.

Other rituals blessed the season for the hunters. Just as with the first salmon, the first elk killed was cut up, boiled, and the meat distributed throughout the village. A freshly killed bear was offered sacrifices of dried salmon, then a chief sprinkled eagle down on the head of the bear. The Bella Coola tribe skinned the bear and then draped the furry mantle backwards on the animal, tapped the body four times and repeated an invitation to the spirit of the dead animal: 'Tell your brothers, your sisters, your uncles, your aunts, and your other relations to come to me.'

MYTHS AND LEGENDS OF THE PACIFIC NORTHWEST

THE TALE OF THE TEN BROTHERS

Haida

TEN BROTHERS WENT OUT TO hunt with their dogs. While they were climbing a steep rocky mountain a thick mist enveloped them, and they were compelled to remain on the heights. By and by they made a fire, and the youngest, who was full of mischief, cast his bow in it. When the bow was burnt the hunters were astonished to see it on the level ground below. The mischievous brother thereupon announced his intention of following his weapon, and by the same means. Though the others tried hard to dissuade him, he threw himself on the blazing fire, and was quickly consumed. His brothers then beheld him on the plain, vigorously exhorting them to follow his example. One by one they did so, some boldly, some timidly, but all found themselves at last on the level ground.

As the brothers travelled on they heard a wren chirping, and they saw that one of their number had a blue hole in his heart. Farther on they found a hawk's feather, which they tied in the hair of the youngest. They came at length to a deserted village on the shores of an inlet, and took possession of one of the huts. For food they ate some mussels, and having satisfied their hunger they set out to explore the settlement. Nothing rewarded their search but an old canoe, moss-grown and covered with nettles. When they had removed the weeds and scraped off the moss they repaired it, and the mischievous one who had led them into the fire made a bark bailer for it, on which he carved the representation of a bird. Another, who had in his hair a bunch of feathers, took a pole and jumped into the canoe. The rest followed, and the canoe slid away from the shore. Soon they came in sight of a village where a shaman was performing.

Attracted by the noise and the glow of the fire, the warrior at the bow stepped ashore and advanced to see what was going on.

'Now,' he heard the shaman say, 'the chief Supernatural-being-who-keeps-the-bow-off is coming ashore.'

The Indian was ashamed to hear himself thus mistakenly, as he thought, referred to as a supernatural being, and returned to the canoe. The next one advanced to the village.

'Chief Hawk-hole is coming ashore,' said the shaman.

The Indian saw the blue hole at his heart, and he also was ashamed, and returned to his brothers.

The third was named Supernatural-being-on-whom-the-daylight-rests, the fourth Supernatural-being-on-the-water-on-whom-is-sunshine, the fifth Supernatural-puffin-on-the-water, the sixth Hawk-with-one-feather-sticking-out-of-

Source

Lewis Spence, *Myths and Legends of the North American Indians*, London: George G. Harrap & Co., 1914, pp. 312–14

the-water, the seventh Wearing-clouds-around-his-neck, the eighth Supernatural-being-with-the-big-eyes, the ninth Supernatural-being-lying-on-his-back-in-the-canoe, and the eldest, and last, Supernatural-being-half-of-whose-words-are-raven. Each, as he heard his name pronounced, returned to the canoe. When they had all heard the shaman, and were assembled once more, the eldest brother said, 'We have indeed become supernatural people,' which was quite true, for by burning themselves in the fire they had reached the Land of Souls.

The ten brothers floated round the coast till they reached another village. Here they took on board a woman whose arms had been accidentally burned by her husband, who mistook them for the arms of someone embracing his wife. The woman was severely burned and was in great distress. The supernatural brothers made a crack in the bottom of the canoe and told the woman to place her hands in it. Her wounds were immediately healed. They called her their sister, and seated her in the canoe to bail out the water.

When they came to the Dju, the stream near which dwelt Fine-weather-woman, the latter came and talked to them, repeating the names which the shaman had given them, and calling their sister Supernatural-woman-who-does-the-bailing.

'Paddle to the island you see in the distance,' she added. 'The wizard who lives there is he who paints those who are to become supernatural beings. Go to him and he will paint you. Dance four nights in your canoe and you will be finished.'

They did as she bade them, and the wizard dressed them in a manner becoming to their position as supernatural beings. He gave them dancing hats, dancing skirts and puffin-beak rattles, and drew a cloud over the outside of their canoe.

> 'Paddle to the island you see in the distance. The wizard who lives there is he who paints those who are to become supernatural beings.'

THE BLUE JAY AND IOI TRILOGY

Chinook

The Story of Blue Jay and Ioi

BLUE JAY WAS A TRICKY, mischievous totem-bird. His sister, Ioi, requested her brother to take a wife from among the dead, to help her with her work in house and field. To this Blue Jay readily assented, and he took for his spouse a chieftain's daughter who had been recently buried. But Ioi's request that his wife should be an old one he disregarded.

'Take her to the Land of the Supernatural People,' said Ioi, when she had seen her brother's bride, 'and they will restore her to life.'

Blue Jay set out on his errand, and after a day's journey arrived with his wife at a town inhabited by the Supernatural Folk.

'How long has she been dead?' they asked him, when he stated his purpose in visiting them.

'A day,' he replied.

The Supernatural People shook their heads.

'We cannot help you,' said they. 'You must travel to the town where people are restored who have been dead for a day.'

Blue Jay obediently resumed his journey, and at the end of another day he

Source

Lewis Spence, *Myths and Legends of the North American Indians*, London: George G. Harrap & Co., 1914, pp. 323–27

reached the town to which he had been directed, and told its inhabitants why he had come.

'How long has she been dead?' they asked.

'Two days,' said he.

'Then we can do nothing,' replied the Supernatural Folk, 'for we can only restore people who have been dead one day. However, you can go to the town where those are brought to life who have been dead two days.'

Another day's journey brought Blue Jay and his wife to the third town. Again he found himself a day late, and was directed to a fourth town, and from that one to yet another. At the fifth town, however, the Supernatural People took pity on him, and recovered his wife from death. Blue Jay they made a chieftain among them, and conferred many honours upon him.

After a time he got tired of living in state among the Supernatural People, and returned home.

When he was once more among his kindred his young brother-in-law, the chief's son, learned that his sister was alive and married to Blue Jay.

Hastily the boy carried the news to his father, the old chief, who sent a message to Blue Jay demanding his hair in payment for his wife. The messenger received no reply, and the angry chief gathered his people round him and led them to Blue Jay's lodge. On their approach Blue Jay turned himself into a bird and flew away, while his wife swooned. All the efforts of her kindred could not bring the woman round, and they called on her husband to return. It was in vain, however: Blue Jay would not come back, and his wife journeyed finally to the Land of the Souls.

The Marriage of Ioi

One night, the Ghost-people from the Shadow-land, intending to buy a wife, took Ioi, the sister of Blue Jay. After a year had elapsed her brother decided to go in search of her. But though he inquired the way to the Ghost country from all manner of birds and beasts, he got a satisfactory answer from none of them, and would never have arrived at his destination at all had he not been carried there at last by supernatural means.

In the Ghost-country he found his sister, surrounded by heaps of bones, which she introduced to him as his relatives by marriage. At certain times these relics would come together and take on human form, but instantly became bones again at the sound of a loud voice.

At his sister's request, Blue Jay went fishing with his young brother-in-law. Finding that when he spoke in a loud tone he caused the boy to become a heap of bones in the canoe, Blue Jay took a malicious pleasure in reducing him to that condition. It was just the sort of trick he loved to play.

The fish they caught were nothing more than leaves and branches, and Blue Jay, in disgust, threw them back into the water. But, to his chagrin, when he returned his sister told him that they were really fish, and that he ought not to have flung them away. However, he consoled himself with the reflection, 'Ioi is always telling lies.'

Besides teasing Ioi, he played many pranks on the inoffensive Ghosts. Sometimes he would put the skull of a child on the shoulders of a man, and the other way around, and take mischievous delight in the strange result when they came 'alive'.

On one occasion, when the prairies were on fire, Ioi asked her brother to extinguish the flames. For this purpose she gave him five buckets of water, warning him that he must not pour it on the burning prairies until he came to the fourth of them. Blue Jay disobeyed her, as he was given to do, and with dire results, for when he reached the fifth prairie he found he had no water to pour on it. While trying to beat out the flames he was so seriously burned that he died, and returned to the Ghosts as one of themselves, but without losing his mischievous nature.

Blue Jay and Ioi Go Visiting

Blue Jay and his sister Ioi went to visit their friends. The Magpie was the first to receive the visitors, and by means of magic he provided food for them. Putting a salmon egg into a kettle of boiling water, he placed the kettle on the fire, and immediately it was full of salmon eggs, so that when they had eaten enough Blue Jay and Ioi were able to carry a number away.

On the following day the Magpie called for the kettle they had borrowed. Blue Jay tried to entertain his visitor in the same magical fashion as the latter had entertained him. But his attempt was so ludicrous that the Magpie could not help laughing at him.

The pair's next visit was to the Duck, who obtained food for them by making her children dive for trout. Again there was twice as much as they could eat, and Blue Jay and Ioi carried away the remainder on a mat. During the return visit of the Duck, Blue Jay tried to repeat this feat also, using Ioi's children instead of the ducklings. His attempt was again unsuccessful.

The two visited in turn the Black Bear, the Beaver and the Seal, all of whom similarly supplied refreshment for them in a magical manner. But Blue Jay's attempts at imitating these creatures were futile. A visit to the Shadows concluded the round, and the adventurers returned home.

THE BIRTH OF SIN, THE SKY DEITY

Haida

THE DAUGHTER OF A CERTAIN CHIEF went one day to dig in the beach. After she had worked some time she dug up a cockle-shell. She was about to throw it to one side when she thought she heard a sound coming from it like that of a child crying. Examining the shell, she found a small baby inside. She carried it home and wrapped it in a warm covering, and tended it so carefully that it grew rapidly and soon began to walk.

She was sitting beside the child one day when he made a movement with his hand as if imitating the drawing of a bowstring, so to please him she took a copper bracelet from her arm and hammered it into the shape of a bow, which she strung and gave him along with two arrows. He was delighted with the tiny weapon, and immediately set out to hunt small game with it. Every day he returned to his foster-mother with some trophy of his skill. One day it was a goose, another a woodpecker, and another a blue jay.

One morning he awoke to find himself and his mother in a fine new house,

Source

Lewis Spence, *Myths and Legends of the North American Indians*, London: George G. Harrap & Co., 1914, pp. 314–16

with gorgeous door-posts splendidly carved and illuminated in rich reds, blues and greens. The carpenter who had raised this fine building married his mother, and was very kind to him. He took the boy down to the seashore, and caused him to sit with his face looking toward the expanse of the Pacific. And so long as the lad looked across the boundless blue there was fair weather.

His father used to go fishing, and one day Sin – for such was the boy's name – expressed a wish to accompany him. They obtained devil-fish for bait, and proceeded to the fishing-ground, where the lad instructed his father to pronounce a certain magical formula, the result of which was that their fishing-line was violently agitated and their canoe pulled round an adjacent island three times. When the disturbance stopped at last they pulled in the line and dragged out a monster covered with piles of halibut.

One day Sin went out wearing a wren-skin. His mother beheld him rise in stature until he soared above her and brooded like a bank of shining clouds over the ocean. Then he descended and donned the skin of a blue jay. Again he rose over the sea, and shone resplendently. Once more he soared upward, wearing the skin of a woodpecker, and the waves reflected a colour as of fire.

Then he said, 'Mother, I shall see you no more. I am going away from you. When the sky looks like my face painted by my father there will be no wind. Then the fishing will be good.'

His mother bade him farewell, sadly, yet with the proud knowledge that she had nurtured a divinity. But her sorrow increased when her husband intimated that it was time for him to depart as well. Her supernatural son and husband, however, left her a portion of their power. For when she sits by the inlet and loosens her robe the wind scurries down between the banks and the waves are ruffled with tempest; and the more she loosens the garment the greater is the storm. They call her in the Indian tongue Fine-weather-woman. But she dwells mostly in the winds, and when the cold morning airs draw up from the sea landward, she makes an offering of feathers to her glorious son. The feathers are flakes of snow, and they serve to remind him that the world is weary for a glimpse of his golden face.

Examining the shell, she found a small baby inside.

The Story of Wakiash and the First Totem-pole

Kwakiutl

THERE WAS ONCE a chief named Wakiash, and he was named after the river Wakiash because he was openhanded, flowing with gifts even as the river flowed with fish. It happened on a time that all the tribe were having a big dance. Wakiash had never had any kind of dance of his own, and he was unhappy because all the other chiefs of the tribe had fine dances. So he thought to himself, 'I will go up into the mountains to fast.' And he made himself ready, and went up into the mountains and stayed there four days, fasting and bathing. On the fourth day, early in the morning, he grew so weary that he lay upon his back and fell asleep. Then he felt something that came upon his breast and woke him. It was a little green frog. The frog said, 'Wake up, that you may see where you are going.'

Wakiash opened his eyes and saw that the frog was on his breast. The frog said, 'Lie still as you are, because you are on the back of a raven that is going to fly with

Source
Natalie Curtis Burlin, *The Indians' Book*, New York: Harper and Brothers, 1907, pp. 299–302

The raven flew and carried the man and showed him all the things of the world.

you around the world, so that you may see what you want, and take it.' And the frog said that he would stay with the man till they came back again to the same place. Then the frog told the man to get ready, and bade the raven to start.

The raven flew and carried the man around the world and showed him all the things of the world. They flew four days, and when they were on their way back Wakiash saw a house with a beautiful totem-pole in front, and heard a noise of singing inside the house. He thought to himself that these were fine things, and he wished that he might take them with him. Now the frog knew his thoughts and told the raven to stop. So the raven stopped and the frog told the man to hide himself behind the door. The man did as the frog told him, and the frog said, 'Stay here, and, when they begin to dance, leap out into the room.'

The people tried to begin a dance, but could do nothing – they could neither dance nor sing. One of them stood up and said, 'There is something the matter with us; there must be something near us that makes us feel like this.'

And the chief said, 'Let one of us, who can run faster than the flames of the fire, go around the house and see.'

So the little mouse came and said that she would go, for she could go anywhere, even into a box, and if anyone were hiding she could find him. The mouse was in the form of a woman, because she had taken off her mouseskin clothes; indeed, all the people in the house were animals, and their chief was the beaver, but they had taken off their animalskin clothes to dance, and so they looked like men.

The mouse ran out, and Wakiash caught her and said, 'Ha, my friend, wait here and I will make you a gift.' And he gave the mouse a piece of mountain-goat's fat. Now this mouse was so pleased with Wakiash that she talked with him and asked him what he wanted, and Wakiash said that he wanted the totem-pole, the house, and the kind of dances and songs that belonged to them. The mouse said, 'Stay here, and wait till I come again.'

Wakiash stayed, and the mouse went in and said to the people, 'I have been everywhere to find if there were a man about, but I could find nobody.' And the chief said, 'Now let us try again to dance.'

They tried three times before they could do anything, and they sent out the mouse each time to see what she could find. But each time the mouse was sent out she talked with Wakiash; and the third time that she went out she said, 'Now make ready, and, when they begin to dance, leap into the room.'

Then the mouse went back to the animals and told them that she could find no one, and so they began to dance, and just then Wakiash sprang in. At once the dancers dropped their heads for shame, because a man had seen them looking like men, whereas they were really animals. And they stood silent for some time, till at last the mouse began to speak and said, 'Let us not wait thus; let us ask our friend what he wants. He must want something or he would not come here.'

So they lifted up their heads, and the chief asked the man what he wanted. Wakiash thought to himself that he would like to have the dance, because he had never had one of his own, though all the other chiefs had dances. Also he wanted the house, and the totem-pole that he had seen outside. Though the man did not speak, the mouse heard his thoughts and told the people. And the chief said, 'Let our friend sit down and we will show him how we dance, and he can pick out whatsoever kind of dance he wants.'

So they began to dance, and when they had ended the chief asked Wakiash

what kind of dance he would like. They were using all sorts of masks. Wakiash wanted most of all the Echo mask, and the mask of the Little Man that goes about the house talking, talking, and trying to quarrel with others. Wakiash only thought to himself; the mouse told the chief his thoughts. So the animals taught Wakiash all their dances, and the chief told him that he might take as many dances and masks as he wished, also the house and the totem-pole. The chief said to Wakiash that these things would all go with him when he went home, and that he should use them all in one dance; also that he should thenceforth have, for his own, the name of the totem-pole, Kalakuyuwish, meaning sky-pole because the pole was so tall. So the chief took the house and folded it up in a little bundle. He put it in the headdress of one of the dancers, and this he gave to Wakiash, saying, 'When you reach home, throw down this bundle; the house will become as it was when you first saw it, and then you can begin to give a dance.'

Wakiash went back to the raven, and the raven flew away with him towards the mountain from which they had set out; but before they arrived there Wakiash fell asleep, and when he awoke the raven and the frog were gone and he was all alone. Then he started for home, and when he got there it was night, and he threw down the bundle that was in the headdress, and there was the house with its totem-pole! The whale painted on the house was blowing, the animals carved on the totem-pole were making their noises, and all the masks inside the house were talking and crying aloud. At once Wakiash's people awoke and came out to see what was happening, and Wakiash found that instead of four days he had been away four years. They went into the house, and Wakiash began to make a dance; he taught the people the songs, and they and Wakiash danced, and then the echo came, and whosoever made a noise the Echo made the same, changing its mouths. When they had finished dancing the house was gone; it went back to the animals. And all the chiefs were ashamed because Wakiash now had the best dance.

Then Wakiash made, out of wood, a house and masks and a totem-pole; and when the totem-pole was finished the people made a song for it. This totem-pole was the first that this tribe had ever had; the animals had named it Kalakuyuwish, 'The pole that holds up the sky', and they said that it made a creaking noise because the sky was so heavy. And Wakiash took for his own the name of the totem-pole, Kalakuyuwish.

Source

Charles Skinner,
*Myths and
Legends of Our
Own Land*, vol.
3, Philadelphia:
J.B. Lippincott
& Co., 1896;
reprinted by
Singing Tree
Press, 1969,
pp. 242–45

TAMANOUS OF TACOMA

Siwash

A GREAT FLOOD BATTERED the lands around Mount Tacoma. The Whulge [Native American name for Puget Sound] was so swollen after long rain that its waters covered the earth. All other men were drowned. The waves pursued a single survivor of the flood, a warrior who tried to climb above the floodwaters. All other men were drowned. The waves pursued the one man as he climbed, rising higher and higher until they came to his knees, his waist, his breasts. Hope was almost gone, and he felt that the next wave would launch him into the black ocean that raged about him, when one of the spirits of the peak, taking pity on him, turned his feet to stone. The storm ceased, and the waters fell away. The man still stood there, his feet a part of the peak, and he mourned that he could not descend to where the air was balmy and the flowers were opening. The Spirit of All Things came and bade him sleep, and, after his eyes were closed, tore out one of his ribs and changed it to a woman. When lifted out of the rock the man awoke, and, turning with delight to the woman, he led her to the seashore, and there in a forest bower they made their home. There the human race was recreated.

On the shore of the Whulge in after years lived an Indian miser, a rare man among his people, who dried salmon and jerked the meat that he did not use, and sold it to his fellow men for haiqua – the wampum of the Pacific tribes. The more of this treasure he got, the more he wanted – even as if it were dollars.

One day, while hunting on the slopes of Mount Tacoma, he looked along its snowfields, climbing to the sky, and, instead of doing homage to the spirit of the mountain, he only sighed, 'If I could only get more hiaqua!'

Sounded a voice in his ear, 'Dare you go to my treasure caves?'

'I dare!' cried the miser.

The rocks and snows and woods roared back the words so quick in echoes that the noise was like that of a mountain laughing. The wind came up again to whisper the secret in the man's ear, and with an elk-horn for pick and spade he began the ascent of the peak. Next morning he had reached the crater's rim, and, hurrying down into the hole, he passed a rock shaped like a salmon. Descending lower, he passed a rock shaped like a camas-root, followed by a third rock bearing the shape of an elk's head.

'These are the messages of a spirit!' he exclaimed, as he looked at them.

At the foot of the elk's head be began to dig. Under the snow he came to crusts of rock that gave a hollow sound, and presently he lifted a scale of stone that covered a cavity brimful of shells more beautiful, more precious, more abundant than his wildest hopes had pictured. He plunged his arms among them to the shoulder – he laughed and fondled them, winding the strings of them about his arms and waist and neck and filling his hands. Then, heavily burdened, he started homeward.

In his eagerness to take away his treasure he made no offerings of haiqua strings to the stone spirits in the crater, and hardly had be begun the descent of the mountain's western face before he began to be buffeted with winds. The angry god wrapped himself in a whirling tower of cloud and fell upon him, drawing darkness after. Hands seemed to clutch at him out of the storm. They tore at his treasure, and, in despair, he cast away a cord of it in sacrifice. The storm paused for a moment, and when it returned upon him with scream and flash and roar he parted with another. So, going down in the lulls, he reached timber just as the last handful of his wealth was wrenched from his grasp and flung upon the winds. Sick in heart and body, he fell upon a moss-heap, senseless. He awoke and arose stiffly, after a time, and resumed his journey.

In his sleep a change had come to the man. His hair was matted and reached to his knees; his joints creaked; his food supply was gone; but he picked camas bulbs and broke his fast, and the world seemed fresh and good to him. He looked back at Tacoma and admired the splendour of its snows and the beauty of its form, and had never a care for the riches in its crater. The wood was strange to him as he descended, but at sunset he reached his wigwam, where an aged woman was cooking salmon. Wife and husband recognized each other, though he had been asleep and she a-sorrowing for years. In his joy to be at home the miser dug up all his treasure that he had secreted and gave of his wealth and wisdom to those who needed it. Life, love and nature were enough, he found, and he never braved the spirits again.

THE YOUTH WHO MARRIED A GOOSE

Haida

A CHIEF'S SON HUNTING DUCKS on the shore of a lake saw two young women swimming. On a log lay two goose skins. He cautiously watched them, then suddenly ran out and sat on the skins. The young women leaped toward them, but when they saw that they were too late, they dropped back into the water and looked at him. After a while they spoke, 'Give us our skins.'

He looked at them and said to the younger and prettier one, 'I will marry you.' But the elder answered, 'No, do not take my sister. Take me. I am the elder.'

'No,' he said, 'I must marry your sister before I give up these skins.' For a long time they stood there in the water, and the young man sat on the log. At last the elder said, 'Well, you shall marry my sister. This lake belongs to my father.'

So he gave her a skin and she put it on. At once a fine goose was swimming on the water. It rose into the air and flew about the other young woman for a while, and then flew straight up into the air and disappeared. Then the chief's son climbed a cedar and placed the other goose skin in a cleft of the tree, and throwing one of his two martenskin blankets on his shoulders he led his wife home to his father.

Now the chief invited the people to see his son's wife and to feast with her, but when they placed food before her she picked up a bit, smelled it and laid it back. One day her mother-in-law began to cook some silverweed-roots, and the Goose woman at once fixed her eyes on this food. She said to her husband, 'Tell your mother to hurry with that food.' When the dish was ready, she ate all, and thereafter they fed her only these roots.

One night while the young man was sleeping, he was awakened by his wife coming into the bed and touching him with her body, which was very cold. The following night he remained awake, but pretended to sleep, and so he saw his wife rise quietly and go out. He followed her along the front of the village and into the woods to the tree where her goose skin was. Soon a goose flew away to the point near the village, and he followed her. He saw a goose's tail above the water. She was diving for eel-grass. Then he went home, and soon she came into the bed.

Now the food in the village was exhausted. One day the Goose woman heard a flock of geese behind the village, and she ran out with her husband and found a pile of food in the woods. They carried it to the village. A few days later more food was brought. But some of the people complained that the geese did not bring enough: they were stingy. And the Goose woman became angry and said she would go. Her husband tried to restrain her, but she ran away, got her skin, and flew up into the air above the village, and passed out of his sight.

Now the chief's son began to cry, wandering about the village and through the woods. He went to Crane, the oldest man in the town, who lived in the last house, and said, 'Old man, do you know the way to my wife?' And Crane answered, 'Yes. She is a supernatural being, to marry her is unthinkable.' Then the young man

The Goose woman became angry and flew up into the air above the village.

Source
Edward Curtis, *The North American Indian,* vol. 11, New York: Johnson Reprint Corporation, 1970, pp. 168–71

gave him a bone drill, some rope and a wedge. He wanted more information.

The old man said, 'Well, the first thing is to take a water-basket. Put into it two stone axes and the point of a salmon-spear. And take a silverside salmon's skin, a whetstone, and a rawhide string, some oil, a comb, a knife and a piece of preserved salmon-roe.' And he explained how these things were to be used. He knew all about the supernatural beings.

When the young man had all things ready, he went again to old Crane, who said, 'Iljo! [a term of address indicating humility in the speaker] The trail begins just behind my house.' So the young man started, and before long he came to a person sitting beside the trail and lousing his body. Whenever he turned, lice fell from the folds of his skin. He was the source of all lice. The chief's son stood there peering at this person, who soon said, 'Iljo! Do not tickle me by looking at me. It was already in my mind that you were coming.' So the young man came out from the bushes and combed and oiled the man's hair and gave him the comb and the rest of the oil. Then the old man said, 'Iljo! This is the trail to your wife.' So the young man went forward.

He travelled on and came to a very small mouse trying to cross a log with a cranberry, which it held in its mouth. He lifted it over the log and it went along happily with its tail curled up over its ears. It crept under a bunch of fern, and the young man sat down and waited. Soon a voice called him, 'The chief woman wishes you to come in!' He raised the fern and saw an entrance, through which he passed into a large house. The chief woman sat there, and she said, 'I am the one whom you helped across the log.' They gave him a dish with a single berry on it. As rapidly as he ate the berry, another took its place. Then the chief woman said, 'I am going to give you a mouse skin, which I formerly used in my hunting.' So from the innermost of four boxes a small skin was taken and given to him. She told him to put it on and practise how he would act; and he started to put it on very carefully, but to his surprise it slipped on easily. Then he climbed the walls and ran about the roof, and when he descended, she said that he acted well. 'Now go along this trail,' she said.

After travelling onward, the young man heard a strange sound. He saw a woman tying cedar-withes about large stones, which she was trying to carry away, but constantly the ropes broke and the stones fell. 'What are you doing?' he asked. And she said, 'I have to carry away all these stones and build the mountains, but my ropes always break.' He gave her some rawhide ropes, which easily supported the load, and she assured him that he was on the right trail to find his wife.

Next he came to an open, mossy place in the midst of which was a knoll, and on its top stood a red pole with human bones scattered about it. He drew out his preserved salmon-roe and rubbed it on the pole; he put on his mouse skin and climbed upward, constantly rubbing the roe above him in order to make the pole sticky so that he could hold fast. When he reached the top, a ladder came down from the sky and he mounted it to a land which looked the same as the earth. There the trail went on.

He heard shouting, and soon came to a running creek filled with silverside salmon. At a shallow place an eagle and a bear sat on opposite sides, and just above this were a kingfisher and a crane on opposite sides. All were catching salmon. The eagle caught them with his claws, and the kingfisher and the crane with their beaks, but the bear had no talons and no beak, and he experienced difficulty in fishing. While the young man watched, the eagle took pity on the bear and gave him one of his talons, and when the next rush of salmon came the bear succeeded in catching a fish. Now came hopping along up the stream a half-man, who had only one leg, one arm, half a head and half a body. He was spearing fish. The chief's son at once went farther upstream and put on the salmon skin he had brought. He swam down toward the half-man, who soon speared him. Then the salmon rushed this way and that, trying to break the line or drag the half-man into the water, but he could not. So with his knife he cut the line. The half-man examined the severed end and said, 'It looks as if some human being had done this.' Then the chief's son, having resumed his proper shape, came down and asked, 'What has happened?' Said the half-man, 'My line is broken and my spear-point lost. It looks as if some human being had done it.' Then the young man gave him the spear-point which he had brought, and the half-man thanked him and gratefully informed him that his wife was in the village near at hand.

Above this place were two old men cutting rotten trees. Now and then they would throw an armful of chips into the stream, and these became silverside salmon, which ran down the river. The chief's son slipped up, and while they were throwing chips into the water, he placed his whetstone in the cut they were making, so that when they resumed their chopping they broke their stone axes. Then they lamented, and wondered what their chief would do to them, and the young man asked what was the trouble. He gave them the two axes he had, and out of gratitude these servants of the Goose chief informed him that his wife was in the village. Soon he found the village, and, as he stood for a while before the largest house, his wife came out and greeted him, and led him in. There in that upper world he remained for a long time, and he saw how the bird people lived.

But he became homesick, and his wife told her father, who invited all the people to a feast. At the end he asked the people, 'Who is going to take my son-in-law home to his father's village?' The loon said, 'I will do it. I will put him close to my tail and will dive with him at the edge of this village, and let him off in front of his father's place.' But the chief said, 'That will not do.' Then the Diver offered to take the young man beneath the water, but the chief objected. The Raven said, 'I will put him under my arm, and when I become tired, I will turn in the air and so become rested.' To this the chief agreed. So the Raven flew away with the young man, and the people watched him. Near the end of his journey the Raven became weary, and said to himself, 'Such a heavy fellow, I think I will let him drop!' So he dropped the young man, who alighted on a reef and turned into the first seagull.

SULKOT-SKANAKWAI: LITTLE-FINGER SUPERNATURAL POWER

Haida

Source
Edward Curtis,
*The North
American Indian*,
vol. 11, New
York: Johnson
Reprint
Corporation,
1970,
pp. 162–68

A CHIEF'S DAUGHTER, THOUGH UNMARRIED, gave birth to a child. So the chief had her placed apart with her son at one end of the village. She built a hut of hemlock boughs and hung an old mat over the doorway. The boy grew very rapidly, and helped his mother by gathering food along the beach. He made a bow and some arrows, and killed small birds, which his mother cooked. When he was old enough to make two pointed arrows, he carved a porpoise on the point of one and a killer whale on the other. At this work he happened to cut his little finger.

His uncles had many daughters, and he used to see them playing at camping in the woods or on the beach. But these, whom he should have had a right to marry,

The rotten canoe slipped into the water and became a large handsome vessel with a carved man in the stern and another in the bow.

would not look at him. Sometimes he would play alone at being a medicine man, with an old mat for a dancing skirt and clam-shells for rattles. One day at low tide he found on the beach a crane with a half-broken beak, and he whittled it to a point, so that the crane could catch fish. Then the bird said, 'Now, my son, I am going to help you. I am going to give you hyil [medicinal herbs].' He took something green from his mouth and gave it to the boy, and also one of his wing feathers he gave, saying, 'When you are angry with anyone, blow on this and send it into his body.' The boy went home and took out his old mat dancing skirt. He spat some of the green medicine on it, and it became a fine elk-skin skirt with puffin-beak rattlers. He spat on his little drum, and it became a great drum with the painting of wasko [a mythical animal].

One evening the boy went about the village peering into the cracks of the houses, and catching sight of a chief's son he blew on the feather. Immediately the youth complained of a sharp pain in his side, and all the shamans were called in; but none could help him. The boy went again to look through the cracks, and saw the shamans working. Two dark men stood beside the door with pitch-pine torches. These guards were Porpoises [to the coastal tribes the porpoise is the very embodiment of keen hearing]. He saw also the tip of his feather projecting from the sick boy's side, and he said to himself, 'I wonder if they can see that thing.' At once the two Porpoise men dropped their torches and ran out to catch whoever it was that could see what was the matter with the sick youth. He ran away and hid in his mother's hut, but they followed and summoned him to the chief's house. So he dressed himself in his dancing skirt and his chief's hat, and while the people waited in the house his great drum came flying through the air, and the baton was beating. They looked for the young shaman, and soon saw his dancing hat sticking up through the floor in the corner of the room. After a while he stood before them. While the drum beat itself, the boy danced and then he pulled out the feather; and the chief's son was well. The boy took the property they paid him and went home, and the drum and the baton flew away.

Now one day he saw his uncles' daughters playing in the woods, and he made himself into a salmonberry bush near the trail. When they started homeward, the youngest cousin, who was lame, came walking last, and her hair caught on the bush. The others went on, and the youth stood before her and said, 'I want to marry you.' He spat his medicine on her leg, and made it sound. So they were married. The youth accumulated great wealth by blowing his feather into the sons and daughters of chiefs and then curing them.

One night the hemlock hut moved strangely. In the morning there stood in its place a great wooden house with carved posts, and with his mother lay Watkadagan [the supernatural being who gives artisans their skills]. In one corner was a half-man hopping about. Now the boy's finger was constantly swelling. Watkadagan said to him, 'My son, go and marry the daughter of Tesqanaya, the supernatural being who lives at Konu. There is no driftwood at that place, so you had better take this.' And he gave the young man a heavy, water-soaked limb. So the young man's wife went home to her parents, and the hopping half-man, Hlkyankaikwaskanakwai, took him beneath his arm and carried him away toward Konu. He had his bow and two arrows, on one of which was carved a weasel, on the other a mouse. These were given to him by the half-man, who said, 'Every time you shoot these, they will come back to you.' On the way they passed through a swampy place, and the half-man

could not cross, because his single foot when he hopped, he sank into the mire. But the young man spat his medicine, and the ground became firm. Leaving him at Konu, the Hopping Supernatural-power returned to his master Watkadagan.

Now the two daughters of Tesqanaya used to go down to the beach every evening, and the youth placed himself in the large club which he was carrying, and lay on the beach like a piece of driftwood. The two girls, finding it, were surprised, and took it home. Tesqanaya had five axes, but one after another he broke four of them in trying to split the stick. With the fifth he cut it, and he placed the pieces in the fire. When the girls went to bed behind the wooden partition, a spark from the fire went flying over it. This was the young man. He stood beside the bed and put his hand on the head of the one he was to marry, and she asked, 'Who are you?' He answered, 'I am Sulkot-skanakwai.' She said, 'Oh, that is the one my father wishes me to marry.' So he went to bed with her.

In the morning Tesqanaya said, 'I wonder what supernatural being that was who talked with my daughter last night. I wonder if it was Sulkot-skanakwai.'

The girl replied, 'That is the one, my father.'

'Well, come out and eat,' he said. So they came and sat by the fire. He said they would first eat berries, but in the dishes which he set out was what looked like burning embers. The girl secretly warned her husband not to eat, but he swallowed his green medicine, dipped his spoon into the dish, and ate the embers. These passed right through him and set fire to the floor beneath him. He moved to another place and repeated the act. Thus he ate all the embers.

The next morning the chief called, 'Well, chief my daughter, tell your husband to get the alder tree behind my house.' The young man started up at once, but the girl clung to him, saying that her father was only trying to kill him. Still he insisted, and she said, 'That tree has a crack which comes together five times, and each time there is lightning. After the fifth time, strike it.' She gave him an axe. So the young man waited, and after the fifth time he began to chop. As the tree fell, it grasped him in the cleft. He was almost dead, and could not control his medicine, but he thought of his father's supernatural power, and immediately a man with a hammer and a wedge appeared and opened the cleft. Soon Sulkot-skanakwai felt a little stronger and rubbed his medicine on himself. The man with the wedge left him, and he tore the tree apart. Inside were the bones of many men. He broke up one side of the tree by stepping on it, and scattered the pieces, saying, 'You will be useful for the people who are to be.' The rest he carried into the house and threw down against the wall, and the chief cried, 'Oh, he has killed one of my powers!'

The next morning the chief said, 'Chief my daughter, I wish your husband would get me the octopus on the point.' The girl began to cry, 'Hajadia [alas]! Every time I get a husband, this is the way you treat him!' While the young man gathered up his two arrows and an octopus stick, she told him, 'If you see water spurt up four times, then shoot the octopus.' So he did this, and after shooting his arrows he thrust the stick under the rock. Then he became unconscious, and found himself in the mouth of the monster and nearly smothered with the thick slime. Again he thought of his father's supernatural power, and a man came with a club and killed the octopus. Half of the body Sulkot-skanakwai tore up and scattered, and the rest he threw into the house. The chief cried, 'Hajadia! He has killed another of my powers!'

The following morning Tesqanaya gave his son-in-law a club and ordered him to kill a sealion. The girl warned him to wait until the sealion had roared four times;

so after the fourth time he shot his arrows, and they came flying back to him. Then he clubbed it to death, and half of its body he tore up and scattered, saying, 'You will be useful for future people.' The rest he brought to the house and threw inside. 'Hajadia!' lamented the chief. 'He has killed another of my powers!'

Thus one by one Sulkot-skanakwai destroyed a monster hair-seal, a great eagle, an enormous horse-clam, and a cockle. Finally, Tesqanaya filled a large chest with water and dropped heated stones into it until the water boiled. Sulkot-skanakwai secretly spat his medicine into it, and then got in, and Tesqanaya clapped on the cover and said, 'Now I will kill you!' But soon the cover was thrown violently off and the young man stood up and broke the box to pieces. From that time Tesqanaya treated his son-in-law kindly.

After a while Sulkot-skanakwai became homesick and told his wife he wished to return to his mother. She informed her father, who promised to provide a canoe. Soon he said, 'I have left a canoe on the beach.' She went down, but quickly returned, saying, 'There is no canoe, only an old rotten one.' He told her to look again, and she went down with her husband. Then she kicked the rotten canoe and said, 'Launch yourself in my father's canoe.' It slipped into the water and became a large, handsome vessel with a carved man in the stern and another in the bow. They had paddles in their hands, and they obeyed the girl's orders, moving the canoe forward and back. Now Tesqanaya gave his daughter five boxes of berries, and said, 'When the carved men become hungry they will paddle the canoe backward. Then you must feed them, and they will go forward again.' He sent five women to be the servants of his daughter, and when the canoe started she and her husband sat in the middle without moving, like great chiefs.

When they reached the village of Sulkot-skanakwai, every house was lighted up with great fires. They landed, and the people came to help them carry up all the things they had brought. They sent back the canoe with its two men, and Sulkot-skanakwai went to his mother and said, 'Mother, go down and call my wife, who is sitting among those things.' She went to the beach, but saw nothing except a small cloud among the objects piled there. When she reported this to her son, he said, 'Well, that is my wife. Go and call her.' So the woman called the little cloud, which rose and floated after her to the house. When the village people came to look at the new wife, nobody could see anything except a cloud sitting beside the young man. Then he said to his wife, 'You had better take off your hat.' She asked him to do it for her, and he removed the cloud, which was her hat. Then the people were astonished at her beauty. Outside peering through the cracks were his cousins, crying because they had not married him.

One day a white sea-otter appeared in the water before the village, and all the men went to shoot it, but they could not strike it. When Sulkot-skanakwai shot, his arrow struck it near the tail, and they threw the otter into the canoe and skinned it. Then the young wife placed the skin in the water and trod on it to wash out a spot of blood. Gradually it slipped away, and she kept following it into deeper water. Suddenly a killer whale dashed up and carried her away. For all the supernatural beings wanted her, and this was a plan to secure her.

Now Sulkot-skanakwai wandered about, weeping, and in the woods he came upon an old man, whom he asked where he could find his wife. The old man answered that he could tell, and Sulkot-skanakwai gave him a drill, some rope, some tallow and a whetstone. Then the old man said, 'I will go with you. We will use my canoe. Skanakakwankidas ['supernatural-power in cradle'] has taken her.' This was a killer whale, who in his house lay constantly in a cradle and had a servant swing him by pulling a rope.

One clear, calm day Sulkot-skanakwai proposed that they start, but the old man said, 'No, this is bad weather.' Again this happened. Then on a rough, rainy day he sent for the young man and said, 'Now it is a fine day. We will go. When you get away from land, all this will disappear and the sun will come out. Get a drill, some rope, and some tallow.' Then they started, and far from land they found fine weather.

'Look for a two-headed kelp,' said the old man. 'That will be the starting of the trail. When you come to the village, beware of an old man who lives near it. He is always watching to keep anyone from entering.'

When they found the double-headed kelp, Sulkot-skanakwai stepped out of the canoe and found himself on a broad trail. He went along and soon heard the sound of bailing out a canoe, and suddenly came upon an old man, Crane, who immediately shouted the alarm. But Sulkot-skanakwai quickly gave him the drill, rope and tallow, and Crane hid him under his broad arm just before the people came running out.

'What is the matter?' they demanded.

'Oh,' answered Crane, 'my drill slipped and I always shout when that happens.'

They insisted that they smelled a strange odour, and searched him over and over, but found nothing.

When they had gone, Crane said, 'When you come to that chief's house, be cautious. The top of his house-pole is always on the watch. And where he gets water, the head of a dogfish also is watching. These may see you. Two men will come for wood. They are full of sores on their skin. When you meet them, spit your medicine on them and rub your tallow over them and heal them.'

So Sulkot-skanakwai went along and escaped the eye of the watchman. Coming behind the woodcutters, he put a stone into the cut they were making in a tree, and they broke their axes. When they began to cry, he put the axes into his mouth and drew them out, better than before. Then he healed their sores. They were grateful, and informed him, 'Tonight they are going to steam the fin for your wife.' For when a person from the earth was taken by the killer whales to be made one of them, they took a fin from the numerous ones that stood in the corner, heated it in the fire, and threw it against the back of that person, so that it stuck there.

Then the woodcutters made a plan for the escape of his wife. They carried him into the house in the midst of a load of wood. Then they brought water, and as if by accident spilled it on the great fire. Immediately the house was filled with steam, and the young man grasped his wife's arm and ran out with her. The two woodcutters followed, and so hindered the pursuers that the fugitives could not be taken. The watcher on the house-pole called out the direction in which they were running, but the woodcutters would stop and swell up so that the others could not get over them. So Sulkot-skanakwai and his wife reached the canoe in which the old man was waiting, and returned safely to the village.

THE BEAVER AND THE PORCUPINE

Haida

BEAVER HAD LAID IN a plentiful store of food, but Porcupine had failed to do so, and one day when the former was out hunting, the latter went to his ledge and stole his provision. When Beaver returned he found that his food was gone, and he questioned Porcupine about the matter.

'Did you steal my food?' he asked.

'No,' answered Porcupine. 'One cannot steal food from supernatural beings, and you and I both possess supernatural powers.'

Of course this was mere bluff on the part of Porcupine, and it in nowise deceived his companion.

'You stole my food!' said Beaver angrily, and he tried to seize Porcupine with his teeth. But the sharp spines of the latter disconcerted him, though he was not easily repulsed. For a time he fought furiously, but at length he was forced to retreat, with his face covered with quills from his spiny adversary. His friends and relatives greeted him sympathetically. His father summoned all the Beaver People, told them of the injuries his son had received, and bade them avenge the honour of their clan. The people at once repaired to the abode of Porcupine, who, from the fancied security of his lodge, heaped insults and abuse on them. The indignant Beaver People pulled his house down about his ears, seized him, and carried him, in spite of his threats and protests, to a desolate island, where they left him to starve.

It seemed to Porcupine that he had not long to live. Nothing grew on the island save two trees, neither of which was edible, and there was no other food within reach. He called loudly to his friends to come to his assistance, but there was no answer. In vain he summoned all the animals who were related to him. His cries never reached them.

When he had quite given up hope he fancied he heard something whisper to him, 'Call upon Cold-weather, call upon North-wind.'

At first he did not understand, but thought his imagination must be playing tricks with him. Again the voice whispered to him, 'Sing North songs, and you will be saved.' Wondering much, but with hope rising in his breast, Porcupine did as he was bidden, and raised his voice in the North songs. 'Let the cold weather come,' he sang, 'let the water be smooth.'

After a time the weather became very cold, a strong wind blew from the north, and the water became smooth with a layer of ice. When it was sufficiently frozen to bear the weight of the Porcupine People they crossed over to the island in search of their brother. They were greatly rejoiced to see him, but found him so weak that he could hardly walk, and he had to be carried to his father's lodge.

When they wanted to know why Beaver had treated him so cruelly, he replied that it was because he had eaten Beaver's food. The Porcupine People, thinking this a small excuse, were greatly incensed against the Beavers, and immediately declared war on them. But the latter were generally victorious, and the war by and by came to an inglorious end for the Porcupines. The spiny tribe still, however, imagined that they had a grievance against Beaver, and plotted to take his life. They carried him to the top of a tall tree, thinking that as the Beavers could not climb he

Source

Lewis Spence,
*Myths and
Legends of the
North American
Indians*, London:
George G.
Harrap & Co.,
1914,
pp. 318–20

would be in the same plight as their brother had been on the island. But by the simple expedient of eating the tree downward from the top Beaver was enabled to return to his home.

KATLIAN AND THE IRON PEOPLE

Haida-Tlingit

WHEN THE IRON PEOPLE, the Russians, came to Alaska in vessels much larger than canoes, they had weapons that smoked and made noises like thunder. On their vessels they had larger weapons that hurled balls of iron that would smash trees into pieces. Faced with this great power, Katlian, the chief of the Tlingits at Sitka, gave the Russians all the furs and skins and other property that they demanded.

Although the Iron People would not go away, there was peace for a time between the Tlingits and the bearded strangers. The Tlingits traded skins for the weapons that thundered, and for cartridges, and they learned to kill animals with these weapons brought by the Iron People.

After a while the Iron People built a village of houses across the inlet and brought their families from their land beyond where the sun sets. One day Katlian's nephew visited the village and saw the daughter of one of the Iron People. He fell in love with her. He followed her to the house where she lived and tried to buy her with furs, but the girl's father angrily sent him away. When Katlian's nephew tried to steal the girl, the Iron People killed him.

This nephew was like a son to Katlian, and at the first opportunity the chief killed the son of one of the Iron People. Baranoff, the leader of these people, sent a message to Katlian to surrender himself, or else all the Tlingits at Sitka would be killed by the weapons that smoked and hurled pieces of metal.

Katlian called his people together and they began building walls out of cedars. They built houses inside these walls, and put flat rocks between the cedars and the walls of the houses. Soon afterwards the Iron People came in a vessel to destroy them. Ten times they fired their large weapons that hurled balls of iron against the wall of cedars and rocks. Baranoff their leader then called out from the ship for Katlian to surrender himself to them, but Katlian replied in a loud voice that he could not do this. The Iron People then fired more shots at the cedar and rock walls.

After they had done this for a while, the Iron People came off the ship in three small boats. They landed on the beach, carrying guns with bayonets. Katlian led his people out to meet them, and, while the Iron People were firing by command, the Tlingits shot into them many times. The Tlingits threw out their empty cartridges quickly and shot again. They killed many of the Iron People. Only those who had charge of the boats got back to the ship. Then the war vessel sailed away.

For two moons, the Tlingits worked to strengthen their little fort, and then the Iron People came again in two war vessels. This time they fired at the cedars and rocks from two directions.

Baranoff then shouted, 'Katlian, are you still alive?'

'Yes,' the chief replied. 'I am not afraid of the cannon you use against me.'

Again the cannon roared, and again the Iron People came to the beach in boats.

While the Iron People were firing by command, the Tlingits shot into them many times.

Source
John R. Swanton, 'Haida Texts and Myths', *US Bureau of American Ethnology Bulletin*, 29 (1905), pp. 108–9

Once more, Katlian led the Tlingits against the invaders, and this time they killed many of them and took their guns, coats, hats and swords. The two war vessels sailed away.

After some time had passed, the Iron People returned in a small ship flying white flags of truce. Without weapons of any kind, Baranoff came to the beach under a flag of peace. 'Katlian,' he called, 'are you still alive?'

Katlian walked out of the fort. He carried no weapons. 'Yes,' he replied, 'I am still alive. I won. Now it is all right for you to kill me.'

'I bring you presents,' Baranoff said. He gave Katlian clothing, food, rum and cartridges. After that the Iron People did not bother the Sitka Tlingits again.

DAYLIGHT ALLOWS HIMSELF TO BE BORN

Haida

S HE WAS THE CHIEF'S DAUGHTER and her name was Tullajat ['orderly woman']. After she reached the age of puberty and before her marriage she went with a young man, and, when the chief learned this, he sent his slave to announce in a loud voice that on the next day all would leave the village and abandon his daughter. For in those days the daughters of high chiefs were very carefully watched, that they might be able to make a good marriage.

The ten uncles of the girl took all the mats and even the cedar-bark roofing from the house. So when the people had gone, she made a little hut of hemlock boughs, but her youngest uncle's wife pitied her, and left some food. When in a few days this was exhausted, she went to the beach at low tide and dug clams. In the fourth clam which she broke open she found an object that looked like a human body. She took it into her hut and cared for it, and it grew very rapidly into a strong boy. Soon he was creeping about. When he began to walk, he said one day, 'Mother, this way, this way,' making the motions of using a bow. So the girl made a bow of hemlock and some little arrows tipped with shell. The boy was pleased, and spent his time shooting about the hut. The next day he brought in a bird which he had shot. Later he killed larger birds, such as cormorants and mallards. Then he brought in a blue jay, which he himself skinned, and the next day he killed and skinned a wren. The next was a woodpecker, and then he shot many other birds and skinned them.

One night the boy awoke and heard someone talking with his mother, and he felt the hut move slowly from side to side. At daylight he saw someone lying with his mother, and the house was a great house of timbers, the carvings of which were alive, winking their eyes and thrusting out their tongues. This person with his mother was Watkadagan [the supernatural being from whom comes the ability of artisans]. Said he, 'Come here, chief my son. Let me dress your hair.' So the boy went to him, and Watkadagan moulded his face until it was beautiful, and when he drew a comb through the hair, it became long and glossy. He said, 'It is well, my son. go and sit on that rock.' When the boy sat on the rock, a fine, sunny day broke. For he was Sun [daylight]. All day he remained there, and in the evening he returned to the house. He said to Watkadagan, 'Father, tomorrow get a stick, and we will go to the beach for an octopus.' So they got the octopus.

Source
Edward Curtis,
*The North
American Indian*,
vol. 11, New
York: Johnson
Reprint
Corporation,
1970,
pp. 155–58

On the following day they went to fish at Nahgyu [a fishing bank]. Watkadagan baited his hook and lowered it, and held it all day without a bite. The boy said, 'Now, father, say this: "The chief of all the halibut, thinking about it and getting it."' Watkadagan repeated it. Then the boy said, 'Father, say this: "The one who has seaweed growing on his ribs, thinking about it and getting it."' And Watkadagan repeated this. Next the boy said, 'Father, say this: "You are looking at it. You have quartz crystal for an eye."' Watkadagan said this, and still waited. 'Say this, Father: "Coming up against the current; you are looking at it, largest one."' Again, 'Say this, father: "Greediest one, you are looking at it."' And, 'Say this, father: "You, the biggest one, going along eating gravel; you are the one who is looking at it."' Now the sun was beginning to sink. 'Say this, father: "The time is nearly past; you are looking at it."' Finally, 'Father, say this: "The hills are spotted with shadow and sunlight; you who are looking at it."' Four times it passed completely round the islands while Watkadagan was drawing up the line. When the line was drawn, in there came up a huge halibut covered with tangled seaweed, among which were hundreds of small halibut. These Watkadagan began to pick off and pile in the canoe. When it was full, he pushed on the gunwales and raised them, and continued to pile up the fish. Thus he did four times. When he had enough, he took the hook from the lips of the great halibut and pressed his hand on its head, and it sank. Then they went home. The woman cut up wood and dried the fish.

The people were starving, and when the learned that the chief's abandoned daughter had food in plenty, they came and begged of her, but she gave only to the aunt who had befriended her. Then all the people returned to Ju and began to fish. One day Tullajat told her youngest uncle to put on a new hat and take his new paddle and go fishing. So he did. She sat on the edge of the terrace and drew up her skirt a little. A wind blew off the land. She drew the skirt a little higher, and the wind increased. Higher still she drew it, and the wind increased. When the skirt was as high as her hips, the wind was so violent that all the canoes were capsized and the men drowned, all except the youngest uncle.

Now Watkadagan prepared to depart, and he said to his young wife, 'Make your home on this creek, and sometimes I will come to visit you.' Then he went.

One day Sun took his blue-jay skin and went out, saying, 'Mother, come out soon and see what I look like.' She went out and saw beautiful blue clouds in the sky. She withdrew into the house, and when Sun came he asked, 'Mother, how did I look?' and she answered, 'Chief, you looked fine.' Then he went out with the wren skin, and she saw brown clouds. 'Mother,' he said when he returned, 'how did I look?' As before she replied, 'Chief, you looked fine.' Next he took the woodpecker skin, and his mother saw reddish clouds. 'Mother, how did I look?' he asked. And she said, 'Chief my son, supernatural beings cannot help looking at you, for you are so pretty.' Last he used a snowbird skin, and his mother saw cumulus clouds.

Then Sun said, 'Now, my mother, I am going to leave you. You must make your home at the head of this creek.' He disappeared. Tullajat went to the head of the creek and made that place her home. She was a supernatural being, but is regarded as belonging to the Raven phratry [the Haida consisted of two phratries, the Raven and the Eagle, with each divided into a large number of clans]. She is called also Skanajat-kida-katlhaskas [supernatural-being-woman princess coming-out], because when an offshore wind blows it is this being who 'comes out' of the woods to the shore and sends the wind, as she did when she destroyed her uncles.

PART 8
CALIFORNIA

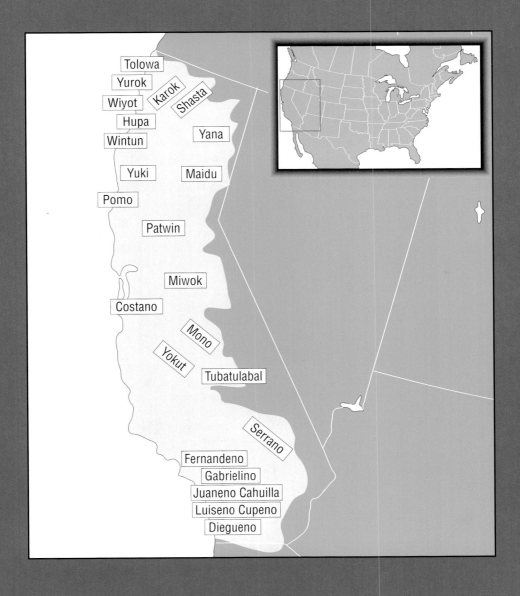

Tolowa
Yurok
Wiyot
Karok Shasta
Hupa
Wintun
Yana
Yuki
Maidu
Pomo
Patwin
Miwok
Costano
Mono
Yokut
Tubatulabal
Serrano
Fernandeno
Gabrielino
Juaneno Cahuilla
Luiseno Cupeno
Diegueno

TRIBES OF
CALIFORNIA

Before the arrival of the first Europeans in the New World, great numbers of Native Americans lived along the Pacific coastal land now known as the state of California. This lengthy region, lying largely between the rugged Sierra Nevada mountain chain to the east and a vast ocean to the west, was home to hundreds of thousands of Native Americans and scores of independent tribes. Many of them traditionally lived in the Great California Valley, a sweeping and fertile land watered by the San Joaquin and Sacramento rivers. Owing to its temperate climate, the region attracted Native Americans for thousands of years; this in turn caused California to become home to an estimated 10–15 per cent of the native population in what is today the United States, while only representing 5 per cent of the land.

The California Culture region is a place of varied topography and, to a lesser extent, climate. While the region corresponds with much of modern California, it does not fit perfectly into that state's present political borders. Native Americans living in the eastern section of California, the land east of the Sierra Nevada, are generally not included among the tribes of the California Culture Group, but rather are included in the Great Basin or Southwestern groups. Along the northern border of California, that it shared with the state of Oregon, tribes are often placed within the Plateau Culture Group or the Northwest Coastal Group. Basically the homeland of the California Culture Group, this area is a long band of land which runs south from the southern border of Oregon through, and including, the Baja Peninsula or Baja California, today a part of Mexico.

Modern estimates place the number of California tribespeople, at the time of white contact, at between 150,000 and 350,000.

This native population was scattered throughout the region, and constituted over 100 tribes. The northwestern part of the region was home to a group of Athapascan-speaking native tribes which included the Tolowas, Mattoles, Hoopas, Wiyots, Yuroks and others. These tribes often borrowed culturally from the peoples of the Northwest Pacific region.

To the south, in central California, a land of oak groves, chaparral-covered foothills and mountains bristling with pine trees, lived the Yukis and a host of tribes which gathered in the mountain lands to the east. These included the Karoks, Shastas and Yanas – tribes often counted among the Plateau peoples. Other tribes in the central region of California, but living closer to the Pacific coast were the Patwins, Miwoks, Maidus, Yokuts and Wintuns. When Europeans arrived in San Francisco Bay in the 1500s, they encountered a tribe known as the Costanoans. Still further south, tribes which came to bear names given to them by early Spanish explorers and mission fathers included the Cahuillas, Fernandenos, Gabrielinos, Juanenos, Luisenos, Nicolenos, Serranos and Tubatulabals. Many of these tribes became known as the 'Mission Indians' with the arrival of the Spanish Catholic-supported mission system of the late 1700s. They could be found in southern California from the Pacific Ocean inland to the mountains and deserts to the east. Other California tribes were located in the border region between modern California and Mexico, such as the Yuman branch of the Hokan language family.

Prehistoric Tribes of California

California has been the site of much archaeological work over the past century. Such work indicates a native population present in the region at a Pre-Projectile Point Stage as early as 30,000 years ago. As was typically the case of such ancient inhabitants of North America, these early arrivals were big-game hunters who were nomadic by circumstance. Clovis and Folsom spear-points have been unearthed. Archaeologists working in southern California have found evidence of a big-game hunting culture known as the San Dieguito Culture. Dating from around 7000 BC, this primitive culture group used chipped-stone tools and weapons, and hunted with stone-tipped spears.

By 5000 BC, the days of the big-game hunting era were typically over, and the native population of California was extensive. The dominant culture of the period was the Desert Culture. These peoples were generally seed-gatherers who collected wild plants, ground them with the aid of milling stones, and supplemented their diets with hunting and fishing as circumstances allowed.

The next phase of development in ancient California was reached between 2000 BC and AD 500. This period, designated as the Middle Period, was marked by a southern California culture which included hunting, fishing, shellfish-gathering and the use of small canoes and boats to hunt dolphins and other aquatic life. These tribal peoples had developed a more sedentary lifestyle, living in larger villages, and yet remaining non-agricultural. Many of these tribes relied on the gathering of acorns as a staple food. Basketry was a practised art among these tribes.

Other native groups of the period included tribes living in the central California coastal region and interior valleys. These tribes were slightly more materialistic and warlike. They fashioned artefacts from bones and antlers, made coiled baskets, bows and arrows, ornamental shell beads, and bone-tipped harpoons for hunting sea life, such as seals, otters and sealions.

In the thousand years prior to the arrival of Europeans on the California coast, from AD 500 to 1500, the region experienced greater population growth and greater variations of tribal units and their culture from one end of the region to the other. In the north, the tribes were mirroring those of the Northwest Pacific region. Others, especially those east of the Sierra Nevada, were being influenced by Great Basin and Plateau tribes. Pottery was becoming common among California tribes, and clay utensils were used to continue the practice of gathering acorns, which had remained a mainstay of the Californians' diet.

Most of the tribes which would make contact with whites by the sixteenth century were in existence by AD 1300, and were becoming permanently located on the lands which they still occupied two centuries later when the Spanish arrived to explore the region. Some groups found their identity in small, tribal units called 'tribelets', which often consisted of an extended family. A typical tribelet numbered around 100 people and was led by a male of the group who held a hereditary title. Each unit, whether a tribe or a portion of a tribe, such as a tribelet, occupied its own land, and did not generally fight with its neighbours over territory. Unlike the Native Americans of other cultural regions of the period, nearly all the tribes of California were largely peace-loving, and not known for coveting the lands of the tribe next door.

Due to the regional variations of California, its native population created a variety of lifestyles, relying on different food sources, materials for homes and clothing styles. However, they tended to hold some elements of their cultures in common. Nearly all tribes shared certain rituals, such as a dance of preparation before going to war, or one of victory after an encounter with an enemy. Most of the California tribes practised a puberty ceremony to mark the passage of a young girl into womanhood with the arrival of her first menstrual period. As was the practice among most tribes of North America, the California groups relied heavily on shamans – a combination of healer and prophet – to direct the spiritual and medicinal activities of the tribe or tribelet.

Tribal Food Sources

Food varied, depending on where a tribe was located in the California Culture region, with some food sources overlapping from one part of the region to another. The tribes of the northern part of California relied heavily on fish, especially salmon, and acorns. Salmon were caught during their annual spring spawning runs by use of a variety of devices, including nets, spears, diverting traps known as weirs, and the more typical method of fishing used today, the hook and line. V-shaped hooks were fashioned from a piece of bone. In his book, *The Native Americans: Prehistory and Ethnology of the North American Indians* (New York: Harper & Row Publishers, 1965, p. 244), Robert Spencer describes the extraordinarily varied methods by which these fisherman brought in their catch:

> Fish were caught in many different ways but netting was by far the commonest method. Seines, often of great length, gill and dip nets all were employed. For taking salmon, a pole and brush weir was constructed across a stream, leaving a foot-wide opening near one bank. Fish ascending the stream had to pass through the narrow aperture and were easily stabbed with a bone-tipped spear. Sometimes a long cylindrical basketry trap was set at the upstream side of the opening. Crushed pulp of the soaproot bulb or leaves of the turkey mullen, dropped into quiet pools formed behind brush dams, stupefied the fish and caused them to float to the surface belly up from whence they were readily gathered.

Individual fishermen, armed with a spear, stood on small platforms which extended out over a swiftly flowing river. Other fishermen worked in groups, manning nets which allowed for massive catches of salmon and other fish, including steelhead, trout and sturgeon. Some tribes caught lamprey eels during spring harvests, using weirs to corral their catch. Eels were highly prized as a delicacy by some California groups. Coastal tribes annually harvested a rich bounty of seafood, combing the warm beach sands and tidal waters for clams, oysters, mussels and scallops. As was the practice of the tribes of the Northwest Pacific Coast region, the women had the responsibility of cutting open the fish and seafish, cleaning the catch and drying the meat. Salmon was typically smoked on large, wooden racks placed over a fire.

The second food considered essential among California tribes was acorns, the smallish nut produced by the tall, sprawling oak trees of the region. Acorns were harvested in the fall when the oak leaves were turning a crisp brown. Gathering was considered women's work, but some tribes allowed men and boys to help out, usually by climbing the great oaks and shaking the limbs and branches, bringing the tree's fruit tumbling to the ground below, where women waited to collect the acorns. White oaks were the favourite and most abundant source of acorns for California tribes. The acorns were stored in large granaries, each of which might hold up to a dozen bushels of the oak nuts.

Once the acorns were collected, much labour was involved in preparing them for consumption. Typically, the acorns were dried and the shells removed. Women then pounded the dried nuts with stone mortars and pestles, grinding the acorns on rock slabs into a fine nut meal. The meal was then spread out and hot water was added, creating a brown paste. By pouring water on the acorn meal, the women were removing tannin, a very bitter, natural substance, from the nuts. They then placed the wet acorn meal in nearly airtight baskets and cooked it by dropping heated rocks into the mixture. This created a mush, which was sometimes shaped into unleavened loaves and baked, then eaten.

Other seeds and wild plants were included in the California diet. Dozens of grass seeds, flowering herbs, roots, tubers and wild bulbs were collected, each in their season. The Luiseno of southern California, for example, collected over 60 varieties of plants and seeds for consumption, including chia seeds, sunflowers, clover, Indian lettuce, watercress, sage and pepper grass. Fruits also were collected and eaten. The Luiseno took the fruit from the prickly pear cactus, using tongs to remove the fruit from the needle-laden cactus. Various other fruits – including wild grapes, choke-cherries and a host of berry varieties – were gathered for food.

Game-hunting was common among California tribes, with deer and elk as the larger quarry. These animals were hunted down by bands of tribesmen carrying bows and arrows, sometimes using dogs to help track their prey. Some tribes, such as the Pomo of central California, hunted deer by herding them toward a hunter known for his skill with a bow. Such a hunter often wore a deerhead mask. Deer meat was usually cut into thin strips and dried in the sun. Hunters also relied on iris-fibre rope snares to catch both large and small game, such as squirrels, rabbits and quail. Waterfowl were also hunted. Native hunters sometimes built 'blinds' along marshes and lakes from which they bagged ducks, geese and swans. While fish, game, waterfowl and seafood were important to the diet of California tribes, they also harvested other animal life for food, such as insects. Among central-California peoples, small, smooth-skinned caterpillars called army worms were caught, roasted or boiled, salted and eaten. When an abundant supply was discovered, the excess catch was sun-dried and stored for winter consumption. Other insects eaten included grasshoppers – which were herded into nets as they fled specially set grass fires – angleworms and hornet grubs. Despite an appetite for insects, the tribes of California usually avoided eating reptiles.

Clothing and Adornments

Given the temperate climate found in most of California, the clothing worn by the Native Americans here was nothing if not limited – literally. Most men spent their days naked, although sometimes they wore loincloths. In northern California, the men might wear a two-piece deerskin outfit. Women wore little more, relying on a native costume of southern California which consisted of an apron, cut smaller at the front than at the back, covering the midsection. Such a garment was made of cords of Indian hemp or perhaps milkweed, plus strips of willow bark. In the northern part of the region, women wore buckskin skirts which only covered them from the waist to the knee. When the weather was cooler or wet, both men and women donned rabbitskin robes or coats of sea-otter skin. Head coverings were rare among California men, and the women wore a cone-shaped hat made of coiled strips of bark. Sandals were worn by both men and women, styled out of fibrous strips of yucca plant, which might take the form of a thick footpad, tied to the foot with pieces of plant-fibre cordage. Such footwear was rare, worn usually while travelling in desert regions or across rugged landscape. Otherwise, men, women and children all went barefoot.

California tribes were not known for their outer adornment, such as jewellery, elaborate hairstyles or intricate tattooing. Hairstyles were undramatic, with both sexes keeping their hair long and untied, a male's hair generally shorter than that of a female. Tattooing was done on both men and women, with the women sporting more such markings than the men. Women often tattooed their chin lines, wrists and the chest area. During special celebrations and dances, men and women painted their bodies and faces with red, white and black paint, in elaborate designs, and adorned themselves with necklaces of shell and bone. For such important rituals, they pierced their noses and ears, using bone pins and shell pendants which they suspended from their nostrils after piercing their nasal septa.

Housing Variations

Depending on the geography, the availability of materials and the climate of their region, housing in California was varied. Southern tribes typically lived in simple, thatched, cone-shaped houses. These round homes were built over a pre-dug circular pit, 60cm (2ft) in depth and approximately 2.5m (8ft) in diameter. Built on a pole frame, these 'straw' houses were fashioned from rushes or arrow-wood, and sometimes from bark strips. During cooler weather, a reed mat was used to cover the lodge door opening.

In central California, houses were often built using slabs of cedar wood, laid upright in a circle measuring 3.5–4.5m (12–15ft) in diameter and propped against a centre pole, then fastened into place. Other lodges included those found along the Russian River basin, where the natives built dome-shaped hogans made of bent saplings. Grasses were used to cover the house in overlapping strips.

In northern California, the tribes were influenced by the peoples of the Northwest Coastal region to build their homes as solid, cedar-plank houses, usually square or rectangular. These homes were perhaps the most substantial of all the California models. These were larger homes, measuring 5.5m by 6m (18ft by 20ft) and covered with a plank roof. The floor of such a home was dug into the earth to a depth of perhaps 1.2m (4ft). Planks were erected to provide steps into the pit, where a dirt floor played host to an extended family unit. Such homes were not as elaborate as those of the Northwestern tribes, but they were the fanciest style in California.

In addition to the houses in which California natives slept, cooked, ate, and raised their children, some tribes constructed other structures in which to practise other social customs. The most common example is that of the sweat-lodge. Such a structure was smaller than the average house. It consisted of a pit 1.2m (4ft) deep, lined with wooden planking and roofed with boards, the only part of the sweat-lodge to show above ground, a wooden floor and a rock hearth. Unlike the sweat-lodges found on the Great Plains, where water was poured on heated rocks to produce steam, a fire was built inside the California lodges to produce the requisite sweating. While such sweat-lodges were important for ritualistic purposes, they also functioned as gathering places for men where they could relax, talk, sleep and even work on their crafts without disturbance from their wives and families.

Arts and Crafts

Chief among the domestic crafts fashioned by California tribes were a variety of elaborately styled baskets, each designed for a specific purpose. Such baskets might be used for collecting plants (there were perhaps eight different basket types used in collecting and processing acorns), food storage and even fishing, where baskets were used as underwater traps to catch unsuspecting fish. Baskets were formed out of a wide variety of materials including hazel, willow and wicker. Such baskets were heavily adorned and painted, with each California tribal group creating their own unique ornamental style of geometric patterns.

California peoples fashioned other handicraft items, both for their practicality and functionality, as well as for their purely ornamental value. Men worked with stone, bone, antler and other materials, and created necessities such as bows and other weapons, arrowpoints and tools. Stone knives were made and used in hunting and for

skinning the hides of dead animals. Many men worked artefacts from elk-horn, including eating-spoons. However, spoons were only fashioned by the men as they were the only ones who used them. Women used shells to scoop their food. Horn was also used to make measuring rules, stone-knapping tools and other items. Bone was used in the making of awls, needles, fish-hooks and harpoons. Tobacco pipes were formed out of clay.

Some tribes were noted for their production of shell beads, and other artistic endeavours. Men formed disc-shaped beads from clam shells; these were typically a popular trade item both within a tribe and without. Such beads sometimes served as money, much like the wampum beads traded among Northeastern tribal groups. Clam-shell beads were strung together and sometimes grouped in units of 10,000, an amount used to pay off personal debts or to give as wedding and special occasion presents. Tribal jewellers also created colourful, glass-like beads from pieces of magnesite. This whitish, carbonite material was placed in a fire, heated until red or yellow, then shaped into cylinders. The cylinders were cut and drilled to be worn on a necklace, and were highly prized. Often a necklace might include only one such cylinder, owing to its value. When a member of a tribe died, sometimes a single magnesite cylinder was included among the items placed in a burial site along with the physical remains.

Village and Social Structures

As with every tribe in North America, the basic unit of each group was the extended family. Such family units typically consisted of six to eight people, including a married couple, their children and an unmarried relative or two, such as a wife's brother or a widowed aunt. Several family units, joined by blood and marriage, constituted a clan or a kinship group, another common societal element among Native American tribal groups. However, the social unit which carried the greatest influence in a tribe was that of the independent village which consisted of several families, generally related to one another through a male lineage. This structure, usually called a tribelet, was formed around a single settlement-village site and several smaller, outlying, or satellite, villages. Each tribelet occupied a designated piece of land, using its forests, streams or coasts for gathering, hunting and fishing for the village's food. The Hupa tribe of northern California, for example, by the time of the first European arrivals, lived in a dozen settlements scattered up and down the banks of the Trinity River. While each settlement site was autonomous, they remained close, with the furthest two villages separated by less than a mile's distance.

Tribelets usually each had a headman or chief, a hereditary position, who co-ordinated the social and civil activities of the unit. He did not have extraordinary power, however, especially when compared to the chiefs found in other tribes elsewhere on the continent. Such leaders were not commonly war leaders, since warfare was not an exalted practice of California tribes. Wars in California among tribes were uncommon.

Even though the tribal structure of California tribes tended to be rather loose, village laws were common and strictly enforced. Tribal sanctions against wrongdoing, such as rape, stealing, adultery, murder or even cursing another, were punishable by clearly delineated fines and other indemnities.

Passage to Adulthood

Californian families commonly had close personal relationships within their societal order. Children were raised with relative freedom, passing time in play, games, swimming and other distractions. They were taught various skills, but their education was rudimentary and sporadic. When a girl experienced menstruation for the first time, she was isolated for ten days, as she was considered unclean. She was forbidden to eat any meat. A public ceremony was carried out on her behalf.

While puberty rites were universal for girls entering the adult world, not all tribes practised a ritual or ceremony when a boy passed into manhood. Some of the tribes that did recognize such a passage rarely celebrated on behalf of a single boy, but practised a rite only when there were enough boys for a group recognition. The

Luiseno tribe, for example, was typical of southern California tribes in the practice of giving young boys a drink which caused them to hallucinate for days at a time, as described by Robert Spencer (*The Native Americans: Prehistory and Ethnology of the North American Indians*, New York: Harper & Row Publishers, 1965, p. 259):

> The initial and central ritual involved drinking a potent decoction prepared from roots of the Jimson weed or Toloache plant. The roots, which had earlier been gathered and dried, were crushed in a special stone mortar and then steeped in water. Administered to each of the initiates, gathered together at night in a special enclosure, the drink quickly produced unconsciousness. Great care had to be exerted not to give too much to a boy because taken in excess the infusion caused death. The period of stupor lasted two to three days or, with too heavy a dose, four. While under influence of the drug, neophytes experienced visions during which they acquired personal guardian spirits. Their revelations usually took the character of visitations by animal spirits from whom the boys obtained supernatural power and at times learned special songs.

Most boys and girls were married young, girls by the age of 15 or 16, boys a couple of years later. A suitable spouse was one who came from a family of an adequate social rank and was related by blood, but not a close relative. Such marriages helped to solidify the bonds between kinship groups. Most California men only had one wife, although polygamy was practised among more wealthy tribesmen. Divorce was generally a simple task, available to those in marriages which did not seem to work well, but marriage dissolution was not taken lightly and was not common.

Most Californians, both male and female, did not live into old age. Those who survived into their 50s or 60s, and older, were generally well respected and given places of honour. Relatives had the responsibility for such an aged member of the tribe, and many such tribal senior citizens often did what they could, helping with household chores, crafting baskets and other utensils, and caring for the children.

Upon death, a person's remains were prepared for burial almost immediately. The body was often wrapped, perhaps in a deerskin which was tied to a piece of wood on which the corpse was laid, and carried out of the home through a special opening in the lodge wall. A shallow grave was dug and lined with wooden planks, creating a coffin-like box for the remains. Most California tribes did not bury a person's goods with the dead body, but might place old items, perhaps broken and useless, in the coffin for burial. A funeral often featured much wailing and loud expressions of sorrow. Close family members often cut their own hair short to show their grief. Once the funeral was complete, an elaborate purification ritual was carried out. A grieving family member might weave a grass necklace and wear it, its purpose being to keep one from having dreams about the newly deceased family member. After death, the name of the deceased one was never spoken again within the hearing of one of his or her family members.

Warfare

Although warfare and strife between California tribes was rare, it did occur. Reasons for such conflict tended toward the personal. Men might take up arms against one another to avenge the murder of a loved one. Another common reason for war among California tribes was the belief that someone was cursing one's family or practising witchcraft to cause death or sickness. Such an alleged activity might bring on a violent reprisal. A fight often did not include many people, sometimes no more than a few kinship groups. The California tribes did not organize warrior societies or military organizations to any notable extent.

The warriors of these tribes carried a variety of weapons into combat. The bow and arrow was the basic unit of the Native American's arsenal, but spears for throwing and stabbing, slings and knives were also used. California tribes did not use shields during their fighting. They did wear protective gear, however, which typically included hardened shirts made of elk skin or even a body armour crafted from pieces of wood. Such protection could break the impact of an enemy's arrow and save a warrior's life.

The tactics of battle used by these far western tribesmen included those common to many other tribal regions. Ambushes and surprise attacks were the strategies of choice. Scalping was not commonly practised among California tribes, but some placed great significance on the action. The Pomo tribe, for example, scalped, and were quite thorough, removing from a vanquished foe a sizeable portion of the top of his head, including the ears. Such scalps were taken back to a village where they were dried and kept as war trophies.

War practice by California tribes tended to be quick, limited and short in duration. Once a series of engagements was carried out between combatants, the participants usually called a halt to the actions, and elected to sit down and engage in formal negotiations of peace. When violence had broken out between clansmen, kinship groups or tribelets of the same tribal unit, a third-party negotiator was selected, one acceptable to all parties. During such peace talks, an assessment of damages on both sides was taken and payments established to compensate all participants for any losses incurred during an attack or other military encounter.

Religion and Mythology

The Californians, as was universally true of all other North American tribes, practised a religion of proscription, rituals, the recognition of the power of one's gods, and a daily physical life which came into regular contact with that of the spirit world. Elaborate ceremonial rituals marked the passing days of the calendar with seasonal regularity. Such ceremonies often lasted for days and were carried out to give protection to the tribe and blessings to the hunt and the harvest. The northern California Hupa, Yurok and Karok tribes, for example, engaged in two quasi-religious rituals called the White Deerskin Dance and the Jumping Dance. Each featured its own songs and dance steps. During the White Deerskin Dance, a ritual which recalled an early time on earth when a race of spirit beings occupied the land, making way for the Native Americans, was practised, detailed in the following account by Alfred L. Kroeber, an American anthropologist who observed the ritual during a field study (*Nature of Culture*, Chicago: University of Chicago Press, 1952, pp. 55–6):

The Deerskin dancers wear aprons of civet cat [a spotted skunk native to the western United States] or a deerhide blanket about the waist, masses of dentalium necklaces, and forehead bands of wolf fur that shade the eyes. From the head rises a stick on which are fastened two or four black and white eagle or condor feathers, so put together as to look like a single feather of enormous length, its quill covered with woodpecker scalp . . . The dancers also hold poles on which are white, light grey, black, or mottled deerskins, the heads stuffed, the ears, mouths, throats, and false tongues decorated with woodpecker scalps, the hide of the body and legs hanging loose . . . The singer in the centre of the line, and his two assistants, add to the costume of the others a light net, reaching from the forehead to the middle of the shoulders and terminating in a fringe of feathers . . . The step of the entire row is merely a short stamp with one foot. At the end of the line and in front of it is a dancer who carries an obsidian blade instead of a deerskin. Over his wolf-fur forehead band is a strap from which project like hooks half a dozen or more curve-cut canine teeth of sealions. From the head hangs down a long loose-woven or crocheted net, painted in diamonds or triangles, and feather fringed . . . These two dancers advance and pass each other in front of the row of deerskins several times during each song, crouching, blowing a whistle, and holding their obsidians conspicuously.

Such a ritual recognized the power of the gods and the spirits over the lives of the members of their tribe. Californians believed in a number of such gods. Various gods had control of various aspects of a tribe's existence. Such gods might include an ancient hero, a being who was the progenitor of the tribe and had worked to bring it into existence. Other gods included those in control of the harvest, or of providing individual wealth and prosperity to men. Despite the importance of such deities, California peoples remained more highly interested in the myriad number of spirits which inhabited the land about them. These beings were more immediate, living on earth in the mountains, rocks, rivers and other physical features of the Native American landscape.

The Luiseno of southern California venerated two primary gods, named Wiyot and Chungichnish. Wiyot was a great culture hero, the embodiment of everything good, and an example of how to behave on earth. He was responsible for introducing the first humans to basket-making and other crafts. Also, he established the original customs and rituals practised by the Luiseno tribe. Chungichnish was a wise deity who carried great power and had established in ancient times the laws of the tribe and how infractions should be punished. He was also credited with establishing certain rituals for the tribe, such as the Jimson weed initiation. Chungichnish oversaw the people on earth through helpers which included spirits that occupied animals, fauna and even the stars. These observers watched the human beings and reported their actions to Chungichnish.

Other Luiseno deities included a man-eating spirit called Takwish. This cannibalistic god roamed the earth as a swiftly moving lightning ball, seeking human victims and eating them. To gain even a glimpse of Takwish was a bad portent, one which signalled doom and destruction to the hapless soul.

The Pomos recognized a vast pantheon of deities. Among them was the god named Kuksu, who resided in the southern half of the earth and had power over illness. He was also considered by some tribes to rule the land of the dead. The Pomos practised a ritual called the Kuksu ceremony – an elaborate dance that included costumed participants who were symbols of Kuksu – which was intended to appeal to the healing god's blessing. Another Pomo ceremony was the Ghost Ceremony. Most California tribes recognized the existence of ghosts, deceased spirits who returned to earth and could cause sickness in any person who actually saw them. During the Ghost Ceremony the men danced, their bodies painted grotesquely and their faces made ghastly by ramming wooden sticks through their noses and cheeks. The dancers represented dead spirits. These frenzied participants danced all night, and created a frightening whirlwind of terror by eating fire, handling live, wriggling rattlesnakes, and throwing frightened little boys over a blazing fire from one dancer to another. Throughout the ritual, the night air was monotonously broken by the endless beat of the footdrum.

Other Pomo gods included Madumda, the creator of the world, and a great flying deity-creature called Gilak, which flew through the skies, searching for someone to attack and consume. Within the assembly of California gods, then, were some who could do good on behalf of the tribes, and some who could bring evil. Shamans played an important in warding off the intentions of evil gods, passing out charms, amulets and potent herbs and medications which could protect from harm.

The role of the tribal shaman – holy man, seer and healer – was therefore important to his people through his knowing and understanding of the nature of the spirit world and how it worked. Shamans were medicine men for the tribes, practising their spiritual and physical healing for a fee. If a patient was not cured within a year after treatment by a shaman, often the payment was refunded. These healers carried out elaborate rituals, each individually designed to remove a specific pain or evil from the body of a sick and suffering person.

Mythology

The legends and supernatural stories of California are broad in scope. Typically, their mythology interprets the universe and the world in which they lived as a three-tiered cosmos. The Upper World was the home of Madumda. From here he observed his world and the people who occupied it. Above the Upper World was a second place where the brother of Madumda lived. The California tribes had very little mythology about this second place and it remained vague to them. The third world was one in which human beings and animals lived. This world, by the mythology of some tribes, had been previously occupied by a race of flying beings, 'Bird People,' who later evolved into various groups including humans, birds, mammals and reptiles.

Among the Luiseno people, myths were devised which explained the creation of the earth and its people. Two beings – Sky Male and Earth Female – were responsible for transforming a void and black universe into a place of light and being. Their conjoining created all things living including human beings, plants and animals. Such myths were unique neither to the Luiseno tribe nor to the tribes of California.

Exclusive to the Luiseno as a California tribe, however, was their mythology regarding the arrival of the First People to California in prehistoric times. These legends hold that the First People arrived in their great sacred valley – today located between Los Angeles to the north and San Diego to the south – where they took up residence. The god Wiyot became the victim of a plot and died at the hands of his own daughter, Frog. With Wiyot's death, the First People ceased to be immortal. When his body was burned, the institution of cremation of the dead was brought into the world of the Luiseno. Their culture hero, Wiyot, was then transformed and resurrected in the form of a moon in the night sky, in the same way as other Luiseno-based myths include other spirits seen as the souls of the dead inhabiting the stars.

MYTHS AND LEGENDS OF CALIFORNIA

THE ORIGIN OF THE WORLD AND OF MAN: THE EARTH DRAGON

Cahto

BEFORE THIS WORLD WAS FORMED there was another world. The sky of that world was made of sandstone rock. Two gods, Thunder and Nagaicho, looked at the old sky because it was being shaken by thunder.

'The rock is old,' they said. 'We will fix it. We will stretch it above far to the east.'

Then they stretched the sandstone rock of the sky, walking on the sky as they did so. Under each of the four corners of the sky they set up a great rock to hold it. Then they made the different things which would make the world pleasant for people to live in. In the south they made flowers. In the east they made a large opening so that the clouds could come through. In the west they made an opening so that the fog from the ocean could come through. To make clouds they built a fire. They said that the clouds would keep people, who were to be made later, from having headaches because of too much sunshine.

Then they made a man out of earth. They put grass inside him to form his stomach. Another bundle of grass they put in the figure to make man's heart. For his liver they used a round piece of clay, and the same for his kidneys. For his windpipe they used a reed. Then they prepared blood for man by mixing red stone, which they pulverized, with water. After making the various parts of man the two gods took one of his legs, split it and made a woman of it. Then they made the sun to travel by day and the moon to travel by night.

But the creations of the two gods were not to endure, for floodwaters came. Every day it rained, every night it rained. All the people slept. The sky fell. The land was not. For a very great distance there was no land. The waters of the oceans came together. Animals of all kinds drowned. The waters completely joined everywhere. There was no land or mountains or rocks, but only water. Trees and grass were not. There were no fish, nor land animals, nor birds. Human beings and animals alike had been washed away. The wind did not then blow through the portals of the world, nor was there snow, nor frost, nor rain. It did not thunder nor did it lighten. Since there were no trees to be struck, it did not thunder. There were neither clouds nor fog, nor was there a sun. It was very dark.

Then it was that this earth with its great, long horns got up and walked down this way from the north. As it walked along through the deep places the water rose to its shoulders. When it came up into shallower places, it looked up. There is a ridge in the north upon which the waves break. When it came to the middle of the world, in the east under the rising of the sun it looked up again. There where it

Source

Edward W. Gifford, *Californian Indian Nights Entertainments*, Glendale, CA: Arthur H. Clark Co., 1930, pp. 79–82

looked up will be a large land near to the coast. Far away to the south it continued looking up. It walked under the ground. Having come from the north it travelled far south and lay down. Nagaicho, standing on earth's head, had been carried to the south. Where earth lay down Nagaicho placed its head as it should be and spread grey clay between its eyes and on each horn. Upon the clay he placed a layer of reeds and then another layer of clay. In this he placed upright blue grass, brush and trees.

'I have finished,' he said. 'Let there be mountain peaks here on its head. Let the waves of the sea break against them.'

The mountains became and brush sprang up on them. The small stones he had placed on its head became large. Its head was buried from sight.

Now people appeared. These people all had animal names, and later, when Indians came to live on this earth, these 'first people' were changed into the animals which bear their names. Seal, Sea Lion and Grizzly Bear built a dance house. One woman was named Whale. She was fat and that is why there are so many stout Indian women today.

The god Nagaicho caused different sea foods to grow in the water so that the people would have things to eat. He caused the seaweed to grow, and also the abalones and mussels, and many other things. Then he made salt from ocean foam. He made the water of the ocean rise up in waves and said that the ocean should always behave in that way. He said that old whales would float ashore, so that the people might have them to eat.

He made redwoods and other trees grow on the tail of the great dragon, which lay to the north. He made creeks by dragging his foot through the earth so that people would have good fresh water to drink. He travelled all over the earth making things so that this earth wold be a comfortable place for men. He made a great many oak trees, so that the people would have plenty of acorns to eat.

After he had finished making everything, he and his dog went walking all over the earth to see how all of the new things looked.

Finally when they arrived at their starting point he said to his dog, 'We are close to home, my dog. Now we shall go back north and stay there.'

So he left this world where people live and now lives in the north.

The two gods, Thunder and Nagaicho, made man out of earth.

HOW THE WORLD WAS MADE COMFORTABLE FOR PEOPLE

Hupa

IN NORTHWESTERN CALIFORNIA the god who made the nice things in this world for people is known as Yimantuwingyai, which in English means He-who-is-lost-to-us-across-the-ocean. He first appeared in a place on the Klamath river. When he came into existence there was a ringing noise throughout the world like the striking of a large bell. Just before he appeared in this world smoke had settled on the mountainsides and rotten pieces of wood fell from the sky. Where they fell there was fire. After he appeared there grew everywhere in the world a race of people who lived there until the Indians appeared, when they went away across the ocean never to be seen again. These people were immortals who did not die. Some of these people were bad and the god who came first did not like them. One of

Source
Edward W. Gifford, *Californian Indian Nights Entertainments*, Glendale, CA: Arthur H. Clark Co., 1930, pp. 112–17

these bad people had all of the deer in his keeping. He kept them inside a mountain through the side of which was a door. The god, not liking this, set out to find a way by which he could let the deer out of the mountain so that everybody could have venison to eat.

He went to the house of the stingy person who kept all of the deer.

He said, 'I am hungry for fresh deer meat.'

The owner of the deer went to kill a deer to give the god some of it to eat. The god secretly watched him to see what he did. He saw the man open a door in the side of the mountain where the deer were kept. The god ran back to the house before the man returned. He put his quiver, in which his arrows were kept, on the roof of the house; then he went inside. When the man brought the deer the god made an excuse to go out.

He said, 'I am going out to take a swim before I eat the deer meat.'

As he passed out he took down his quiver from the roof. In it had grown a plant called wild ginger, of which the deer are very fond. He now went secretly to the door behind which the deer were kept. He opened the door and laid the ginger on the ground. The deer came out and smelt the ginger and scattered all over the country. In that way it became possible for everybody to have deer meat to eat, instead of only the one stingy person who had them all the in the beginning.

Then the god thought that it would be a nice thing if he could have some sort of fish for people to eat everywhere. A woman who lived across the ocean toward the north had all of the salmon in the world, in a pond there. Although she ate plenty of fish herself she would not allow the fish out of the pond for fear other people might catch them. The god arrived at this selfish woman's house. He was very polite to her and called her his niece. She gave him fresh salmon for the evening meal. The next day the god, having spent the night there, told the woman he would like some eels to eat. When she went to catch them he followed to spy upon her. Having found out what he wished to know he hurried back before the woman arrived with the eels. She cooked the eels and called to him to come and eat.

After he had remained at the woman's house for two nights he again felt hungry for salmon. When she went for them he followed to see what she would do. He saw the fishing platforms projecting out over the water and many fish nets nearby. He also saw the nets for catching surf fish.

The next day he said he was hungry for surf fish. He watched her get them as he had done before. Then she cooked them for him between two sticks.

Now that the god had found out what to do to get the various kinds of fish for people to eat, he made a flute of wood. He told the flute that when he went out it should play, so that the woman would think he was still there.

He looked around to see the best place for digging a ditch from the pond to the ocean, so as to let the salmon and other fishes out. He dug a ditch with a sharp stick. When the ditch was finished the water rushed out, carrying the fish with it, so that they were able to swim to all parts of the world. The stingy old woman ran along after her salmon, telling them to come back, but they went swimming away just the same. Every year this old woman follows the salmon up the Klamath river and the Trinity river, when they swim up those rivers to lay their eggs. They speak of her as Salmon's grandmother. She is believed to appear in the form of a small yellow-breasted bird, a flycatcher.

The god travelled over the world making things comfortable for people. As he was going along to the south he saw someone coming toward him carrying a heavy load. This person had no eyes.

When the god saw him he said, 'Eh, old man, the load has nearly worn you out.'

The old man sat down, falling over as he did so.

'Help me carry it,' he said.

'All right,' said the god. 'Push the load up on my back while I sit under it.'

When the blind man pushed the load on the god's back he untied the strap by which it was held, so that the load fell. If the god had not jumped out quickly the load would have fallen upon him and cut him to pieces, for it was a load of sharp, black rock called obsidian, of which arrowpoints are made. The blind man felt around to see if he had killed the god, for this old man was in the habit of killing people by letting the load fall upon them, when they offered to help him carry it.

He could not find the body of the god, and he said to himself, 'This one I did not kill.'

Then the old man arranged the pieces of sharp stone in the bundle again.

Now the god spoke to him, 'Come, it is your turn. Let me push the load on your back.'

The old man was afraid, now.

'No, I will let nobody push the load on to me.'

Nevertheless the god threw him on the ground and pushed the load of sharp stones on to him, so that they stuck into him and cut him all to pieces. In that way the god got rid of this bad cannibal who killed and ate people.

Further on to the south the god found a man who was trying to catch passing travellers with a hook. As the god came along he grabbed the man's hook and allowed himself to be drawn quite close to the bad man. Then he suddenly let go.

Then he said to the man with the hook, 'Come, let me catch you with the hook.'

The old man said, 'No.'

But the god took the hook out of his hand and caught him with it and killed him.

Then the god said, 'People will travel the trails in safety now, since I have killed the cannibals.'

Further on he saw someone making a seesaw. This man asked the god to sit on the seesaw. After the god did so he suddenly let it down with a bang. but the god was too quick for him and jumped off in time to avoid being hurt.

Then the god said to this bad man, 'Let me seesaw with you.'

The man objected, but nevertheless the god put him on the seesaw, which was of sharp stone. He let the seesaw down hard and this evil man was killed by it.

Another man who was splitting a log of wood tried to get the god to stand in the cleft, intending to let the log spring shut on him suddenly. This man, who was also blind, was a cannibal, too, and caught people this way. When he thought that he had caught the god he brought a big basket pot and set it where he thought the god's blood would be dripping after he had been squeezed in the log. Then he set the wedge in the log. He felt around for the body of the god but could not find it.

Then the god said to him, 'Come, you step into the crack.'

The blind man did not want to do this, but the god pushed him in, and let the log spring shut on him.

The god said, 'When people are going to build a house they may split logs this way, but they must not kill people to eat, as this wicked person has been doing.'

This god tried to arrange for Indians to live forever, or at least to live again once after they had died. But people did not like this scheme and the god failed to arrange it, so that now people die and do not come to life again.

Finally, after he had done all that he could to make this world a comfortable place for Indians to live in, he went away across the ocean and was never seen again. He lives there today.

YO-SEM-I-TE, LARGE GRIZZLY BEAR

Yosemite-Miwok

WHEN THE WORLD WAS MADE, the Great Spirit tore out the heart of Kay-o-pha, the Sky Mountains, and left the gash unhealed. He sent the Coyote to people the valley with a strong and hardy race of men, who called their home Ah-wah-nee, and themselves, the Ah-wah-nee-chees.

The Ah-wah-nee-chees lived the simple life, which knows no law but to hunt and kill and eat. By day the trackless forests rang with the clamour of the chase. By the flaring light of their fires the hunters gorged themselves upon the fresh-killed meat, feasting far into the night. They made war upon the tribes that lived beyond the walls of Ah-wah-nee and never knew defeat, for none dared follow them to their rock-ribbed fastness. They were feared by all save the outcasts of other tribes, whose lawless deeds won for them a place among the Ah-wah-nee-chees. Thus the children of Ah-wah-nee increased in number and strength.

As time went by, the Ah-wah-nee-chees, in their pride of power, forgot the Great Spirit who had given them their stronghold and made them feared of all their race. And the Great Spirit, turning upon them in his wrath, loosed his evil forces in their midst, scourging them with a black sickness that swept all before it as a hot wind blights the grain at harvest time.

The air of the valley was a poison breath, in which the death shade hovered darkly. Before the Evil Spirit medicine men were powerless. Their mystic spells and incantations were a weird mockery, performed among the dying and the dead; and when at last the Evil One passed onward in his cursed flight, the once proud and powerful band of Ah-wah-nee-chees was like a straggling pack of gaunt grey wolves. Their eyes gleamed dully in their shrunken faces, and their skin hung in loose folds on their wasted bodies.

Those who were able fled from the valley, which was now a haunted place, eerie with flitting shadows of funeral fires and ghostly echoes of the funeral wail. They scattered among the tribes beyond the mountains, and Ah-wah-nee was deserted.

A vast stillness settled upon the valley, broken only by the songs of birds and the roar of Cho-look when Spring sent the mountain torrents crashing over his head. The mountain lion and the grizzly roamed at will among the rocks and tangled chinquapin, fearless of arrows; the doe led her young by an open path to the river, where trout flashed their colours boldly in the sun. In the autumn the choke-cherries and manzanita berries dried upon their stems, and ripened acorns rotted

With his instinctive love of conflict roused, the young chief seized a broken limb and gave the grizzly blow for blow.

Source
Bertha H. Smith, *Yosemite Legends*, San Francisco: Paul Elder and Co., 1904, pp. 3–10

to dust upon the ground after the squirrels had gathered their winter store. The homeless Ah-wah-nee-chees circled wide in passing the valley.

Over beyond To-co-yah, the North Dome, among the Mo-nos and Pai-u-tes, a few of the ill-fated Ah-wah-nee-chees had found refuge. Among them was the chief of the tribe, who after a time took a Mo-no maiden for his bride. By this Mo-no woman he had a son, and they gave him the name of Ten-ie-ya. Before another round of seasons, the spirit of the Ah-wah-nee-chee chieftain had wandered on to the Land of the Sun, the home of happy souls.

Ten-ie-ya grew up among his mother's people, but the fire of a warrior chief was in his blood and he liked not to live where the word of another was law. The fire in his blood was kept aflame by the words of an old man, the patriarch of his father's tribe, who urged him to return to Ah-wah-nee, the home of his ancestors, and gather about him the people whose chief he was by right of birth.

So Ten-ie-ya went back across the mountains by a trail abandoned long ago, and from the camps of other tribes came those in whose veins was any trace of Ah-wah-nee-chee blood; and, as before, the number was increased by lawless braves of weaker bands who liked a greater freedom for their lawlessness. Again, under the favour of the Great Spirit, the Ah-wah-nee-chees flourished and by their fierce strength and daring became to other tribes as the mountain lion to the wolf and the coyote and the mountain sheep.

And it chanced that one day while Ten-ie-ya and his warriors were camped near Le-ham-i-te, the Canyon of the Arrow-wood, a young brave went out in the early morning to the kale of ke-kee-too-yem, the Sleeping Water, to spear fish. His lithe, strong limbs took no heed of the rocks in his path, and he leaped from boulder to boulder, following the wall that rose sheer above him and cut the blue sky overhead.

As he reached the base of Scho-ko-ni, the cliff that arches like the shade of an Indian cradle basket, he came suddenly upon a monster grizzly that had just crept forth from his winter cave. The grizzly knows no man for his friend; least of all, the man who surprises him at the first meal after his long sleep. The rivals of Ah-wah-nee were face to face.

The Ah-wah-nee-chee had no weapon save his fish spear, useless as a reed; yet he had the fearlessness of youth and the courage of a race to whom valorous deeds are more than strings of wampum, piles of pelt or many cattle. He faced the grizzly boldly as the clumsy hulk rose to its full height, at bay and keen for attack. With his instinctive love of conflict roused, the young chief seized a broken limb that lay at his feet, and gave the grizzly blow for blow.

The claws of the maddened brute raked his flesh. The blood ran warm over his glistening skin and matted the bristled yellow fur of the grizzly. The Ah-wah-nee-chee fought bravely. While there was blood in his body, he could fight; when the blood was gone, he could die; but with the traditions of his ancestors firing his brain, he could not flee.

Furious with pain, blinded by the blows from the young chief's club and by the blood from the young chief's torn flesh, the grizzly struggled savagely. He, too, was driven by the law of his breed, the universal law of the forest, the law of Indian and grizzly alike – which is to kill.

Such a battle could not last. With a low growl the crippled grizzly brought himself together and struck with the full force of his powerful arm. The blow fell short.

Urging his waning strength to one last effort, the Ah-wah-nee-chee raised his club high above his head and brought it down with a heavy, well-aimed stroke that crushed the grizzly's skull and sent him rolling among the boulders, dead.

That night as the Ah-wah-nee-chees feasted themselves on bear meat, the story of the Young chief's bravery was told, and told again; and from that hour he was known as Yo-sem-i-te, the Large Grizzly Bear.

In time the name Yo-sem-i-te was given to all the tribe of Ah-wah-nee-chees, who for fearlessness and lawlessness were rivaled only by the grizzly with whom they shared their mountain fastness. And when, long afterward, the white man came and took Ah-wah-nee for his own, he gave it the name by which Ten-ie-ya's band was known; and Cho-look, the high fall that makes the earth tremble with its mighty roar, he also called by the name of the Large Grizzly Bear, Yo-sem-i-te.

Hum-moo, the Lost Arrow

Yosemite-Miwok

TEE-HEE-NEH WAS THE FAIREST of the daughters of Ah-wah-nee, and the happiest, for she was the chosen bride of the brave Kos-soo-kah.

When she went forth from her father's lodge to bathe in the shadowy depths of Ke-koo-too-yem, the Sleeping Water, her step was light as the touch of a windswept leaf upon the rocks. When she stooped to lave her cheeks in the cool spray, her dark hair fell about her shoulders like a silken web, and the water mirror showed her a pair of laughing eyes of the colour of ripened acorns, and in them the soft light of an Indian summer day. The sound of her voice was as the patter of rain on green leaves, and her heart was fearless and full of love.

No other woman of the tribe could weave such baskets as grew by the magic skill of her fingers, and she alone knew the secret of interweaving the bright feathers of the red-headed woodpecker and the topknots of mountain quail. Her acorn bread was always sweetest, the berries she gathered ripest, the deerskin she tanned softer than any other; and all because of the love in her heart, for she knew that Kos-soo-kah would eat of her bread and fruit, would drink from the baskets she wove, and would wear upon his feet the moccasins she made.

Kos-soo-kah was a hunter, fearless and bold, sure with bow and spear, always fortunate in the chase. In his veins ran the blood that surges hot when there are daring deeds to do, and of all the young chiefs of Ah-wah-nee he had the greatest power among his people. Like the wooing of the evening star by the crescent moon was the mating of Tee-hee-neh with Kos-soo-kah; and when the young chief gathered together robes of squirrel and deerskin and of the skins of waterfowl, arrows and spearheads, strings of coral and bear teeth, and gave them as a marriage token to Tee-hee-neh's father, the old chief looked upon him with favour.

This was their marriage. But before Tee-hee-neh should go with Kos-soo-kah to his lodge there must be a great feast, and all day long Ah-wah-nee was astir with signs of preparation.

From many shady places came a sound like the tap-tap-tapping of woodpeckers, where the older women sat upon smooth, flat rocks pounding dried acorns into

Source
Bertha H. Smith,
Yosemite Legends,
San Francisco:
Paul Elder and
Co., 1904,
pp. 21–30

She went forth from her father's lodge to bathe in the shadowy depths of the Sleeping Water.

meal to make the acorn bread; and the younger women went with their baskets to the meadows and woods for grass seeds, herbs and wild honey.

Early in the morning Kos-soo-kah left his lodge and gathered about him the strongest of the young braves to go forth into the forest and net the grouse, and seek the bear and deer in their haunts, for this was the man's share of the marriage feast. While his hunters strung their bows and fastened arrowheads to the feathered shafts, Kos-soo-kah stole away for a last word with Tee-hee-neh, his bride; and when they parted it was with the promise that at the end of the day's hunt Kos-soo-kah should drop an arrow from the cliff between Cho-look, the high fall, and Le-ham-i-te, the Canyon of the Arrow-wood. By the number of feathers it bore, Tee-hee-neh could tell what the kill had been.

The morning mists were still tangled in the pines when Kos-soo-kah and his hunters began to climb the trail that cut into the heart of the forest. From a covert spot Tee-hee-neh watched her lover disappear through the cleft in the northern wall, where the arrow-wood grows thick; then she joined the other women and worked with a light heart until long shadows stretched across the meadow and warned her of the hour when she was to be near the foot of Cho-look to receive the message from Kos-soo-kah.

Far over the mountains Kos-soo-kah laughed loud with a hunter's pride as he bound to his swiftest arrow all the feathers of a grouse's wing. Sped by a hunter's pride and a lover's pride he leaped along the rocky trail, far in advance of the youthful braves of his band who bore among them the best of the kill. Eagerly he watched the western sky, fearful lest the sun's last kiss should tinge the brow of Tis-sa-ack before he reached the cliff whence his bow should let fly the message to the waiting one below.

The frightened quail fluttered in his path unseen. A belated vulture, skimming the fading sky, seemed not to be in motion. So swiftly Kos-soo-kah ran, the wind stood still to let him pass.

He reached the valley wall at last, his strength well spent but still enough to pull his bow to a full half-circle. Poised for an instant, the feathered shaft caught on its tip a sun ray, then flew downward; but though mighty and sure the force that sent it, no message came to the faithful Tee-hee-neh.

Hour after hour she waited, the joy in her heart changing to a nameless fear as the blue sky faded grey, and the grey went purple in the thickening dusk, and yet no sign, no sound of the returning hunters.

'Kos-soo-kah! Kos-soo-kah!' trembled her voice in the stillness. Only a weird echo answered, 'Kos-soo-kah.'

Perhaps they had wandered far, and Kos-soo-kah could not reach the cliff till the night shadows had crept out of the valley, and over the tops of the mountains. Perhaps even now he was returning down the Canyon of the Arrow-wood. This she whispered to a heart that gave no answering hope.

She would go forward to meet him, and hear from his lips the message which the arrow failed to bring. As she hurried along the narrow trail, clinging to the slanting ledges, pushing aside the overhanging branches, she called and called, 'Kos-soo-kah!'

Now and again she stopped to listen for the sound of voices, or of footsteps, but only the cry of a night bird or the crackling of dry twigs stirred the still air.

Trembling with uncertainty and fear, she reached the top of the sharp ascent.

There by the light of the stars she saw fresh footprints in the loose, moist earth. Her heart told her they were his; her quick eye told her they went toward the cliff, but did not return. Crouching there beside them, she called again, 'Kos-soo-kah!' Not even an echo answered the despairing cry.

Slowly she crept forward, following the fresh trail to the edge of the wall. She leaned far over, and there on a mound of fallen rock lay her lover, motionless, nor answering her call. Tight in his grasp was the spent bow, the sign of a promise kept.

As she looked, there came again to Tee-hee-neh's mind the dull roar of rending rock, the low moan of falling earth, that ran through the valley at the sunset hour. Now she knew that as Kos-soo-kah drew his bow to speed the messenger of love, the ground beneath his feet had given way, carrying him with the fatal avalanche.

The girl's heart no longer beat fast with fear. It seemed not to beat at all. But there was no time for grief; perhaps Kos-soo-kah had not ceased to breathe. On the topmost point of rock she lighted a signal fire, and forced its flames high into the dark, flashing a call for help. It would be long, she knew, before any one could come; but this was the only chance to save Kos-soo-kah.

Hours passed. With feverish energy she piled dry branches high upon the signal fire, nor let its wild beckonings rest a moment. At last old men came from the valley, and the young braves from the mountains bearing with them the carcasses of deer and bear.

With their hunting-knives they cut lengths of tamarack, and lashed them together with thongs of hide from the deer killed for the marriage feast. By means of this pole they would have lowered over the edge of the cliff a strong young brave but that Tee-hee-neh pushed him aside and took his place. Hers must be the voice to whisper in Kos-soo-kah's ear the first word of hope; hers the hand to push aside the rocks that pinioned his body; hers the face his slowly opening eyes should see.

They lowered her to his side; and, loosing the cords that bound her, she knelt beside him, whispering in his ear, 'Kos-soo-kah!' No sound came from the cold, set lips. The wide-open eyes stared unseeing at the sky. Tee-hee-neh knew that he was dead.

She did not cry aloud after the manner of Indian women in their grief, but gently bound the helpless form with the deerskin cords and raised it as high as her arms could reach when the pole was drawn upward; then waited in silence until she was lifted by the willing hands above.

When she found herself again at Kos-soo-kah's side, she stood for an instant with eyes fixed upon the loved form, there in the cold, starless dawn of her marriage day; then with his name upon her lips she fell forward upon his breast. They drew her away, but the spirit of Tee-hee-neh had followed the spirit of Kos-soo-kah.

The two were placed together upon the funeral pyre, and with them was burned all that had been theirs. In Kos-soo-kah's hand was the bow, but the arrow could not be found. The lovers had spirited it away. In its stead they left a pointed rock lodged in the cliff between Cho-look, the High Fall, and Le-ham-i-te, the Canyon of the Arrow-wood, in token of Kos-soo-kah's fulfilled pledge. This rock is known to the children of Ah-wah-nee as Hum-moo, the Lost Arrow.

THE LAND OF THE DEAD

Yokut

ALONG TIME AGO a woman died. Her husband buried her, but he could not bear the thought of her death. He wanted to get her back. He knew that very soon she would leave the grave and go to the island of the Dead. So he dug a hole near her grave and stayed there, watching.

On the second night he saw his wife come up out of the ground, brush the earth from her, and start off to the island of the Dead. He tried to seize her but he could not hold her. She slid through his hands and went on. He followed and attempted many times to hold her, but she always escaped.

Once when he had overtaken her, only to have her slip through his fingers, she turned to him and said, 'Why are you following me? I am nothing now. Do you think you can get my body back?'

'I think so,' he answered.

'I think not,' she replied. 'I am going to a different kind of a place, now.'

The woman then went on, saying nothing further to her husband who continued following her. Soon they arrived at a bridge. On the other side of the bridge was the island of the Dead. The dead had to pass over this bridge in order to arrive at the island. Sometimes when the island became overcrowded with dead people, the chief would send a little bird to the bridge. As the dead walked along the bridge, the bird would suddenly flutter up beside them, which would frighten them and cause many to fall off the bridge into the river. There they turned to fish.

The dead wife passed over the bridge and entered the island. The chief of the island approached her.

'You have a companion?' he asked.

'Yes, my husband,' she replied.

'Is he coming here?' he asked.

'I do not know,' she answered. 'He is alive.' Then the chief sent his men to the husband on the other side of the bridge.

'Do you want to come to this country?' they asked.

'Yes,' he said.

They replied, 'Wait. We will see the chief.'

So the men went back to their chief.

'He says that he wants to come to this country,' they told the chief. 'We think he does not tell the truth. He intends to get his wife back.'

'Well, let him come across,' the chief answered.

He intended to send the bird to the bridge to frighten the man as he crossed, and so cause him to fall into the river. But the bird was not able to scare the man, and so he soon arrived on the other side and entered the Island of the Dead.

The chief did not want him to stay. He said, 'This is a bad country. You should not have come. We have only your wife's soul, and we cannot give her back to you.'

But the man stayed on the island for six days, and watched the dead people dancing all the time.

Then the chief sent him home, saying, 'When you arrive home, hide yourself. Then after six days, come out and make a dance.'

Source

Edward W. Gifford, *Californian Indian Nights Entertainments*, Glendale, CA: Arthur H. Clark Co., 1930, pp. 185–87

So the man returned to his parents.

'Make me a small house. In six days I will come out and dance.'

But the man was in such a hurry to come out and tell all the people of what he had seen in the island of the Dead that he came out on the fifth day. He danced all night, telling the people about the island. He told them that even though the little bird who was sent to the bridge did all he could to keep too many people from entering the island, every two days the island became full. Then the chief would gather the people and say to them, 'You must swim.' The people would stop dancing and bathe. While bathing the little bird would appear and frighten them, causing some to turn to fish and others to ducks. In this way the chief made room for the new dead who were continually coming over the bridge.

Early in the morning the man stopped dancing, and went to bathe. There a rattlesnake bit him and he died. So he went back to the island of the Dead and he is there now.

It is through him that we now know about the island where the dead go.

On the other side of the bridge was the Island of the Dead.

Kom-po-pai-ses, Leaping Frog Rocks

Yosemite-Miwok

FOREVER AND FOREVER the Three Brothers sit looking over each other's shoulders from the north wall of Ah-wah-nee (today in Yosemite National Park).

The Indians likened these peaks to frogs sitting back upon their haunches ready to leap, and called them Kom-po-pai-ses, the Leaping Frog Rocks. This the white man did not know when he named them the Three Brothers.

The story of the Three Brothers is history, not tradition. It has to do with the coming of the white man to Ah-wah-nee, and the downfall of Ten-ie-ya, the last chief of the Ah-wah-nee-chees.

Across the plains that billow away toward the sea, Ten-ie-ya watched the approach of the white stranger, having always in mind the words of the old man who was his counsellor when he left the land of his Mo-no mother and returned to Ah-wah-nee to rule over his father's people.

The patriarch had heard the call of the Great Spirit, bidding him to the happy land of the West, and had told Ten-ie-ya many things. This, last of all, 'Obey my word, O Ten-ie-ya, and your people shall be many as the blades of grass, and none shall dare to bring war into Ah-wah-nee. But look you ever, my son, against the white horsemen of the great plains beyond; for once they have crossed the western mountains, your tribe will scatter as the dust before a desert wind, and never come together again. Guard well your stronghold, O Ten-ie-ya, lest you be the last of the great chiefs of Ah-wah-nee.'

The faded eyes had the light that comes when the call of the Great Spirit sounds very near, and the feeble hand of the patriarch trembled as he raised his pipe above his head, and said, 'Great Spirit, I pray be good to my son, the chief of the Ah-wah-nee-chees. Toward the pines, north, cold wind treat him kindly; toward the rising sun, east, great sun shine upon his lodge in the early morning; toward the place where the sun goes in winter, south, bless my son; toward the

Source
Bertha H. Smith, *Yosemite Legends*, San Francisco: Paul Elder and Co., 1904, pp. 57–64

land of the setting sun, west, waft on the breezes a peaceful sleep. And, lowering my pipe, I say, kind mother earth, when you receive my son into your warm bosom, hold him gently. Let the howl of the coyote, the roaring of the bear and the mountain-lion, and the sound of winds swaying the tops of the pine trees, be to him a sweet lullaby.'

Because of these last words of the dying seer, Ten-ie-ya guarded his mountain retreat as a she-bear guards the refuge of her young. With vague foreboding he saw the white horsemen coming nearer. They took the land that the Great Spirit had made for the people of his race. They burrowed into it like moles, and washed the sands of its rivers, searching for something yellow and shining that the Indian neither knew was there nor cared to know. They grazed their horses and their cattle upon the broad stretches that had been the Indian's hunting-ground since time began. They even went so far, these pale-faced strangers, as to steal Indian women for their wives. And always they made their camps nearer and nearer to Ah-wah-nee.

While the vigour of youth remained, Ten-ie-ya did not fear these men of an alien race. He only hated them. With his band of lawless Grizzlies he stole forth in the night and drove away their horses to kill for food; and as they feasted, drunk with the taste of warm blood, their spirits were made bold, and the deep gorge rang with shouts of defiance.

But Ten-ie-ya grew old, and the white horsemen of the plains, now strong in number, were at the very walls of Ah-wah-nee. The words of the dying patriarch were ever in his ears, and he knew that the evil day was come.

At last the white men climbed the western mountains, offering gifts in the name of the Great Father, their chief; and when they went away they led Ten-ie-ya captive to their camp. The young braves fled from Ah-wah-nee, across To-co-yah, the North Dome, to the home of the Mo-nos. It was well that Ten-ie-ya should go to the plains, they said; but they were young and could find plenty in the mountains; they would not go to be herded like horses in the white man's camp.

Though he appeared to yield, the spirit of Ten-ie-ya was not broken. Like a wild beast in captivity, he chafed under restraint. With the cunning of his race, he watched his chance; and when it came, he returned to his stronghold in the Sky Mountains, bearing in his heart a fiercer hate for the white man, a hate made keener by defeat, a hate that burned for revenge.

But an evil spell seemed cast upon the children of Ah-wah-nee. They were scattered, and they did not rally round their chief. Again the white horsemen climbed the western mountains, this time without gifts. But day and night signal fires had burned upon the mountain tops; and when the messengers of the Great Father entered Ah-wah-nee they found the valley deserted, save for five dark figures that darted like shadows from tree to rock at the base of a jagged spur of the northern wall.

Feeling themselves secure because of the swollen river that lay between, the five scouts came into the open when discovered, and mocked the strangers; then disappeared up the side of a cliff so straight and pathless that no white man could follow. By fair promises carried to them by an Indian guide they were induced to come into camp, and three of them were found to be sons of Ten-ie-ya.

It does not speak for the faith of white men that one of the brothers was killed while held as hostage until the aged chief should come in and deliver himself to the

messengers of the Great Father; and that only an uncertain aim saved another who tried to escape through the Canyon of the Arrow-wood, where his father was hiding. When he saw it was useless to resist further these fearless, faithless horsemen of the plains, who had stolen his lands and his women, who would not let him live in peace in his mountains, Ten-ie-ya came down from Le-ham-i-te, the Canyon of the Arrow-wood, by a trail that led into the valley through the branches of a giant oak.

The first sight that met the gaze of the twice-conquered chieftain was the dead body of his youngest son. He spoke no word, but lines of sorrow appeared in the hard, old face; and secretly, in the heart of the night, he had the young chief's body carried away – none knew where. Once more he tried for his liberty; once more was captured. Then in a passion of grief and rage, he turned his bare breast to his captors, and cried, 'Kill me, white chief, as you have killed my son, as you would kill all my people if they would but come to you. You have brought sorrow to my heart. For me the sun shines no more. Kill me, white chief, and when I am dead I will call my people, that they shall come and avenge the death of their chief and his son. My spirit will follow your footsteps forever. I will not leave the spirit world, you will not see me, but I will follow you where you go and you will know it is the spirit of the old chief, and you will fear me and grow cold. This is the message of the Great Spirit.'

But Ten-ie-ya's hour was not yet come. He was to die, for an act of treachery, at the hands of the Mo-nos, his mother's people. Even so, the prophecy of the seer was fulfilled, for the white horsemen of the plains had crossed the western mountains, the tribe was scattered, never to come together again, and Ten-ie-ya was the last great chief of the Ah-wah-nee-chees.

Because his three sons were captured at its base, the triple peak in the northern wall was given the name Three Brothers.

WHY WE ARE NOT ABLE TO VISIT THE DEAD

Shasta

ONCE UPON A TIME Woodpecker fell into the fire and was burned to death. Her husband saw what happened, but he could do nothing to save her. As he looked at the fire into which she had fallen and burned up, he thought he saw her ghost rise up toward the sky. He went out in back of the house until he found the trail of the ghost. The trail led up and up, until it was lost in the sky.

Woodpecker's husband followed the ghost of his wife along this trail until he reached the sky. He saw the ghost proceed along the milky way. He tried to overtake her to catch her and bring her back to earth with him, but during the day she far outdistanced him. In fact, she left him far behind in the trail. When night came the ghost camped on the trail and then her husband would almost come up to her. But always, before he could reach her, the day commenced and she set off again.

Finally the ghost reached the Other World, and soon after her husband came. He found all the dead people dancing and having a fine time, his wife's ghost included. He watched all this for a long time, then he addressed the firetender.

'May I get back my wife?' he asked.

Source
Edward W. Gifford, *Californian Indian Nights Entertainments*, Glendale, CA: Arthur H. Clark Co., 1930, pp. 189–90

'No,' the firetender answered.

After a while he fell asleep; and when he awoke it was daytime and all the dead people had gone to sleep. They looked like patches of soft white ashes on the ground. The firetender then approached Woodpecker's husband and handed him a poker.

'Poke the various sleeping ghosts,' he said. 'The one that gets up and sneezes when you do this will be your wife.'

So Woodpecker's husband followed this advice. He found his wife and picked her up and started home. At first she weighed nothing, but as they approached the earth she grew heavier. She grew so heavy that before he was able to reach his house he dropped her. The ghost immediately ran back to the Other World.

Woodpecker's husband then started all over again along the trail to the Other World, and, as the first time, succeeded in getting hold of his wife in the Other World. But again, as he neared home, he was forced to drop her, because of her heaviness, and again the ghost ran back to the Other World.

A third time Woodpecker's husband followed his wife to the Other World. This time, however, the firetender told him that he might not try again.

'Return home, and in a short time you will be allowed to come and live with your wife,' he told him.

So Woodpecker's husband was forced to follow these instructions, and returned home and went to sleep. He died, and then as a ghost returned to the Other World for good.

If Woodpecker's husband had succeeded in bringing back safely to our world the ghost of his wife, today everyone would be able to visit the Other World without dying first.

THE TWO-HEADED MONSTER
Chilula

The two-headed monster chased him around until his breath was nearly gone.

Source
Edward W. Gifford, *Californian Indian Nights Entertainments*, Glendale, CA: Arthur H. Clark Co., 1930, pp. 194–96

IN A FARAWAY VILLAGE, where once many people had lived, there now reigned a two-headed monster. The hillside leading from the forest down to the creek was white with the bones of people killed by him.

In another village four brothers and an old woman lived. One day the oldest and wisest of the brothers decided to go down to the creek. While walking along its bank he heard something making a noise on the hill on the other side of the creek. As he kept on he wondered what it was that was making that noise.

Then the two-headed monster appeared from out of the hill-forest and proceeded to chase him about. He ran, but soon his breath gave out, and he felt as though he was about to die. Still the monster chased him and he was forced to continue running until he dropped dead from lack of breath. The monster then picked up his body and carried it across the creek and up the hill to the house where he lived. This house was so covered with moss that no one could see it. The beings who eat people lived there.

Meanwhile, the old woman and the three remaining brothers became worried when the brother did not return. When two days passed and still he did not return, another of the brothers set out. Soon he came to the bank of the creek and

headed to the north, as his brother had done. And then, like his brother, he heard something making a noise. It was the monster, who when going along made a noise in the forest like the blowing of the wind. The monster killed this second brother also, and carried him across the stream and up the hill to the house hidden by moss.

When neither the first nor the second brother returned, the third brother made ready to go. He never returned.

Now there was only the youngest brother left, with the old woman. He was only a little fellow, yet he said to his grandmother, 'Today I am going.'

She replied, 'My grandchild, why do you say that? They will eat us all.'

But he would not stay, and when the grandmother saw this she looked for his belt. When she found it she took it out and bade him put it on. It was very wide.

'When you are about to lose your breath do this,' she told him, motioning for him to loosen his belt.

So he started out, following the same direction as was taken by his three brothers, who had gone off and never returned. When he came to the bank of the creek and was walking along he heard something making a noise. Off across the creek in the hill-forest the redwood trees were moving back and forth. It was the coming of the monster. When the monster saw him he started after him, chasing him around and around, until his breath was nearly gone. When he was almost about to die, he loosened his belt, as his grandmother had told him, and the monster fell apart, dead! It was the magic thing in his belt which had done it. Then the young brother went across the stream and followed the track up the hillside, covered with the bones of people killed by the monster, to the house hidden by moss. He went in.

An old woman and a boy were sitting there. Beside these two lay a net, made for catching the people which these persons ate.

'Something made a noise,' the boy said to the old woman. Then he turned to pick up the net, but the younger brother loosened his belt, and the boy fell in two parts.

The old woman then took up the net, and the young brother did the same thing to her, and she died.

The young brother said, 'People shall not live this way. They shall not eat people. They shall live right.'

He set fire to the house and burned it. Then he set out to the southward, where his grandmother lived.

'I have come back, grandmother,' he said.

'I am glad you came back, grandchild,' she replied.

'I killed them,' he said, and returned the belt to her.

'My body is glad,' she said.

Her grandchild was left to her, and they lived well after that.

THE ROLLING SKULL

Yana

WILDCAT'S WIFE HAD JUST GIVEN BIRTH to a baby, so Wildcat did not go deer-hunting, as usual. Instead he went with his wife and child to gather pine-nuts. They came to a place where there were many trees loaded with pine-nuts.

'I shall climb up for them here,' said Wildcat. He climbed the tree and began throwing the pine cones down one after another. While doing this he began thinking of a dream he had had the night before. He dreamed that he was throwing himself down from a tree. So now he threw down one shoulder, then the other. Then he threw down one thigh, then the other. Then he threw down his backbone, until he had nothing left but his skull. Meanwhile, below, Wildcat's wife noticed blood dripping from the pine tree. She looked up and became afraid and ran off home.

'I don't know what he is going to do,' she cried. 'He had thrown his own members down, and bounds about in the tree with nothing but his skull. Blood is dripping down from the tree. I am afraid.'

All the people were afraid!

'Let us run off to save ourselves,' they said. 'He might cause us all to die.' So they ran away to the south, and hid in a sweat-house. They put a sandstone rock on the roof to keep others out. Meanwhile, Wildcat's skull was calling to his wife. Upon receiving no answer he bounded down to the ground. He saw his child, left by his wife when she had fled in terror, and swallowed it. Then he bounded home only to find there were no people there. He bounded about to every house, but there were no people anywhere. He was very strong and cut up brush and trees as he went along.

'Ah! Where is it that you have all gone, running away to save yourselves?' he cried. 'I'll find you.'

He bounded about until he found their tracks, and then followed them to the south. He bounded along until he arrived at the sweat-house.

'Let me in, you people, I want to enter,' he called.

The people inside whispered to one another, saying, 'Don't say anything. Don't let him in.'

When he saw that the people would not let him in the skull went some distance away and then with a great rush came back intending to burst into the house. But he could not, for it was too strong. He tried this many times, but, although the sweat-house shook, it was too strong for him to break in.

Suddenly he got an idea. He bounded high into the air, intending to burst into the house through the smokehole. But he was not able to because of the sandstone rock, which the people had placed over the opening. Wildcat's skull then bounded down and lay on the ground.

'Why should I try to burst into the house?' he asked. 'It is too strong for me. Where shall I go?'

He bounded north and met some people. He killed them and went rushing on. He met more people and killed them, rushing on as before.

Coyote, who was coming along, heard the rushing sound, and said, 'That must be the human skull. I am going to meet him. I hear that he is killing the people.'

Source

Edward W. Gifford, *Californian Indian Nights Entertainments*, Glendale, CA: Arthur H. Clark Co., 1930, pp. 198–201

As Coyote neared the skull he began to sob. The skull lay quiet a while, listening to the person crying. Coyote stopped in front of it and said, 'I hear that you were bad in the south. Why are you acting that way?'

The skull spoke. 'I dreamed that I threw my body down. I dreamed that I was bounding about, merely a skull.'

'I have seen a person that way before, acting like you because of a bad dream, and I have caused him to be a person again,' said Coyote, speaking to the skull, who lay there, big-eyed, consisting of nothing but his eyes.

Then Coyote continued.

'I put wood and rocks into a hole, and I built a fire down in the hole. When the rocks were hot, I got some pitch and smeared that skull with it, and then I put it down in a hole. When the pitch had all sputtered away that skull stretched out until it became a person again.'

Wildcat's skull begged Coyote to do the same thing to him. But when Coyote placed him in the fire hole and he became heated, he attempted to burst out, but could not, and so died.

CHIPMUNK, THE GIANT-KILLER

Miwok

YAYALI, THE GIANT, set out in search of food. He searched everywhere, over all the hills, shouting in a deep, loud voice as he went along. He started up the mountain, looking all the time for someone to eat.

Far up in the mountains Chipmunk, thinking that his wife's brother was approaching, answered the giant's call and went to meet him. When he approached and saw who it was coming toward him he knew indeed that he had made a sad mistake. Yayali made Chipmunk lead the way to his house, although Chipmunk tried in vain to get the giant to enter the doorway before him. But Yayali would not hear of it.

'You are the owner of the house,' he said. 'You lead into your own house. I am not the owner of it.'

As Chipmunk led the way to the door the giant reached into his basket for a stone, which he threw at Chipmunk, striking him on the back and killing him.

After he had killed Chipmunk, the giant called to the Chipmunk's wife to help him bring in the meat. He then made himself at home and married Chipmunk's widow. Chipmunk's widow had a daughter whom she hid in a pit, fearful lest the giant discover the child and eat her.

Every day the giant left to go into the hills in search of more people. As he departed he rolled big boulders against the door, against both ends of the house, and also one over the smokehole at the top of the house, where the smoke emerges. This was so his wife could not escape. Then he went into the hills to capture more victims.

When he returned he would say to his wife, 'Cook and eat this food, or I will kill you.'

She answered always, 'Yes,' and the giant thought that she ate the fat people, but instead she ate the deer meat which Chipmunk had provided for her.

After some time she gave birth to two giants.

Source
Edward W.
Gifford,
*Californian
Indian Nights
Entertainments,*
Glendale, CA:
Arthur H. Clark
Co., 1930,
pp. 205–9

When the giant had departed for the day in search of food and while the two little giants slept, she would take her daughter from the pit and hold her in her lap. The thought of Chipmunk's sad end depressed her and used to make her cry all day, while the giant was away. When he returned in the evening, she hid her daughter in the pit again. She feared the giant, but she could not escape, because the boulders which the giant put against the doors were too heavy for her to push away. So each day she sat in the house and cried.

Far away in another place Chipmunk's brother dreamed about him one night.

'I think I will visit him,' he said. 'I will see how he fares. I dreamed that he was sick.'

So he set out for his brother's house, telling no one that he was leaving. At last he arrived only to find the house blocked by the large boulders.

He called out to his sister-in-law, 'I have come. Why are these large boulders against the door?'

Then his sister-in-law answered from within, saying, 'Come in. The giant killed your brother. He closes the door with those large boulders each time he goes out.'

He rolled aside the boulders at each end of the house and entered. His sister-in-law told him that the giant had killed his brother and she pointed out to him the giant's two sons. Her brother-in-law then inquired about her daughter, and she told him that she had placed her in the hole so that the giant would not discover and eat the child.

Then he told her to crush some obsidian. He said, 'I am going to help you escape. But the giant has many brothers, who will probably follow you and try to catch you, while you are on your way home. Throw the crushed obsidian in their eyes. I shall not go with you. I shall remain here.'

Chipmunk's brother next killed the two young giants, hitting them with a stick 'in the ankle', the place where, his sister-in-law told him, the young giants kept their hearts. He then gouged out their eyes and threw them into the fire, putting one in each of the four corners.

The giant's wife crushed the obsidian as her brother-in-law told her, and placed it on a deer hide. Then Chipmunk's brother told her to start for home. He warned her especially not to lose the obsidian.

'If they catch you,' he said, 'you can use it. Throw it in their eyes.'

Following his advice she started. He, meanwhile, proceeded to dig holes, one toward the south, one toward the east, one toward the north, and one toward the west, so that he might conceal himself and dodge from one to the other in case he were pursued by the giant. He made holes all around the house, both inside and outside, After he had finished digging the holes he thought about the giant and wondered when he would return. He went into the hills, cut a hard manzanita stick, and sharpened one edge of it. Then he walked around. Soon the giant appeared, coming over the hill. As he approached the house, Chipmunk's brother stepped inside.

The giant saw him and said to himself, 'There is another victim.' He was glad that he had another person to kill, and he followed close behind him into the house.

Chipmunk's brother now asked the giant, 'What do you do first, when you come home?'

The giant replied, 'I dance. Just watch me dance.'

Then Chipmunk's brother went into the holes he had dug and came forth in different places. The giant tried to catch him and followed him about, but

Chipmunk's brother was too quick for him and dodged into the holes. The giant chased him around the house. Every time that the giant neared him, he jumped into a hole, appearing again in another part of the house.

He told the giant, 'You cannot catch me unless you dance. After you dance, I will let you catch me. I want to see you dance first.'

Chipmunk's brother stayed outside, while the giant danced. He shouted at the giant and said, 'Dance more. Jump higher through that smokehole. I like to see you dance.' The giant did as Chipmunk's brother told him. While he danced, Chipmunk's brother with his manzanita stick climbed on top of the house. Suddenly he struck the giant across the neck, chopping his head off with the sharp stick. The head rolled down close to the spring near the house and the body of the giant collapsed inside of the house.

But the giant had many brothers, and they also dreamed of their brother one day. So they all set out for his house. Arrived there they perceived meat scattered about the rocks and trees. They did not know that this was their brother, whom Chipmunk's brother had cut up after killing, and scattered around. So they set to and cooked and ate this meat, thinking it to be some of their brother's victims. The youngest giant, having eaten all he could, went to the spring to drink, and there discovered the giant's head where it had rolled after Chipmunk's brother cut it off. Then they knew that they had eaten their own brother.

'Who could have killed him?' they cried.

They decided to sleep and see whether they would dream about it.

It was the youngest brother's dreams that set them off in pursuit of Chipmunk's widow. Many times they overtook her, only to have her escape when she blinded them by throwing the crushed obsidian in their eyes. By the time they had picked it out of their eyes, she was far ahead of them.

At last Chipmunk's widow reached the house of her father, Lizard. Once she was safely within his doors, with the giants in hot pursuit, Lizard spat on the house and turned it to stone.

Then Lizard called upon the wind to destroy the giant's brothers, but they blew the wind back. Lizard next called upon the snow for aid, but the giants melted the snow by shouting, and when the hail was summoned they stopped the hail by shouting. But at last Lizard called upon the flood, which succeeded in drowning them.

Thus came to an end Yayali, the giant, and his many brothers.

Source

Charles Skinner, *Myths and Legends of Our Own Land*, vol. 3, Philadelphia: J.B. Lippincott, & Co., 1896; reprinted by Singing Tree Press, 1969, pp. 259–60

BRIDAL VEIL FALL

Yosemite-Miwok

THE VAST RAVINE OF YO SEMITE (Grizzly Bear), formed by tearing apart the solid Sierras, is graced by many waterfalls raining down the mile-high cliffs. The one called Bridal Veil has this tale attached to it.

Centuries ago, in the shelter of this valley, lived Tutokanula and his tribe – a good hunter, a thoughtful saver of crops and game for winter, a wise chief, trusted and loved by his people. While hunting, one day, the guardian spirit of the valley – the lovely Tisayac – revealed herself to him, and from that moment he knew no peace, nor did he care for the well-being of his people; for she was not as they were:

her skin was white, her hair was golden, and her eyes like heaven; her speech was as a thrush song and led him to her, but when he opened his arms she rose lighter than any bird and vanished in the sky.

Lacking his direction Yo Semite became a desert, and when Tisayac returned she wept to see the corn lands grown with bushes and bears rooting where the huts had been. On a mighty dome of rock she knelt and begged the Great Spirit to restore its virtue to the land. He did so, for, stooping from the sky, he spread new life of green on all the valley floor, and smiting the mountains he broke a channel for the pent-up meltings of the snows, and the water ran and leaped far down, pooling in a lake below and flowing off to gladden other land. The birds returned, the flowers sprang up, corn swayed in the breeze, and the people, coming back, gave the name of Tisayac to South Dome, where she had knelt.

Then came the chief home again, and, hearing that the spirit had appeared, was smitten with love more strong than ever. Climbing to the crest of a rock that spires three thousand feet above the valley, he carved his likeness there with his hunting-knife, so that his memory might live among his tribe. As he sat, tired with his work, at the foot of the Bridal Veil, he saw, with a rainbow arching around her, the form of Tisayac shining from the water. She smiled on him and beckoned. His quest was at an end. With a cry of joy he sprang into the fall and disappeared with Tisayac. Two rainbows quivered on the falling water, and the sun went down.

Legend of the Geysers

Wappo

From a time longer than a man's memory, the various peoples of the valley of the Russian River lived at peace with one another. With hunting and fishing, with clover, wild oats, and acorns, with the various roots, berries, and fruits provided by Nature, they lived a happy, contented life. The dense chaparral which covers the mountains and lines the canyons of the region surrounding the Geysers effectually concealed the wonderful springs. It was since the Spaniards and Mexicans began to settle in the country and fatten their immense herds upon the rank herbage that the Indians were compelled to put forth greater exertions for food.

Two of their young men were hunting on the south side of the river, when they caught sight of an unusually large grizzly bear. Simultaneously they fired their sharp-barbed arrows into the monster's side. He dropped as if dead, but well knowing it to be a habit of the grizzly to fall to the ground upon receiving the slightest wound, they again let fly their flint-headed shafts, and again struck the bear. Sorely wounded, the animal instinctively staggered toward the thick underbrush, leaving a trail of blood behind. Sure of their game, the hunters followed the bloodstains into the chaparral and up the canyon. Here and there the weary monster lay down to rest for a moment, and upon arising left a gory pool to attest the severity of his hurt. The thews [muscles] and sinews of the California grizzly almost give him a charmed life. The eager hunters would several times have given up the chase, but fresh indications of the bear's weakness, the hope of so rich a prize, and the fear of the ridicule of their companions, spurred them forward. The wounded animal never once swerved from a direct course up the canyon. Mile after mile he tottered straight forward, although

Source
Stephen Powers, *Contributions to North American Ethnology*, vol. 3, Washington DC: Department of the Interior, US Government Printing Office, 1877, pp. 201–3

They found themselves standing on the brink of the Witches' Cauldron, in the midst of the hissing, seething geysers.

his fast-ebbing life frequently caused him to stumble and fall. Just as his merciless pursuers were ready to turn back, baffled and discouraged, they saw him writhing in agony on a little, open grassy plot half a mile distant. Most of their route, until now, had been through close-timbered forests, thick-set with chaparral and scrub-oak.

The sun had moved far down the heavens, and the lofty western mountain shut out his beams from the gorge. At sight of their dying game, the Indians gave a loud, exultant shout. The grizzly startled by the sound rose from the ground, and with the last glimmering ray of life plunged into the ravine ahead. Running across the intervening space, the hunters saw his lifeless body in the bottom of the gorge. In their eager haste they had not noticed the thousand minute jets of steam issuing from the hillside, nor did they hear the hoarse, rushing sound that filled the canyon with a continuous roar, until just as they reached the body.

Halting, amazed, they found themselves standing on the brink of the Witches' Cauldron, in the midst of the hissing, seething Geysers. One horrified, ghastly look at the smoky, steaming hillsides; one breath of the puffing, sulphurous vapour; one terrified glance at the trembling, springy earth, and the frightened hunters darted back down the canyon.

With stoical scepticism, the aged chief and council listened to the tale the hunters told as the trio gathered around the campfire. Earth that smoked! Water that boiled and bubbled without fire! Steam that issued from holes in the ground with a noise like the rushing of the storm-wind! Impossible! But the two young braves were noted for courage and truthfulness, and at last they prevailed on a score of their fellows to return with them. It was all true. There lay the dead bear by the black, seething waters that were hotter than fire could make them. After a thorough examination, the medicine men concluded that the strange mineral waters must have rare healing properties. Booths of willows were erected over the jets of steam, and the sick laid thereon. The canyon became a favourite healing spot, and all the Coast Range tribes came hither with their invalids. Many wonderful cures were effected, and yet, occasionally, things happened that convinced the superstitious medicine men that the place was under the control of an evil spirit.

Finally, one cloudy night a strange, rumbling sound rose through the darkness, and the earth trembled violently. After that no one approached the spot for many days.

It is a common belief among the Coast Indians that evil spirits frequently dwell within the bodies of grizzlies. It was now universally believed that the spirit of the slaughtered bear had charge of the Geysers. There were many sick and dying with a strange plague, or pestilence that had suddenly appeared among the tribe. Something must be done. Many urged a return, at all hazards, to the medicinal springs; others held that the angry demon of the gorge had sent the pestilence upon them. At last a grey-haired seer whose hand was skilled in all cunning craft was persuaded to try to appease the spirit by making a graven image near the Witches' Cauldron. Enough of the idolatrous traditions of their ancestors were remembered to enable them to have faith in this strange attempt at propitiation.

Day after day the good old sculptor went all alone to the canyon, and chiselled away the rock until the semblance of a human face appeared. As the work neared completion, he often lingered later, in his anxiety to finish the statue. It was believed that when the task was entirely ended the demon would retire, and let the people be healed.

A few more days and the finishing strokes would be made on the figure.

Everyone was full of hope. The old man was working at the dawn, and when the evening came and the twilight shadows stole down the mountain and up the ravine he had not returned.

Suddenly a weird, hollow moan seemed to tremble on the shuddering air, and at the next instant the earth shook so violently that the cliffs toppled from their base. The terrible shocks were felt several times during the night, and when the sun arose the old seer was gone from earth. The cold, stony face of the image alone remained. Not the slightest trace was ever discovered of the faithful sculptor, yet during the night new springs had burst forth three-quarters of a mile down the river. Here the sick were brought, and from that day to the present time the Indians used only the lower springs. Scaffolds are raised above the steam-jets three or four feet, and willows and brush are laid across. On these the sick are placed, and the mineral vapours encircle and heal them.

As to the geysers in the great valley of the Russian River, the Indians continued to firmly believe that the wrathful demon still holds sway, and they can never be induced to approach the gorge of the main Geysers.

THE BEAR AND THE DEER

Nishinam

AT FIRST ALL THE ANIMALS ate only earth, but afterward the clover grew, and then they ate that also. There were no men yet, or rather all men were yet in the forms of animals. One day the bear and the deer went out together to pick clover. The bear pretended to see a louse on the deer's neck, and the deer bent down her head to let the bear catch it, but the bear cut her head off, scratched out her eyes, and threw them into her basket among the clover. When she went home and emptied her basket, the deer's children saw the eyes, and they knew they were their mother's. So they studied revenge.

On another day, when the bear was pounding earth in a mortar for food, as acorns are now pounded, the deer's two children enticed the bear's children away to play, and persuaded them to enter a cave beneath a great rock, Oamlam (high rock), on Wolf Creek, near Bear River. Then they fastened them in with a stone, and made a fire which roasted them to death. When the bear came and found them, she thought they were asleep and sweating, but it was the oil on their hair, and when she pawed them the hair came off. Thereupon she flew into a great passion, tore them to pieces, and devoured them.

Then she pursued the deer's two children to destroy them. She called out to them that she was their aunt and would do them good, but they flew and escaped up the great rock, Oamlam, and it grew upward with them until the top of it was very high. The bear went round behind the rock and found a narrow rift where she could crawl up, but the deer's children saw her coming, and they had a red-hot stone, which they cast down her throat and slew her. Then they took this same stone and threw it to the north, and manzanita-berries fell down; to the east, and pine-nuts fell down; to the south, and one kind of acorns fell down; to the west, and another kind of acorns fell down. Thus they had now plenty of food of different kinds, and they ate earth no more.

Source

Stephen Powers, *Contributions to North American Ethnology*, vol. 3, Washington DC: Department of the Interior, US Government Printing Office, 1877, pp. 341–43

After this, while they were yet on the rock, the deer's children thought to climb into heaven, it had grown so high. The big one made a ladder that reached the sky, and, with bow and arrow, he shot a hole up through, so that the little one could climb up into heaven. But the little one was afraid, and cried. So the big one made tobacco and a pipe, and gave them to the little one to smoke as he went up the ladder, whereby the smoke concealed the world from him, and his heart was no longer afraid. And this is how smoking originated. So the little one climbed up through the hole into heaven, and went out of sight; but presently he returned down the ladder, and told his brother that it was a good country above the sky, with plenty of sweet grass, and buds of trees, and pools of water, and flowers for them to sleep on. Upon that they both climbed the ladder and went above the sky.

Presently they saw their mother by a pool of water cooking, and they knew it was she, because she had no eyes. Now, the big brother was a deer, but the little one was a sap-sucker. So these two made a wheel to ride on, that they might pursue their mother, for they were not well pleased to see her without eyes. But they were punished for this act of wickedness, for the wheel went contrary with them, turned aside, and plunged into a pool of water, so that they were drowned.

THE GREAT FIRE

Chenposel

THERE WAS ONCE A MAN who loved two women and wished to marry them. Now these two women were magpies (atch-atch), but they loved him not and laughed his wooing to scorn. Then he fell into a rage and cursed these two women, and went far away to the north. There he set the world on fire, then made for himself a boat, wherein he escaped to the sea and was never heard of more.

But the fire which he had kindled burned with a terrible burning. It ate its way south with frightful swiftness, licking up all things that are on earth – men, trees, rocks, animals, water, and even the ground itself. But the Old Coyote saw the burning and the smoke from his place far in the south, and he ran with all his might to put it out. He took two little boys in a sack and ran north like the wind. So fast did he run that he gave out just as he got to the fire and dropped the two little boys.

But he took Indian sugar (honeydew) in his mouth, chewed it up, spat it on the fire, and so put it out. Now the fire was out, but the coyote was mighty thirsty, and there was no water. Then he took Indian sugar again, chewed it up, dug a hole in the bottom of the creek, covered up the sugar in it, and it turned to water, and the earth had water again. But the two little boys cried because they were lonesome, for there was nobody left on earth.

Then the coyote made a sweat-house, and split out a great number of little sticks, which he laid in the sweat-house over night. In the morning they were all turned to men and women, so the two little boys had company, and the earth was re-peopled.

Source
Stephen Powers, *Contributions to North American Ethnology*, vol. 3, Washington DC: Department of the Interior, US Government Printing Office, 1877, p. 227

BIBLIOGRAPHY

Alexander, Hartley Burr, *The Mythology of All Races*, New York: Cooper Square
 Publishers, Inc., 1964

Beach, William W., *The Indian Miscellany: Containing Papers on the History, Antiquities, Arts,
 Languages, Religions, Traditions, and Superstitions of the American Aborigines*, Albany: J.
 Munsell Publishing Co., 1877

Boas, Franz, *Ethnology of the Kwakiutl*, Washington DC: Government Printing Office,
 1921

Brinton, Daniel G., *The Myths of the New World*, Philadelphia: David McKay, 1896

Burland, Cottie, *North American Indian Mythology*, London: Paul Hamlyn Limited, 1965

Burlin, Natalie Curtis, *The Indians' Book*, New York: Harper and Brothers, 1907

Bushnell, David, 'The Choctaw of Bayou Lacomb, St Tammany Parish, LA', *BAE
 Bulletin*, 48 (1909)
  'Myths of the Louisiana Choctaw', *American Anthropologist*, 12 (1910)

Coolidge, Mary Roberts, *The Rain-Makers: Indians of Arizona and New Mexico*, Boston:
 Houghton Mifflin Co., 1929

Curtin, Jeremiah, *Creation Myths of Primitive America*, New York: Benhamin Blom, 1898

Curtis, Edward, *The North American Indian* (20 vols), New York: Johnson Reprint
 Corporation, 1970

Cushing, Frank Hamilton, *Zuni Folk Tales*, New York: G.P. Putnam's Sons, 1901

De Angulo, Jaime, *Indian Tales*, New York: A.A. Wyn, Inc., 1953

Dorsey, George A, 'Traditions of the Caddo', *Carnegie Institution*, 41 (1905)

Dorsey, J.O., 'Two Biloxi Tales', *JAFL*, 6 (1893)

Driver, Harold E., *Indians of North America*, Chicago: University of Chicago Press, 1961

Dunn, Jacob P., *True Indian Stories* (with glossary of Indiana Indian names),
 Indianapolis: Centinel Printing Co., 1908

Eastman, Charles A., *Old Indian Days*, New York: McClure Company, 1907

Emerson, Ellen R., *Indian Myths*; or, *Legends, Traditions, and Symbols of the Aborigines of
 America*, Boston: J.R. Osgood and Co., 1884

Farb, Peter, *Man's Rise to Civilization*, New York: E.P. Dutton & Co., Inc., 1968

Fewkes, J. Walter, 'How the Medicine Man was Born,and How He Turned a Man into
 a Tree', *JAFL*, 3 (1884)

Fiedel, Stuart J., *Prehistory of the Americas*, New York: Cambridge University Press, 1987

Fletcher, Alice C., *Indian Story and Song from North America*, Boston: Small, Maynard,
 and Co., 1900

Fletcher, Sidney E., *The American Indian*, New York: Grosset & Dunlap Publishers, 1954

Forbes, Jack D., editor, *The Indian in America's Past*, Englewood Cliffs, NJ: Prentice-Hall,
 Inc., 1964

Foster, J.W., *Prehistoric Races of the United States of America*, Chicago: S.C. Griggs & Co.
 1874

Gatschet, Albert S., 'Some Mythic Stories of the Yuchi Indians', *American Anthropologist*, (OS) 6 (1893)

Gifford, Edward W., *Californian Indian Nights Entertainments*, Glendale, CA: Arthur H. Clark Co., 1930

Gill, Sam D., *Native American Religions, An Introduction*, Belmont, CA: Wadsworth Publishing Co., 1982

Greenlee, R.F., 'The Milky Way', *JAFL*, 58 (1945)
'Men Visit the Sky to see God', *JAFL*, 58 (1945)

Grinnell, George Bird, *Pawnee Hero Stories and Folk-Tales*, New York: Forest and Stream Publishing Company, 1889
Blackfoot Lodge Tales: The Story of a Prairie People, New York: Charles Scribner's Sons, 1892
By Cheyenne Campfires, New Haven, Conn: Yale University Press, 1926

Halbert, Henry S., 'Nanih Waiya, the Sacred Mound of the Cocktaws', *Publications of Mississippi Historical Society*, 2 (1899)

Hale, Horatio, *Iroquois Book of Rites*, Philadelphia: D.G. Brinton, 1883

Hirschfelder, Arlene, and Paulette Molin, *The Encyclopedia of Native American Religions: An Introduction*, New York: Facts On File, 1992

Hultkrantz, Ake, *Native Religions of North America: The Power of Visions and Fertility*, San Francisco: Harper & Row Publishers, 1987

Johnson, Elias, *Legends, Traditions, and Laws of the Iroquois, or Six Nations*, Lockport, NY: Union Printing and Publishing Co., 1881

Josephy Jr, Alvin M., *The Indian Heritae of America*, Boston: Houghton Mifflin Company, 1991
500 Nations: An Illustrated History of North American Indians, New York: Alfred A. Knopf, 1994

Kate, H., 'The Hero with the Horned Snake', *JAFL*, 2 (1889)

Kroeber, Alfred L. *Nature of Culture*, Chicago: University of Chicago Press, 1952

Leland, Charles, G., *The Algonquin Legends of New England*, Boston: Houghton, Mifflin, and Company, 1884

Lummis, Charles F., *The Man Who Married the Moon and Other Pueblo Indian Folk Stories*, New York: Century Co., 1894

Mails, Thomas E., *Plains Indians: Dog Soldiers, Bear Men and Buffalo Women*, New York: Bonanza Books, 1973

Martin, Paul S., *Indians Before Columbus: Twenty Thousand Years of North American History Revealed by Archeology*, Chicago: University of Chicago Press, 1947

Mooney, James, 'Myths of the Cherokees.' *BAEAR*, 19 (1900)
'The Cherokee Play Ball'. *BAEAR*, 24 (1907)

Nusbaum, Aileen, *Zuni Indian Tales*, New York: G.P. Putnam's Sons, 1926

O'Bryan, Aileen, 'The Dine: Origin Myths of the Navajo Indians', *Bulletin of the Bureau of Ethnology*, 163 (1956)

Palmer, William R., *Pahute Indian Legends*, Salt Lake City: Deseret Book Co., 1946

Powers, Stephen, *Contributions to North American Ethnology*, vol. 3, Washington DC: Department of the Interior, US Government Printing Office, 1877

Prince, John, 'Notes on Passamaquoddy Literature', *Annals of the New York Academy of Science*, 11 (1898) and 23 (1901)

Radin, Paul, The Trickster: *A Study in American Indian Mythology*, New York: Bell Publishing, Inc., 1956

Russell, Frank, 'Myth of the Jicarilla Apache', *JAFL*, 11 (1898)

Salomon, Julian Harris, *The Book of Indian Crafts and Lore*, New York: Harper and Brothers, 1928

Schoolcraft, Henry R., *North American Indian Legends*, Philadelphia: J.B. Lippincott & Co., 1856

Skinner, Charles, *Myths and Legends of Our Own Land* (3 vols), Philadelphia: J.B. Lippincott & Co., 1896; reprinted by Singing Tree Press, 1969

Smith, Bertha H., *Yosemite Legends*, San Francisco: Paul Elder and Co., 1904

Smith, E.A., *Myths of the Iroquois*, *BAEAR*, 2, 1881

Speck, Frank G., 'The Creek Indians of Taskigi Town', *American Anthropological Society Memoirs*, 2, 2 (1907)
    'Penobscot Tales', *JAFL*, 48 (1935)

Spence, Lewis, *Myths and Legends of the North American Indians*, London: George G. Harrap & Co., 1914

Spencer, Robert F., *The Native Americans: Prehistory and Ethnology of the North American Indians*, New York: Harper & Row Publishers, 1965

Swanton, John R., 'Haida Texts and Myths', *US Bureau of American Ethnology Bulletin*, 29 (1905)
    'Adoption of the Human Race' and 'Creation', *BAE Bulletin*, 42 (1924–5)
    'The Celestial Canoe', *BAE Bulletin*, 42 (1924–5)
    'How Rabbit Fooled Alligator', *BAE Bulletin*, 88 (1929)
    'Myths and Tales of the Southeastern Indians', *BAE Bulletin*, 88 (1929)
    'The Walnut-cracker', *BAE Bulletin*, 88 (1929)
    The Indians of the Southeastern United States, Washington, DC: US Government Printing Office, 1946
    The Indian Tribes of North America, Washington DC: Smithsonian Institution Press, 1952

Time-Life Inc., *Indians of the Western Range*, Alexandria, VA: Time-Life Books, 1995
    Keepers of the Totem, Alexandria, VA: Time-Life Books, 1993

Waldman, Carl, *Atlas of the North American Indian*, New York: Facts on File Publications, 1985
    Encyclopedia of Native American Tribes, New York: Facts On File Publications, 1988

Wissler, Clark, *Indians of the United States*, Garden City, NY: Doubleday & Co., Inc., 1966

Wolfson, Evelyn, *From Abenaki to Zuni: A Dictionary of Native American Tribes*, New York: Walker and Co., 1988

Wood, Charles Erskine Scott, *A Book of Tales: Being Some Myths of the North American Indians*, New York: Vanguard Press, 1929

Wright, Harold Bell, *Long Ago Told: Legends of the Papago Indians*, New York: D. Appleton & Co., 1929

INDEX